Adaptation in Young Adult Novels

Adaptation in Young Adult Novels

Critically Engaging Past and Present

Edited by
Dana E. Lawrence and Amy L. Montz

BLOOMSBURY ACADEMIC
NEW YORK • LONDON • OXFORD • NEW DELHI • SYDNEY

BLOOMSBURY ACADEMIC
Bloomsbury Publishing Inc
1385 Broadway, New York, NY 10018, USA
50 Bedford Square, London, WC1B 3DP, UK

BLOOMSBURY, BLOOMSBURY ACADEMIC and the Diana logo are trademarks of
Bloomsbury Publishing Plc

First published in the United States of America 2020

Volume Editors' Part of the Work © Dana E. Lawrence and Amy L. Montz 2020
Each chapter © Contributors 2020

For legal purposes the Acknowledgments on p. vii–viii constitute an extension
of this copyright page.

Cover design: Eleanor Rose
Cover images (clockwise from top left): Mary Wollstonecraft Shelley (1797–1851)
© Culture Club / Getty Images; Jane Austen. (1775–1817), engraving, 1873
© Getty Images; Charles Dickens (1812–1870), engraving, 1870 © Getty Images;
Charlotte Bronte (1816–1855). Photo © Hulton Archive / Getty Images; F. Scott
Fitzgerald (1896–1940). Photo © Minnesota Historical Society / CORBIS / Getty Images;
William Shakespeare (1564–1616), engraving, 1877 © Getty Images

All rights reserved. No part of this publication may be reproduced
or transmitted in any form or by any means, electronic or mechanical,
including photocopying, recording, or any information storage or retrieval
system, without prior permission in writing from the publishers.

Bloomsbury Publishing Inc does not have any control over, or responsibility for, any
third-party websites referred to or in this book. All internet addresses given in this
book were correct at the time of going to press. The author and publisher regret any
inconvenience caused if addresses have changed or sites have ceased to exist, but can
accept no responsibility for any such changes.

A catalog record for this book is available from the Library of Congress.

ISBN: HB: 978-1-5013-6177-7
ePDF: 978-1-5013-6179-1
eBook: 978-1-5013-6178-4

Typeset by Newgen KnowledgeWorks Pvt. Ltd., Chennai, India

To find out more about our authors and books visit www.bloomsbury.com
and sign up for our newsletters.

Contents

Acknowledgments — vii

"Both Flesh and Monument": The Immortal Life of Literature through Adaptation   *Dana E. Lawrence and Amy L. Montz* — 1

Part One   Representation Matters — 15

1   Re-visioning Rosaline; or, Romeo and Juliet Are Dead   *Fiona Hartley-Kroeger* — 17

2   Inhabiting the House of Edith Wharton's Fiction: Rewriting the Captive Woman in Deborah Noyes's *The Ghosts of Kerfol*   *Indu Ohri* — 33

3   Rewriting *The Great Gatsby*: Questioning Identity and Morality in Sara Benincasa's *Great*   *Lisa M. Valenzuela* — 49

4   LGBTQIA Fairy Tales: Queering *Cinderella* in Lo's *Ash* and Donoghue's "The Tale of the Shoe"   *Dalila Forni* — 63

5   "Wherever the Flame Was Brightest": Identity and Assimilation in Rick Riordan's Greek Mythological Adaptations for Young Adults   *Saffyre Falkenberg* — 79

Part Two   Literature and Popular Culture — 95

6   *Jane Eyre* in Space: Adapting Brontë's Novel for Young Adult Fans of Sci-Fi and Fantasy   *Tara Moore* — 97

7   Megan Shepherd's The Madwoman Trilogy and the Female Voice: The Twenty-First-Century Young Adult Adaptation of *Frankenstein* and the *Frankenstein* Franchise   *Melanie A. Marotta* — 111

8   Austen, Wollstonecraft, and Zombies: Female Autonomy in Jane Austen's Popular Canon   *Eileen Totter* — 125

9   A Twist in Time or a Break in Narrative: Adapting the Disney Classic Canon for a Young Adult Audience   *Michelle Anya Anjirbag and Madeleine Hunter* — 139

Part Three Making the Past Present   153

10 Rewriting Nineteenth-Century New York City for the Modern
    Teen   *Amy L. Montz*   155

11 Find Our Past Voice: Reimagining the Nineteenth-Century Feminist in
    Young Adult Literature   *Brett Carol Young*   169

12 A Tale of Two Women: Representing Femininity in Charles Dickens's
    A Tale of Two Cities and Sarah Rees Brennan's *Tell the Wind and
    Fire*   *Maya Zakrzewska-Pim*   183

13 "In fair Verona, where we lay our scene": Adaptation, Literary Tourism,
    and Locating Juliet   *Dana E. Lawrence*   197

14 From Ancient to Modern Myth: Storytelling in Jesmyn Ward's *Salvage
    the Bones*   *Madeleine Tulip*   213

Notes on Contributors   229
Index   233

Acknowledgments

This collection was born out of a conversation about adaptation and young adult literature, and versions of our texts were presented at the Children's Literature Association Conference in 2018. We began soliciting abstracts at that conference and have been excited by the promise of this collection since. We are proud of our contributors' work and the continuance of work being done on this important subject. Adaptations are often denied place among canonical literatures, and adaptations of canonical literatures in particular are sometimes viewed as sacrilegious. We are grateful for the serious and thoughtful contributions in this collection about a subject dear to our hearts.

We would like to thank the team at Bloomsbury for seeing the great potential in this collection and working tirelessly with us on revisions. Further, we would like to thank each of our contributors for meeting deadlines (sometimes quite sudden!) and giving us amazing work. Dean Walter Collins III at the University of South Carolina Lancaster provided funding for the indexing, and we are grateful for his support.

Amy: I would like to thank Catherine Whalen and Kasey Grier for their amazing work with the National Endowment for the Humanities 2017 Summer Institute's American Material Culture: Nineteenth-Century New York, as well as my fellow participants whose intelligence, drive, and contributions to our discussions helped to inspire my paper and, further, this collection. I would also like to thank the Department of English at the University of Southern Indiana and the College of Liberal Arts for continued contributions to my scholarship, most particularly in the form of a Liberal Arts Research Award (LARA) that granted time (one-course release for the semester) to work on my chapter and this collection. I'd like to thank my family, especially Anthony Rintala, Byron Montz, and my cadre of canines, for continued support, and finally Dana Lawrence for her tireless efforts on this book, her excitement for our work, and random phone calls at all hours of the morning with editing questions. This collection simply would not exist without her.

Dana: I would like to thank USC Lancaster for providing financial support for my 2013 travel study course, "Shakespeare in Italy," the preparation for which introduced me to the scholarly world of literary tourism. I must also thank Professor Kaetrena Davis Kendrick, who was instrumental in helping me develop the final tourism-centered project for the "Shakespeare in Italy" course and who has been a tireless supporter of and sounding board for my teaching and research endeavors. Additional thanks go to the Research and Productive Scholarship committee at USC Lancaster and the Provost's office of the University of South Carolina for funding subsequent travel to Italy to conduct on-site research of Shakespeare tourism sites.

I would like to thank my husband, Nick, for enabling my extended absences so I could complete this project and for being a cheerful reader of my work in progress, and my kids, Cooper and Hayden, for at least pretending to be interested in Mama's work. As always, thanks go to Debbie Brogden, Mike Eatman, Barbara Etsell, Linda Hamby, and Chuck Hamby for their continuing enthusiasm and support for my journey into and through the strange and challenging world of academia. Finally, to my collaborator, Amy, I offer hugs and chocolate and my forever friendship. You're brilliant and wonderful, and this project wouldn't have even gotten started without you!

"Both Flesh and Monument": The Immortal Life of Literature through Adaptation

Dana E. Lawrence and Amy L. Montz

In *A Theory of Adaptation*, Linda Hutcheon argues that "An adaptation is not vampiric: it does not draw the life-blood from its source and leave it dying or dead, nor is it paler than the adapted work. It may, on the contrary, keep that prior work alive, giving it an afterlife it would never have had otherwise."[1] Hutcheon's refusal to see adaptation as "vampiric" is particularly inspiring for those of us who do work on adaptations. The idea of an "afterlife" of texts, of seeing what comes before as an inspiration for what comes now, is, by its very definition, keeping works "alive." Adaptations for young adults, in particular, have the added benefit of engaging the young adult reader with both then and now, past and present—functioning as both "monuments" to history and the "flesh" of the reader's lived experience. While this is true for adaptations in general, it is especially important for those written with young adults in mind. Such adaptations allow young readers to make personal connections with texts that might otherwise come across as old-fashioned or irrelevant. This is essential for reaching the target audience, because, as Andrea Coldwell has observed, "Teen readers, even more than readers of other ages, value the ways that reading reflects aspects of themselves. That is, interest in reading seems to result from interest in shaping oneself as a reader."[2] The hope is, of course, that the young adult reader will approach both text and context, both original and adaptation, to explore the importance of a theme, or a writer, or a novel and see the historical, cultural, and literary connotations presented. Adaptation is about these connections—connective tissues leading from one text to another, one author to another, one time to another. We see an adaptation and we are invited to remember and engage with the source, and we are encouraged to visit the source text for the first time, or once again.

For these reasons, we present essays that explore relationships between texts and contexts that see the connections between canonical and young adult literature. As adaptation simultaneously reimagines and reinscribes a literary canon, the engagement with the canon is a key aspect of the adaptive qualities of the text. The author's familiarity with the source of the adaptation—whether text, context, author, or place—lends new life to the canonical text. In "Seven Types of Intertextuality," Robert S. Miola understands adaptations as "literary progeny that bear direct and immediate descent from originary texts and that exist in a very conscious counterpoise of tribute and criticism … If an author's revision of his or her own work asserts his or her power and domination, then the reviser of another's work enacts a rebellion and usurpation."[3] What remains unique about the adaptation is this tension between tribute and criticism, particularly when issues of race, gender, and other aspects of diversity are brought into play. Seeing the past through new eyes means we must examine the past in all its defects. It means engaging with our predecessors and the rights—and wrongs—of their literatures.

Adaptation in Young Adult Novels: Critically Engaging Past and Present explores the "afterlife" of texts and contexts. These historical and literary phenomena argue that adapting the classics is a way to engage young adult readers with their cultural past and to see how that past can be rewritten in order to emphasize what can be changed, what and who benefits from change, and how they, too, can be agents of change. These adaptations empower young readers, making them more culturally, historically, and socially aware through the lens of literary diversity.

Telling the Truth, Sometimes: Adapting Chaucer for Contemporary Teens

Kim Zarins's 2016 adaptation of Geoffrey Chaucer's *The Canterbury Tales, Sometimes We Tell the Truth*, offers an excellent example of how adaptation can simultaneously respect and interrogate a canonical text while also using that text as a vehicle for critical engagement of both its historical significance and its continuing relevance for young adult readers. The novel follows a group of high school seniors on their road trip from Canterbury, Connecticut, to Washington, DC. The characters are based on those in Chaucer's classic, and Zarins rewrites the tales and the characters to reflect a more contemporary audience. For example, Chaucer (the writer) and Chaucer (the pilgrim) are now Jeff Chaucer, a teenager struggling with his writing and his bisexuality. Several of the characters are rewritten as female characters to call attention to the inadequacy of gender representation in Chaucer's text, in which only the Wife of Bath, the Prioress, and a Second Nun are women. Further, characters from Chaucer's text are now their 2016 high school counterparts: the Knight is the popular football player, for example, while the Pardoner is Pard, a gay teenager at ease with his identity and feelings for Jeff. Their Civics teacher declares a storytelling competition to keep the group in line, and we get the tales, and the characters, through Jeff's narrative eye.

We chose this text not only because it is an exceptional text but also because Chaucer is often called "The Father of English Literature" and *The Canterbury Tales* one of the first major works in English vernacular. Chaucer himself, as Zarins says in her afterword, was in fact a rewriter. Zarins notes of Chaucer's audience that "Readers were not obsessed with originality as much as we are today and, like a proto-fanfiction culture, had something like a passion for retellings."[4] Zarins takes this to heart in her rewrite and examines cultural moments such as the craze for zombies, *Twilight*, and the Harry Potter franchise through her characters' tales.

It would be impossible to focus on all of Zarins's rewrites here, so we decided that focusing on the most direct of the rewrites, Alison/Alisoun (The Wife of Bath), would highlight our argument most specifically. Zarins's Alison is described in the DRAMATIS PERSONAE as a "Venus with a gap-toothed smile; her favorite color is red."[5] Describing her as a "Venus" offers her an overt sexuality that is mythological. She is a sexual creature to aspire to, someone people, gay, straight, bi, genderqueer, are obsessed with. Taking this from Chaucer's Wife of Bath, who herself is a sexualized creature, Zarins also reiterates Alison's "gap-toothed smile." This smile, "gat-tothed" in Chaucer, is a further symbol of her sexuality, according to a medieval audience.[6] The focus on the color red for Alison is another callback to Alisoun, who is often pictured as red of hue, sanguine according to the medieval humors, as well as wearing red stockings. This demonstrates both Alisoun's sexuality and also her wealth, as red would have been a difficult color to dye. For Zarins's Alison, we see a glimpse of red stockings as an homage to her source material, but also a point of her own fashion sense.

Some of her statements shock her peers, but they take it in stride, as it seems to be part of Alison's personality. Jeff tells us,

> Unlike Briony, with the blonde hair, the bikini body, the baby blue eyes, Alison isn't that kind of pretty. But she's got your attention like no one else. I don't just mean clothes, though today's outfit is cowboy boots, red stockings, and a lacy baby-doll dress, all on a five-foot-eleven-inch body. I mean *her*. When Alison flashes that gap-toothed smile like she's up to something, you want to be up on it with her. You want to be the one who says the funny line that makes her tip her chin and laugh with nothing held back. And maybe, I love her with something like tenderness, because in this large, lonely world, she's the only girl who has ever grabbed my ass.[7]

Giving Alison an untraditional prettiness, based on the canonical detail of that "gap-toothed"/"gat-tothed" smile, presents Alison as real. She's not a Queen Bee; throughout the text she is seen as kind and even sympathetic as well as sexually free. She kisses Pard—even knowing he is gay—on top of Jeff's lap, is kind to Jeff after he tells the story of the death of his sister, and tells both a prologue and a tale to the group, like her source.

Her prologue, like the Wife of Bath's, is about her sexual exploits. While Alisoun boasts, "sith I twelf yeer was of age . . . Housbondes at chirche-dore I have had five,"[8] Alison tells us of her experience of a statutory rape, with an 18-year-old boy when she is only 12. Both Alisoun and Alison emphasize the pleasure they take in their sexual experiences, even in the face of social scrutiny and assumptions about their character, and both derive a sense of authority from that experience. Alisoun tells her fellow pilgrims, "Experience, though noon auctoritee / Were in this world, were right y-nough to me / To speke of wo that is in marriage."[9] No one in the group knows more about marriage than she does, and this expertise extends to include biblical exegesis and responses to men's disparagement of women. In response to expectations of chastity in women, Alisoun asks, "where comanded [God] virginitee?"[10] then "Men may conseille a womman to been oon, /But consillying is no comandement. / He putte it in oure owne juddgement; / For hadde God comanded maydenhede, / Thanne hadde he dampned weddyng with the ded."[11] Alisoun has no interest in what men think about her or what she chooses to do with her body, and not even the threat of violence will stop her from arguing against Jankyn's misogynist attacks, reading from his ever-present *Book of Wicked Women*. Noting that though there are many examples of good women in the Bible and in mythology, not a single one was included in this text, Alisoun again addresses her audience, "Who peyntede the leon, tel me who? / By God, if wommen hadde writen stories, / As clerkes han withinne hire oratories, / They wolde han writen of men moore wikkednesse / Than al the mark of Adam may redresse."[12] Again, Alisoun asserts her authority and proves her point with descriptions of her unfaithful fourth husband and the wicked Jankyn in her Prologue and, later, in her tale of a rapist knight.

Alisoun's fifth and most-recent husband, Jankyn, had twenty years to her forty, and she describes her lust for him without shame: "me thoughte he hadde a paire / Of legges and of feet so clene and faire / That al myn herte I yaf unto his hold."[13] In fact, Alisoun's lust for Jankyn is so powerful that she is willing to put up with his verbal and physical abuse for it: "But in oure bed he was so fressh and gay / . . . That thogh he hadde me bete on every bon, / He doude wynne agayn my love anon."[14] Though Alisoun knows that Jankyn mistreated her, she is also adamant that she knew what she was doing and, in the end, got what she wanted. Though Alisoun is confident in her expertise and is unapologetically sexual, both her Prologue and Tale serve as arguments against a patriarchal culture that not even she can escape. Her experience is her source of authority, but that experience came at the expense of her body over the course of at least thirty years (given her first marriage at age 12 and her marriage to Jankyn at around age 40). So, it is no surprise that Alisoun's answer to the question, "What do women want?" is sovereignty, autonomy, and power. Alison, too, is confident in her sexuality and uses it to get what she wants. However, like Alisoun, the empowerment that she locates within her sexuality must share space with the trauma of abuse at the hands of her lovers. Also like Alisoun, Alison describes her initial attraction to her friend's much older brother, "Pete." Though she was only in sixth grade at the time, she felt "mature" walking with him, and she makes it clear that the physical attraction is mutual.[15] After having sex—characterized as consensual—in his car in a parking garage, Alison and "Pete" join the rest of their group at the Liberty Bell. While she tells us she is complicit in the sex, and enjoys it immensely, we as readers, and the peers as listeners, know that the young age when she lost her virginity makes the sex not consensual but rape.

The unfairness of the situation, of both women being taken advantage of not only by men but by a patriarchal structure that controls their sexual access, is not lost on the reader, the peers, and, one imagines, even Alisoun's listening audience. Alison's tale, that she lost her virginity in the back seat of a car with the man who drove her and her friends to Philadelphia, is full of sadness as well as matter-of-factness. When she realizes she has lost her underwear somewhere in the car, she tells "Pete" to be on the lookout for them, but he "Makes a face when I describe them—pink with Hello Kitty—and I'm embarrassed I wore them on the trip. Like maybe he'll never want to do it again, because I'm such a kid."[16] This small detail, these childlike panties with Hello Kitty on them, reiterates how incredibly young Alison is, as well as her awareness of her youth. She calls herself a "kid," especially in the eyes of her statutory rapist, but later tells us they continue to have sex throughout the summer.

When she arrives at the Liberty Bell, sans underwear and having lost her virginity, Alison sees herself like the very symbol of Revolution before her: "Cracked, but still the icon of freedom," because "instead of getting scrapped as used-up goods, it became a monument."[17] When she compares herself to a broken bell that somehow became a national symbol of freedom, Alison determines that losing her virginity will not define her as "used-up goods." In fact, the purpose of her Prologue is to ask her peers if she should contact "Pete" again now that she is of legal age.

Resoundingly, they are quiet. Jeff and Pard both say no.

We see Alison challenge patriarchy like her predecessor both in her prologue and tale—a tale that is a near-recreation of Alisoun's from Chaucer's text—and also when the group arrives at the Washington Monument. There, at the largest phallic-shaped monument in America,

> we watch as Alison strides right into the shallow water. Her joking smile is replaced with this radiant, almost determined look on her face as she turns to face the Washington Monument. She stands tall as a Valkyrie with her fist high above her head, posed in a warrior's salute, and she unfurls her red stockings, which stream behind her flowing hair. There's a certain unflinching core I've never seen in Alison before as she looks up at the monument towering over her, but not leaving her in shadow.[18]

Jeff, watching Alison as she is caught up in the moment, compares her to the Columbia Pictures credits in which a woman stands triumphant. Jeff sees her as "a symbol, both flesh and monument, for all time," and notes, "It's like that now. Alison's so perfect. So complete," and calls Alison's stance a "face-off" with the Washington Monument.[19] This scene is a direct callback to the scene with the Liberty Bell, in which Alison is "Cracked, but still the icon of freedom." She understands that something is wrong about her loss of virginity—not the virginity itself, as she enjoys the sex with "Pete," but, rather, the fact that she loses it so young. The undercurrent of tension in her tale has to do with how "Pete" abandons her and how she understands it, saying, "I don't want him to get in trouble for something I wanted as much as he did, so I don't text much."[20] While for Alison, her desire for "Pete" excuses her behavior, the reader and her peers know it in no way excuses his. When Alison has her "face-off" with the Washington Monument, she stands against the duality of sexism she has faced: as a young victim of statutory rape and as a culture that would see her actions as those of a seductive Lolita. For Alisoun, we understand that 12, while young, is still an acceptable age to get married in the 1300s, according to Church and law. We, the readers, know better now, for both Alison and Alisoun.

The sympathy that the Prologue invokes in the reader and Alison/Alisoun's peers is in some ways lost by her tale, which is the recovery of a rapist's reputation through his marriage to a once-ancient hag now turned beautiful lady. In Zarins's novel, "Alison ends with a flourish, but we're quiet and uneasy."[21] Alison claims her ending is "'better this way. For everyone.'"[22] As a direct retelling of The Wife of Bath's Tale—the rape, the knight's judgment, the loathly lady, the reward at the end—Alison's text has historically been problematic. While Chaucer's audience may not see the problems with forgiveness from rape for a Knight, the highest of his social class, they clearly see a problem with rape itself. The King is ready to execute his knight, and it is only the women of the court who ask for a torturous exercise instead. One assumes the Queen does not expect the knight to discover what women truly want. But because he has, she must agree to the bargain struck. Who, then, is at fault with this tale? The rapist? The Queen for staying the execution? The teller (Alisoun/Alison)? Chaucer for scripting it? No. Rather, Alison's face-off with the Washington Monument brings to mind the history of injustices against victims of sexual assault. Alison stares down the Washington Monument, waves high her red stockings, and is, to Jeff, both "flesh and monument." In this moment, we see the purpose, truly, of adaptive texts. To become both flesh and monument, real and iconic, to review and reenvision a story for a new audience is to breathe life into characters, into stories, into cities, into authors. To become flesh and monument is to understand that adaptation is *as important as* the originary texts, as they exist together, happily.

Defining Adaptation: Process, Palimpsest, and Perception

Definitions of "adaptation" continue to evolve as the range of texts thought to fit within its scope grows broader and more diverse. Once limited to written texts and performances, the category of adaptation has expanded to include fashion, tourism, social media, recipes, and more. The question of whether there can be a common definition of "adaptation" or even what constitutes adaptation continues to be up for debate. Linda Hutcheon, whose 2006 book, *A Theory of Adaptation*, provides our introductory quote and is cited in most adaptation scholarship since its publication, offers a three-part definition:

In short, adaptation can be described as the following:

- An acknowledged transposition of a recognizable other work or works
- A creative and an interpretive act of appropriation/salvaging
- An extended intertextual engagement with the adapted work.

Therefore, an adaptation is a derivation that is not derivative—a work that is second without being secondary. It is its own palimpsestic thing.[23]

Hutcheon's definition of adaptation as process and product is both more inclusive—moving beyond easily recognized adaptation genres to include music, video games, and visual art—and restrictive. She specifies that adaptation requires extended engagement with a source text, which excludes allusions and musical sampling, due to their brevity and superficiality. Hutcheon also excludes sequels, prequels, and fan fiction, because "[t]here is a difference between never wanting a story to end . . . and wanting to retell the same story over and over in different ways."[24] For Hutcheon, repetition is a core characteristic of adaptation, though her understanding of "repetition" seems narrowly focused on plot, given the fact that sequels, prequels, and fan fiction all tend to focus on specific characters—backstories, alternative endings, reimagined relationships, and lives beyond the ending of the source texts—and usually announce their palimpsestic relationship to the source text.

Julie Sanders, in *Adaptation and Appropriation* (2006), likewise emphasizes acknowledgment of and sustained engagement with source texts in her definition of "adaptation." Sanders makes a distinction between adaptation and appropriation, which "frequently affects a more decisive journey away from the informing source into a wholly new cultural product and domain."[25] Appropriation, like adaptation, requires a source text, "[B]ut the appropriated text or texts are not always as clearly signaled or acknowledged as in the adaptive process."[26] Acknowledged by whom, though? Christopher L. Morrow considers how adaptation functions when the author does not acknowledge it as such or, as in the case of Ron Rash's novel, *Serena*, actively distances his work from the supposed source text, Shakespeare's *King Lear*. Morrow argues that authorial acknowledgment and intertextuality should not be the only criteria for identifying and analyzing adaptation and explores the ways in which "publishers, reviewers, readers, and the marketplace can acknowledge and construct relationships between adaptations and source texts."[27] Building upon Morrow's work, John R. Severn examines the effect of "unannounced adaptations," that is, a work that "neither announces itself as an adaptation nor attempts to conceal its status as an adaptation" in order to make the audience's gradual recognition of intertextuality part of the desired effect of the text.[28] Whereas Hutcheon, Sanders, Morrow, and others assert that source acknowledgment is essential to critical analysis of the commentary being made in an adaptation, Severn argues that identifying a specific source text actually limits the interpretive possibilities. Like Hutcheon, Severn emphasizes the process of adaptation as inextricably linked to adaptation as product. For Severn, though, the experience of an audience gradually recognizing a work as an adaptation reveals adaptation's "queer potential," which lies in its ability to "destabilize categories of identity."[29]

Alongside these questions about what constitutes adaptation and who decides are the myriad ways of describing the process of adaptation (oftentimes blurring the line between process and product, perhaps influenced by Hutcheon's three-part definition). Robert Stam draws upon Darwinism to compare adaptation to evolution: "Do not adaptations 'adapt to' changing environments and changing tastes, as well as to a new medium, with its distinct industrial demands, commercial pressures, censorship taboos, and aesthetic norms?"[30] Sanders also sees adaptation as a temporal and cultural process, though she calls it "a form of collaboration."[31] John Bryant's "fluid-text approach" aligns with Hutcheon's description of adaptation as palimpsest, in which all of the source texts and cultural influences are layered rather than merged: "a *work* is the sum of its versions; *creativity* extends beyond the solitary writer, and *writing* is a cultural event transcending media."[32] However, "fluid text" serves as an umbrella term, under which adaptation ("an announced retelling") is differentiated from an "adaptive revision" (similar to the distinction made by Sanders). Along similar lines, David Buchbinder defines adaptation according to the adapter's end goal: "'adaptations *of* an originary text and 'adaptations *from*' such a text (the latter idea sometimes phrased, in film credits, as 'based on' or 'inspired by' an originary text)."[33] Ultimately, Timothy Corrigan notes, there can be no single definition of "adaptation." The term itself is continually adapted to account for new media, new ways of thinking about author and audience, and new understandings of the complexity of the field. For this reason, Corrigan argues, "scholars and practitioners accordingly need to change and refocus regularly."[34] "Adaptation," it turns out, is as multilayered as the adaptations it attempts to define.

We do not seek to add to existing definitions and theories of the term; instead, we take to heart Kamilla Elliot's admonition: "Adaptation, which Hutcheon and others define as 'repetition with variation,' has produced a great deal of critical and theoretical repetition with very little variation. Joining argumentative repetition, scholars often fail to cite prior work upon which they build, exacerbating the sense of scatter and fruitless repetition."[35] In *Adaptation in Young Adult Novels*, we acknowledge and expand upon the work of adaptation scholars, examining not only what "counts" as an adaptation but also how adapted texts simultaneously claim and challenge the authority of canonical authors and the ways in which adapters utilize that authority to both perpetuate a text's canonical status and interrogate the limitations of that canon.

Adaptation and Young Adult Novels: Channeling and Challenging Authority

Anja Müller argues that "adaptations of canonical texts in children's literature are an important test case where an 'original' certified as belonging to a so-called 'high culture' is transported to a genre or medium with a still highly contested cultural status."[36] A fine line exists between the assumptions of quality among adaptations and the presumed quality of young adult novels, in particular. But we prefer to see the quality of young adult novels, going by Lee Talley's definition of "Young Adult" in *Keywords for Children's Literature* as, ultimately, works that are "potent and transformative."[37] Because it is written for a younger age group, the genre's role in a literary canon is often called into question, as all genre fiction often is. We instead see in the proliferation of novels for young adults evidence of a literate audience craving stories about agency, development, and journey. Whether through a fantastic landscape or a contemporary high school, young adult novels' ability to be "potent and transformative" drives the genre, and readers have flocked to the novels en masse.

Adaptation is not a new phenomenon to the literary world, but its proliferation in the genre of young adult fiction over the past several years has brought it into the critical spotlight. In *Reinventing Childhood Nostalgia: Books, Toys, and Contemporary Media Culture*, Elisabeth Wesseling sees adaptation as a return to the desires of youth, in this case, nostalgia, and notes, "Nostalgia is generally considered to be a merely reactionary form of resistance against modernity that cannot ever have constructive effects on the shaping of contemporary society and culture."[38] But it is not nostalgia alone that causes a text to be adapted for contemporary readers. In their discussion of the rewrites of *Alice in Wonderland*, Sonya Sawyer Fritz and Sara K. Day see Alice as a "particularly useful case study for a larger phenomenon: the ongoing and increasingly prevalent adaptation and appropriation of Victorian source material in media for twenty-first-century children and young adults."[39] Further, they argue:

> Certainly, these adaptations indicate a set of financial or consumer-driven considerations, motivated by the possibility of capitalizing on child readers as a new audience; at the same time, adaptations for young people allow us to more closely interrogate the construction of child readers as it specifically pertains to Victorian and neo-Victorian literature.[40]

Like Day and Fritz's collection, Benjamin Lefebvre's *Textual Transformations in Children's Literature: Adaptations, Translations, Reconsiderations* looks at both children's and young adult texts and argues, "These postmodern twists on canonical nineteenth- and early twentieth-century texts not only demonstrate a certain amount of playfulness toward the notion of a sacrosanct 'original' text, but they also lead to new and complex conversations about authorship, adaptation, and fidelity in the age of YouTube."[41] Like other postmodern genres that rewrite originals—neo-Victorianism, for example, or the defiant steampunk genre—adaptation can be seen as a postmodern genre, with roots going back to Geoffrey Chaucer and William Shakespeare. We propose to look at these "new and complex conversations about authorship, adaptation, and fidelity" for young adults because, in part, this age group plays the most with fandom, fan fiction, and defiance of the sacrosanct.

At the same time, as scholarship on reading like Andrea Coldwell's shows, teens are exploring their tastes and their roles as readers. Further, they are exploring the role of readership in their lives. What does it mean to be a reader in the age of YouTube, to parrot Lefebvre? Or, in the age of *The Cursed Child*, a Harry Potter, J. K. Rowling-approved sequel to the books? In the age of fan fiction and *The Lizzie Bennet Diaries*? Young adults are saturated by adaptations and, as evident by the market for them, are hungry for more.

The question then becomes, are authors demeaning the source material through adapting these texts and contexts for a young adult audience? Anja Müller in her *Adapting Canonical Texts in Children's Literature* understands that there is a proliferation of adaptation, but thinks it is "important to appreciate adaptations as artistic creations in their own right" when so often for readers and critics, "the underlying hope seems to be to guide the young reader 'home,' that is to the original."[42] *Adaptation in Young Adult Novels* argues that both are important and essential, the original and the adaptation, but also argues that the adaptation can shed light on important aspects of injustice and inequality that the original may hint at (or not) but not fully discuss. Our focus on canonical texts in particular for this collection argues for a refreshing new look at classics to see how they are being perceived, and reworked, in the twenty-first century. And, our focus on young adult novels, as opposed to film or multimedia adaptations, looks to the importance of the novel for young adults today, as well as notes the gap in adaptation scholarship that has, until now, mainly focused on cinematic or multimedia adaptations of classics for a children's rather than young adult audience.

In Part One: Representation Matters, the chapters examine adaptations in which marginalized and underrepresented voices are brought to the forefront in order not only to critique the source texts but also to address contemporary concerns about diversity, sexuality, and economic inequalities. Fiona Hartley-Kroeger considers novels in which Shakespeare's Benvolio and Rosaline replace Romeo and Juliet as lovers, questioning *Romeo and Juliet*'s status as one of the world's greatest love stories and turning Romeo's generic Petrarchan mistress into a fully realized heroine who *doesn't* die for love. In Indu Ohri's chapter, gender and class inequalities in Edith Wharton's short story, "Kerfol," are explored in Deborah Noye's *The Ghosts of Kerfol*, through the eyes of peripheral characters who not only solve the mystery of Kerfol's haunting but also subvert power imbalances to prevent the oppression of women. Rather than changing perspectives by featuring different characters as narrator, Sara Benincasa's *Great* adapts *The Great Gatsby* for modern readers by rewriting Nick as a teen girl (Naomi) and delving into the damaging effects of social media. Lisa Valenzuela's chapter emphasizes the ways in which Naomi's struggles with her sense of identity in the face of peer pressure reflect the concerns of contemporary young adult readers.

Both Dalila Forni and Saffyre Falkenberg are concerned with issues of representing diversity in European literary traditions. In her chapter, Dalila Forni analyzes two queer retellings of the Cinderella tale, stressing the importance of depicting nonheteronormative love stories and nonbinary characters in positive ways in young adult literature. Forni notes that queer adaptations of fairy tales not only allow LGBTQIA readers to see themselves in canonical texts, but, because of the historically social function of fairy tales, such adaptations can also effect positive change on the perceptions of queer people and relationships more broadly. Finally, Saffyre Falkenberg is likewise interested in the positive effects of seeing diversity in young adult literature. In her reading of Rick Riordan's series adapting Greek mythology, Falkenberg identifies some of the problems that come with representation for the sake of representation. Noting the ways in which Riordan, a white man, relies on stereotypes and whitewashes colonial history, Falkenberg points to Riordan's recent imprint to highlight the importance of self-representation, in the spirit of the #ownvoices movement.

Part Two, Literature and Popular Culture, probes the intersections of canonical texts and popular culture. Tara Moore studies the ways in which *Jane Eyre* "travels"— literally and figuratively—through speculative fiction adaptations of Charlotte Brontë's novel. Observing the choices adapters make in addressing the more problematic elements of *Jane Eyre*, Moore contends that, by introducing the novel to young adult readers via popular forms of genre fiction, adaptations extend the life of the text and, ideally, inspire young readers to seek out the "original" Jane. Turning her attention to the mother of science fiction, Melanie Marotta takes a look at Mary Shelley's influence on popular culture and the ways in which her biography informs Megan Shepherd's postmodern feminist adaptation of *Frankenstein*, *A Cold Legacy*. Eileen Totter compares Seth Grahame-Smith's *Pride and Prejudice and Zombies* with Steve

Hockensmith's sequel, *Dreadfully Ever After*, both of which unabashedly tap into the widespread interest in zombies in popular culture. Totter argues that, while both novels reimagine Elizabeth Bennet as an archetypal young adult dystopian heroine, only Hockensmith moves beyond the shock value of violence to create a dystopian version of Austen's novel in order to provide a sharp critique of social inequalities. Framing the Walt Disney Company's filmic fairy-tale adaptations as canonical texts in themselves, Michelle Anya Anjirbag and Madeleine Hunter examine Disney's series of spin-off novels for young adults, *Twisted Tales*. Anjirbag and Hunter assert that these novels, which offer alternative versions of the canonical films, not only extend the life of the source texts but also function to extend the interest of Disney's young audience. These novels, they argue, tap into adolescents' sense of nostalgia for their childhood, but offer darker narratives that undermine the films' happy endings and reflect teen readers' struggle to reconcile childhood and impending adulthood.

Finally, in Part Three, Making the Past Present, each chapter locates the space (physical or metaphorical) where adaptations bring canonical texts into direct contact with present-day readers. Amy L. Montz reads New York City as a canonical text, citing its representation as such in young adult novels set in the city during the nineteenth century. Montz explores the paratextual material in Jennifer Donnelly's *These Shallow Graves* and Katherine Howe's *The Appearance of Annie Van Sinderen*, paying particular attention to the novels' Author's Notes and Bibliographies. Pondering the texts' emphasis on historical accuracy and the research conducted to ensure it, along with lists of suggested supplementary texts for inquisitive readers, Montz argues that these novels recognize the intellect of young adult readers and their desire to be a part of the physical spaces of the novels they love. Likewise interested in the interactions of readers and texts, Brett Carol Young contends that Megan Shepherd's *The Madman's Daughter*, an adaptation of H. G. Wells's *The Island of Dr. Moreau* and the first book in Shepherd's Madwoman Trilogy, embeds a modernized teen girl protagonist within a neo-Victorian adaptation not only to connect with readers but also to serve as a guide for young adults who may be unfamiliar with the novel's context. Young argues that such embedded characters can teach inexperienced readers how to read canonical texts by introducing them to the similarities between the past and the present through the figure of a Victorian girl who expresses a modern feminist perspective. Maya Zakrzewska-Pim also examines the ways in which Sarah Rees Brennan's adaptation of Charles Dickens's *A Tale of Two Cities* emphasizes the parallels between the themes of her Victorian source text and its modernized historical adaptation. In particular, Zakrzewska-Pim is interested in Brennan's feminist revision, which emphasizes a rejection of traditional gender roles and issues of consent.

The final two chapters merge past and present by bringing canonical texts into a contemporary setting. Dana E. Lawrence reads Suzanne Selfors's meta-retelling of *Romeo and Juliet*, *Saving Juliet*, through the lens of literary tourism. In both meta-retellings, which feature a protagonist reading or performing the source text, and literary tourism, in which visitors get to enact their own vision of a text, the role of the author—in this case, Shakespeare—is usurped by the modern reader/visitor. The canonical text becomes one with the experience of the new storyteller, and the authority of literary history is simultaneously sustained and questioned. In Madeleine Tulip's analysis of Jesmyn Ward's *Salvage the Bones*, the Medea myth is likewise usurped by the novel's protagonist; however, Ward's adaptation of this familiar story is unannounced, and Tulip identifies the appropriation of the Medea tale by the novel's narrator, Esch, who, along with Ward, uses the Greek myth to correct the modern American myth of Hurricane Katrina and its effects.

Whether the desire for retellings and adaptations comes directly from a teen audience's wish to see themselves in the canonical texts they encounter in school or libraries or whether publishers and authors saw an untapped market ripe for the rewriting, it doesn't matter. What does matter is that these adaptations of canonical texts, places, myths, and stories offer their teen audience the chance to engage with stories and see their worth, sometimes centuries after they were written. The choices made by authors to rethink gender, sexuality, and class, among other markers of identity, help to make the original texts *more* relatable, not less. By seeing herself in a queer version of Cinderella, a reader can then take that knowledge of adaptation and discover the original fairy tale in a new light. Reading *The Great Gatsby* in high school with its male narrator may become more enjoyable knowing that the essence of the character is one yearning for that which they cannot have. Is that then not adolescence?

Notes

1 Hutcheon, *A Theory of Adaptation*, 176.
2 Coldwell, "Imagining Future Janeites," n.p.
3 Miola, "Seven Types of Intertextuality," 16.
4 Zarins, *Sometimes We Tell the Truth*, 426.
5 Ibid., n.p.
6 Chaucer, "Prologue," line 603.
7 Zarins, *Sometimes We Tell the Truth*, 8–9.
8 Chaucer, "Prologue," lines 4–6.
9 Ibid., lines 1–3.
10 Ibid., line 62.
11 Ibid., lines 66–70.
12 Ibid., lines 692–6.
13 Ibid., lines 597–9.
14 Ibid., lines 508–11.
15 Zarins, *Sometimes We Tell the Truth*, 157.
16 Ibid., 159.
17 Ibid.
18 Ibid., 406.
19 Ibid.
20 Ibid., 159.
21 Ibid., 171.
22 Ibid., 172.
23 Hutcheon, *A Theory of Adaptation*, 8–9.
24 Ibid., 9.

25 Sanders, *Adaptation and Appropriation*, 26.
26 Ibid., 26.
27 Morrow, "Acknowledgement," 138.
28 Severn, "All Shook Up," 549.
29 Ibid., 542.
30 Stam, "Introduction," 3.
31 Sanders, *Adaptation and Appropriation*, 47.
32 Bryant, "Textual Identity," 47.
33 Buchbinder, "From 'Wizard' to 'Wicked,' " 135.
34 Corrigan, "Defining Adaptation," 34.
35 Elliot, "Literary Film Adaptation," 24.
36 Müller, "Introduction," 2.
37 Talley, "Young Adult," 228.
38 Wesseling, *Reinventing*, n.p.
39 Fritz and Day, "Introduction," 2.
40 Ibid., 5.
41 Lefebvre, "Introduction," 1.
42 Müller, "Introduction," 2.

Bibliography

Bryant, John. "Textual Identity and Adaptive Revision: Editing Adaptation as a Fluid Text." In *Adaptation Studies: New Challenges, New Directions*, edited by Jørgen Bruhn, Anne Gjelsvik, and Eirik Frisvold Hanssen, 47–67. New York: Bloomsbury, 2013.

Buchbinder, David. "From 'Wizard' to 'Wicked': Adaptation Theory and Young Adult Fiction." In *Contemporary Children's Literature and Film: Engaging with Theory*, edited by Kerry Mallan and Clare Bradford, 127–46. New York: Palgrave Macmillan, 2011.

Chaucer, Geoffrey. "The Wife of Bath's Prologue." In *The Riverside Chaucer*, 3rd ed., edited by Larry D. Benson, 105–16. Boston: Houghton Mifflin, 1987.

Chaucer, Geoffrey. "The Wife of Bath's Tale." In *The Riverside Chaucer*, 3rd ed., edited by Larry D. Benson, 116–22. Boston: Houghton Mifflin, 1987.

Coldwell, Andrea. "Imagining Future Janeites: Young Adult Adaptations and Austen's Legacy." *Persuasions On-Line* 35, no. 1 (Winter 2014): n.p.

Corrigan, Timothy. "Defining Adaptation." In *The Oxford Handbook of Adaptation Studies*, edited by Thomas Leitch, 23–35. Oxford: Oxford University Press, 2017.

Elliot, Kamilla. "Literary Film Adaptation and the Form/Content Dilemma." In *Narrative across Media: The Languages of Storytelling*, edited by Marie-Laure Ryan, 220–43. Lincoln: University of Nebraska Press, 2004.

Fritz, Sonya Sawyer, and Sara K. Day. "Introduction." In *The Victorian Era in Twenty-First Century Children's and Adolescent Literature and Culture*, edited by Fritz and Day, 1–17. New York: Routledge, 2018.

Hutcheon, Linda. *A Theory of Adaptation*. New York: Routledge, 2006.

Lefebvre, Benjamin. "Introduction: Reconsidering Textual Transformations in Children's Literature." In *Textual Transformations in Children's Literature: Adaptations, Translations, Reconsiderations*, edited by Lefebvre, 1–6. New York: Routledge, 2013.

Miola, Robert S. "Seven Types of Intertextuality." In *Shakespeare, Italy, and Intertextuality*, edited by Michele Marrapodi, 13–25. Manchester: Manchester University Press, 2004.

Morrow, Christopher L. "Acknowledgment, Adaptation and Shakespeare in Ron Rash's *Serena*." *South Central Review* 30, no. 2 (2013): 136–61.

Müller, Anja. "Introduction: Adapting Canonical Texts in Children's Literature." In *Adapting Canonical Texts in Children's Literature*, edited by Müller, 1–8. New York: Bloomsbury, 2013.

Sanders, Julie. *Adaptation and Appropriation*. London: Routledge, [2006] 2010.

Severn, John R. "All Shook Up and the Unannounced Adaptation: Engaging with Twelfth Night's Unstable Identities." *Theatre Journal* 66, no. 4 (2014): 541–57.

Stam, Robert. "Introduction: The Theory and Practice of Adaptation." In *Literature and Film: A Guide to the Theory and Practice of Film Adaptation*, edited by Robert Stam and Alessandra Raengo, 1–52. New York: Blackwell, 2005.

Talley, Lee A. "Young Adult." In *Keywords for Children's Literature*, edited by Philip Nel and Lissa Paul, 228. New York: New York University Press, 2011.

Wesseling, Elisabeth. *Reinventing Childhood Nostalgia: Books, Toys, and Contemporary Media Culture*. New York: Routledge, 2017.

Zarins, Kim. *Sometimes We Tell the Truth*. New York: Simon Pulse, 2016.

Part One

Representation Matters

1

Re-visioning Rosaline; or, Romeo and Juliet Are Dead

Fiona Hartley-Kroeger

Something Is Rotten with *Romeo and Juliet*!

"Romeo and Juliet are just two rich kids who've always gotten every little thing they want. And now, they *think* they want each other …. It's Shakespeare making fun of love."[1] When asked to articulate her unimpressed reaction to *Romeo and Juliet*, Eleanor, one half of the eponymous duo in *Eleanor & Park*, voices a persistent stance within millennial receptions of *Romeo and Juliet*: that Romeo and Juliet's doomed romance engenders cynicism rather than sublime catharsis, nostalgia, or affection for the play. There is something wrong with the play, or more precisely with its reputation as the ultimate love story, that frustrates its audience and instills a powerful need for creative correction. Romeo and Juliet themselves prove impossible vehicles for this correction: they are dead, crushed by clichéd sentimentality, and cannot be the vehicles of *Romeo and Juliet*'s resurrection. Since the turn of the millennium, however, a micro-trend of *Romeo and Juliet*-inspired young adult novels have been published that feature not the eponymous star-crossed lovers but Rosaline, Romeo's initial object of poetic adoration, and Romeo's cousin, Benvolio. In *Still Star-Crossed* by Melinda Taub and *Prince of Shadows* by Rachel Caine, as well as Stacey Jay's duology of *Juliet Immortal* and *Romeo Redeemed*, Rosaline and Benvolio serve as doubles for the doomed Romeo and Juliet in efforts to resolve frustrations with the play and its ubiquitous but unsatisfactory reputation as the greatest love story ever told. These transformations engage directly with events of Shakespeare's play, with special focus on Rosaline as a replacement romantic heroine for the dead, idealized Juliet, drawing on Rosaline as the distant, chaste, silent beloved of the Petrarchan sonnet tradition in order to illuminate a need for women to survive and tell their own stories.

A number of scholars have positioned the act of retelling and adapting Shakespeare as an enterprise particularly congenial to feminist "re-vision," a term coined by Adrienne Rich to describe "the act of looking back, of seeing with fresh eyes, of entering an old text from a new critical direction."[2] For Rich, re-vision is "an act of survival," of understanding how women "have been led to imagine ourselves, how our language has trapped as well as liberated us; and how we can begin to see—and therefore live—afresh."[3] Re-vision enables women writers to reimagine possibilities for fictional women—possibilities beyond the fears of losing their youth and beauty, or of dying young and thus remaining beautiful eternally—and thereby to imagine possibilities for themselves and other women who read their work. As Marianne Novy observes, "Using fiction as a form of criticism, they [women rewriting Shakespeare] let characters escape plots that doom them to an oppressive marriage or to death ..., and they imagine stories for figures who are silent or demonized in Shakespeare's version."[4] Shakespeare's uber-canonical body of work is a high-profile locus for re-vision, and Julie Sanders argues that working in prose narrative is a way for women rewriters of Shakespeare to set themselves apart from "their male-authored dramatic precursors" and "assert the innovative and creative aspect of their work."[5] Juliet is one of those "image[s] of Woman" who die young and beautiful that Rich's woman writer finds "in books written by men"; but in the beautiful, idealized, dead girl, "precisely what she does not find is that absorbed, drudging, puzzled, sometimes inspired creature, herself."[6] Re-visioning *Romeo and Juliet* in prose narrative, then, is a powerful and productive act of feminist imagination. Choosing Rosaline for the focus of re-vision is particularly apt: re-visioning Rosaline, the silent Petrarchan mistress of poetry written by Romeo, written by Shakespeare, is a *double* act of liberation that has emerged as a powerful and popular opportunity for feminist adaptation in recent young adult fiction.

Romeo and Juliet Is for Teens, and Other Frustrations

Because of the young age of its protagonists, *Romeo and Juliet* is frequently associated with youth (rightly so) and therefore (perhaps less rightly) a youthful audience. Young readers and viewers most often encounter *Romeo and Juliet* in an educational context: it is foisted upon them under the assumption that they will find the adolescent characters relatable and sympathetic and the play, therefore, interesting. A young audience is expected, as Abigail Rokison puts it, to "identify with the play's central themes of generational conflict, violence, rebellion, and first love."[7] John Stephens and Robyn McCallum note that *Romeo and Juliet* is one of Shakespeare's most frequently "reversioned" plays.[8] But *Romeo and Juliet*'s cultural primacy, its position as the Shakespeare play (or retelling) *par excellence* for young readers—not necessarily for teens only—seems to be a twentieth-century development. The first edition of Charles and Mary Lamb's *Tales from Shakespeare* (1807)[9] places *Romeo and Juliet* as the seventh tale in the second volume—hardly a position of special emphasis. The first edition of E. Nesbit's *The Children's Shakespeare* (1897)[10] places *Romeo and Juliet* second. Some nineteenth- and early-twentieth-century retellings for children do not include *Romeo and Juliet* at all.[11] Several twentieth-century republications of the Lambs and Nesbit, however, have reordered the retellings to place prime emphasis on *Romeo and Juliet*. In a single-volume edition of the Lambs' *Tales*, published in 1901, the tales have been rearranged: *Romeo and Juliet* is now the first tale.[12] Similarly, the Opie Library's 1997 selection of E. Nesbit retellings begins with *Romeo and Juliet*.[13] These editorial reorderings give new priority to *Romeo and Juliet* as the first tale readers will encounter, strongly suggesting that young readers are supposed to like *Romeo and Juliet* as an individual work and as a gateway drug, as it were, to Shakespeare.

Yet a significant set of young adult adaptations presume frustration and dissatisfaction with *Romeo and Juliet*, even as they reward the implied reader's assumed affection for the language and, at the very least, a baseline familiarity with the story. W. B. Worthen locates this baseline familiarity, and its accompanying frustration, in "a contact narrative: Shakespeare in school."[14] Worthen finds that this first contact, this "celebration of school Shakespeare as an instrument of potentially transformative class ambition structuring mass education," cannot "overcome the inherent mystification of the project."[15] None of the participants interviewed for the Nature Theater of Oklahoma *Romeo and Juliet*, a "dedramatize[d]" production reconstructed from the participants' unaided memories of the play, can explain *why* they are forced to read *Romeo and Juliet* in school.[16] They share a frustration with the experience that lingers even when the play's exact events have been forgotten. Worthen describes this frustrated, imperfect remembrance of *Romeo and Juliet* as "the introjection of loss, an unhealing wound ... *Romeo and Juliet*, Shakespeare, are sites of shaming failure: the failure of the memory to store a culturally licensed narrative more completely."[17] In Worthen's argument, school contact with *Romeo and Juliet* fails to produce acquisition of cultural capital, and knowledge of their own inability to connect with the play results in shame for readers and viewers.

Millennial transformations of *Romeo and Juliet*, however, are motivated not by shame but by frustration and a conflicted kind of affection for the characters and Shakespeare's language. For underlying all of them is a desire to have a "do-over": to restage the tragedy in a way that allows the lovers, whoever they are, to live. The authors rely on frustration with the ways in which Romeo and Juliet are, again and again, barely thwarted and doomed to tragedy by the flimsiest of coincidences and mishaps. All of the lovers' attempts to escape the relentless feud their families' enmity has locked them into, and to define their own destinies, merely deliver them into the even more relentless machinations of a plot from which they cannot escape. The chance meeting at Capulet's ball; the tidy, direful formulation of "My only love sprung from my only hate";[18] the plague in Mantua that causes Friar Laurence's messenger to turn back; Romeo's arriving at the tomb *just* too soon; and Juliet's awakening *just* too late—all these turning points piled on each other are almost farcical in their sheer volume and relentlessness. What results for the audience or reader, especially given the play's ubiquitous reputation as the greatest love story ever told, is a frustration with that story. So appropriation is a chance to do it over; to do it right. Given the extent to which *Romeo and Juliet* is oversold and hypersaturated with cultural familiarity, foregrounding the minor (or non-) characters Rosaline and Benvolio brings a freshness to the act of retelling or transforming the tale.

Enter Rosaline: The Petrarchan Mistress in the Sonnet Sequence and *Romeo and Juliet*

Rosaline is not, technically, a character in *Romeo and Juliet*. She never speaks; she does not appear in the *dramatis personae*. She is a name for Romeo to spin into poetic platitudes, the archetypal distant mistress of the English love sonnet tradition who "hath sworn that she will still live chaste."[19] In Romeo's first appearance, it is she whose indifference "lengthens Romeo's hours," "Not having that which, having, makes them short,"[20] and makes him "Out of her favour where I am in love."[21] Like Dante's Beatrice or Petrarch's Laura, Rosaline is an unattainable object of erotic desire for the poet; Romeo's unfulfillable, unrequited desire for her prompts the writing of poetry. Early modern sonnet writing, inspired by Petrarch's sonnet sequence, enables the male poet-speaker to create an identity for himself: a creative identity instigated by desiring someone he cannot have. Astrophil, the eponymous speaker of Sir Philip Sidney's *Astrophil and Stella*—the touchstone sonnet sequence of Shakespeare's day, published posthumously in 1591 and briefly, extensively imitated by sonneteers of varying abilities—exemplifies the poetic pose of the "man on fire": driven by unrequited love for Stella, Astrophil uses his feelings as inspiration for writing poetry about his frustrated desire, and in doing so inhabits the persona of the rejected lover-poet. Sonneteering is as much, if not more, about creating the identity of the desiring speaker as it is about its ostensible object; "the 'Lady' of sonnet tradition," as Catherine Bates puts it, "is not so much a being, however idealized, as an element within a structure, a position, a 'You' to which the 'I' can orient itself and relate. Her job is quite functional. She is there purely to create a relational field and, in so doing, enable subjectivity."[22] Pining for Rosaline, writing poetry about her, is a means for Romeo to define himself, to construct his own subjectivity.

Rosaline further serves this "relational field" as the catalyst for Romeo and Juliet's meeting: her name, which Romeo reads on the Capulet guest list,[23] prompts him and his friends to gate-crash the Capulet feast. Rosaline's name occasions the very meeting that drives all thought of her from Romeo's mind. For once Romeo falls in love with Juliet, Rosaline and the version of love she enables are no longer attractive to him. Mercutio attempts to conjure the poet Romeo by reciting sonnet clichés, bidding him "Speak but one rhyme and I am satisfied."[24] Mercutio's taunts culminate in a catalog of Rosaline's body parts in a parody of the blazon, a common sonnet device that, as Nancy Vickers describes, "figuratively dismembers the female body."[25]

> I conjure thee by Rosaline's bright eyes,
> By her high forehead and her scarlet lip,
> By her fine foot, straight leg, and quivering thigh,
> And the demesnes that there adjacent lie
> That in thy likeness thou appear to us.[26]

Mercutio mocks Romeo's self-oriented obsession with the Petrarchan mistress and with clichéd sonnet language. But Mercutio's conjuring fails to produce Romeo-as-poet, for Romeo's identity, now that he has met Juliet, has shifted: no longer the perpetuator of a tired, ubiquitous sonnet tradition, Romeo's request to "Call me but love, and I'll be new baptis'd:/ Henceforth I never will be Romeo"[27] reveals a willingness to shed his former subjectivity ("Madman! Passion! Lover!"[28]), along with the Montague name. Rosaline's name, and his own former identity as her frustrated lover, he has forgotten—"I have forgot that name, and that name's woe."[29]

Once Romeo discards the mantle of poet-lover, Rosaline's presence in the text—which is defined by her absence, her distance, her lack of response to Romeo's overtures, and her replacement in his affections—operates as a benchmark against which to measure Romeo's love for Juliet, and Juliet's reciprocal, enthusiastic love for Romeo. Distant, unfeeling Rosaline contrasts with Juliet, the passionate, innocent lover who reciprocates Romeo's feelings and acknowledges her own, despite the norms of polite society. "Fain would I dwell on form: fain, fain deny/ What I have spoke,"[30] says Juliet, aware that the spontaneous expression of her feelings is improper but aware, too, that denying them is pointless. In this willingness to honestly acknowledge and act on her feelings, Juliet rejects the maidenly forms of coyness of which Rosaline, the Petrarchan mistress, is an extreme version. "Her I love now," explains Romeo to a skeptical Friar Laurence, "Doth grace for grace and love for love allow./ The other did not so."[31] Friar Laurence, unable to find fault with this logic, responds with a dig at Romeo's erstwhile use of love poetry as self-creation, noting, "O, she knew well/ Thy love did read by rote that could not spell."[32] Rosaline, he says, refused to reciprocate Romeo's love because that love was merely a reproduction of sonnet clichés and not genuinely felt.

Rosaline thus serves as a basis for comparison with Juliet, a placeholder for authentic desire, and a commentary on Romeo's clinging to a clichéd courtly love poetic tradition—a tradition he participates in because he does not have the lived experience to understand real love or articulate it in an authentic and persuasive way until he falls in love with Juliet, and she with him. Since Rosaline is a placeholder, the enabler of a field of relations with no subjectivity of her own, and a name that stands for a poetic tradition but is not attached to a real character, she can become anything the creative purposes of adaptation want her to be.

The Petrarchan Mistress Embodied: A Blank Space

Rosaline's lack of definition as a character—because she is not a character—leaves her as a convenient space that writers can adapt for a wide range of purposes and interpretations. Rosaline makes an appearance in Mary Cowden Clarke's *Girlhood of Shakespeare's Heroines* series in "Juliet; The White Dove of Verona." An overeducated foil for Juliet and Juliet's untrained but intuitive love of beauty and emotions, Rosaline is a self-satisfied know-it-all, overly pleased with her own intellect and opinions, both impressive and ridiculous to her Capulet relatives. Cowden Clarke's Tybalt calls her an "affected young pedant" (though not to her face).[33] Juliet, by contrast, is "no reader,— she fed her thoughts with things, rather than with studies, and gained ideas from objects, instead of from books."[34] Rosaline cares only for study and for her own moral and intellectual excellence. If Juliet is too inclined to passion, Rosaline is too inclined to reason and too conscious of the impression she creates. She deems love and courtship a waste of time because they distract from the "high pursuits" to which she has chosen to dedicate herself.[35] Her "sublime style of lofty humility"[36] renders her superiority ironic, but (unlike many later writers) Cowden Clarke takes Rosaline's Petrarchan chastity seriously. As Erica Hateley notes, Cowden Clarke seeks to "render the playwright's version coherent with and for a nineteenth-century female readership, not necessarily to displace it."[37] The archetypally distant, unavailable Petrarchan mistress becomes a smug, wealthy, beautiful scholar who opts for chastity and the (literally) holier-than-thou lifestyle it affords.

Cowden Clarke uses Rosaline's disdain for courtship in general, and Romeo in particular, on the grounds that "I should have no time I could call my own, were I to admit his attentions,"[38] to prime Juliet, in a move of emotional perversity, to be receptive to love. Juliet pities this unknown lover, as yet unnamed (but whom the audience knows to be Romeo), and "now, for the first time, asked herself what her own feelings would be, were she to discover that she had inspired such a passion."[39] The prospect of inspiring passion transforms Juliet, hitherto a lively, curious child, into an object of art who "seemed awaiting,—like the clay Pandora, the touch of Prometheus,—the vital fire of Love, which was to make her, from a dreaming child into a sentient, passionate woman."[40]

Neither Rosaline nor Juliet, in Cowden Clarke's version, is a good model for her readers to emulate. Juliet is too passionate and susceptible to self-destructive love. Rosaline appears too smug and passionless because she cares nothing for earthly things; while condemning as soulless the sort of woman who would choose the "drudgery" of marriage,[41] she has perhaps neglected aspects of her own soul. Though her role in Cowden Clarke's tale is nuanced, Rosaline remains opaque and unfocused; she serves to prime Juliet for romantic susceptibility, not as a protagonist in her own right.

More recently, around the turn of the millennium, Sharman Macdonald's play, *After Juliet*, imagines Rosaline as a vengeful heir to Tybalt's anti-Montague rage.[42] *Romeo's Ex: Rosaline's Story*, by Lisa Fiedler, reformulates her as a career-oriented healer-in-training; Rebecca Serle's modern-day Rosaline is Romeo's possessive would-be girlfriend in *When You Were Mine*. In Rosamund Hodge's magical, radically reimagined post-apocalyptic world of *Bright Smoke, Cold Fire*, Rosaline (Runajo) is a novice tasked with helping to preserve the last city standing. The novels explored in this chapter use the Rosaline-shaped space to critique the play's idealization of the dead lovers, who are tricked by dramatic chance into (to borrow a phrase from Sandra M. Gilbert and Susan Gubar) "kill[ing] themselves into art."[43] Their critiques aim particularly at Juliet and her fate, seeking to reorient the star-crossed lovers' plot away from tragedy toward comedy and a version of romantic fulfillment that prioritizes maturity, resourcefulness, and vitality in pursuit of self-actualization.

Stacey Jay's duology of *Juliet Immortal* and *Romeo Redeemed* is a continuation story, based on the premise that *Romeo and Juliet* as we know it is an erroneous version of true historical events. Romeo and Juliet themselves do not die but become enemies embroiled in a cosmic battle between good and evil, love and death. Embedded in the premise is a critique of the plot machinery of *Romeo and Juliet*. Jay replaces one improbable plot with another, but hers gives the characters some agency to escape the confines of Shakespeare's events by moving across time and space, in and out of other bodies, and through multiple, simultaneous versions of reality. Exactly how much agency they gain is questionable, however, for both Juliet and Romeo willingly enter the service of cosmic factions that control their actions. The fracturing, multiplying versions of reality in Jay's novels recalls Graham Holderness's observation that

"Shakespeare now exists in an environment of textual multiplicity. The text is multiple, iterable, subject to an inevitable law of change."[44] All versions of events, in the story as told by Jay, are simultaneously true; they do not collapse when the characters—or perhaps their souls or essences—shift into a different reality. Shakespeare's *Romeo and Juliet* and Jay's novels coexist; knowledge of the one informs knowledge of the other, and the reader can contain multiple experiences of *Romeo and Juliet* simultaneously.

In *Juliet Immortal*, Juliet reveals that Romeo actually helped Shakespeare write the play and "twisted [the] story to fit his agenda."[45] Juliet, inhabiting a text born from frustration with her story's unearned reputation, rails against popular receptions of *Romeo and Juliet* that "further the goals of the Mercenaries—glamorizing death, making dying for love seem the most noble act of all, though nothing could be further from the truth."[46] Jay's books argue instead for love as an empowering force that, liberated from the totalitarian confines of plot, *can* end happily. But the argument is complicated by the ever-multiplying versions of reality and the friction between the characters' agency and the constraints of greater cosmic forces—even when those forces act in their favor.

Rosaline serves as a proxy for Juliet in the second book, *Romeo Redeemed*. Her identity provides an alternate-past space for a modern-day girl named Ariel, who falls in love with Romeo (Juliet and Benvolio having been paired up in the previous book, *Juliet Immortal*, during which Ariel serves as a host body for the incorporeal Juliet). When Ariel and Romeo arrive in an alternate past, Ariel finds herself in the body of Rosaline, the former object of Romeo's affection—or rather, Jay casts them as versions of the same person. Ariel realizes, "Rosaline is what I could have been if I'd been born in a different time, raised a different way, taught different things."[47] Compelled by necessity to stay in the past, Ariel absorbs Rosaline into her own identity, and she and Romeo are able to live happily ever after. For Jay, the empty space of the Petrarchan mistress functions much as it does in the sonnet sequence: as a useful enabler of someone else's subjectivity. When confronted with her alternate self from the future, Rosaline becomes subsumed, her identity absorbed by the more forceful version of herself. The Petrarchan emptiness manifests as a shell for her alternate self to step into, a placeholder for someone else to become.

The Petrarchan Mistress Speaks: *Still Star-Crossed*

While Benvolio and Rosaline are relegated to period-correct identities for the modern-day love interests of Juliet and Romeo, respectively, in Jay's books, they take a more central role in *Still Star-Crossed* by Melinda Taub. As dual protagonists, they share the narrative's focalization in this direct sequel to the events of *Romeo and Juliet*. The novel picks on the lingering social tensions between the Capulets and the Montagues: Shakespeare's "glooming peace"[48] is short-lived, and the twin (or perhaps rival) golden statues of Romeo and Juliet are fresh fodder for desecration, insult, and bloodshed. Prince Escalus attempts to impose order on the city by superseding the reluctant heads of the families and arranging a second union between them: namely, marriage between Rosaline Capulet and Benvolio Montague. The pair are thus literally replacements for Romeo and Juliet within the world of the novel and in Taub's critique of the tragedy that purports to end civil strife but does not guarantee peace.

Escalus's plan does not go well. The script he attempts to write for Rosaline and Benvolio is continually thwarted by internal factors (their mutual personal and family-mandated dislike and Rosaline's progressively requited childhood love for Escalus) as well as external (news of the betrothal sparks rioting, and a not-dead-after-all Count Paris schemes to use the chaos to usurp his kinsman's throne). Instead, Rosaline and Benvolio decide to find out who is inciting the continued violence, bring the perpetrator to the Prince's justice, and thus bring peace to the city and negate the necessity of their marriage. They embark on a sleuthing plotline that allows them to bicker their way into a romance after all.[49] Taub layers plot machinery in an implicit critique of the relentless series of coincidences and disastrous timing that doom Romeo and Juliet. The plot of *Still Star-Crossed*, while constraining the characters in certain directions toward an end predetermined by genre (bickering, mystery-solving romance), allows the characters enough agency to respond to their circumstances in a reasonable, productive manner that contrasts with the ominous, destructive passion of their cousins.

Taub's third-person narration is written in contemporary English, but the characters mimic the conventions of early modern language when speaking or thinking. This difference between narration and "spoken" language both weakens and makes visible the division between drama and novel forms. It is an uneasy hybrid text that never collapses back into drama, but conjures it up every time a character speaks. This ever-present reminder of textual multiplicity foregrounds the background work of appropriation: the characters on the page of a novel have a degree of authorially determined interiority that, in a performance text, requires an actor or a more participatory reader to interpret. This is not to say that a novel must be read passively; merely that by virtue of form, the reader/audience experience is mediated differently. As Worthen puts it, "A reader [of plays] can imagine the richly ambiguous interplay of materialized assertion and nuance, the complex armature of embodiment, posture, and gesture, certainty and uncertainty, the dialectic of opportunity and agency enlarging and implementing Shakespeare's writing onstage."[50] The reader of a novel does this too, but the experience, instead of being mediated through an observed performance, is mediated through another layer of written text. The hybridity of *Still Star-Crossed* calls attention to this mediation and constantly reminds the reader that this is a work of appropriation across literary forms as well as across time and language. Rosaline, as a focalizer, is thus a dual subject: she is not only a character in a novel but also analogous to an actor mediating between text and audience.

Language also serves to explicitly mark Rosaline and Benvolio as doubles—echoes, or perhaps mirrors—for their dead kin. When forced to camp out of doors during the course of their investigation, Rosaline and Benvolio echo the language of the lovers in *Romeo and Juliet*, who are reluctant to bid farewell after their first and only night together:

JULIET
Wilt thou be gone? It is not yet near day.

It was the nightingale and not the lark
That pierc'd the fearful hollow of thine ear.
Nightly she sings on yond pomegranate tree.
Believe me, love, it was the nightingale.
ROMEO
It was the lark, the herald of the morn,
No nightingale.[51]

In *Still Star-Crossed*, Benvolio attempts to wake the sleepy Rosaline: "'Day is here, lady. Dost thou not hear the lark?' She rolled over, her arm flopping across his face. 'Hush,' she mumbled. ''Tis not the—'"[52] The contrast between the tragic lovers, reluctant to be parted, and the bickering pair who have spent a decidedly unromantic and uncomfortable night out of doors is comical and emphasizes their practical yet playful personalities. "Perhaps 'tis the lark," Rosaline acknowledges.[53] Benvolio momentarily channels the reformed Kate the Shrew in addition to Romeo in his reply, "I am ready to declare it any bird thou say'st."[54] The scene is equally poignant and humorous, assuming an audience familiar with the Shakespearean scene; without that familiarity, its humorous aspect dominates as the pair banter their way into heroism. Innocent, passionate Romeo and Juliet are dead; older, wiser, wittier Rosaline, a speaking, thinking subject, survives to save her city and embark on a lifetime of companionable bickering with an equally sanguine Benvolio.

The Mistress in the Margins: *Prince of Shadows*

Prince of Shadows by Rachel Caine is a prequel and first-person retelling of *Romeo and Juliet* from Benvolio's point of view. Like Taub, Caine foregrounds the civil conflict in her adaptation, depicting the two houses as alike not only in dignity but also in their modus operandi as violent, tyrannical, even abusive families. This highly restrictive social and familial hierarchy justifies Romeo and Juliet's desire for escape as well as for secrecy; these are not families who forgive disobedience. Rosaline enters Benvolio's life as the unwilling recipient of Romeo's love poetry. Benvolio's exasperation with Romeo mirrors many readerly frustrations, and his respect for and interest in Rosaline offers an indirect portrait of a level-headed, self-controlled, highly literate young woman. This version of Rosaline both inhabits and resists the distant, cold Petrarchan mistress identity. She is the object of Romeo's poetry, transformed by his imagination into a construct on which to hang his dreams of love. Alas for Romeo, she is also a real character—and one unimpressed by his literary efforts, which she dismisses as "awful drivel."[55] Rosaline's own bookishness does not predispose her to admire poetry and behavior that is "by th' book."[56] Adding insult to injury, she tells Benvolio, "Your cousin reads by rote and cannot spell."[57] Friar Laurence attributes precisely this critique to Rosaline in 2.3.84, and coming from her own mouth in *Prince of Shadows*, it becomes a protest against being fixed in the Petrarchan mistress status (by a bad poet, no less).

The other ways in which Caine's narrative objectifies Rosaline, however, further complicate her subjectivity. Rosaline *is* an active participant in the events of the book, not as a poetic construct but as a body and mind with an awareness of its relation to others and the agency to think and act within the constraints of her circumstances. But her narrative participation occupies a double space of being under the male gaze and, simultaneously, protesting the multivalent constraints of that gaze. The blazon tradition haunts Caine's Rosaline. Benvolio's perspective is hyperaware of Rosaline's physicality: he is constantly catching a "glimpse" of "flashing dark eyes" or "the shape of her fingers" or "a glossy dark fall" of hair.[58] Though he is no poet, his gaze replicates the blazon on her living body. In *Prince of Shadows*, Mercutio's taunting catalogue of conjures, closely following Shakespeare's in 2.1.17-20, is thus doubly crude and reveals the violence inherent in the blazon's poetic dismemberment.[59] "Rosaline's bright eyes ... her high forehead and her scarlet lips ... her fine foot, straight leg and quivering thigh, and the domains that there adjacent lie"[60] are simultaneously poetic clichés and body parts belonging to an actual woman whose body is constantly subject to the whims of others. Rosaline's body is also subject to the violent abuses of Tybalt (her brother in this version) and the senior Capulets; her mind is constantly under threat of expulsion to a nunnery "that held to the belief that women should be dumb beasts, content to parrot the responses given to them and mortify their sinful flesh."[61] The constant threat of violence from both Montagues and Capulets, and even Benvolio's gaze, confines her living female body within social and literary boundaries.

Though Benvolio's narration appreciates her as a thinking and acting subject, Rosaline rails at the partial picture of her gendered subjectivity that Benvolio's point of view allows. "You know nothing about us, Benvolio Montague," she rages in a rare moment of open conflict. "We live our lives in terror, not in safety—terror of our fathers, who may beat or kill us with any reason or none at all ... terror of other women whispering rumors that destroy us, with no defenses possible. You have swords to defend your honor. We have *nothing*."[62] This outburst exposes the constraints imposed on Rosaline by the conventions of her world, even as it mourns the silencing of women's voices in literature and life. In defiance of this objectification, Rosaline's writing emerges in the margins, in diary entries and correspondence that punctuate (and puncture) the narrative and its male voice. Most of the novel is in the first person, focalized through Benvolio. The diary entries, however, come directly from Rosaline's own hand: she is the focalizer and writer of these documents. Though they are often destroyed or undelivered, imposing silence on her once again, the diary entries resist the roles that men try to confine her to: poetic placeholder, love interest, sister, property. In these moments of resistance to male narration, Rosaline the Petrarchan mistress and Rosaline the object of the male gaze become Rosaline the author.

Rosaline's emotional and poetic literacy, combined with Benvolio's clever, controlled forms of rebellion and self-definition, form the hinge on which Caine's appropriation turns. This version of Rosaline is a reader of poetry, yes, but a critical reader, and one whose vitality comes from self-actualization, not from loving or poetically defining someone else. "I'd thought that a bookish aging virgin would have hoarded love poems to greedily warm her in the cold," observes Benvolio, "but Rosaline clearly held her own source of heat. She radiated it like a bonfire."[63] Rosaline has a rich inner life that Benvolio (and thus the reader) can appreciate but not wholly fathom, a sovereignty of self that is vulnerable to oppression but is part of what helps her survive where Caine's (and by extension Shakespeare's) Juliet is consumed when Romeo abandons literary passion for living, breathing love. Rosaline and Benvolio, in Caine's adaptation, lay bare the dangerous fragility of Romeo and Juliet's love, even before the farcically obstructive plot drives them to their deaths.

Caine accounts for the deadly accumulation of tragic coincidences by having Mercutio cast "a plague on both your houses" as a magical curse.[64] Repentant on his deathbed, Mercutio tells Benvolio that "Love is the curse."[65] Mercutio's curse of destructive love accounts for the relentlessness of the plot machine and the inability of Romeo and Juliet to escape from it. Against this backdrop, Caine asks: What happens if you put two *other* characters in what looks like exactly the same position as Romeo and Juliet and subject them to what looks like the same plot machinery? Benvolio and Rosaline are able to thwart the curse because of their greater age, their more thoroughly developed individual identities, and their awareness of the curse's existence. Their love, when they admit to it, is founded in mutual esteem and attraction, rather than the uncanny, unnatural, irresistible love that is "too like the lightning"[66] of their cousins. They are saved by an orientation toward love that prioritizes the beloved's well-being and cognizance that life can differ from art. This is a lesson Shakespeare's Romeo and Juliet appear to be learning, as Juliet repeatedly diverts Romeo away from sonnet cliché declarations in their early courtship, but do not have the time or maturity to put into practice. Rosaline and Benvolio, as more mature, self-controlled, literate versions of their cousins, are saved by being able to act on understanding the difference between loving someone (literally) on paper and loving someone in real life.

Conclusions

Even when partially or wholly liberated from Petrarchan mistress status in these re-visions, Rosaline never fulfills her resolution "to live chaste."[67] The female figure who declares uninterest in marriage becomes a romantic heroine under the dictates of the revised or continued plot. Megan Lynne Isaac notes that young adult appropriations in the twentieth century often deemphasize the sexuality that charges *Romeo and Juliet*.[68] Is Rosaline's sexuality—heterosexuality—an indication that the tables have turned on what is considered acceptable for teen readers? This seems likely, given the vast and rapid changes the young adult landscape has undergone since the 1990s. Sexuality and desire are more likely to be celebrated—at least in *Romeo and Juliet* adaptations—as natural parts of a fully realized life. Textual transformations have tremendous potential "to complicate what it means to recognize the presence of eroticism in literary representation" and to explore and "interrogate our own flashes of transhistorical erotic identification as readers."[69] This set of adaptations suggest that it is still of interest, even at this cultural moment, to tell *Romeo and Juliet* stories that validate the main characters' heterosexual desire for one another, no matter who the main characters are.

Other, less central characters are more likely sites for "queer desires and acts";[70] *Prince of Shadows* gives Mercutio a male lover, though that relationship ends in tragedy to fuel the curse plot.

Revising *Romeo and Juliet* as Rosaline's story, often pairing her with Benvolio, is a way for authors to grapple with frustrations with *Romeo and Juliet* and its cultural cachet, particularly the gendered cultural baggage that surrounds Juliet as an idealized dead heroine. Drawing on the sonnet tradition to which Shakespeare's Rosaline belongs, authors transform the Petrarchan mistress figure—who exists only to define the male poet-speaker—into a protagonist with a subjectivity of her own. Although the embodiment and self-realization of the Petrarchan mistress are revolutionary acts in and of themselves, Rosaline is never just herself: She functions as a more mature double for Juliet, whose life and death haunt the narratives. In foregrounding an active, self-actualized, self-aware heroine who *survives*, the novels critique the constraints that doom Romeo and Juliet within the play and the subsequent cultural reverence for the lovers' suicides. Heroism, they suggest, is not about dying for love but living for (or in spite of) it.

Notes

1. Rowell, *Eleanor & Park*, 44.
2. Rich, "When We Dead Awaken," 18.
3. Ibid.
4. Novy, *Transforming Shakespeare*, 1.
5. Sanders, *Novel Shakespeares*, 4.
6. Rich, "When We Dead Awaken," 21.
7. Rokison, "Romeo and Juliet for the Young Viewer," 42.
8. Stephens and McCallum, *Retelling Stories, Framing Culture*, 256.
9. Lamb and Lamb, *Tales from Shakespeare Vol. 1 and 2*.
10. Nesbit, *The Children's Shakespeare*.
11. For content comparisons, see Richmond, *Shakespeare as Children's Literature*.
12. A copy of this edition housed at the Folger Shakespeare Library bears a bookplate proclaiming that it was "Awarded to Alice Morwood. Attendance and conduct." That this edition was awarded in an educational context for exemplary behavior underscores Shakespeare's importance as a bearer of cultural capital and also *Romeo and Juliet*'s presumed appeal to young readers. Charles Lamb's preface envisions the *Tales* as a conduct manual for young girls; Alice Morwood's prize suggests an ongoing association between Shakespeare retellings and models of good female behavior. See Hateley, *Shakespeare in Children's Literature*.
13. Nesbit, *The Best of Shakespeare*.
14. Worthen, *Shakespeare Performance Studies*, 58.
15. Ibid.
16. Ibid., 56.
17. Ibid., 64.
18. Shakespeare, *Romeo and Juliet* (abbreviated henceforth as *RJ*), 1.5.137.
19. Ibid., 1.1.215.

20 Ibid., 1.1.161-62.
21 Ibid., 1.1.166.
22 Bates, "Desire, Discontent, Parody," 107.
23 *"My fair niece Rosaline," RJ*, 1.2.70.
24 Ibid., 2.1.9.
25 Vickers, "Members Only," 5.
26 *RJ*, 2.1.17-21.
27 Ibid., 2.2.50-1.
28 Ibid., 2.1.7.
29 Ibid., 2.3.42.
30 Ibid., 2.2.88-9.
31 Ibid., 2.4.81-3.
32 Ibid., 2.4.83-4.
33 Cowden Clarke, *The Girlhood of Shakespeare's Heroines*, 461.
34 Ibid., 457.
35 Ibid., 461.
36 Ibid.
37 Hateley, "Sink or Swim?" 439.
38 Cowden Clarke, *The Girlhood of Shakespeare's Heroines*, 462.
39 Ibid., 463.
40 Ibid.
41 Ibid., 462.
42 Though this essay focuses on young adult novels, the play merits note as an early Rosaline re-vision for youth. Abigail Rokison observes that most transformations of Shakespeare for children are prose novels, not drama (57). *After Juliet* is one of the few transformative appropriations of *Romeo and Juliet* for the stage, written specifically for youth performers. Macdonald credits her daughter, Keira Knightley, with the "original idea" to write a play focused on Rosaline (1). Knightley performed the role of Rosaline in the premiere.
43 Gilbert and Gubar, "The Queen's Looking Glass," 201.
44 Holderness, *Tales from Shakespeare*, 7.
45 Jay, *Juliet Immortal*, 17.
46 Ibid.
47 Jay, *Romeo Redeemed*, 335.
48 *RJ*, 5.3.304.
49 Their dynamic as a couple is frequently informed by Shakespeare's reluctant or bickering lovers, notably Beatrice and Benedick of *Much Ado about Nothing*.
50 Worthen, *Shakespeare Performance Studies*, 53.
51 *RJ*, 3.5.1-7.
52 Taub, *Still Star-Crossed*, 207.
53 Ibid.
54 Ibid., 208, after Shakespeare, *RJ* 3.5.19-22: "I'll say yon grey is not the morning's eye,/ 'Tis but the pale reflex of Cynthia's brow./ Nor that is not the lark whose notes do beat/ The vaulty heaven so high above our heads" and *Taming*, 4.5.22-3: "What you will have it named, even that it is,/ And so it shall be so for Katherine."
55 Caine, *Prince of Shadows*, 41.
56 *RJ*, 1.5.109.
57 Caine, *Prince of Shadows*, 41.

58 Caine, *Prince of Shadows*, 149, 151, 198.
59 See Vickers, "Members Only," 5.
60 Ibid., 194, after *RJ*, 2.1.17-20.
61 Ibid., 150.
62 Ibid., 318–19.
63 Ibid., 41.
64 Ibid., 245, after *RJ*, 3.1.100-101 and 108, "A plague o' both your houses."
65 Ibid., 249.
66 *RJ*, 2.2.119.
67 Ibid., 1.1.215.
68 "The perversity of canonizing *Romeo and Juliet* and then refusing to acknowledge one of the very themes that makes it attractive to young audiences speaks volumes about our society" (Isaac, 65).
69 Varnado, "'Invisible Sex!,'" 42 and 47–8.
70 Ibid., 48.

Bibliography

Bates, Catherine. "Desire, Discontent, Parody: The Love Sonnet in Early Modern England." In *The Cambridge Companion to the Sonnet*, edited by A. D. Cousins and Peter Howarth, 105–24. Cambridge: Cambridge University Press, 2011.

Caine, Rachel. *Prince of Shadows*. New York: New American Library, 2014.

Cowden Clarke, Mary. *The Girlhood of Shakespeare's Heroines*. New York: G.P. Putnam's Sons, [1851] 1873.

Fiedler, Lisa. *Romeo's Ex: Rosaline's Story*. New York: Henry Holt, 2006.

Gilbert, Sandra M., and Susan Gubar. "The Queen's Looking Glass." In *Don't Bet on the Prince*, edited by Jack Zipes, 201–8. London: Routledge, 1987.

Hateley, Erica. *Shakespeare in Children's Literature: Gender and Cultural Capital*. London: Routledge, 2009.

Hateley, Erica. "Sink or Swim?: Revising Ophelia in Contemporary Young Adult Fiction." *Children's Literature Association Quarterly* 38, no. 4 (2013): 435–48.

Hodge, Rosamund. *Bright Smoke, Cold Fire*. New York: Balzer & Bray, 2016.

Holderness, Graham. *Tales from Shakespeare: Creative Collisions*. Cambridge: Cambridge University Press, 2014.

Isaac, Megan Lynn. *Heirs to Shakespeare: Reinventing the Bard in Young Adult Literature*. Portsmouth: Boynton/Cook, 2000.

Jay, Stacey. *Juliet Immortal*. New York: Delacorte Press, 2011.

Jay, Stacey. *Romeo Redeemed*. New York: Delacorte Press, 2012.

Lamb, Charles, and Mary Lamb. *Tales from Shakespeare Vol. 1 and 2*. London: Thomas Hodgkins, 1807.

Lamb, Charles, and Mary Lamb. *Tales from Shakespeare*. London: Sands, 1901.

Macdonald, Sharman. *After Juliet*. London: Faber and Faber, 2001.

Nesbit, E. *The Best of Shakespeare*. Edited by Iona Opie. Oxford: Oxford University Press, 1997.

Nesbit, E. *The Children's Shakespeare*. Edited by Eric Vredenburg. London: Raphael Tuck, 1897.

Novy, Marianne (ed.). *Transforming Shakespeare: Contemporary Women's Re-Visions in Literature and Performance*. New York: St. Martin's Press, 1999.

Rich, Adrienne. "When We Dead Awaken: Writing as Re-vision." *College English* 34, no. 1 (October 1972): 18–30.

Richmond, Velma Bourgeois. *Shakespeare as Children's Literature: Edwardian Retellings in Words and Pictures*. Jefferson: McFarland, 2008.

Rokison, Abigail. "Romeo and Juliet for the Young Viewer—Interpretation and Adaptation." *New Review of Children's Literature and Librarianship* 15, no. 1 (2009): 42–66.

Rowell, Rainbow. *Eleanor & Park*. New York: St Martin's Griffin, 2013.

Sanders, Julie. *Novel Shakespeares: Twentieth-Century Women Novelists and Appropriation*. Manchester: Manchester University Press, 2001.

Serle, Rebecca. *When You Were Mine*. New York: Simon Pulse, 2012.

Shakespeare, William. *Romeo and Juliet*. Edited by Brian Gibbons. London: Arden Shakespeare, 2008.

Shakespeare, William. *The Taming of the Shrew*. Edited by Barbara Hodgdon. London: Arden Shakespeare, 2010.

Sidney, Sir Philip. "Astrophil and Stella." In *The Broadview Anthology of British Literature: Concise Edition, Vol. A*, 2nd ed., edited by Joseph Black, Leonard Conolly, Kate Flint, Isobel Grundy, Don LePan, Roy Liuzza, Jerome J. McGann, Anne Lake Prescott, Barry V. Qualls, and Claire Waters, 731–40. Peterborough: Broadview Press, 2017.

Stephens, John, and Robyn McCallum. *Retelling Stories, Framing Culture: Traditional Story and Metanarratives in Children's Literature*. New York: Garland/Taylor and Francis, 1998.

Taub, Melinda. *Still Star-Crossed*. New York: Delacorte Press, 2013.

Varnado, Christine. "'Invisible Sex!' What Looks Like the Act in Early Modern Drama?" In *Sex before Sex: Figuring the Act in Early Modern England*, edited by James M. Bromley and Will Stockton, 25–52. Minneapolis: University of Minnesota Press, 2013.

Vickers, Nancy. "Members Only: Marot's Anatomical Blazons." In *The Body in Parts: Fantasies of Corporeality in Early Modern Europe*, edited by David Hillman and Carla Mazzio, 3–21. New York: Routledge, 1997.

Worthen, W. B. *Shakespeare Performance Studies*. Cambridge: Cambridge University Press, 2014.

2

Inhabiting the House of Edith Wharton's Fiction: Rewriting the Captive Woman in Deborah Noyes's *The Ghosts of Kerfol*

Indu Ohri

Introduction

As a home designer, Edith Wharton was sensitive to the link between married women's role in the domestic sphere and the isolation arising from the limits on their economic, intellectual, and sexual autonomy. Critics have found this theme particularly applicable to the trapped upper-class wives held captive by possessive husbands in "The Duchess at Prayer" (1898), "The Lady's Maid's Bell" (1902), and "Kerfol" (1916). Inhabiting the house in Wharton's ghost stories is a miserable experience for women who venture outside to pursue their sexual desires. In Barbara White's words, these stories illustrate Wharton's sympathy for "claustrophobic ladies"[1] punished with death, harassment, or imprisonment for their affairs. Wharton's existence as an unhappily married woman living in The Mount with her mentally declining husband and beloved dogs buried in a nearby pet cemetery may have inspired her to write "Kerfol."[2]

Deborah Noyes's *The Ghosts of Kerfol* (2008) expands on "Kerfol" by reworking it from a servant's perspective and adding four linked chapters that track various hauntings at the titular estate. In her guidebook *The Writing of Fiction* (1925), Wharton promotes an idea of originality that also serves as a theory of adaption, since it fits with Noyes's process of rewriting "Kerfol" for young adults. She declares, "[t]rue originality consists not in a new manner but in a new vision. That new, that personal, vision is attained only by looking long enough at the object represented to make it the writer's own."[3] Noyes achieves this originality in engaging with Wharton's sympathetic representation of a woman excessively punished on the suspicion of adultery, Anne de Cournault. As Wharton phrases it in *The Age of Innocence* (1920), "'when such things happened' it was undoubtedly foolish of the man, but somehow always criminal of the woman."[4] Noyes extends Wharton's strategy of employing the supernatural to critique the transhistorical double standard that made physical, emotional, and legal violence against cheating women acceptable.

In the introduction to her anthology, *Gothic!: Ten Original Dark Tales*, Noyes remarks, "You may wonder, Why take a literary form that revels in rot and tailor it to *you* ... teen readers? By its nature there's something gothic about coming of age."[5] Anne's youthfulness in Wharton's story gives Noyes the opportunity to reenvision this tale as a novel about a series of young adults experiencing the nightmare of adolescence. In *The Ghosts of Kerfol*, Noyes's coverage of an intense period in the lives of teenage girls growing into adulthood focuses specifically on their emergence into sexual maturity. The cheating woman provides the nexus for her to expand on Wharton's depiction of various types of violence against female characters undergoing the horrors of young love, desire, and heartbreak. "Kerfol" is the perfect vehicle for Noyes to critique the abuse of cheating women, because she can extend Wharton's nuanced portrayal of its insidious effects on teenagers, including domestic violence, animal abuse, and sexual objectification. She renders the nightmare that Perrette, Anne, and Suze endure for their transgressive desires by developing Wharton's technique of interweaving several eras to show the mistreatment of young women and other oppressed populations over time.

While the cheating woman is commonly found in Wharton's ghost stories, Noyes offers young adult readers a "new vision" of this character as she experiments with narrative form, intertextuality, and diverse perspectives. She explores the penalties that Anne and Suze suffer for infidelity to highlight the discrepancies in men's and women's transhistorical punishments. Most importantly, Noyes's final chapter transmutes the captive woman from the upper-class ladies inhabiting Wharton's houses of fiction into a servant girl, Perrette. She innovates on "Kerfol" by adding marginalized populations to the narrative—the working-class Perrette and the disabled Gavin—and makes them heroes who resolve the estate's haunting. Her novel valorizes the deaf boy who offers compassion to Perrette and the spectral servant held imprisoned as the new captive woman. While Wharton captures the perspectives of a servant girl and female deaf-mute in "The Lady's Maid's Bell" and "Mr. Jones," they are helpless witnesses or victims of male abuse. In contrast, Noyes combats the sense of futility that pervades these ghost stories when women are left victimized, ineffective, or dead and ultimately unable to enact change. Perrette and Gavin's heroism not only brings the overlooked Others in Wharton's ghost stories to the forefront, but it also gives them the power to end Kerfol's legacy of female victimization.

Another important aspect of Noyes's reenvisioning is her assumption that young people who read her novel are highly literate and perceptive, since she adds multiple perspectives and intertexts appropriate to each period in which the hauntings take place. These intertexts, which include Breton folklore, Romantic Gothic poems, and Irish ballads, allow Noyes to elaborate on Wharton's objection to the unfair stigmatization of cheating women by revealing its presence throughout four centuries. In three of the chapters, female characters who cheat on their cross-class partners are punished in different ways. Noyes's characters pursue these affairs for different purposes—Anne for passion and Suze for desire—but in each case, the penalties are heavily disproportionate to their wrongs. The men mistreat these women by objectifying them, controlling them, and abusing them for their sexual transgressions; in fact, their intentions appear threatening because—whether chivalrous or abusive—they end up harming the female characters. *The Ghosts of Kerfol* critically examines the methods, degrees, and violence of the punishments that unfaithful women suffer, since they are too severe and one-sided when applied to just one gender.[6]

"What Judge, What God, Would Hear Us?"

Wharton's *The Writing of Fiction* draws a sharp distinction between the novel and the short story because the former is concerned with situation, while the latter is focused on character. She insists that "one of the fiction-writer's essential gifts is that of discerning whether the subject which presents itself to him, asking for incarnation, is suited to the proportions of the short story or of the novel. If it appears to be adapted to both the chances are that it is inadequate to either."[7] She includes a section on writing ghost stories in which she links the supernatural with Brittany (modern Armorica), heightening the atmosphere of "Kerfol," since it is located in an eerie location identified as the origin of ghost stories: "[Supernatural fiction] seems to have come from the mysterious Germanic and Armorican forests, from lands of long twilights and wailing winds; and it certainly did not pass through French or even Russian hands to reach us."[8] *The Ghosts of Kerfol* is "adapted to both" forms as a series of interconnected short stories that center on episodic ghostly encounters while charting the overarching plot of resolving Kerfol's haunting. Noyes admits that she modeled the structure of *The Ghosts of Kerfol* on her other major intertext, *The Red Violin* (1998).[9] In the film, the violin-maker, Nicolo Bussoti, varnishes his masterpiece with his deceased wife's blood; henceforth, this cursed object brings tragedy uniquely suited to the situations of its four different owners. The hybrid form of *The Ghosts of Kerfol* allows Noyes to use Wharton's inner tale as the starting point for the five hauntings of Kerfol. She also turns Anne's dog collar/necklace into a cursed object that various men bestow on women as an emblem of the transhistorical reality of male domination.

While the following synopsis of "Kerfol" will facilitate my analysis of Wharton's original and Noyes's adaption, it also highlights the story's focus on Anne's status as a cheating woman who endures harsh mistreatment. The story opens with a frame tale in which the narrator visits Kerfol at his friend Lanrivain's suggestion and encounters a pack of ghost dogs that silently follow him. After Lanrivain's wife admits that no living dogs reside at Kerfol, the narrator consults *A History of the Assizes of the Duchy of Brittany. Quimper, 1702* and shares a third-hand summary of its contents. He condenses the relevant historical account found in the book, which has been adapted from the legal records of Anne's trial for the murder of her husband, Yves. During the early seventeenth century, the elderly Yves married a young bride from an impoverished noble family. Although Yves showers her with presents such as a necklace/collar and a pet dog, his frequent absences and her confinement at Kerfol leave Anne so lonely that she befriends their neighbor, Hervé de Lanrivain. Out of jealousy, Yves cruelly strangles Anne's dog with the collar (which she had given to Hervé) to warn her of the fate she will suffer if she is unfaithful. Yves kills a series of abused dogs Anne harbors and she plans to flee Kerfol with Hervé out of terror, but the ghost dogs kill their murderer before the two can escape. The court finds Anne's testimony about Yves's death so baffling that it delivers her to her husband's family and they imprison her in Kerfol until she dies a madwoman.

Besides inspiring the structure of *The Ghosts of Kerfol*, the multicultural cast of *The Red Violin* may have influenced Noyes to provide a greater diversity of viewpoints than those featured in "Kerfol." Wharton's inner tale is already an adaption of the judicial records of Anne's trial presented by a male narrator; thus, the patriarchal legal system and the narrator both frame Anne's words. Critics have pointed out the double-edged nature of the legal framework that tries to silence Anne and yet allows for the recovery of her voice.[10] The narrator's editorial role aligns him with the male authorities who try Anne because he inserts his speculations about their feelings; for instance, Anne, "when questioned as to her reason for going down at night to open the door to Hervé de Lanrivain, made an answer which must have sent a smile around the court."[11] Her prosecutors initially suspect the lovers conspired to murder Yves, but Anne's testimony generates so much uncertainty that they relinquish responsibility for punishing her. Wharton's fascination with the notorious murder trials of affluent women like Madeleine Smith and Lizzie Borden may be reflected in her crafting of Anne's testimony. Besides offering sensationalism, Anne's trial creates doubt and forces readers to fill in the narrative blanks about her guilt.[12] Wharton's interest in the upper-class woman tried for murder and her abused dogs highly restricts the scope of her social critique.

In contrast, the combination of short story and novel forms in Noyes's adaption allows for multiple perspectives from diverse young adult characters, starting with her reinterpretation of "Kerfol" as the first chapter, "Hunger Moon." Perrette's narrative offers a more immediate and sympathetic viewpoint of Anne's situation from another teenager who relates to the cheating woman's desires. As an heiress from an old New York family, Wharton was raised to regard servants with a mixture of affection and condescension. Her ghost stories are sometimes told from the perspective of working-class women serving the wealthy, like the domestics in "The Duchess at Prayer" and Alice Hartley in "The Lady's Maid's Bell." Ann Mattis and Sherrie Inness argue that Wharton's portrayal of these servants uncovers her ambivalence about the American class system and the reformation of the master–servant relationship of her day.[13] In "Hunger Moon," Noyes follows the conventions of the Edwardian ghost story by rewriting "Kerfol" from the perspective of the maid waiting on the captive woman. She builds on references to the nameless "maids" who testify at Anne's trial and makes them her protagonists: the newcomer, Perrette; her admirer, Youen; and her mentor, Maria. The conflict between Perrette's account of their marriage and the legal transcripts that understate or deny Yves's brutality suggests that these records—and Wharton's narrator's interpretation of them—are unreliable. Perrette's inside access to Kerfol and her mistress allows her to bring Yves's abuse of his wife, servants, and dogs to light.

Since Perrette's working-class status in Renaissance Brittany leaves her subject to Yves and Anne's authority, she initially blames her mistress's affair for placing everyone at risk of violent retribution. When Yves threatens to beat Perrette, Maria warns her, "Do you not see now ... he has the right to do much worse? And exercises it. You'll learn how to walk and where to stand. Where not to stand. The best of us, the wisest, are hidden in plain sight."[14] Maria informs Perrette that their patriarchal master is in charge of not only administering punishment to his servants but also regulating its severity to the utmost cruelty. Although her training requires Perrette to learn her place as a ghostly figure ready to obey Yves's orders, her loyalties get divided between her tyrannical master and rash mistress. Her ambivalence regarding Anne consists of concern for her mistress's plight as a captive woman and wariness of becoming too close to someone with power over her. The tensions in their relationship arise from the fact that they double each other as teenagers who are sold into Yves's service by impoverished fathers and engage in parallel romances with men Yves punishes. In Wharton's ghost stories, the economic, sexual, and intimate tensions between mistresses and maids can generate the hostility and closeness that Perrette harbors toward Anne.[15] Perrette resents Anne for confiding in her about her feelings for Hervé, conscious that their relationship is defined by class disparities rather than affection. She protests, "I wanted to know what would become of me, of everyone in this doomed house. I wanted fair warning if she meant to turn the master's wrath upon us all, but it was not my right."[16] Perrette's self-interest leads her to victim blame Anne, given that she knows her mistress's foolhardy actions in secretly meeting Hervé and adopting dogs will provoke Yves to massacre everyone for Anne's misbehavior.

Although Anne's carelessness endangers everyone, Perrette allies with her mistress because she recognizes their shared victimization at the hands of a man who regards both as his property and turns his wife into a captive woman. Yves showers Anne with gifts such as the necklace/dog collar to flaunt his economic control in an elaborate performance that highlights his sense of ownership over his wife and servants. Their discussion of one such incident reveals Perrette and Youen's indignation at his emotional abuse of Anne and implicitly aligns them with her as a fellow sufferer of Yves's tyranny:

> I realized this was an established dance they were doing, we were all doing, for could any do other than his or her part? There was no script, but no matter. Neither was there liberty or uncertainty .... He clasped it round her neck, encircling her with powerful arms, his gaze daring her not to look away, though she did. She always did, Youen told me later, when we met by the well before supper. And always looked at the edge of tears. "He's a bully," the stable boy pronounced.[17]

This added scene dramatizes Yves's presentation of the necklace to Anne in order to underscore his dominance over his subordinates: she is expected to act grateful and they must admire his largesse as part of their unwritten social scripts. The necklace's doubling as a collar for Anne's dog and its murder weapon provides a more brutal illustration of Yves's power over her. Noyes extends the necklace's importance in later stories by turning it into a cursed object that marks women as victims of patriarchal violence for their sexuality. Another scene taken mostly verbatim from Wharton indicates that Yves treats Anne like the objects he lavishes on her when he says, "I would have you inside now … I depart soon, and a man with a treasure does not leave the key in the lock when he goes out."[18] His confinement of his wife under the pretense of guarding her illustrates how overbearing men isolate women while pretending to act in their best interests.[19] Yves's metaphor of Anne as a "treasure" only he can access reflects Wharton using her architectural knowledge to explore the oppression of married women confined to the home in spatial terms. While Noyes adapts this scene in "Hunger Moon," I will later document how she also builds on Wharton's key imagery as an important motif and intertextual element in her portrayal of the objectification of the Jazz Age heiress, Suze Cole.

The excessiveness of Yves's violence against Anne for her flirtation with Hervé shows that the abuse extends beyond her to encompass others in the community, including her lover, dogs, and servants. "Kerfol" reflects Wharton's lifelong love of dogs and feeling of being "secretly afraid of animals—of all animals except dogs, & even of some dogs. I think it is because of the *usness* in their eyes, with the underlying *not-usness* which belies it" (quoted in Haytock 2012).[20] In her study on animals, Noyes similarly writes that people can only overcome the barrier between humans and dogs and inhabit their "skin" through an act of imagination.[21] Perrette highlights the parallels between Anne and her first dog as victims of domestic violence, noting that "[t]he necklace was twisted thrice round the dog's slender throat" while Anne's "shoulders—bruised, I knew, tender under fine fabric—moved with silent sobs."[22] Noyes elaborates on a red herring from "Kerfol" when Perrette suspects that Yves murdered Hervé; however, it is relatively common for a wronged husband to kill his rival as punishment. The real horror of Yves's actions lies in the fact that he relentlessly targets Anne and her pets *after* Hervé's death without verifying her affair. His paranoia implies that Anne's underlying transgression is prizing her dogs over Yves, to the point that she disobeys her husband and secretly adopts them. The dogs play a crucial role in the triangulations of desire between Yves, Anne, and Hervé, since they function as intermediaries in Anne's affair and victims of Yves's fury.[23]

Perrette's allusions to her grandmother's narratives about werewolves, elf princes, and archangels suggest that the medieval writer Marie de France's Breton lais could be read as intertexts for "Hunger Moon." Like Wharton and Noyes, Marie narrates supernatural tales in which she sympathizes with unhappy wives whose adulterous affairs are often mediated by animals. For instance, the lay "Laüstic" closely mirrors the plot of "Kerfol": a noblewoman in love with a neighboring knight talks to him nightly at her window, lying to her suspicious husband that she is listening to a nightingale's song. He orders his servants to set traps, and, when he catches the bird, "wrung its neck (it took but a slight / twist) and he hurled it at [his wife] so / that the drops of its blood spattered below / her breast on her linen tunic."[24] Despite being wronged, the husband's murder of the nightingale makes him the inhumane one for crushing his wife's spirit and ending the affair. His punishment of the nightingale appears gratuitous because it is an innocent victim that does not deserve to be killed for facilitating their romance.

Similar to Anne, Perrette suffers for desiring the Renaissance bad boy (a poacher's son) who disobeys Yves in trying to protect Anne and her animals from the master's violence, a situation that we can connect to another of Marie's lais. Perrette's metaphor figuring both Youen and Yves as shapeshifting werewolves that blur the human–animal divide evokes "Bisclavret," in which the wife's terror at being sexually possessed by a monster leads her to commit adultery. She grows "alarmed and filled with fear / to learn that her husband was a were / wolf. How ghastly! How could she / and such a creature have intimacy?"[25] Although she and her lover leave her husband trapped in his werewolf form, Bisclavret's human behavior convinces the king of his identity and the monarch brings the treacherous lovers to justice. Perrette muses, "Youen became my *loup-garou*, and this was a girl's fancy, feverish and exciting but never horrible. Grand-mère's version, on the other hand, was a beast that stalked in shadow, ripping the dogs to ribbons. Youen was not our monster. It was Master, two-faced and terribly transformed."[26] Like Bisclavret's wife, Perrette fears Youen is the evil werewolf from her grandmother's stories, but she realizes that this metaphor captures her desire for her brooding love interest instead. While Marie emphasizes the nobility of animals, Perrette perceives their bestial side in calling Yves a "monster" that lures Anne so he can catch her meeting Hervé and kill everyone as punishment. Perrette is indirectly disciplined for her attraction to Youen and role in shielding Anne when Yves batters Youen so badly for disclosing Hervé's death that he is reduced to a "blathering idiot."[27]

Though Yves dies before he can slay Anne, she is punished by everyone—the legal system, the church officials, and her in-laws—for her sexual transgressions, except the loyal Perrette, who stays to care for her mistress and becomes the next captive woman. The shapeshifting imagery conveys an intense identification between human and animal throughout Noyes's novel; however, it can only reveal more about *human* nature rather than animal subjectivity. Similar to "Kerfol," the ghost dogs surprise even Noyes's Anne when they band together and attack Yves in a show of feral savagery, though their act is morally just because his victims target him out of revenge as well as to protect her. However, they cannot safeguard Anne from the institutionalized sexism that holds her responsible for this crime, largely due to her passion for Hervé. Instead of Wharton's male narrator relating Anne's trial, Perrette's eyewitness account questions whether a patriarchal justice system can fairly punish an alleged adulteress and murderer. Perrette shares Anne's sentence of being confined to Kerfol out of mutual loyalty and grief, and both end up unwilling to risk being close after suffering punishment for their tenderness toward Youen, Hervé, and the dogs: "To touch, to know affection, was to suffer, and we would not bring that upon ourselves, upon each other. For what judge, what God, would hear us? I will labor till my last days in obscurity—like paw prints in rainfall, like Milady in her madness—fade and be forgotten"[28] The unfair means and severity of punishment throughout "Hunger Moon" render Perrette skeptical that a just human "judge" or God can possibly exist; thus, she becomes the new captive woman haunting Kerfol.

"You Have the Look of Someone Damned"

In the next two chapters, Noyes represents the aesthetic and sexual objectification of Suze Cole during two time periods and by men from three different eras to illustrate the continuity of the oppression of young women across several centuries. The first male character to objectify her is Noyes's reworking of Wharton's narrator, Victor, an emasculated artist who suffers fits of "nerves" due to the trauma of his father's death. Victor and his mother rent Kerfol while she tries to reestablish their wealth in order to provide for her son, a penniless Romantic artist and son of an executed nobleman. Victor lives at a time when tyrannical aristocrats—as exemplified by Yves—have lost their brutal privileges after mistreated peasants rebelled during the French Revolution. As a male artist, Victor is sensitive to Kerfol's "romantic" nature and supernatural influence, which inspire him to produce magic portraits in which he sexually objectifies female subjects. This setting invests Victor with the visionary powers to see other female characters across time and enhanced creative abilities, since he draws the sketch of Anne that Wharton's narrator describes as well as Suze's portrait:

> Unlike the lady in the crayon drawing, the painted girl was a clear translation of fantasy. This long-necked blonde was his match, Victor imagined, sweet and arrogant with a knack for withholding. A careless, slightly dangerous girl with a pout…She deserved whatever delight he might offer, for the sadness in her eye—less defined than that of the woman in the sketch but more subtle in the end, more masterful—made him want to protect her. *You have the look of someone damned*, he thought. Someone who doesn't know it yet.[29]

Victor's painting of Suze initially resembles the Romantic femme fatale, who uses her beauty, mystery, and supernatural powers to seduce men and women, such as John Keats's La Belle Dame sans Merci and Geraldine in Samuel Taylor Coleridge's "Cristabel" (1816). Victor associates the castrating blade of the guillotine with women like his mother and the working-class Marguerite, whom he resents for mocking his fears, artwork, and sexuality. Hence, he tries to contain Suze's power by viewing her as a male "fantasy" that he objectifies in painting her wearing the cursed necklace. Victor's portrait of a future murder victim transforms Suze into a beautiful muse he "kills" into an art object that reflects his creativity and conceals the castrative threat of death from him.[30] Although he produces the fatal portrait, Victor desires to fulfill the fictionally constructed role of his father as a hero and save Suze from her fate of being strangled by Yves's ghost.

However, Victor's failure to destroy the magic portrait reveals the underlying problem of young men sexually objectifying women and attempting to wield power over them like he does by painting Suze. In this way, Noyes indicates the need to change young men's perception of and behavior toward women they find attractive, and she will later extend this theme to her representation of Gavin as a modern teenage boy. On the anniversary of Yves's murder, Victor notices parallels between himself and the ghost dogs as mute, ineffectual, and traumatized victims of violent punishment who act passive in the face of futility:

> In the end, it was as if [the dogs] held in common one memory so deep and dark that nothing since had seemed worth a growl or a wag, rather like Victor's own

notions of his father under the blade of the guillotine. How could he wish to be a man after that knowledge? Didn't death not dwarf all expectations? All ambition?[31]

The dogs may feel hopeless knowing that even though they tried to shield Anne from Yves, they could not prevent her being shut up in Kerfol for life. The sight of them standing around his painting out of a desire to save Suze inspires Victor to destroy the magical portrait that will facilitate her death and take "pleasure" in the thought of rescuing her. Victor's endeavor to obliterate his sexually objectifying image entails "slapping" Suze's face, "slashing" her eyes, and covering her in bloody "red cadmium" paint.[32] He implicitly believes in the same sexist outlook that motivates Yves's violence against Anne and Suze; thus, he cannot protect her from being "damned." The blurring of male chivalry and violence reinforces the notion that both endanger women, since they originate from the same misogynistic attitude that results in Suze's death.

In the next chapter, this misogynistic attitude creates an era of false sexual freedom for young women such as Suze, since men exploit her for their emotional, financial, and physical gratification. She is the young adult version of a heroine from a realist Wharton novel as an heiress who faces disgrace for refusing to fulfill men's desires and pursuing her own erotic longings instead. Suze's future inheritance is doubtful due to her wealthy grandparents disapproving of her mother's marriage and her father working as a Wall Street stockbroker three years before the Crash of 1929. She repeatedly alludes to lines from Edward Lear's nursery rhyme "The Owl and the Pussy-cat" (1871) that offer a childish version of her wish-fulfillment fantasy and hints at her secret pregnancy: "The Owl and the Pussy-cat went to sea / In a beautiful pea-green boat, / They took some honey, and plenty of money, / Wrapped up in a five-pound note."[33] Suze dreams of marrying her working-status lover, a shipwright named Stan, and sailing away with her family's riches. When her father gives Suze the cursed necklace, she reacts ambivalently because he tries to bribe her with "one more shiny gemstone"[34] into forgetting Stan and she implicitly agrees to try after he places it on her as part of their understanding. He is patronizing in presenting her with a necklace meant to gain his daughter's complicity; in turn, Suze feels "ashamed"[35] knowing it is too late to buy her off—she is carrying the baby of the lover who abandoned her.

Noyes uses the ancient Breton legend of Dahut to represent the shaming of Suze for exercising her sexual and financial autonomy in a society that would stigmatize her as a fallen woman and unwed mother. She extends Wharton's single reference to Anne's hometown of Douarnenez by referring to a local legend about the seaside city of Ys and its ruler, Princess Dahut.[36] Dahut's father, King Gradlon, overlooks her wild parties and promiscuity until she steals his silver key to the dyke protecting Ys for her lover (the devil) and submerges the city in the Bay of Douarnenez. During Suze's first meeting with her demon lover, Yves's ghost, he examines her wearing the necklace at a party and criticizes this "[t]houghtless, pretty thing" for displaying her body to attract male admiration: "If you were my…daughter…I'd beat you senseless."[37] Suze's possession of the necklace and her sexual misbehavior suggest that she recalls Anne for

Yves, who assumes an inappropriate role in threatening her and later punishing her for infidelity. After the frightened Suze seeks out her friends for help, a local named Tres tries to use the Dahut legend to seduce her.[38] She rightly suspects that Tres wants to steal her necklace, though the narrative insinuates he may be Yves (the devil) in disguise, who tempts her at a time when her pregnancy leaves her emotionally vulnerable and isolated from her family.

In a metafictional seduction scene, Suze fulfills her destiny of being "damned" because the cheating woman holds the illusion of having sexual autonomy when she will actually be punished by the very man who seduces her. Although she revels in male attention, Suze is horrified once she examines Victor's magic portrait and sees men's objectifying view of her firsthand: "The artist had captured [the necklace's] glint and rich waved contours well and crisply, and the likeness thrilled and terrified her."[39] She cheats on Stan while carrying his child by sleeping with Tres, in a complex seduction scene that contains multiple omens she is going to be punished. We see the extent of Suze's hypersexuality as she recalls her infidelities to Stan, consents to sleeping with Tres, and listens to his rendition of the devil's temptation of Dahut:

> Conjuring Stan was something she did often, at the petting parties her older college friends had invited her to and later at her own parties. (*She's the queen of parties,* blowhard Peg always said.)
> "… if you love me, you will make me a gift,"—Tres yanked the dusty sheet off the daybed—"of the silver key that unlocks the gates of the sea."
> She let her dress fall round her ankles, and with her eyes closed, she could almost conjure it, the smell and feel of Stan's skin, the veins in his wrists as he smoothed the hanging hair from her face. The cushions were a silky chill beneath her back, and his weight a warmth. There was no moon tonight, and she could make out nothing in the painting, though she knew it was there.[40]

Dahut's theft of her father's "silver key" echoes Yves's metaphor of using a key to lock up Anne (his "treasure") in Kerfol as well as his view that he must guard his commodity and sexual possession. Suze offers Tres her father's "silver key" by inviting him to Kerfol knowing that he wants to steal her necklace and giving him sexual access to her body. Tres continues to recite Dahut's punishment for stealing the key out of desire for the demon lover: she betrays her father, Ys is submerged, and everyone drowns. The horror in the devil/Tres's actions is that he tempts Dahut/Suze to have sex and then reveals how he is going to punish her while they are *committing that very act*. Suze's accomplice in the act of cheating should not be allowed to penalize her for it, and yet this often happens in Faustian narratives such as the Dahut legend. The following day, Suze examines the magic portrait predicting her doom for wearing the necklace before Yves strangles her with it. Years later, a tour guide explains that "strange holes and mounds had appeared all over the grounds in the night"[41] that Suze died, as Anne's dogs bury the necklace to protect other women from its curse.

"A Girl Who Shines so Well on Her Own"

In the final chapter, Noyes adds the greatest diversity of perspectives to "Kerfol" by depicting an architectural restorer named Gavin resolving the hauntings with help from Perrette's ghost and his dog, Cleo. They work together to exorcise the ghosts of Wharton's characters and redirect the focus of the narrative to themselves as worthy of acknowledgment. Noyes transforms Wharton's upper-class captive woman into Perrette and foregrounds the servant who waits for someone to recognize her worth and help liberate her from captivity. She highlights how a deaf teenager like Gavin occupies a secondary role in modern society and thinks "living in a hearing world's something like living in a world with ghosts anyway. Everyone's on the other side of a veil of silence, speaking mystery."[42] Gavin's infatuation with Perrette also suggests that young men's sexual attitudes toward their love interests must change if the cycle of violence against women is to end.

Gavin's social invisibility, respect for the female characters, sensitivity to animals, and appreciation of history make him the perfect ally for Perrette. The reality of Kerfol's haunting does not bother him because he has reconciled himself to his mother's death and feels like he inhabits "a world with ghosts." While restoring a wing of Kerfol, Gavin fires the workers who objectify women, "stuffing their mugs with their wives' lunches and trolling for porn on Erik's laptop."[43] His remark that he and Clio "understand each other, and I'll never punish Clio with a leash unless she crosses me"[44] conveys his appropriate response to disciplining his dog with restraint, not violence. Perrette's fear of being forgotten at the end of "Hunger Moon" proves to be unfounded; she can finally appear to someone open to her presence. Although Perrette despairs that no judge or God will give her a fair "hearing," Gavin's struggle with his disability makes him sympathetic to her plight and sensitive to her ghostly presence. He perceives Perrette through his mother's favorite song, "She Moved Through the Fair," in which the speaker's fiancée dies and her ghost appears in his dreams promising "It will not be long, love, till our wedding day."[45] While Gavin's attraction to Perrette fosters his desire to help her, he recognizes that his mother's spirit is better situated to care for Perrette and lead her to the afterlife.

In contrast to Yves, Gavin respects the unique subjectivity of animals enough to give Clio the freedom to interact with Anne's dogs, which is a necessary element for exorcising the ghosts of Kerfol. He recalls, "I was eleven and nearly brained [his Uncle Sean] with a shovel while we were digging [his sister's]'s cat's grave and he unwittingly made her cry. 'It's the runt quiet ones, not the big barkers, you have to worry about.'"[46] The metaphor of him as a dog highlights the fact that while Gavin may be silent due to his deafness, he is willing to fight injustice and inflict severe punishment on *behalf* of women, not *to* them. As previously discussed, both Wharton and Noyes recognize that dogs are Others that seem to act human while having a wildness that makes them inaccessible to people. Clio's naming after the muse of history suggests that she can mediate between Gavin, the dogs, and Perrette in helping the estate come to terms with its traumatic past. Gavin remarks, "It's making me uneasy, Clio tearing up and down the lawn like she's in some sort of crowded dog park or something. They say animals and babies see angels and ghosts and whatnot, which makes me think of that girl again, her mouth stained bright with berry juice."[47] It is imperative for a dog to occupy Kerfol because Clio's animal nature and supernatural perception enable her to communicate with the ghost dogs where the other human characters have failed. The ghost dogs lead Clio to the cursed necklace's location and she steers Gavin to Perrette, who helps them escape Kerfol when the haunting intensifies.

The crucial scene in which Gavin must choose whether to objectify Perrette emblematizes how young men's sexuality needs to undergo transformation if women are to be treated with respect. Gavin and Perrette are connected in several ways because they constitute the only first-person narrators, their stories bookend the novel, and they escape unscathed from the ghosts of Kerfol. Furthermore, only those who have read "Hunger Moon" will know that Perrette's consumption of berries represents the unfulfilled desire for Youen that keeps her trapped. After she saves him, Gavin reacts like a naive boy approaching his crush and considers offering her the cursed necklace:

> I imagine leading her out of the dark wood by the hand, kissing her in the rain, presenting her with Clio's shiny find to watch how gems rest against that white, white throat. Sadness settles over me instead. I turn the piece over in my hands, and it's sharp. It's heavy. It's a glorified dog collar—a pretty noose—not something I'd weight Clio with, much less a girl who shines so well on her own.[48]

At this moment of decision, Gavin has an epiphany as a teenager emerging into adult sexuality when he recognizes that he should treat his crush with dignity, rather than domination or ownership. Gavin finds that he has to check his controlling impulses and show compassion for Perrette as an individual, even though this choice leaves him wistful that he cannot fulfill his fantasy of young love.

In an ending that subverts the typical young adult romance, the boy must place the girl's wishes before his desires by providing her with the validation she needs to depart for the afterlife and no longer haunt Kerfol. Unlike Yves, Victor, and Suze's father, Gavin refrains from bestowing the cursed necklace on Clio and Perrette, realizing it is a "glorified dog collar" that the male characters fasten on women to mark them as sexual and economic objects. His respect for their autonomy enables him to recognize Perrette as a strong and capable woman who will be restricted if he fetters her in "a pretty noose," both literally and mentally. While Perrette does not commit the other female characters' sexual transgressions, Gavin would punish her by subjecting her to the misogynistic beliefs that men use to restrict, penalize, and slut-shame women. His actions also illustrate that a modern teenage boy is capable of breaking the cycle of female victimization after nearly four centuries. The ghost dogs will continue to wander Kerfol indefinitely in Wharton's story, whereas Noyes settles the haunting with the emancipation of a woman held captive by historical erasure. Perrette's confinement at Kerfol for sympathizing with Anne and desiring Youen can end now that she may own her sexuality without the fear of male judgment or control.

Notes

1. White, *Edith Wharton*, 53.
2. I want to thank the staff at The Mount for helping me research Wharton's life and literary interests. I am especially grateful to Anne Schuyler for showing me Wharton's library and true crime books.
3. Wharton, *Writing of Fiction*, 17–18.
4. Wharton, *Age*, 132.
5. Noyes, "Introduction," x.
6. I am indebted to Rohin Ohri for his insights into the various facets of legal punishments.
7. Wharton, *Writing*, 33.
8. Ibid., 29.
9. Noyes, "Author Snapshot."
10. See Haytock, "Dogs"; Ohler, "Sexual Violence"; Waid, *Edith Wharton's*, 173–203; Fedorko, *Gender*, 48–68; and Schiesari, *Beasts*, 16–37 for scholarly readings of "Kerfol."
11. Wharton, "Kerfol," 107.
12. The husbands' doubt about their wives' guilt in committing murder is central to Wharton's play "The Shadow of a Doubt" (1901) and her story "Confession" (1936). In the former work, Mr. Derwent captures this sentiment perfectly: "Well, it can't be pleasant for the most adoring husband to feel that there's even the shadow of a doubt about his wife" (39).
13. Mattis, "Gothic," 218–19; Inness, "Loyal," 338.
14. Noyes, *Ghosts*, 17–18.
15. See Inness, "Loyal"; Blackford, "Haunted"; and Mattis, "Gothic."
16. Noyes, *Ghosts*, 28.
17. Ibid., 21–2.
18. Ibid., 24; Wharton, "Kerfol," 107.
19. Yves's imagery also invokes the Breton legend of Bluebeard leaving a key to a forbidden door so that he can later justify murdering his wife for opening it.
20. For more on Wharton's petkeeping and its influence on "Kerfol," see Haytock, "Dogs"; and Adams, *Shaggy*, 141–94.
21. Noyes, *One Kingdom*, 86–8.
22. Noyes, *Ghosts*, 37.
23. For readings that apply this interpretation to Anne's love of dogs, see Schiesari, *Beasts*, 16–37; and Haytock, "Dogs."
24. Marie de France, "Laüstic," lines 76–80.
25. Marie de France, "Bisclavret," lines 95–8.
26. Noyes, *Ghosts*, 48.
27. Ibid., 57.
28. Ibid., 58.
29. Ibid., 74.
30. Bronfen, *Over Her*, 64.
31. Noyes, *Ghosts*, 83.
32. Ibid., 85.
33. Lear, "The Owl," lines 1–4.

34 Noyes, *Ghosts*, 96.
35 Ibid.
36 Like *The Ghosts of Kerfol*, another neo-Victorian work that uses Breton folklore and the Dahut legend to condemn the shaming of fallen women is A. S. Byatt's *Possession* (1990).
37 Noyes, *Ghosts*, 100.
38 Wharton, "Kerfol," 101. See Byatt, *Possession*, 148 and Guyot for variations on the Dahut legend.
39 Noyes, *Ghosts*, 108.
40 Ibid., 113.
41 Ibid., 120.
42 Ibid., 152.
43 Ibid., 143.
44 Ibid., 145.
45 Colum, "She Moved through the Fair," 171.
46 Ibid., 145.
47 Ibid., 151.
48 Ibid., 162.

Bibliography

Adams, M. *Shaggy Muses*. New York: Ballantine Books, 2007.

Blackford, Holly. "Haunted Housekeeping: Fatal Attractions of Servant and Mistress in Twentieth-Century Female Gothic Literature." *Lit: Literature Interpretation Theory* 16, no. 2 (2005): 233–61.

Bronfen, Elizabeth. *Over Her Dead Body: Death and the Aesthetic*. Manchester: Manchester University Press, 1992.

Byatt, A. S. *Possession*. New York: Random House, 1990.

Coleridge, S. T. "Christabel." In *Coleridge: Selected Poems*, edited by Richard Holmes, 101–20. London: HarperCollins, 1996.

Colum, Padraic. "She Moved through the Fair." In *An Irish Literature Reader: Poetry, Prose, Drama, Second Edition*, edited by Maureen O'Rourke Murphy and James MacKillop, 170–1. Syracuse: Syracuse University Press, 2006.

de France, Marie. "Bisclavret." In *The Lais of Marie de France*, translated by David R. Slavitt, 47–54. Alberta: AU Press, 2013.

de France, Marie. "Laüstic." In *The Lais of Marie de France*, translated by David R. Slavitt, 89–92. Alberta: AU Press, 2013.

Fedorko, K. A. *Gender and the Gothic in the Fiction of Edith Wharton*. Tuscaloosa: University of Alabama Press, 1995.

Guyot, C. *The Legend of the City of Ys*. Amherst: University of Massachusetts Press, 1970.

Haytock, Jennifer. "The Dogs of 'Kerfol': Animals, Authorship, and Wharton." *Journal of the Short Story in English* 58 (2012): 175–86.

Inness, Sherrie. "'Loyal Saints or Devious Rascals': Domestic Servants in Edith Wharton's Stories 'The Lady's Maid's Bell' and 'All Souls.'" *Studies in Short Fiction* 36, no. 4 (1999): 337–49.

Lear, Edward. "The Owl and the Pussy-cat." In *How Pleasant to Know Mr. Lear! Edward Lear's Selected Works*, edited by Myra Cohn Livingston, 110–11. New York: Holiday House, 1982.

Mattis, Ann. "Gothic Interiority and Servants in Wharton's *A Backward Glance* and 'The Lady's Maid's Bell.'" *Twentieth-Century Literature* 58, no. 2 (2012): 213–37.

Noyes, Deborah (ed.). "Introduction." In *Gothic!: Ten Original Dark Tales*, viii–xi. Cambridge: Candlewick Press, 2004.

Noyes, Deborah. *One Kingdom: Our Lives with Animals*. Boston: Houghton Mifflin, 2006.

Noyes, Deborah. "Author Snapshot and Book Giveaway: Deborah Noyes on *The Ghosts of Kerfol*." Interview by Cynthia Leitich Smith, *Cynsations*, October 2008. https://cynthialeitichsmith.com/2008/10/author-snapshot-book-giveaway-debora/ (accessed September 21, 2019).

Noyes, Deborah. *The Ghosts of Kerfol*. Cambridge, MA: Candlewick Press, 2008.

Ohler, Paul. "Sexual Violence and Ghostly Justice in 'The Lady's Maid's Bell' and 'Kerfol.'" *Edith Wharton Review* 32 nos. 1/2 (2016): 40–56.

The Red Violin. 2003. Directed by François Girard. USA: Lionsgate. DVD.

Schiesari, Juliana. *Beasts and Beauties: Animals, Gender, and Domestication in the Italian Renaissance*. Toronto: University of Toronto Press, 2010.

Waid, Candace. *Edith Wharton's Letters from the Underworld*. Chapel Hill: University of North Carolina Press, 1991.

Wharton, Edith. "The Duchess at Prayer." In *The Collected Short Stories of Edith Wharton*, 2 vols, edited by R. W. B. Lewis, 229–44. New York: Charles Scribner's Sons, 1968.

Wharton, Edith. "Confession." In *The Collected Stories of Edith Wharton*, edited by Anita Brookner, 583–619. New York: Carroll and Graf, 1988.

Wharton, Edith. "Kerfol." In *The Ghost Stories of Edith Wharton*, 92–117. New York: Simon & Schuster, 1997.

Wharton, Edith. "The Lady's Maid's Bell." In *The Ghost Stories of Edith Wharton*, 188–218. New York: Simon & Schuster, 1997.

Wharton, Edith. "Mr. Jones." In *The Ghost Stories of Edith Wharton*, 12–35. New York: Simon & Schuster, 1997.

Wharton, Edith. *The Writing of Fiction*. New York: Simon & Schuster, 1997.

Wharton, Edith. *The Age of Innocence*. Edited by Michael Nowlin. Broadview, 2002.

Wharton, Edith. "The Shadow of a Doubt: A Play in Three Acts by Edith Wharton." *Edith Wharton Review* 33, no. 1 (2017): 113–257.

White, Barbara. *Edith Wharton: A Study of the Short Fiction*. Boston: Twayne, 1991.

3

Rewriting *The Great Gatsby*: Questioning Identity and Morality in Sara Benincasa's *Great*

Lisa M. Valenzuela

In her young adult novel, *Great*, Sara Benincasa reinvents F. Scott Fitzgerald's *The Great Gatsby* with a cast of teenagers, set against a backdrop of opulence and wealth that easily keeps pace with the Roaring Twenties of Gatsby's era. Just as Fitzgerald's characters struggle to reconcile their identities with the social and financial extravagance of the Jazz Age, Benincasa's cast of characters seeks to navigate the equally lavish lifestyle of the twenty-first-century Hamptons, all the while under the watchful, and often brutal, eye of social media. Though *Great* clearly relies on Fitzgerald's novel, it does not mean that this piece has nothing new to say. Benincasa continues what Fitzgerald began through an examination of the unchecked extravagance and prejudice of the wealthy elite, and the damage that can be done by those who believe themselves untouchable. While Fitzgerald comments on this behavior through his creation of the thoroughly self-centered characters, Tom and Daisy Buchanan, he portrays a world in which there is no punishment for the sins of the wealthy. In contrast, Benincasa picks up this discussion where *The Great Gatsby* leaves off. Through the focus on the narrator, Naomi, and her struggle with identity, Benincasa ensures that the boundaries of social constructs are pushed to the point of breaking and the selfish deeds of the rich do not go unpunished. As the novel progresses, Benincasa's work provides a retelling that allows young adult readers to see their own struggles with identity played out through Naomi's efforts to solidify her own sense of belonging.

A cursory examination of Benincasa's work reveals that the plot of *Great* is nearly identical to that of *The Great Gatsby*. Just as Nick Carraway describes the brief affair between Gatsby and Daisy during that fateful summer in East and West Egg, Naomi narrates the relationship between Jacinta and Delilah. This connection crosses the barriers of literary canon and time, drawing parallels between the stories, as these characters struggle with questions of identity and find themselves embroiled in a love triangle that questions the rules of the Hamptons' hierarchy. While these plot elements effectively connect the two texts, the most notable similarity between the original novel and *Great* lies in the power struggle that exists between those social forces that shape the identities of the characters and their desire to follow their own paths. However,

Great continues *The Great Gatsby*'s interrogation of these power dynamics through the depiction of the search for self that envelops its main characters.

Themes of self-discovery and the development of self in young adult literature are often played out through the adolescent struggle to find oneself in the midst of competing demands and roles. Critic Roberta Seelinger Trites notes that this struggle arises from multiple relationships and societal expectations: "During adolescence, adolescents must learn their place in the power structure. They must learn to negotiate the many institutions that shape them: school, government, religion, identity politics, family, and so on. They must learn to balance their power with their parents' power and with the power of the other authority figures in their lives."[1] This struggle to find a sense of belonging is especially difficult as teens attempt to reconcile familial influences with their own desires to establish a unique sense of self that reflects their own beliefs. Much of this development occurs within the warring factions of parental rules, sexual desires, and adolescent rebellion. As Benincasa expands upon the theme of power, she not only makes the original novel accessible to her adolescent readers, she also speaks to their own struggles in which "[t]hey learn to negotiate the levels of power that exist in the myriad social institutions within which they must function."[2] Each character is subjected to both the common roles of the teenager, including student and child, as well as the power dynamics that come with being a member of the wealthy elite. While Trites notes that "[p]ower is a force that operates within the subject and upon the subject in adolescent novels," she indicates that these same constructs can be harnessed, allowing teenagers the ability to be "liberated by their own power and by the power of the social forces that surround them in these books."[3] *Great*'s characters are not helpless against these powers. Instead, their exploration of the social constructs of the Hamptons allows them to both examine and acknowledge these forces in an act of what Lacan refers to as "*assomption*: the individual's active assumption of responsibility for the role into which society casts her."[4] Once the characters recognize their own role in these power structures, they are able to either accept their place or resist it to enact change.

Like *The Great Gatsby*, Benincasa's *Great* has one narrator who directs the readers through the twists and turns of a doomed love story. The most noticeable difference between the narrators is the gender change. While Fitzgerald relies on a male narrator to tell Gatsby's story, Benincasa chooses a female narrator to describe the events in the novel. In her discussion of the importance of gender in the role of narration, Maria Nikolajeva notes that "[m]asculine narration, … represents the dominant, empowered, conservative, conformist, normative narrative voice."[5] Though Nick is merely a visitor in East Egg, his "masculine voice implies [a confirmation of] the existing norms of power."[6] Nick's gender not only allows him a privileged place to tell the story of the other characters, it also grants him an authority to shape the norms presented in the novel. Unlike its predecessor, *Great* both questions and challenges existing power structures through a female narrator. While Benincasa's novel certainly supports Nikolajeva's assertion that feminine writing is self-reflective, Naomi's feminine voice engages her environment in a manner that elicits change both inwardly and outwardly. While Nick is limited to the role of storyteller for

Gatsby, Naomi is both narrator and protagonist. Rather than focus on the disastrous relationship between Jacinta and Delilah, the novel revolves around Naomi's own struggle to develop a sense of self. As the story unfolds, Naomi is forced to confront the warring factions of her family, which include a mother who represents the greed and deception of the wealthy, and a father who values kindness and honesty. While this dichotomy can be seen in *The Great Gatsby* in the conflict of Nick's Midwestern values and the behavior of his Hamptons companions, much of the story focuses on the follies of Gatsby and Daisy, with very little opportunity for change among the characters. In contrast, these dynamics are fully explored through Naomi's own story, opening the door to the possibility of growth that challenges the established norms of the Hamptons.

When Naomi first arrives in the Hamptons, she fully expects to have the same tiresome experience that is typical of her summers with her mother. As if rehearsing a well-known play, Naomi dutifully take her role as the sulky teen, ever at odds with her socialite mother. This is immediately evident when Naomi steps down from the helicopter dressed in her standard wardrobe of a worn Cure T-shirt and "a jet-black pair of vintage Doc Martens with slouchy black socks."[7] This image is a stark contrast to Naomi's mother, Anne Rye, who wears "a silk scarf and silk dress, [with] white open-toe high heels from Ferragamo."[8] This depiction effectively highlights the competing styles and, more importantly, the values of Naomi and her mother. Naomi's own observations after a cursory examination of her mother's attire reinforce this conflict as she notes that she is not simply "some weird Goth kid," that she actually likes these clothes, but that there is also a desire to set herself apart from her mother: "But did I wear all that black because I was kind of hoping it would freak my mother out a little? You're damn right I did."[9] As she is still considered a child and subject to the rules and expectations of her mother, Naomi seeks to assert her power through wearing clothes that are a visual contradiction to her mother that "fits right in with the rail-thin priestesses of New York high society."[10] This small act of rebellion is a means through which Naomi can differentiate her own identity outside of the parameters of her mother's expectations.

Though she continues to reject her mother's expectations at the start of the novel, as the plot progresses, Naomi begins to let her guard down and participate in the lifestyle that she had formerly disdained. As she becomes lulled into a sense of comfort and belonging, Naomi's newfound friendships, attire, and attitudes will challenge her self-perception. The first indication that Naomi is struggling to reconcile her parents' vastly different lifestyles with her own identity emerges at the start of the novel as Naomi tries to make sense of her feelings about Delilah Fairweather. Though they are "from different tribes that spoke different languages and had different customs," Naomi finds it difficult to resist the draw of Delilah.[11] With her stereotypical model features, including "perfect tanned skin and abnormally huge blue eyes," Delilah falls naturally into the beautiful world of the Hamptons.[12] Like *The Great Gatsby*'s Daisy, Delilah has an otherworldly beauty that both sets her apart and makes those around her desire to be part of her circle: "She always seemed to have one foot in this world and one foot in some other rarified realm where magical elves twirl inside sparkling soap bubbles that float on the surface of an enchanted sea."[13] Despite her beauty, Delilah seemingly breaks the stereotypes of the socially elite, as "she treated [Naomi] kindly, ... [and] had a way of training her eyes on you and making you feel like you were the only important person in her entire life."[14] This disparity between Delilah's social status and her behavior causes Naomi to question her own preconceived notions of the Hamptons' social structures and norms: "Different tribes or not, Delilah Fairweather was exactly the sort of person you want to think 'you're just lovely'—not that I'd ever admit that to any of my friends back home, where we called the popular, beautiful girls the Beasts."[15] Rather than feeling rejected by the Beasts of the Hamptons, Naomi finds that friendship with someone like Delilah might be possible. Like her counterpart, Nick, and his initial impression of Daisy, Naomi is drawn into the social scene of the Hamptons through the ethereal beauty and kindness of Delilah and the promise of acceptance into a world where she had previously felt like an outsider. This acceptance will prove to be a point of contention for Naomi, for the further she slips into her role with the Hamptons' elite, the more she must confront her own self-perception and reexamine the values and norms that have shaped her identity up to this point.

As she settles into the rhythm of life in the Hamptons, Naomi, though loathe to admit it, wonders what it would be like to actually take part in the local social scene, rather than sit on the outside, watching. Naomi admits that though Delilah had included her in parties and outings in past summers "as if [she] were her real friend and not just the daughter of her mother's ex-caterer," she had never felt at home in this environment.[16] Though she dutifully tags along on these outings, Naomi finds she has little in common with Delilah's friends, and her quiet demeanor leaves her with the reputation of a "good listener," a quality that soon provides her with "an arsenal of wealthy teenager tales" and secrets.[17] As interesting as the sins of the wealthy can be, Naomi feels like an outsider among these teens. It is this feeling of isolation that further solidifies her desire to belong, even if it means becoming someone that she is not. Interestingly enough, it is not until she meets Jacinta Trimalchio that Naomi is able to fully immerse herself in the Hamptons' social scene.

Like her counterpart, Jay Gatsby, Jacinta Trimalchio arrives on the Hamptons' scene in an air of mystery. Though her name is synonymous with social media fame, little is known about her life or identity, leading to fanciful conjecture on the part of her fandom. Benincasa's use of the name Trimalchio is no accident; literary critic, James W. L. West III noted that Fitzgerald's first draft of *The Great Gatsby* was tentatively named *Trimalchio* or *Trimalchio in West Egg*, after an ancient character in the *Satyricon*, by Petronius.[18] In the section "The Banquet of Trimalchio," Petronius paints a picture of Roman society and wealth through the title character's lavish dinner parties.[19] However, like Jacinta, Trimalchio is not all that he seems. As a freedman, Trimalchio is merely playing at being a member of the upper class.[20] In essence, he is a fraud. Like her namesake, Jacinta is also an impostor. In reality, all that is certain concerning Jacinta is that she has successfully intrigued the young socialites of the Hamptons through her blog, *The Wanted*. Though she never reveals her face on the blog, she becomes an icon and commentator for the fashion world of New York. Despite having no prior knowledge of *The Wanted* or its author, Naomi immediately senses that there is something more to Jacinta's "gorgeous otherworldly façade" than what can be found online.[21] During their first meeting, Naomi notes that under the "wig and layers of makeup, Jacinta was the most authentic person at the party."[22] Admittedly, this description of Jacinta is ironic considering the lengths that she goes through to create both her online and her Hamptons' persona. However, it foreshadows the interrogation of truth and identity that will unfold throughout the novel. Like Gatsby, Jacinta's deception will become the catalyst that reveals the hypocrisy of Delilah and her friends.

Through Jacinta, Benincasa's novel effectively examines the power that the internet and social media have on shaping the means through which teenagers come to develop a sense of self, as well as a relationship with the world around them. As social media platforms grow at an exponential pace, they have come to represent the expectations that teenagers both hold themselves to and the lens through which they see and judge others. Social influencers have a god-like authority that exhorts their followers to shape themselves in their internet perfect image. The ultimate problem with this obsession with online personas is that they do not exist. They are merely snapshots of life, carefully edited to convey an unattainable version of prosperity and perfection. Given this ability to deceive, the internet becomes a powerful place for Adriana DeStefano to recreate herself into Jacinta Trimalchio in an attempt to reconnect with Delilah. Through careful manipulation of her blog, Adriana begins to infiltrate the glamour of the New York elite and establish herself as a fashion icon and influencer, Jacinta. Ironically, her followers are made up of the same group that had rejected Adriana when her family lost their fortune. However, Jacinta is careful to bury any remnants of that past and establish an online persona that becomes the voice of teenage fashion with the ability to predict and establish the up-and-coming social celebrities. Jacinta's word becomes law. Though they know nothing about her, including what she looks like, her followers eagerly read her posts, searching for the next new trend to emulate.

While it is undeniable that Jacinta is responsible for deceiving her audience, and later Delilah and Naomi, this deception would not have been possible had it not been for the susceptibility of her followers. This instinct to follow the guidance of an internet celebrity is not a new phenomenon, but is, instead, the result of the turmoil that teenagers have when attempting to reconcile their sense of self with the pressure of achieving perfection based on the expectations of social media. Trites notes that these social expectations "derive their power from the discourse people use."[23] In this instance, Jacinta's blog is the discourse that informs the behaviors of her readers and, in doing so, is responsible for "regulating social power."[24] Inherent in this discourse is the ability to both "repress and to empower their constituents."[25] Just as *The Wanted* can shape the behavior of its fan base, it can also provide its followers with the power to either enforce these expectations or undermine them. In this manner, social media not only has the ability to dictate and control trends, but it can also be used a means to elicit change. As the novel progresses, social media will be the means through which Jacinta and, finally, Naomi challenge the social constructs of the Hamptons.

Naomi's first opportunity to meet this enigmatic internet personality presents itself the day after she arrives at her mother's home. This meeting is the catalyst that forces Naomi to explore her own values and establish a sense of self based on her own terms.

In an effort to rekindle a relationship with Delilah, Jacinta throws a lavish party at her temporary home in the Hamptons. From the moment that Jacinta's invitation arrives at her house, Naomi is drawn into a series of events that will challenge her perceptions of her mother's world and the people that she has kept at a careful distance throughout her childhood. Interestingly, Naomi makes the decision to attend the party, an action she would never have considered in her previous summers, based on the carnival theme that is reminiscent of childhood favorites, such as cotton candy and Ferris wheels. This is an ironic choice given that Naomi's attendance at this party precipitates her own movement from childhood to adulthood. The attraction of the childish atmosphere soon fades, leaving Naomi to explore the very adult world of the Hamptons' social scene. It is at this party that Naomi succumbs to this lavish lifestyle, leaving behind her preconceived notions of Delilah and her friends in order to fully participate in summer in the Hamptons. In doing so, Naomi opens the door to experiences and growth that signal her movement from childhood insecurities to a self-assured adult.

In order to truly find acceptance in the Hamptons, Naomi must transform her outward appearance to match those of Delilah and her friends. This transformation begins when Naomi is forced to abandon her typical wardrobe of black concert tees and Doc Martens in order to don the uniform of the wealthy elite to join the festivities. When Naomi begins to get ready for the party, her mother insists on examining her wardrobe. After finding only clothes with "cartoon characters, a band, or a snotty saying on the front," Naomi's mother reveals that she has already purchased "some Marc Jacobs basics" for just such an event.[26] In this moment, Naomi is faced with the fact that her style, which reflects her personality, is unacceptable for the Hamptons' social scene. Instead, in order to play the part of the socialite partygoer, Naomi must give up a piece of her own identity. Despite her initial trepidation with this process, Naomi allows her mother to dress her and do her hair. The result, though positive, is a double-edged sword. The more Naomi succumbs to this role, the easier it becomes for her to assimilate to the Hamptons' lifestyle. However, accepting this role does not come without a cost. As Naomi slips into her place among her Hamptons' friends, she finds that she begins to sacrifice parts of herself that had previously been integral to her identity.

The transformation that begins with her clothing continues as Naomi attends Jacinta's first summer party. Like Gatsby, Jacinta uses extravagance and spectacle as a means to attract a crowd that is sure to include the focus of her admiration: Delilah Fairweather. As the partygoers of the Hamptons gather for the festivities at Jacinta's carnival, they come to represent the social norms of the wealthy that Naomi typically keeps at arm's length. Like those revelers that Nick encounters at Gatsby's parties that "preserved a dignified homogeneity and assumed to itself the function of representing the staid nobility of the countryside," Naomi suddenly finds herself immersed in a world governed by glamour and excess.[27] This party marks Naomi's first tentative steps into the Hamptons' social scene, as she is determined to be a participant, not merely a witness to the revelries: "I made a split-second vow to myself that I wasn't going to be Naomi the confession receptacle at this party. I was going to—participate, whatever that meant."[28] Naomi's decision to step outside of her usual role at these events indicates that she is expanding her sense of self by experimenting with behavior that goes against her typical responses to these scenarios. This party, and her subsequent meeting with Jacinta, becomes the catalyst for Naomi exploring new roles, both socially and sexually.

As Naomi becomes willing to set aside her preconceived notions about her new friends' lifestyle, she further immerses herself in this new persona through her summer romance with Jeff Byron, a fellow member of the Hamptons' social scene. In Jeff, Naomi finds the means to explore a side of herself that had previously gone untouched. At 17, Naomi has never been part of a romantic relationship and, in fact, knows very little about her own sexuality. Any talk of sex is limited to what she hears of her best friend Skags' relationships; Naomi is merely a bystander. Through her budding relationship with Jeff, the novel explores Naomi's own desires to establish a connection with someone that moves beyond the realm of friendship. Jacinta's party provides the perfect moment for Naomi to make this connection with Jeff at the top of a Ferris wheel, where she experiences her first kiss. In that moment, Naomi feels that she has reached a milestone in her life, "like [she had] checked off a box on the grand list of Things You Must Do While You Are a Teenager."[29] Though the exploration of romantic love and sexuality are common themes in young adult novels, *Great* moves beyond using these topics to explore coming-of-age scenarios and, instead, examines how the dynamics of these relationships can shape, and even challenge, the development of identity.

While this milestone is the first of many that Naomi will experience during her interactions with Jeff, this first kiss will send ripples of change far beyond their immediate relationship. The first noticeable change occurs in Naomi's friendship with Delilah. Initially, Naomi is ecstatic at this turn of events. However, she soon realizes that she has no one to confide in: "Then I immediately wanted to text somebody and tell them, but who was I going to tell? Certainly not my mother, and definitely not my dad. Skags would just say that straight make-outs were gross. I wished I had a girly girlfriend I could tell."[30] As exciting as her first kiss is, Naomi realizes that her position as an outsider in the Hamptons has left her without an outlet to share her thoughts and experiences. Her tense relationship with her mother all but eliminates any chance that Naomi will feel the need to share this first with Anne. Her friendship with Skags is also eliminated, as Naomi predicts a less than enthusiastic response to her new romance. Instead, Naomi longs for a friendship that she would typically have responded to with disdain.

In a turn of events that will force her to rethink her estimation of the Hamptons and its inhabitants, Naomi awakens to an unexpected text from Delilah. During their exchange of texts, Naomi falls into a comfortable rhythm of gossip about her interactions with Jeff. This simple act opens a door for Naomi that had previously been shut, though admittedly by her own preconceived notions, allowing her access to a world that she had worked to keep at arm's length. Now Naomi finds herself questioning her previous position on this friendship: "The weirdness of girly-texting with Delilah Fairweather was actually less intense that I'd thought it would be. Could I be getting used to talking to her like a real friend? And if I were used to talking to her like a real friend, did that mean she was a real friend?"[31] Although this friendship is clearly out of

Naomi's typical comfort zone, she finds herself considering the possibility of making a genuine connection with Delilah, an event that she had avoided in previous summers. This revelation is not without its discomfort for Naomi. To accept this turn of events, Naomi must set aside her doubts and resist the desire to question these changes:

> Since when did I happily and comfortably swill champagne with the sons and daughters of America's finest families? I started to analyze the previous evening the way I always do the morning after a party, but I stopped after a few seconds. Maybe it was my hangover. Or maybe it was something else—a conviction that I was going to do things differently this summer. Maybe I didn't need to overthink everything.[32]

In this moment, Naomi's outlook begins to shift, allowing her to let her guard down. She tries to enjoy her time in the Hamptons and her unexpected relationships with Jeff and Delilah. In what can only be perceived as an outward acceptance of this new attitude, as Naomi dresses for the day, she chooses to wear one of the Marc Jacobs outfits, not only because "it would give [her] mother a little bit of a thrill" but because she was opening herself up to the idea that she could feel like she belonged this summer.[33]

Naomi's decision to acclimate herself to her new role in the Hamptons is not without its consequences. As she becomes further immersed in the lives of her new friends, Naomi finds herself playing a role that conflicts with her own moral compass. As she grapples with these conflicting emotions, Naomi is forced to make a choice between conformity and isolation. This becomes more difficult as Naomi becomes wrapped up in both the relationship between Jacinta and Delilah, and her own budding romance with Jeff. As she spends more time with these newfound friends, Naomi finds that she has less time for those individuals who make up her life in Chicago, including her best friend Skags. Though she admits that she "could've tried harder to call Skags or at least try to text back and forth," Naomi notes that "something else was always coming up—a clambake, or a day at the village spa with Jacinta and Delilah, or a long bike ride with Jeff."[34] Naomi is soon surprised to find that while she "usually spent all summer wishing [she] were back in Chicago, … at some point that summer [she] stopped thinking about home."[35] These distractions prove to be so time-consuming that Naomi even forgets to check in with her dad. This is a surprising turn of events, given that in previous summers, Naomi had regularly called home with complaints about her mother and life among the Hamptons' residents. When her dad finally calls her to check in, Naomi finds that her relationship with her father is strained in a way that she is unaccustomed to, so much so that she finds herself annoyed with him. In addition to lying to him concerning her lack of SAT study time, Naomi finds that she is suddenly defensive and annoyed with her father. This is a new and disturbing sensation for Naomi: "I'm not used to feeling irritated with my dad, so I figured I'd get off the phone before I said something crappy."[36] This sudden irritability comes with Naomi's continued exploration of friendships and activities that are typically a direct contradiction to her previous opinions and behavior. Rather than focusing on studying for the SAT to prepare for early admittance to Harvard, as she would have usually done, Naomi has found that there are many other things to keep her occupied:

> It was just that there were always other things to do, like hang out with the girls or go night-swimming at the beach with Jeff or go biking around the neighborhood with Jeff or go hiking on some of the old horse trails with Jeff. ... And at night—especially at night—there were other things to do with Jeff.[37]

As Naomi explores this new side of her life, she finds that her former priorities, including keeping in touch with her dad and best friend, have fallen away. Study sessions are replaced with social activities with Jacinta and Delilah, as well as sexual experimentation in her relationship with Jeff. However, Naomi struggles to reconcile this new behavior with her former beliefs and identity.

Admitting that she is enjoying time with her friends in the Hamptons contradicts Naomi's previous sense of self. While Naomi had typically viewed herself as an outsider when she was with her mother and the wealthy teenagers of the Hamptons, she soon finds herself abandoning her own sense of style, as well as priorities. Naomi's choice to adapt to this new world stems from more than a simple desire to find acceptance; it is a product of an isolation versus conformity to power structures. In order to be accepted, Naomi must adapt to her surroundings, even if that means behaving in a manner that is outside of her comfort zone. Though she appears to make these choices of her own volition, Naomi is driven by the desire to find approval from her new friends, rather than risk further isolation. While Naomi certainly has a sense that her new friends' values and behaviors are problematic, her concern is overshadowed by her desire to finally feel included. However, as the novel's ending unfolds around her, Naomi is forced to reconsider the lifestyle that she has immersed herself in over the summer.

Though Jacinta's deception clearly sets the tragedy of the novel into motion, Delilah is not without guilt in this turn of events. She engages in a romantic relationship with Jacinta, but Delilah's participation is a product of her own selfish nature. Initially, it appears that Benincasa's decision to replace Gatsby with a female character will allow the novel to push the boundaries of sexual norms and open up a dialogue concerning the resistance that these sexual identities meet when faced with heteronormative expectations. Naomi's commentary certainly confirms that this nontraditional relationship will be problematic for Delilah: "I had a very strong feeling that Senator and Mrs. Fairweather would prefer to be swallowed whole by a monster than to have their picture perfect, all-American image besmirched by a lesbian daughter."[38] The Fairweathers' likely response to Delilah's behavior represents not only her parent's desire to impose their own value systems on their daughter but also the social structures that reinforce this heteronormative behavior. Her father's position as a politician, as well as her family's wealth, ensures that Delilah's choices have the ability to reiterate the values of the status quo. By involving this character in a nontraditional relationship, the novel should push the boundaries of social constructs. However, as Skags points out, Delilah's involvement with Jacinta is not based on mutual attraction. Instead, it is a means for Delilah to maintain her position of social power: "And what Delilah and Jacinta have is not a real relationship. They are mutually obsessed. Well, Jacinta is obsessed with Delilah, and Delilah is also obsessed with Delilah, so it all works out for them."[39] As long as Jacinta caters to Delilah's need for adoration, the relationship remains beneficial without truly breaking social boundaries. In fact, Skags is quick to note that even if their relationship has moved into sexual behavior, "given Republican Barbie's natural inclination toward straight white douches like her dad—it is all Jacinta doing stuff to Delilah."[40] Jeff affirms that Delilah's behavior is self-serving by noting that she is simply using Jacinta to punish Teddy for his cheating escapades with a local waitress named Misti. Rather than being genuinely invested in this relationship, Jacinta is "Delilah's pet for the summer, someone for her to play with."[41] While Benincasa's decision to change the gender of Gatsby has the potential to challenge gender norms, Delilah's behavior, instead, reaffirms the social structures that are inherent in the Hamptons' social circles. A relationship with Jacinta is only acceptable as long as it panders to Delilah's desire to remain in a position of power. Once Teddy ruthlessly reveals Jacinta's identity in an attempt to reassert power over the situation, Jacinta is no longer useful to Delilah and is summarily abandoned. Instead of challenging heteronormativity, this relationship becomes a means to reinforce these norms.

The aftermath of both Teddy and Delilah's rejection of Jacinta mirrors the events of *The Great Gatsby*, as two of the characters end up dead by the novel's closing. Like her counterpart, Myrtle, Misti is killed in a hit-and-run accident. Just as Gatsby attempts to protect Daisy, Jacinta does not initially reveal Delilah's role in the incident. Instead, she maintains the hope that Delilah truly does love her and will come to be with her regardless of her past. The striking difference in this ending comes when Jacinta finally admits to herself that she has misjudged Delilah. When it becomes apparent that she will likely be blamed for Delilah's crime, Jacinta's despair leads her to take her own life. The forces that have sought to separate her from Delilah have finally suppressed Jacinta's attempts to reinvent herself into a member of Hamptons' society. In doing so, the novel notes that the development of identity is closely tied to the power structures that are responsible for maintaining the status quo. Despite her attempts to buy acceptance through gifts and extravagant parties, Jacinta is unable to fully gain entrance into Delilah's world. The perfect persona that she had carefully cultivated through her blog cannot stand up to the scrutiny of life outside of the internet. Although Jacinta's blog has become the discourse that informs the fashion choices of the East Hamptons' teens, once it becomes clear that she does not actually belong to their world, she is summarily abandoned by all who had previously admired her. Jacinta's lack of wealth and social status is enough to condemn her. As she has spent all of her inheritance on impressing Delilah and the rest of the Hamptons' residents, Jacinta does not have the means to defend herself. She is tried and convicted by a jury of her peers who uphold the law and the status quo of the wealthy. Jacinta accepts her place as the Other by taking her own life and, in doing so, allows the wealthy elite to reestablish their social order. Like Gatsby's, Jacinta's death is met with little fanfare.

While Jacinta's suicide initially appears to follow the pattern of *The Great Gatsby* in which justice is not served and the Other is punished for defying societal expectations, as *Great* closes, Naomi becomes the vehicle through which these norms are interrogated and subverted. Though Naomi has struggled to reconcile her own identity throughout the novel, Jacinta's death propels her into self-reflection and the revelation that she does not truly belong in the Hamptons. While Naomi has found acceptance from her East Hamptons' friends, it was at the cost of her own values and beliefs. In that moment, Naomi not only realizes that her newfound acceptance was based on superficial aspects, such as clothing and appearance, but also notes that the inclination to pursue success at any cost is a common theme among her new friends. Though Delilah and Teddy must know that implicating Jacinta in Misti's death will have destructive consequences, they use their status as the children of politicians and businessmen as a buffer from punishment. As these events unfold, Naomi comes to realize that the privilege that is afforded to the wealthy causes Delilah and her friends to believe that they are impervious to the repercussions of Misti's death.

Though Naomi has briefly allowed herself to be taken in by the privilege and lifestyle offered to her by her mother's social status, these events prove to be a permanent breaking point for her. In a true coming-of-age moment, Naomi separates herself from her mother and the rest of the Hamptons and returns home to Chicago on a flight the next day. This separation is effectively depicted in Naomi's change from her Marc Jacobs clothes to the outfit that she had worn when she first arrived for the summer. As she sheds the frilly dress and dons her Cure T-shirt and Doc Martens, "[i]t felt like slipping back into [her] real skin instead of the plastic facsimile [she'd] been wearing all summer long."[42] Just as Nick returns to his Midwestern values at the end of *The Great Gatsby*, Naomi turns back to a lifestyle based on her father's example of hard work and kindness. Though Trites's discussion of power in young adult novels would suggest that Naomi's identity is still a product of the forces that seek to repress and shape her into an acceptable adult by her father's standards, her rejection of the power structure inherent in the Hamptons' lifestyle indicates that her development of self is still a choice.[43] Naomi chooses to follow those values that reflect her father's sensibilities, while simultaneously pushing back against the social norms that were responsible for the death of Jacinta. This in itself is an indication that despite the apparent power of the social structures that seek to repress the Other, those brave enough to question the status quo can successfully reject these expectations and choose their own path.

It is Naomi's persistence in questioning the established norms of the wealthy that leads to an ending that is a stark departure from Gatsby's story. Naomi does not sit idly by and allow Delilah and Teddy to escape into the safety of their wealth and social status. Instead, with the help of Jacinta's suicide note, Naomi uses the blog that initially granted Adriana DeStefano access to Delilah's world as a weapon to mete out some form of justice. Just as Jacinta helped to solidify Delilah as a local celebrity among her peers, her last video message uses the truth about Misti's death to undermine Delilah's social status. Though Jacinta, like Gatsby, defends the object of her affection even in her last moments, Delilah will still be forced to face the repercussions of her actions. Though it is unlikely that this video will result in criminal charges, Naomi has at least ensured that Delilah will be forced to endure the whispers and rumors that tainted Jacinta's memory. Though this ending is not entirely happy, *Great* manages to provide an outlet for justice to be served on some level. In doing so, the novel highlights the notion that the status quo can, and should, be challenged. As Naomi comes to terms with Jacinta's death and her role in the events that summer, she also learns about herself. Her attempts to gain acceptance among the teenagers in the Hamptons lead Naomi to question her own belief systems and the role her parents' values have on the development of her sense of self. In the end, Naomi is able to reconcile her own identity with the conflicting lifestyles of the Hamptons and Chicago. The realization that she can choose her own path in life leads to closure for both Jacinta and Naomi, as she can now enter adulthood on her own terms.

Though her adaptation of *The Great Gatsby* is certainly faithful to the original, Benincasa's *Great* moves beyond interrogating the conflict that arises between East Coast and Midwestern values, and instead focuses on the forces that shape the identity of the novel's characters. While Nick Carraway simply draws attention to societal norms and limitations without challenging them, *Great* uses Naomi's struggle with developing a sense of self to both interrogate these issues and push the boundaries of the status quo that seeks to repress the Other. As she bears witness to the doomed relationship of Jacinta and Delilah, Naomi comes to realize that the privilege that she experiences comes with a price. However, unlike Nick, Naomi chooses to not stand idly by as Delilah and Teddy go unpunished. Instead, Naomi finally accepts that she does not truly belong in the Hamptons, with its "fancy people who spend their days pretending, and their nights dreaming, that their pretense is real."[44] Naomi ends the summer on her own terms by embracing her own values and resting in the knowledge that she had "done right by Jacinta."[45] As she follows her "best friend. [Skags] out into the late-summer sunshine," Naomi does so with the conviction that it is sometimes better to live life outside the lines.[46]

Notes

1 Trites, *Disturbing the Universe*, x.
2 Ibid., 3.
3 Ibid., 7.
4 Fink, *The Lacanian Subject*, 46–8, summarized in Trites, *Disturbing the Universe*, 5–6.
5 Nikolajeva, *Power, Voice and Subjectivity*, 121.
6 Ibid.
7 Benincasa, *Great*, 24.
8 Ibid.
9 Ibid., 25.
10 Ibid., 24.
11 Ibid., 11.
12 Ibid., 12.
13 Ibid., 14.
14 Ibid.
15 Ibid., 12.
16 Ibid., 15.
17 Ibid.

18 West, "Introduction," xvii.
19 Ibid.
20 Ibid.
21 Benincasa, *Great*, 83.
22 Ibid., 87.
23 Trites, *Disturbing the Universe*, 22.
24 Ibid.
25 Ibid.
26 Benincasa, *Great*, 25.
27 Fitzgerald, *The Great Gatsby*, 44.
28 Benincasa, *Great*, 75.
29 Ibid., 23.
30 Ibid., 93–4.
31 Ibid., 104.
32 Ibid.
33 Ibid., 105.
34 Ibid., 144.
35 Ibid.
36 Ibid., 148.
37 Ibid., 147.
38 Ibid., 186–7.
39 Ibid., 189.
40 Ibid.
41 Ibid., 172.
42 Ibid., 247.
43 Trites, *Disturbing the Universe*, 19–20.
44 Benincasa, *Great*, 4.
45 Ibid., 262.
46 Ibid., 263.

Bibliography

Benincasa, Sara. *Great*. New York: Harper Teen, 2014.
Fink, Bruce. *The Lacanian Subject: Between Languages and Jouissance*. Princeton, NJ: Princeton University Press, 1995.
Fitzgerald, F. Scott. *The Great Gatsby*. New York: Scribner, 2004.
Nikolajeva, Maria. *Power, Voice and Subjectivity in Literature for Young Readers*. New York: Routledge, 2010.
Trites, Roberta Seelinger. *Disturbing the Universe Power and Repression in Adolescent Literature*. Iowa: University of Iowa Press, 2000.
West, James L. W., III. "Introduction." In *Trimalchio: An Early Version of* The Great Gatsby, *by F. Scott Fitzgerald*, edited by James L.W. West III, xiii–xxii, Cambridge: Cambridge University Press, 2002.

4

LGBTQIA Fairy Tales: Queering *Cinderella* in Lo's *Ash* and Donoghue's "The Tale of the Shoe"

Dalila Forni

The Power of Fairy-Tale Retellings for Young Adults

Both cultural studies scholars and sociologists argue that products addressed to young audiences (books, films, toys, songs, etc.) shape children's perception of gender identity and gender relationships. As a consequence, fairy tales are one of the potential "cultural markers" that may affect children's, teenagers', and adults' perceptions of what is culturally legitimate and what is not. As Christina Bacchilega has noted, despite being an ancient form of art, fairy tales pervade popular culture and become an indirect agent of cultural transmission and transformation. Fairy tales affect "the making of who we are and of the world we are in. … fairy tales interpellate us as consumers and producers of transformation"; they encourage readers to consider new possibilities and to seek changes, while indirectly transforming our social world.[1] For this reason, according to Jack Zipes, fairy tales have a strong influence on socializing processes and are thus an attractive and long-lasting form of narration.[2]

Neal A. Lester identifies an "early indoctrination" concerning gender roles, identity, and sexual orientations that impacts children's and kids' perception of what is morally suitable in Western society.[3] In particular, "children's texts perpetuate a limiting heteronormalcy that negatively impacts identity development for those that do not fit in this model of behavior and desire."[4] As part of the complex system of gender socialization from an early age, fairy tales may indirectly work on broadening gender labels and on deconstructing traditional stereotypes. Moreover, this literature works on social and personal awareness, promoting visibility and empowerment. Indeed, fairy tales are now presenting a new consciousness that fits contemporary times as they address new perspectives that can be interpreted through a sociological, cultural, and pedagogical analyses.

Historically, fairy tales have been used as an educative tool in order to transmit specific values or moral lessons to children,[5] but this power can also facilitate the transformation of moral standards and promote new values. Fairy-tale retellings can help the reader consider different perspectives, encourage empathy, and reflect the reader's own experiences concerning gender identity and sexual orientation. Therefore, this literary genre, if adapted to contemporary times, may support gender diversity and indirectly construct an open-minded, inclusive collective imagination. Young adult novels and short stories based on fairy tales are particularly successful instruments to achieve this goal. As Anne Kerchy notes, young adult fairy tales "craft a relational model of identity."[6] Kerchy highlights young adult retellings of fairy tales' educative function that, in this chapter, will be linked to a queer perspective.

Adolescence is a particularly sensitive period of life marked by questions about identity, love relationships, and sexuality.[7] Literature works as an effective tool in helping young adults dealing with emotional insecurities related to identity and sexuality. According to Beth Younger, young adult novels may serve as a source of information as they portray teen characters negotiating cultural standards of gender and sexuality.[8] However, most of the young adult texts addressing love or sexual relationships offer values linked to the dominant society that fail to respect different shades of identity and attraction. Because adolescence is an intersectional time that builds bridges between childhood and adulthood, young adult texts can challenge heteronormativity by reconsidering identity from different perspectives.[9] If gender identity is built from a very early age both directly and indirectly, gender dynamics are confirmed (or reassessed) during adolescence. For this reason, literature for young adults should provide rich, complex, and inclusive models in order to provide a wide spectrum of identities and sexualities with which to identify. Specifically, teenagers can find in lesbian, gay, bisexual, and queer characters a safe opportunity to explore their own experience, identity, and desires and to stimulate their personal growth and empowerment thanks to positive models presented in books.[10]

Queer Retellings

Queer adaptations or retellings of fairy tales aim to challenge the heteronormativity that usually characterizes conventional children's and young adult texts.[11] Classical versions of fairy tales are known worldwide and appear familiar for many generations of readers. However, their representations of sexuality usually deal with heteronormative patterns and fixed gender roles.[12]

Even if fairy tales have been historically devoted to the fulfillment of heteronormativity, a growing number of queer retellings presenting diverse gender and sexual identities is now offered to young readers.[13] To begin with, "queer" is an open umbrella term that covers a wide spectrum of meanings.[14] In some cases, it may be used as a synonym for LGBTQIA (Lesbian, Gay, Bisexual, Transsexual, Queer, Intersex, and Asexual), acknowledging no differences along the continuum of sexualities and gender identities. For others, "queer" is the rejection of those classifications that try to categorize identity: "Queer theorists recognize sexual and gender identities as social, multiple, variable, shifting, and fluid; and while they allow for movement among such identity categories, they advocate for movement outside of these categories as well."[15] According to Annamarie Jagose, queer signifies "those gestures or analytical models which dramatize incoherencies in the allegedly stable relations between chromosomal sex, gender, and sexual desire."[16] The term includes a destabilization of long-lasting dichotomies such as male versus female, straight versus gay, and so on. Queerness works against what is familiar to present unexpected and unfamiliar situations or identities. Overall, "queer" indicates those notions or practices that demonstrate that gender and sexual identity is not a natural quality but a cultural construction that may change in time and space, questioning dominant cultural norms and labels.[17]

In this chapter, "queer" will be used as a term indicating fluid or marginalized identities that resist hegemonic discourses about gender or sexuality.[18] As suggested by Kay Turner and Pauline Greenhill in their collection, *Transgressive Tales: Queering the Grimms*, normative sexual dynamics—such as heterosexual love and marriage—should be overcome in order to focus on the deepest struggles of the tale, where far more intricate non-normative, unexpected desires and identities are presented.[19] Fairy-tale symbols, despite presenting Western values, hide complex and multiple meanings, multifaceted identities, and ambiguous situations that may arouse young adult readers' curiosity concerning identity and sexuality. As a matter of fact, the significance of a fairy tale often lies not in its text but in its reception and interpretation.[20] Consequently, fairy tales are not part of a morally transparent genre that wants to teach lessons, but rather an ambiguous and transgressive form of art that might be interpreted differently. Thus, a "different" interpretation should be encouraged in order to reassess gender-related issues and to include a wider audience that is rarely represented in classical fairy tales or in most of their modern reinterpretations.

Consequently, just as feminist retellings of fairy tales unsettle patriarchal values, queer readings of fairy tales are needed to contest heteronormative relations and identities and expand fairy-tale signifiers to reflect contemporary sensibilities. Queer retellings are necessary in order to break stereotypical representations of nonconventional identities or relationships, to represent those readers who were not represented when the original story was written, and to make a tale more contemporary, giving the reader the opportunity to reflect upon modern issues and to work against the expected, most of all with a young adult reader.[21] Queer retellings of fairy tales offer an opportunity to undo and recreate the connection between tradition and transgression, working on cultural values through popular narrations. Maria Micaela Coppola addresses the value of modern revisions:

> the text is no longer considered as the deposit of a hidden, unique meaning which the interpreter has to unveil. On the contrary, it is perceived as the receptacle of performances of meaning that are conveyed by multiple interactions with determined readers.[22]

This disruption of social norms through queer texts is particularly appropriate for young adult audiences questioning their own identity and sexuality. Tales focusing on awareness and self-discovery may encourage young readers to personally interpret their own lives through a queer lens and to overcome gender and sexual standards proposed by society.

Queer Desires

The present chapter compares two retellings of *Cinderella* that counteract gender stereotypes, reconsider female desires, and offer new approaches to sexual orientations for young adult readers. *Ash*, a novel by Malinda Lo, and "The Tale of the Shoe," a short story by Emma Donoghue, challenge binary understandings of gender and sexuality. In each text, a female protagonist falls in love with another female character instead of marrying Prince Charming; however, the girls are not explicitly defined as lesbians but could be considered bisexual, pansexual, or, simply, queer. This inability to categorize the girls' sexuality is particularly significant in this analysis, because both *Ash* and "The Tale of the Shoe" leave the readers free to interpret the texts following their own desires. The absence of labels allows a larger audience to identify with the character, since no specific limits are set in their portrayal and development. In addition, the lack of fixed classifications allows readers to think outside of the box, so to speak, and consider different shades of sexual orientations and identities.

Since the 1970s, female characters with nonstandard gender roles or sexual orientations in young adult fiction have increased in number and quality: novels on the topic are richer, deeper, stronger, and less stereotypical. Through the last decades, lesbian characters in fiction for young adults have become more and more independent, strong, and self-confident. The earliest novels tended to represent only stereotypical queer characters, thinking that mere presence was enough to count as inclusive. More recently, writers and readers felt an urgent need to see complex, progressive characters as well. Thus, standards concerning authenticity, diversity, depth, and complexity of the character and their experience gradually increased in queer young adult fiction.[23] Nevertheless, books on LGBTQIA topics are still considered, produced, and categorized as "issue books" by editors, booksellers, and readers.[24]

With this in mind, scholars have tried to catalogue queer fiction for younger audiences. In particular, Caroline E. Jones, examining depictions of female love relationships in fiction for young adults, created three different (and partially chronological) categories: traditional texts, mediating texts, and progressive texts.[25] First, traditional texts are usually addressed to heterosexual audiences and are based on a stereotyped representation of homosexual characters, who are usually persecuted or extremely fragile. These texts, in Lee Edelman's words, "are designed to educate audiences unfamiliar or uncomfortable with lesbianism and/or to eroticize the lesbian as a facet of male heterosexual pleasure."[26] Second, mediating texts may deconstruct stereotypes, but homosexual characters are portrayed as types. The main character overcomes difficulties and accepts her/his orientation. In this case too, the texts address heterosexual readers and approach queer identities as Other. Finally, most of the young adult novels featuring lesbian characters published in the twenty-first century fall in the category of progressive texts. In this case, the characters are usually well-developed as they are explored considering professional and personal awareness, raising themes such as race, ethnicity, and social class. Moreover, for Christine A. Jenkins, in progressive texts the bi/lesbian character does not hate herself for her sexual orientation: When she is out, she is serenely aware of her sexuality; when she is not out, she is not victimized and peacefully accepts her orientation.[27]

Nonheteronormative novels or short stories for young adults usually depict a young queer character in their teens who is slowly becoming aware of their sexual orientation and/or identity. These works often criticize social paradigms linked to heteronormativity, and, in addition to relationships, female pleasure and desire may be the focus of the books as well. This is also a particularly unusual element in heterosexual literary works, in which female sexual desire (both heterosexual and queer) is often repressed or punished.[28] Consequently, female love relationships are usually depicted as platonic or unrealistic. In general, women and adolescent girls are rarely represented in literature as sexual beings. Authors usually focus on the romantic side of a love relationship, avoiding sex altogether. For this reason, Jones points out that any queer young adult novel that is sexually explicit would likely be labeled pornography. If sexuality is generally perceived as an uneasy theme in young adult literature, in queer literature, sexual desire is even less freely represented since it is perceived as a taboo topic.[29]

Nevertheless, queer retellings may offer the possibility of showing realistic female love relationships and desires while counteracting conservative sexual values and heteronormativity. As argued by Jones, young adult texts featuring queer identities present a new perspective on traditional love stories and rewrite female figures from a different perspective. Women are not passively looking and waiting for Prince Charming but actively take part in love affairs that are not necessarily related to male figures. In queer retellings for young readers, women are not passive and desireless but actively show their feelings and passions.

Similarly, Younger points out that lesbian young adult novels offer young readers a new perspective on female sexuality while deconstructing heterosexism: female desires are not punished or considered a taboo topic but are sensibly expressed in the pages of young adult queer novels.[30] Moreover, she underlines the importance of presenting alternative desires to teenagers and young adults through literature in order to accompany them in a process of self-awareness and consciousness. As a matter of fact, queer young adult works are usually bildungsromans of growth and self-discovery, "a safe space where young people can read about themselves and discover options, alternatives, and information."[31]

Malinda Lo's *Ash*

In Malinda Lo's 2009 young adult novel, Ash is raised by her stepmother and her stepsisters after the death of her mother and father. The girl, treated by her stepfamily as a servant, loves to imagine a fairy world, the one her mother used to tell her about before going to bed. Wandering in the woods, Ash meets fairies and becomes particularly close to a male fairy, Sidhean. In the woods, the protagonist meets a girl too: Kaisa, the King's huntress. While her stepsisters have parties in the city in order to find a rich husband, Ash enjoys hunting and chatting with her new friend. When a royal ball is set in order to find a proper wife to the Prince, Ash asks Sidhean, the male fairy, to make her wish come true: she would like to go to the feast without being recognized by her stepfamily and meet Kaisa there. The fairy does make her wish come true but warns Ash that, in return, she will be his property. At the end of the novel, Ash must pay a sacrifice in order to be free and live happily with her huntress.

The novel should be classified as a progressive text—according to Jones's categories—since it presents homosexuality simply as a different way of being in a love relationship; different sexualities are completely natural in the fairy world. For example, when Kaisa and Ash are dancing together during the ball, people are surprised and describe it as "one of the more unusual things to happen at a Yule Ball,"[32] but they are simply curious, not shocked. As a consequence, Ash does not question her sexual orientation; she is a self-confident female character whose identity is considered beyond her sexual and romantic preferences. Ash does not even feel the need to come out and she is not directly defined as "lesbian," "bisexual," or "pansexual" in the novel. This choice was not made to ban this aspect but to be consistent with a world in which sexuality does not need to be defined. For instance, some of the fairy tales told by the two girls portray same-sex relationships. This detail indirectly shows that the imaginary world where the action takes place is not characterized by homophobia. The characters spontaneously talk about the nonheteronormative relationships that populate ancient fairy tales as well. Queerness is not an exception but is considered part of the norm, or ordinary.

Though Ash is not concerned about Kaisa's gender, she is worried about her social class: Ash is a poor orphan who works as a servant in her stepmother's house, while Kaisa sits next to the King during the ball on Yule night. However, Ash's worries are not due to class aspirations—she is not interested in becoming rich. When, during the ball, the Prince asks her to dance, she is not excited by the idea of meeting him. Thus, she refuses power, money, and storybook romance to choose a different path. Lo presents a powerful metaphor for accepting one's identity during the ball: while Ash is wearing a mask, Kaisa prefers to show her face. However, at the end of the night, Ash too wants to be herself and show her identity, taking off her mask. This can be interpreted as a metaphor for coming out: removing the mask in order to show one's inner, secret, fragile identity. Similarly, the attic where Ash lives serves as the proverbial closet: the girl is restricted to her own room; however, at the end of the novel, she manages to leave her attic/closet and set off to new worlds, adventures, and relationships.

Despite the portrayal of a world free of homophobia, Ash's character is not explored deeply as a woman, even less as a bi/lesbian woman, and there is a lack of focus on the love relationship between the two main characters. Their love and physical story is not explored in detail, but most of the focus addresses Ash's thoughts and fears. We partially know Ash's feelings while she is falling in love. We partially share her anxieties, and there are few moments in which the two girls are together when we can see their relationship growing. Ash and Kaisa's love story reaches its highest point at the end of the book, but more than a happy ending, Lo's novel offers an open ending, focusing only on the process of falling in love but not on the dynamics of a queer relationship. So, young adult readers are not offered an in-depth account of female dynamics during a love story at different levels but are just encouraged to imagine a possible development of the story without addressing it. Readers are not provided with a portrayal of nonheteronormative relationships but have to imagine them on their own. This fact could be due to the source of the novel: in classic fairy tales, too, the relationship between the protagonist and their lover is only hinted at and the reader does not know what will happen after the happy ending, when the love relationship finally begins. Similarly, Lo ends the narration at a very traditional point: even if marriage is not considered, the novel ends with the two girls' fulfilment of their love story.

Although our society is more and more open to LGBTQIA topics, coming out and dealing with sexual orientation is still not easy. Since Ash presents an ideal land where homophobia does not exist, the novel does not manage to depict the anxieties of real people in the real world. As Jon Wargo highlights in his analysis, the novel's "compromising sexuality and sometimes utopian overtones of gay assimilation position readers to acknowledge that this narrative journey is purely fantastical."[33] On the one hand, it is positive to present to young readers a world where all sexual orientations are accepted; on the other, it is not completely realistic and the risk is not representing the readers. Young adults need to be understood and to read about both their fears and their goals. Lo presents a positive, idealistic model; however, a world where sexual orientation has no influence on individuals' social life is desirable, but not realistic yet. Ash's world mixes fantasy and reality but forgets the culture in which the book was produced and does not deal with some of the troubles adolescents may face in their lives. Thus, the text does not relate to the real experience of queer teenagers but instead simply portrays a fantasy-like world that cannot be compared to our present, Western world.

Although the novel presents a clear queer interpretation of the *Cinderella* fairy tale, in the book the only relationship that is defined as queer (meaning: peculiar) is the one with Sidhean. The protagonist says, "Sidhean, for many years, you have been my only friend, though such a friendship is by definition a queer one, for your people and mine are not by definition meant to love one another."[34] This is particularly interesting because the term "queer" is linked to a male/female relationship and not a same-sex relationship. This relationship overturns the reader's perspective: what is usually considered "strange" or "different" is now the norm, and what is usually perceived as the norm is now defined as queer or bizarre. Thus, Lo offers a new point of view, giving a peculiar connotation to accepted relationships and normalizing those that are usually considered as different.

Wargo notices the strong heterosexual influence on the novel and states that "the transition into queer sexuality requires the payment of compulsory heterosexual love."[35] In order to live happily ever after with the huntress, Ash has to give herself to the fairy. Sidhean takes the place of the Fairy Godmother and helps Ash to go to the ball, where she wants to meet her beloved. Ash promises she will be his, but, at the end of the book, she begs to be set free. Sidhean agrees that in payment for her freedom, he requires the girl for one night. In this final part of the book, Lo presents one of the few scenes of sexual intimacy, even if vaguely described:

> He stepped back and extended his hand to her. She asked, "Will I die?" He answered, "Only a little," and she put her hand in his, and she felt the ring between their palms, burning like a brand … [Ash] turned her palm up to the sunlight and saw a pale, circular scar.[36]

In the novel, heterosexual consummation is necessary to be free and to experience female love. Female desires are still linked to patriarchal values that must be satisfied before Ash can be set free to seek empowerment and independence. Moreover, the scar will mark the girl's body forever and will remind her of her sacrifice, symbolically fastening her to heterosexuality. The scar, as a Scarlet Letter, will testify to her (undesired) encounter with Sidhean and mark her faults in wishing to be free. In addition, when Kaisa and Ash kiss for the first time, Ash feels Sidhean's pain: the magic moment is invaded by a male, undesired presence. Despite living in a world free of homophobia, intimate female desires and passions are interrupted and ruined by an external presence that reminds of Ash's sacrifice and suffering in order to be free. Female love can be experienced only after a tribute to patriarchy.[37]

Again, young adult fiction avoids depictions of physical and sexual encounters and, in particular, lesbian novels are more focused on romance than sexuality; passion and desire are not described directly.[38] Indeed, Ash focuses more on love as a platonic force, and, as in a heterosexual relationship, love helps Ash grow up: at the beginning of the book she is 12 and completely absorbed by the fairy-tale world described by her mother. After meeting Kaisa, Ash slowly distances herself from magic and from her past. Her dreams, once populated by fairies, now feature the girl. Ash leaves the magic world to enter adulthood and to experience a loving relationship. Kaisa makes her exist as a woman: "no one else had paid the slightest attention to her all night, and Ash felt as though the huntress had suddenly called her into being."[39] Thus, Ash's journey goes from an innocent infancy to a passionate adolescence that is not completely shown to the reader. However, considering the target audience of the book, an in-depth analysis of desires, doubts, fears, and emotions would perfectly suit *Ash*. As previously stated, teens seek themselves in the pages of young adult books as they are experiencing an intersectional phase between childhood and adulthood, when complex changes take place. For this reason, it is necessary to provide a portrayal of their experiences, fears, and accomplishments without taboos, to accompany them in their growth without filters.

While Kaisa's portrayal goes beyond gender roles, the love relationship between the two girls is partially stereotyped and represents the canonical male–female relationship in same-sex couples. In particular, Kaisa takes on the "male role." She is taller than Ash—Ash often looks up at her—she is more active (Kaisa flirts with her and goes to visit her when she's home alone), and she is a huntress. She does not wear dresses, but hunting clothes, and she is portrayed as independent and, in some cases, a cold person. Finally, Kaisa tells Ash a fairy tale about the love story between two girls, making the girl aware of her sexuality. Thus, we can define Kaisa as Ash's Prince Charming, rather than her Princess Charming. Even if this characteristic shows an important opening to different gender roles, this choice leads to a stereotyped representation of a lesbian couple linked to heteronormativity. Ash and Kaisa clearly imitate heterosexual couples composed of a male and a female member, usually perceived as opposing poles concerning gender standards. Ash is the female partner who has to be seduced, while Kaisa is the strong male partner who has to flirt with the girl and win her over. *Ash* retells the Cinderella fairy tale from a queer, feminist perspective, presenting two nonheterosexual characters and their love story. The text could be labeled as progressive, even though some stereotypes concerning gender identity and sexuality are presented through the story.

"The Tale of the Shoe" by Emma Donoghue

Kissing the Witch (1993) is a collection of twelve retellings of classical fairy tales and an original story from the author Emma Donoghue. The text is not always labeled as young adult fiction, but it could be interpreted as a crossover collection that blurs the line between what is adult and what is not;[40] its complex topics linked to identity, sexuality, and self-discovery may appeal and stimulate young adult readers. The tales presented in the collection are connected through a narrative chain,[41] where different narrators are linked together: after a story is told in the first person by the protagonist, a secondary character is prompted to tell her own story and gives life to a new narration. The collection of short stories might be considered what Stephen Benson defined as a "post-Carter generation" of fairy tales:[42] Donoghue focuses on issues such as love, identity, and sexuality and gives voice to female characters of the canon. As considered by Martine Hennard Dutheil de la Rochere, the stories "derail the straight path of female destiny encoded in tales."[43] The author questions the canon and rewrites it from a new perspective through subversive plots that encourage social and cultural critique.

Although it has been labeled and approached as a feminist text, in Donoghue's tales female identity is deconstructed and rebuilt through new gender standards that encourage a queer approach in their attempt to broaden the boundaries of identity.[44] The collection counteracts gender stereotypes linked to femininity and female desire and deconstructs gender hierarchies while offering a new, nonbinary perspective. In most of the stories, desires are not fixed but often shift and evolve with the growth of the character and disrupt the fixity of notions regarding gender, love, and sexuality. In the collection's first story, "The Tale of the Shoe," the plot follows the best-known versions of the tale but "subverts the myth of heterosexual desire usually perpetrated in *Cinderella*."[45] The main character does not fall in love with Prince Charming, as in traditional versions of Cinderella, but falls in love with an older female character, reconsidering standards linked both to gender and to age.

While in canonical Cinderella tales violence is perpetrated by the stepmother and/or stepsisters and inflicted on the protagonist, Donoghue's tale deals with more complex and intimate forms of violence. The author reconsiders female bonds in a new light, since no evil sisters or stepmothers are presented in her retelling and violence is usually self-inflicted by Cinderella. At the beginning of the tale, the protagonist hears internal voices that tell her how to behave and what to do: she is forced to do the house chores not by her sisters or her mother but by her intimate thoughts and beliefs. Most portrayals of Cinderella adhere to the canon constructed by heteronormalcy since she behaves as a woman "should" behave. However, Donoghue's version presents a far more complex figure who directly faces psychological issues such as social exclusion, unstable psychological and physical conditions, grief, mourning a loss, and self-inflicted punishments.[46] What strikes most in this retelling is the absence of evil characters, who are internalized by the girl because of her need to follow social values and norms. Society and its strict norms are the main villains of the short story. Indeed, Cinderella suffers a subtle form of abuse: self-rejection. According to Hennard Dutheil de la Rochere, "in this modern-day reinterpretation of the tale in psychological terms, the heroine is not punished for her bad character or manners, but under the only too real spell of depression."[47] From this perspective as well, Donoghue's retelling reflects modern topics concerning identity and self-awareness.

If most of the traditional versions of *Cinderella* present Prince Charming as a source of happiness and liberation, Donoghue's version introduces a female stranger who will help Cinderella emancipate herself from social construction through an inner transformation. The unknown figure offers multiple interpretations at different levels: she represents the witch, the fairy godmother, and the prince. She is mysterious, fascinating, protective, and caring at the same time. Moreover, she gently prompts the girl to explore her desires and follow her wishes, so that she will change her destiny and the fairy-tale ending: "She showed me the sparkle in my eyes, how wide my skirt could spread, how to waltz without getting dizzy. I was lithe in green satin now; my own mother would not have recognized me."[48] In addition, Cinderella is not passively saved by the character, but she is encouraged to make her own decisions without being pushed or obliged to follow a precise path. For instance, Cinderella refuses the Prince's proposal on her own, without knowing the mysterious character's feelings for her:

> I could hardly hear him. The voices were shrieking, Yes yes yes say yes before you lose your chance you bag of nothingness. I opened my teeth but no sound came out. There was no harm in this man; what he proposed was white and soft, comfortable as fog. There was nothing to be afraid of. But just then the midnight bell began to toll out the long procession of years, palatial day by moonless night. And I leapt backward down the steps, leaving one shoe behind. The bushes tore my dress into the old rags. It was perfectly silent on the lawn. She was waiting for me in the shadows.[49]

With the help of this unknown character, Cinderella can free herself from the conventional, monolithic, and patriarchal voices that she was obsessed with; can find her own identity; and can overcome her sadness. In this version of the tale, it is not a male character who saves the protagonist but a strong, mature woman who indirectly rescues the young girl. Indeed, in her analysis of the tale, Hennard Dutheil de la Rochere notes "the beneficial influence of the woman who has helped the narrator overcome her misery. Her arrival is seemed in terms of warmth, suggesting both physical comfort and emotional-wellbeing."[50] Mutual help and mutual love experienced by the characters help them to find self-awareness and to disrupt social canons.

Thanks to her rescuer, Cinderella can reach adulthood and self-awareness, both emotionally and physically. On the one hand, Donoghue's tale is a coming of age and coming out retelling: the protagonist's emancipation and self-discovery are the main topics of the tale. On the other hand, "The Tale of the Shoe" is a story of "erotic fulfillment"[51] as well. Donoghue often introduces love and sexual metaphors to portray the two characters' desires:

> The helper eases her tension by claiming to be a fairy who can use her little finger like a magic wand to do spectacular things. The sexual joke, which plays with the idea of the body as capable of wielding a very special kind of magic, is more than a queer … reinterpretation of the traditional motif of the wand, since it celebrates lesbian love as the sire of magic in the otherwise simple, ordinary and homely world of Donoghue's tale.[52]

In the tale, female love is presented in an apparently heteronormative context as a possible happy ending. Cinderella is not only "saved" by the stranger but also falls in love with her despite the Prince's proposal to marry him. The girl chooses queerness, a different, unknown path instead of safety, wealth, and canonical love. This choice gives the reader the chance to imagine multiple paths to well-known tales usually characterized by fixed developments and structures, such as heterosexual marriage. Cinderella explores her own identity and decides to accept it, disregarding social (and literary) constructions of gender aspirations and sexual orientation.

In "The Tale of the Shoe," Donoghue challenges different categories: not just gender and sexuality but also class and age. In this specific case, the term "queer" could be considered effective at different levels: queerness is not simply related to sexuality and identity; it is a subversive response to oppressive cultural and social standards. This topic may be particularly intriguing for young adult readers and their common desire to discover themselves and to overthrow cultural ideals and expectations. Thus, Donoghue challenges social constructions and etiquettes from both a gender and a cultural perspective.[53] For instance, during the ball, Cinderella behaves according to social constructions regarding femininity, but she appears annoyed by the artificial self she has to show to the guests. Social pressure increases the protagonist's feeling of inadequacy: Cinderella is literally sick of social norms, so much so that she vomits her dinner. After this highly symbolic event, where the protagonist refuses cultural values that do not suit her, the Prince asks her to marry him. In this specific point of the story, the author highlights the artificiality of heterosexual romance of fairy tales: Cinderella recognizes that the Prince's proposal took place in a fairy-tale atmosphere but decides to refuse it.[54] In addition, during the proposal, the protagonist hears inner voices that suggest she accept the marriage: again, social norms are inflicted not by evil characters but by the girl herself. Heteronormative social standards urge the girl to accept the proposal in order to be complete; without marriage, she would be "a bag of nothing."[55] However, Cinderella's process of self-discovery *is* complete: the girl decides to run away from Prince Charming and chooses the old stranger's love. Despite the constant, destructive influence of cultural standards, the girl manages to subvert them and finally offers a possible, alternative model to young readers.

Conclusions

The two retellings discussed in this chapter offer a new perspective on the story of *Cinderella*. Despite their different lengths and structures, the two works present a queer reading of canonical, heterosexual values usually perpetrated in fairy tales. Both of the authors focus on problematic episodes in the original source in order to stimulate new possibilities and represent categories that are usually forgotten or hidden. In particular, the works give voice to different, minority female identities that can be described as queer. *Ash* and "The Tale of the Shoe" subvert gender dynamics and sexual desires not only by presenting feminine experiences but also by highlighting the existence of female love stories, so as to emphasize the original tale's limits in a contemporary context.[56] The two stories are particularly fascinating and compelling for young adult audiences: queer retellings of fairy tales allow younger readers to rethink the canon, imagining different possibilities that could have taken place. The two tales overthrow one of the most well-known fairy tales in order to prove that different identities, desires, and passions are now possible and legitimate. Queer retellings deconstruct what is already known—such as heteronormative standards, roles, and aspirations—and inclusively accompany young readers through the difficult process of self-discovery they must face during adolescence, offering them new possibilities to explore.

Notes

1. Bacchilega, *Fairy Tales Transformed*, 2–3.
2. Zipes, *Why Fairy Tales Stick*, 94.
3. Lester, "(Un)Happily Ever after," 55.
4. Ibid., 58.
5. Greenhill et al., *The Routledge Companion to Media and Fairy-Tale Cultures*; Cambi, *Itinerari nella fiaba. Autori, testi, figure*.
6. Kerchy, *Postmodern Reinterpretations of Fairy Tales*, 11.
7. Trupe, *Thematic Guide to Young Adult Literature*, 212.
8. Younger, *Learning Curves*, ix.
9. Ibid., xiv.
10. Ibid., 52.
11. Lester, "(Un)Happily," 56.
12. Seifert, "Introduction: Queer(ing) Fairy Tales," 17.
13. Ibid., 16.
14. Jagose, *Queer Theory*; Bernini, *Le teorie queer*.
15. Blackburn, Clark, and Nemeth, "Examining Queer Elements," 14.

16　Jagose, *Queer Theory*, 7.
17　Blackburn, Clark, and Nemeth, "Examining," 18.
18　Orme, "Mouth to Mouth," 124.
19　Turner, "Introduction," 3.
20　Ibid., 7.
21　Jones, "From Homoplot to Progressive Novel," 76.
22　Coppola, "The Gender of Fairies," 128.
23　Jones, "From Homoplot," 91.
24　Ibid., 74.
25　Ibid., 75–80.
26　Edelman, *No Future: Queer Theory and the Death Drive*, 152.
27　Jenkins, "Young Adult Novels," 147–8.
28　Younger, *Learning*, xiii.
29　Jones, "From Homoplot," 75–6.
30　Younger, *Learning*, 71.
31　Ibid., xv.
32　Lo, *Ash*, n.p.
33　Wargo, "Sexual Slipstreams," 45.
34　Lo, *Ash*, n.p.
35　Wargo, "Sexual," 46.
36　Lo, *Ash*, n.p.
37　Wargo, "Sexual," 47.
38　Younger, *Learning*, 49.
39　Lo, *Ash*, n.p.
40　Cart, *Young Adult Literature*, 111.
41　Hennard Dutheil de la Rochere, "Queering," 15.
42　Orme, "Mouth," 116.
43　Hennard Dutheil de la Rochere, "Queering," 14.
44　Orme, "Mouth," 117.
45　Hennard Dutheil de la Rochere, "Queering," 14.
46　Ibid., 18.
47　Ibid., 18–19.
48　Donoghue, *Kissing the Witch*, 5.
49　Ibid., 6–7.
50　Hennard Dutheil de la Rochere, "Queering," 17.
51　Ibid., 19.
52　Ibid., 22.
53　Ibid., 20; Coppola, "The Gender," 126.
54　Hennard Dutheil de la Rochere, "Queering," 23.
55　Donoghue, *Kissing*, 7.
56　Coppola, "The Gender," 134.

Bibliography

Bacchilega, Cristina. *Fairy Tales Transformed? Twenty-First-Century Adaptations and the Politics of Wonder*. Wayne: State University Press, 2013.

Bernini, Lorenzo. *Le teorie queer*. Milan: Mimesis, 2017.
Blackburn, Mollie V., Clark, Caroline T., and Emily Nemeth. "Examining Queer Elements and Ideologies in LGBT Themed Literature: What Queer Literature Can Offer Young Adult Readers." *Journal of Literary Research* 47, no. 1 (2015): 11–48.
Cambi, Franco (ed.). *Itinerari nella fiaba. Autori, testi, figure*. Pisa: ETS, 1999.
Cart, Michael. *Young Adult Literature: From Romance to Realism*. Chicago: Neal-Schuman, 2006.
Coppola, Maria Micaela. "The Gender of Fairies: Emma Donoghue and Angela Carter as Fairy Tale Performers." *Textus. English Studies in Italy* XIV (2001): 127–42.
De Lauretis, Teresa. "Queer Theory: Lesbian and Gay Sexualities. An Introduction." *Differences. A Journal of Feminist Cultural Studies* 3, no. 2 (1991): iii–xviii.
Donoghue, Emma. *Kissing the Witch: Old Tales in New Skins*. New York: Harperteen, 1999.
Edelman, Lee. *No Future: Queer Theory and the Death Drive*. Durham, NC: Duke University Press, 2004.
Greenhill, Pauline, Jill Terry Rudy, Naomi Hamer, and Lauren Bosc (eds.). *The Routledge Companion to Media and Fairy-Tale Cultures*. New York: Routledge, 2018.
Jagose, Annamarie. *Queer Theory: An Introduction*. New York: New York University Press, 1996.
Jenkins, A. Christine. "Young Adult Novels with Gay/Lesbian Characters and Themes 1969–92: A Historical Reading of Content, Gender, and Narrative Distance." In *Over the Rainbow: Queer Children's and Young Adult Literature*, edited by Ann Michelle Abate, and Kenneth Kidd, 147–63. Ann Arbor: University of Michigan Press, 2011.
Jones, E. Caroline. "From Homoplot to Progressive Novel: Lesbian Experience and Identity in Contemporary Young Adult Novels." *The Lion and the Unicorn* 37, no. 1 (2013): 74–93.
Hennard Dutheil de la Rochere, Martine. "Queering the Fairy Tale Canon: Emma Donoghue's *Kissing the Witch*." In *Fairytale Reimagined: Essays on New Retellings*, edited by Susan Redington Bobby, and Kate Bernheimer, 13–30. Jefferson, NC: McFarland, 2009.
Kerchy, Anne. *Postmodern Reinterpretations of Fairy Tales: How Applying New Methods Generates New Meanings*. Lewiston: Edwin Mellen Press, 2011.
Lester, Neal A. "(Un)Happily Ever after: Fairy Tale Morals, Moralities, and Heterosexism in Children's Texts." *Journal of Gay & Lesbian Issues in Education* 4, no. 2 (2005): 55–74.
Lo, Malinda. *Ash*. Boston: Little Brown, 2009.
Orme, Jennifer. "Mouth to Mouth: Queer Desires in Emma Donoghue's *Kissing the Witch*." *Marvels & Tales* 24, no. 1 (2014): 116–30.
Seifert, Lewis C. "Introduction: Queer(ing) Fairy Tales." *Marvels & Tales* 29, no. 1 (2015): 15–20.
Trupe, Alice. *Thematic Guide to Young Adult Literature*. Westport: Greenwood, 2006.
Turner, Kay, and Greenhill Pauline. "Introduction: Once Upon a Queer Time." In *Transgressive Tales: Queering the Grimms*, edited by Kay Turner and Pauline Greenhill, 1–24. Detroit: Wayne State University Press, 2012.
Ulivieri, Simonetta. "Modelli e messaggi educativi al femminile nella fiaba." In *Itinerari nella fiaba*, edited by Franco Cambi, 237–54. Pisa: ETS, 1999.
Ulivieri, Simonetta (ed.). *Educazione al femminile*. Milan: Guerini, 2007.
Wargo, Jon M. "Sexual Slipstreams and the Limits of Magic Realism: Why a Bisexual Cinderella May Not Be All That Queer." *Bookbird* 52, no. 1 (2014): 44–8.

Younger, Beth. *Learning Curves: Body Image and Female Sexuality in Young Adult Literature*. Lanham: Scarecrow Press, 2009.
Zipes, Jack. *Fairy Tales and the Art of Subversion: The Classical Genre for Children and the Process of Civilization*. London: Routledge, 1983.
Zipes, Jack. *Why Fairy Tales Stick: The Evolution and Relevance of a Genre*. New York: Routledge, 2006.

5

"Wherever the Flame Was Brightest": Identity and Assimilation in Rick Riordan's Greek Mythological Adaptations for Young Adults[1]

Saffyre Falkenberg

Classical Greek mythology saturates contemporary popular culture, but this permeation is especially prevalent in young adult literature. Over the last decade, numerous novels and even entire book series featuring elements of Greek mythology have appeared on the market. These books utilize either characters or plotlines from classical myths in a modern setting, transport entire myths to a modern setting, or retell myths in a classical Greek setting influenced by modern beliefs and values. Despite whatever differences exist between the adaptation and the source material, these books for young adults all function as adaptations because they are still—however loosely—tethered to the source texts of Greek mythology. Of all the mythological adaptations written for young adult readers, Greek mythology is by far the most prevalent and the most popular. Though otherworld mythologies are equally as rich and significant in their literary value, Greek tales reign in mythology adaptations for young adults because of the cultural capital they carry in America and Western civilization as a whole: "[M]otivations for preserving Greek myths for young audiences, such as a desire to pass on cultural tradition ... have proven strong enough to ensure mythology's place within children's literature."[2] However, like many other adaptations of classic literature for young adults, storylines and characters must be updated to reflect the contemporary culture's evolving values.

Of the many Greek mythological adaptations for young adults, Rick Riordan's *Percy Jackson and the Olympians* (2005-9) and *The Heroes of Olympus* (2010-14) stand out from the rest in terms of their popularity. These books borrow classical characters and plotlines, transporting the myths into a modern setting. While *Percy Jackson and the Olympians* adapts only the Greek myths, *Heroes of Olympus* blends Greek and Roman mythologies. Each series contains five books, and each book builds toward an overall plot; in *Percy Jackson and the Olympians*, the demigods are trying to stop Kronos from rising and destroying the world, while the demigods in *Heroes of Olympus* are trying to stop Gaea from doing the same. The books not only use mythological figures, mainly members of the Greek pantheon, but also revisit many plots of classical myths, such as defeating Medusa in *The Lightning Thief*, within the overarching plot of each series.

In many cases, authors present the Greek mythological tradition to younger generations in stories they can understand, featuring characters they relate to within the current social order.[3] In this way, these new adapted mythologies fulfill the four functions of mythology as outlined by Joseph Campbell: Mythology inspires a sense of awe at the universe, it offers explanations for natural phenomenon, it teaches people how to live in their societies according to accepted standards of behavior, and it teaches people how to live human lives in all stages of development within their societies.[4] These stories, then, teach young people how to exist in the world in which they live. It is for this reason that many modern retellings of Greek myths incorporate diverse voices and minority perspectives to make them fit within the context of multicultural society as it exists now. Young adults, especially those in marginalized subject positions, often feel as if they do not belong in the world in which they live. Alexander Leighton writes that young adults "by their nature are in a state of 'in-between,' neither fitting into the world of childhood nor adulthood," and being treated as other because of race, sexuality, gender, or disability only serves to heighten those feelings of not belonging.[5] *Percy Jackson and the Olympians* and *Heroes of Olympus* both feature characters of color, disabled characters, and queer characters. In *Percy Jackson and the Olympians*, all of the demigods have learning disorders: namely, dyslexia and attention deficit disorder. While there are characters of color in this series, none of them are main characters. *Heroes of Olympus*, on the other hand, includes characters like Piper McLean, who is Cherokee Nation; Leo Valdez, who is Mexican-American; Hazel Levesque, who is African American; and Frank Zhang, who is Chinese-Canadian. Likewise, *Heroes of Olympus* also has Nico di Angelo, who comes out as gay. Although Nico is also a fairly prominent character in *Percy Jackson and the Olympians*, he does not come out until the fourth book in the *Heroes of Olympus* series, *House of Hades*. While diversity in all children's and young adult literature is extremely important, diversity in Greek mythological adaptations for young adults presents unique challenges. Including diverse representations of sexuality and disability is important because it implies cultural acceptance. Because Greek mythology is so intertwined with Western culture, updating these myths to including diverse perspectives signifies that these perspectives are both important and "normal" in Western society. While including racial and ethnic diversity in Greek mythological adaptations is also important for the same reasons that it is important to see representations of diverse sexualities and disabilities, it is also more problematic, given the context. Including representations of marginalized identities in young adult literature can demonstrate acceptance, "normalizing" identities that have previously been othered. However, depending on the context in which these representations are included, representation of marginalized identities may not celebrate diversity as intended but instead encourage conformity. By showing characters of diverse races and ethnicities taking part in a very Westernized mythological framework, the underlying message seems to be in favor of assimilation to Western values and beliefs in favor of the minority group's own cultural values and beliefs.

Adapting Greek Myths for Young Adults

Though there are many different definitions for adaptation, Julie Sanders writes that adaptations are "reinterpretations of established (canonical or perhaps just well-known) texts in new generic contexts or perhaps with relocation of an 'original' or source text's cultural and/or temporal setting, which may or may not involve a generic shift."[6] She also writes that "adaptation is frequently involved in offering commentary on a source text."[7] Thus, according to Sanders's definition, adaptation may change the genre or setting of a previously established work in order to offer commentary on it or otherwise interpret it in some way. This process is different from the literary device of intertextuality, where authors merely make mention of or allude to previous texts in order to enrich their own, entirely separate works. Based on Sanders's definition of adaptation, the Greek mythological adaptations that are so popular among young adult readers thereby serve two purposes: to refer back to the source texts to inspire interest in classical literature and to recontextualize these stories for contemporary society by integrating diverse voices and identities. Another way to think about adaptation is to think about the process rather than the product. In discussing the ways that adaptations are consciously constructed, Linda Hutcheon says, "[A]daptation is an act of appropriating or salvaging, and this is always a double process of interpreting and then creating something new."[8] Riordan has embraced the double process in both series, as both borrow characters and plotlines and revise them to fit an entirely new context of his own creation. However, it is within this act of "creating something new" that these works express messages of cultural assimilation rather than cultural acceptance by including characters of color embracing an overtly Western imperialistic paradigm. The double process, then, can also be a double-edged sword.

Adapting any work of classic literature, not just Greek mythology, for children or young adults functions primarily to educate young people about the original work, either inspiring them to seek out the original or at least providing them with enough cultural capital to be familiar with the story and characters. By referring back to Greek mythology within the framework of the overall story, authors can encourage readers to seek out more material without sacrificing the clarity of their own stories. Thus, young adult readers are able to understand, enjoy, and relate to the adaptations without necessarily needing any prior knowledge of Greek mythology; however, the story itself may motivate them to seek out mythology in order to gain a deeper understanding of the adaptation itself because they want to fully immerse themselves in this world the adaptations supposedly "create." Leighton writes that "this rediscovering constitutes the continuation of the shaping power and influence of the original texts throughout time."[9] By being in a familiar format and using age-appropriate language, adaptations are ultimately more accessible to young adult audiences. Their accessibility has the power to make teenage readers feel more comfortable with classical mythology and may inspire them to pursue the more complex source texts as a result.

Greek mythology, though, is already very familiar to many Western audiences; indeed, American culture has appropriated many other elements of Greek culture, ranging from architecture to government. Many white Americans might then identify with Greek culture to some extent because they see their own culture reflecting the Greek traditions, feeling a sense of ownership over Greek mythology the same way they feel ownership over other appropriated cultural elements. As Anne Morey and Claudia Nelson claim in their article about *Percy Jackson and the Olympians* and America's culture wars, "Those American architects who emphasize the classical roots of federal design have done so in part to express a particular relationship to the past, visually claiming to be the heirs of the great tradition and thus to have what it takes to be at the center of an empire."[10] Just as these architects might be visually claiming an inheritance from past generations, adaptations of Greek myths for young adults are a way to claim this inheritance in a literary sense. Thus, there is a desire to pass Greek mythology on to children because of Greek culture's significance to white American culture and the Western world in general, thereby inspiring younger generations to seek out or at least be able to know and reference culturally significant source texts. One of the primary imperatives for adapting classical texts for young adults is to ensure or enable some kind of familiarity with culturally relevant works or even to inspire young adults to seek out the original texts. David Buchbinder refers to this idea as "shared cultural inheritance."[11] What this idea fails to recognize, however, is that the culture of the United States is not homogeneous, meaning there is no singular shared culture to act as an inheritance.

In this way, the endeavor to adapt classic texts for children and young adults in order to provide them with cultural capital reveals the types of voices and the types of narratives deemed worthy to adapt. In other words, the source texts that get adapted into stories aimed at young readers reveal something about the culture in which the adaptations are created. Buchbinder says that "[t]here remains the sense of an imperative that young people ought to be familiar with the literary texts that form part of 'their' cultural inheritance and, importantly, form a significant part of the cultural capital available to them."[12] The literary canon privileges the voices of white, heterosexual, cisgender, middle-class, able-bodied men. If these narratives and these voices are the sources for the majority of adaptations for children and young adults, then that sends a message to all children that these are the voices and the stories that matter, the ones that adults consider to be culturally worthy. To mitigate these messages, many authors, like Riordan, choose to "update" these classics by including characters of diverse races, ethnicities, genders, sexualities, and abilities. Ultimately, including diverse characters in an adaptation of a classic for children or young adults is a very clear and intentional interpretative choice made by the author. Amplifying or adding the voices of characters of marginalized subjectivities makes a statement about the gaps or "deficiencies" of the source text. For example, Sanders writes that adaptations "have a deep political and literary investment in giving voice to characters or events which appear to have been oppressed or repressed in the original."[13] However, just like novels with female main characters are not necessarily feminist, the mere presence of diverse voices does not mean the novel is automatically inclusive. It is the way in which these voices and characters are present in the context of the narrative that determines the book's messages of inclusivity—or exclusivity.

Young Adult Literature's Diversity Problem

Authors write these adaptations for young adults specifically because teenagers are in a transitory period of discovering their own identities, meaning Greek mythological adaptations serve to instill Western beliefs and even a sense of the "superiority" of Western culture because myths "explai[n] why the world is the way it is and why people behave the way they do."[14] Indeed, the sheer prevalence of these Greek mythology adaptations implies that Western culture is somehow "better" or more "worthy" of study, in addition to supporting Western cultural values themselves.

Additionally, because young people are still forming their identities, diversity helps minority teenagers find characters with whom they can identify. For example, children's and young adult book author Walter Dean Myers writes about his own reading experience as a teenager, saying that "there was something missing. I needed more than the characters in the Bible to identify with, or even the characters in Arthur Miller's plays or my beloved Balzac. As I discovered who I was, a black teenager in a white-dominated world, I saw that these characters, these lives, were not mine."[15] Diversity thus allows young adults to see themselves in literature and perhaps feel more comfortable with their own emerging identities. Diversity in Greek mythological adaptations also recontextualizes myths to reflect the values of the new West. However, the presence of racial diversity in Greek mythological adaptations does not undermine the idea that these retellings function to instill the idea of the West's supposed superiority; rather, the presence of racial minorities in mythological adaptation supports the assimilation to Western cultural norms.

None of this is to say that there should not be more diversity incorporated into young adult literature. A lack of diversity has always been an issue in children's and young adult literature, prompting the creation of programs like We Need Diverse Books and Diversity in YA to promote diverse literature and diversity in publishing. In fact, lack of diversity in young adult literature is a problem that is getting worse with time, not better. According to an article published by *The Guardian*, fewer and fewer young adult books by authors of color have been published in the UK since 2010.[16] The issue is also that tokenism and stereotypical portrayals of minority and marginalized characters are huge issues in young adult literature. It is not enough to simply mention that a character's skin is brown or that a character is gay if these facts do not impact the character or the narrative because this does not reflect the real, lived experiences of marginalized people. In fact, this type of nonrepresentation can leave a bad taste in readers' mouths because it appears authors want "credit" for including diversity in their books without doing the hard work of considering how that diversity will affect the narrative in a realistic way. It is thus important for authors to consider how they are including minority characters in their books: if their characterization relies on tired stereotypes, that is a problem. Relying on stereotypes or tokenism sends a negative message to all young people who may encounter the story, implying that these stereotypes are the only way someone in that subject position can be. Additionally, scholars and educators must critically examine works in order to determine what kind of messages are being rhetorically conveyed within a narrative: are they messages of cultural acceptance or cultural assimilation? Only then can young adult literature solve its diversity problem and move beyond tokenism, stereotypes, and cultural assimilation.

Imperialism and Assimilation in Young Adult Literature

Much of the scholarship related to the study of colonialism, imperialism, and assimilation in the fields of children's and young adult literature centers on theoretical conceptions of children's literature as an inherently colonial practice. In *The Case of Peter Pan, or the Impossibility of Children's Fiction*, Jaqueline Rose's highly influential book on the subject of adult–child relationships, she writes, "Literature for children is, therefore, a way of colonising ... the child."[17] This concept of children's literature as a form of colonization went on to influence decades of scholarship on children's literature. Indeed, many times, Rose's statement that children's literature is itself a colonial practice is taken as a point of fact. Take, for example, Perry Nodelman's article on children's literature, colonialism, and Orientalism, which cites Rose in its introduction.[18] Nodelman describes the way that adults colonize children through literature, saying, "[W]e woo them to our values. We tell them that their true happiness consists in pleasing us, bending to our will, doing what we want. We plant the seeds of wisdom in them. And we get very angry indeed when they dare to gaze back."[19] This particular quote is disturbing in its use of language; in addition to Nodelman's argument for the innate imperial nature of children's literature, his use of the verb "woo" implies an inherently sexual relationship between children and adults carried out through children's literature. Nodelman expands on these ideas of the adult–child relationship as inherently colonial in his later book, *The Hidden Adult*. Though this book is mainly concerned with defining children's literature, Nodelman expands on the imperialistic relationship between adults and children by drawing comparisons between the field of children's literature and the qualities of Orientalism as described by Edward Said.[20] Thus, if Rose, Nodelman, and other scholars are to be believed, all children's literature, regardless of author or multicultural subjects, engages in colonizing and assimilating child readers.

If, as these authors argue, children's literature is inherently an imperialistic endeavor, then young adult literature might be a way for adolescents to "gaze back," so to speak. To "gaze back" means to challenge or question the status quo, the norms that are placed upon oneself. Young adult literature very frequently has as its protagonists young people who are frustrated by their roles within the society in which they live, as well as the rules of those societies. Throughout many young adult novels, these protagonists rebel against, question, and "gaze back" at the institutions and individuals oppressing them. Thus, all young adult literature—not just adaptations—has a unique opportunity to challenge social norms for its adolescent readers, presenting other possibilities for viewing and living within the world instead of just repeating and reinforcing normative perspectives. However, much of young adult literature rarely lives up to this potential: "[E]ven those YA texts that most strongly resist dominant social norms typically end up simultaneously enforcing them."²¹ Thus, even though young adult literature has the potential to be transgressive for its adolescent audiences, it does not live up to this potential as often as it should. Riordan's works are a prime example of this idea. On the surface, *Percy Jackson and the Olympians* and *Heroes of Olympus* may seem rather groundbreaking because of the presence of so many marginalized characters. However, reading past the surface and looking at the messages present within the narratives, it becomes clear that, rather than encouraging cultural pluralism and inclusivity, the books advocate for cultural assimilation by including so many characters of color enthusiastically participating in a very Americanized and Westernized system.

However, there are many issues that arise when making a direct comparison between the relationships between children and adults and the vast and multifaceted relationships between the oppressed and their oppressors in all of their individual spatial and temporal contexts. Nodelman himself recognizes the insufficiency of the metaphor when he says that the metaphor of children standing in for the oppressed ultimately breaks down because "the implied reader is being 'colonized' as a child in the process of becoming a colonizer."²² Many other scholars have likewise pointed out the issues in comparing children to colonized subjects. In her article on the topic, Clare Bradford concisely points out the primary issue with the comparison:

> By conflating children with colonised peoples, scholars who use this language seem to condone a strategic forgetting of the materiality of colonisation, its deleterious effects on the lives and cultures of colonised people, its repercussions in the present. ... To refer to children's literature as a site of colonisation is, then, to mute, to downplay, even to trivialise the effects of colonisation on Indigenous peoples.²³

While Bradford—rightly, I might add—refuses to acknowledge all children's literature as being innately colonial, tactics of colonization can be and are used by writers, whether intentionally or not, to assimilate all child readers into the dominant culture. This process of literary assimilation can work either by reinforcing colonial beliefs of superiority for children in powerful subject positions or by breaking down or denying the individual multicultural identities of child readers of marginalized subject positions. Because of this potential for rhetorics of assimilation, books with multicultural characters must be evaluated beyond the mere presence of diversity.

If multicultural literature for children and young adults is supposed to celebrate diversity and promote cultural pluralism, characters of color and the white characters surrounding them must thereby function in the narrative in such a way as to achieve those goals. However, multicultural literature for children and young adults fails at both of these goals, falling into traps of tokenism and even perpetuating harmful, racist stereotypes. Often, the rhetorics of assimilation in multicultural literature for children and young adults are not explicit, and many multicultural narratives celebrated for their "inclusivity" actually contain pernicious messages for white children and children of color. In their study of multicultural picture books, Bogum Yoon, Anne Simpson, and Claudia Haag identify two commonalties in picture books with messages of assimilation: "a transition by the main character from resistance to a new culture to assimilation" and "a focus on the United States as the land of opportunity."[24] Although their study is on multicultural picture books, I believe the principles they discuss can easily be applied to multicultural children's and young adult literature as well, and it is my aim to demonstrate how both *Percy Jackson and the Olympians* and *Heroes of Olympus* include these elements within their narratives.

"The Heart of the Flame": Riordan's Works and Americentrism

From the very beginning of Riordan's *Percy Jackson and the Olympians* series, it is apparent that the narrative is steeped in ideals of the superiority of Western civilization. When Percy finally makes it to Camp Half-Blood, he understandably has a lot of questions about the idea that the myths he learned about in school are real. Chiron, Percy's centaur mentor and, in Greek mythology, the trainer of heroes such as Theseus, Achilles, and Jason, explains the continued existence of the Greek pantheon in this way:

> The gods move with the heart of the West. ... What you call "Western civilization." Do you think it's just an abstract concept? No, it's a living force. A collective consciousness that has burned bright for thousands of years. The gods are part of it. You might even say they are the source of it, or at least, they are tied so tightly to it that they couldn't possibly fade, not unless all of Western civilization were obliterated. The fire started in Greece. Then, as you well know ... the heart of the fire moved to Rome, and so did the gods. ... The gods simply moved, to Germany, to France, to Spain, for a while. Wherever the flame was brightest, the gods were there. They spent several centuries in England. ... Like it or not ... America is now the heart of the flame. It is the great power of the West.[25]

This passage includes a lot of imperialistic imagery and metaphors. First, Chiron brings up the idea that Western civilization is "a living force," though it is unclear precisely what he means by this, and goes on to say that the gods themselves are separate from this mysterious force. Next, Chiron describes Western civilization as a "collective consciousness." The idea of a collective consciousness shared between an entire society is just another way of describing cultural assimilation, implying that all people in a society have a shared set of beliefs and values despite any individual differences between them based on race or ethnicity. An additional problem with this passage is the way it completely whitewashes centuries of imperialism. Chiron says the gods "moved" to Rome and, later, to other countries, also saying that the gods "spent several centuries in England." The gods did not "move" anywhere; they were forcibly imposed upon indigenous peoples by colonizers and assimilated into the local religious systems in the case of Rome and assimilated into the literary tradition in the case of England.

Thus, it is clear from Chiron's explication of the system Percy is now entrenched in that Western civilization is somehow privileged or superior because of the continued presence of the gods.

In addition to the blatant imperialism within the new social order of demigods that Percy enters into, many of the books in the *Percy Jackson and the Olympians* series and the *Heroes of Olympus* series utilize famous American monuments and cultural centers within the narratives in order to emphasize the fact that the gods, and thus their dealings with humans, are within a distinctly American context now. Indeed, the new home of the gods, the new Mount Olympus, so to speak, is on the fictional six hundredth floor of the Empire State Building. Some of the other famous American monuments, locations, and museums the demigods visit throughout both series are the Metropolitan Museum of Art, the Gateway Arch, the Las Vegas Strip, the National Museum of Natural History, the Hoover Dam, the Carlsbad Caverns, and the Grand Canyon. In addition to these monuments and notable places in the United States, there are many mountains that take the place of Greek mountains in the adapted myths, such as Mount Tamalpais, Mount St. Helens, Mount Diablo, and Pikes Peak. All of these various locations function as symbols of the natural order that Percy and the other demigods are trying to save: "Since it is Kronos's stated aim to destroy the gods, what Percy is ultimately saving is not merely the Olympian status quo but Western civilization itself."[26] By working to save the gods, and thus Western civilization, in all of these very nationally charged locations, the narrative is reinforcing the importance of the status quo and the necessity of this so-called "collective consciousness" of assimilation in the West. These characters are supposedly fighting to save the world; however, much of the fighting is central to not only the United States but also locations in the United States that symbolize national pride and/or culture. In the same way that the adaptation itself preserves a "shared cultural inheritance," the characters themselves are doing the same by carrying out the fight between good and evil in these culturally significant locations that again presume a kind of homogeneous American culture.[27]

Tokenism, Stereotyping, and Assimilation: Riordan's Characters of Color and the Greek Tradition

In adapting Greek myths for young adult readers, Riordan handles his characters of color in three ways: they are tokenized, they reflect harmful stereotypes, or they conflate their own heritages with the Greek system of which they are now a part. Sometimes, one character might reflect a combination of these qualities. The tokenism is easiest to see in the *Percy Jackson and the Olympians* series, as all of the core characters are white. Notable characters of color from the *Percy Jackson and the Olympians* series are Charles Beckendorf, a son of Hephaestus, and Ethan Nakamura, a son of Nemesis. However, the roles that these characters play in the overall narrative are very minor, and their identities as Black and Japanese-American, respectively, make little to no difference in the story. Leo and Hazel are likewise two examples of tokenized minority characters in the *Heroes of Olympus* series. Overall, the series contains more characters of color in the core group of demigod characters than the *Percy Jackson and the Olympians* series, but that does not necessarily mean the representation of minority characters is any better. The only time Leo's ethnicity is described is when he first appears in *The Lost Hero* and Riordan characterizes him as "a Latino Santa's elf."²⁸ Likewise, Hazel's identity as a black girl plays little part in the narrative; the struggle of growing up Black in America is only hinted at as Hazel reflects on how the other kids at her school are teasing her about her mother: "Hazel didn't understand how other black kids could be so mean. They should have known better, since they themselves had to put up with name calling all the time."²⁹ One problematic aspect of this reflection, however, is that it takes place in the past; Hazel grew up in the 1930s in New Orleans, ending up in the present day through a series of events that would take too long to explain here. By only ever briefly touching on racism in the context of a past event, it rhetorically argues that racism itself is a thing of the past. These characters, then, become the token minority characters of the series, since their races and ethnicities play little to no difference in the actual narrative itself.

Another issue that comes into play with Riordan's characters of color is the tendency to utilize harmful stereotypes in the characterization. These stereotypes are not necessarily present within any of the core group of demigods; rather, the family members of the characters of color tend to be simplistic caricatures. This phenomenon is most easily seen with Hazel's mother, Marie Levesque, and Frank's grandmother, Grandma Zhang. Hazel's mother, who goes by Queen Marie, is a "voodoo priestess," a very stereotypical role for a black woman associated with the supernatural to fill. Additionally, despite the books' reliance on gods, goddesses, and magic from other traditions, voodoo is not portrayed favorably in the narrative: "Queen Marie had always told Hazel her *gris-gris* was 'bunk and hokum.' She didn't really believe in charms of fortune telling or ghosts. She was just a performer, like a singer or an actress, doing a show for money."³⁰ Additionally, her magical powers and other supernatural encounters she has are attributed to her relationship with the Greek and Roman pantheons, not the voodoo religion. Throughout Hazel's various flashbacks, essentially everyone she comes into contact with also expresses fear and disgust at Queen Marie because of her status as a voodoo practitioner. Likewise, Frank's grandmother is portrayed as intense, harsh, and exacting. She is also very traditional, prohibiting Frank from expressing emotion because "[m]en do not cry" and emphasizing their Chinese roots, which Frank generally finds to be uninteresting.³¹ Her harsh and unsympathetic treatment of him is stereotypical of Chinese matriarchs, offering little complexity to a character who is integral to Frank's story arc. Based on the characterization of both Marie Levesque and Grandma Zhang, it is apparent that, while Riordan might introduce complexity and nuance into his protagonists of color, he relies on tired stereotypes for secondary characters of color.

The messages of assimilation become explicit at several points in the narrative, especially in the context of Piper's Cherokee heritage and Frank's Chinese heritage. When it comes to these two traditions, Riordan explicitly conflates both Cherokee and Chinese cultures with the Greek cultural tradition on multiple occasions throughout the *Heroes of Olympus* series. Although, when it comes to the Greek and Roman myths from the *Percy Jackson* and *Heroes of Olympus* books, "Riordan approaches the sacred stories of various cultures with both mild irreverence and a deep respect," the Cherokee and Chinese cultures tend to be treated with more irreverence than respect in the *Heroes of Olympus* series, given their conflation with the Greek tradition.[32] The first time this conflation of cultures happens is when Frank is learning about his family history and status as a demigod from his grandmother. His grandmother explains: "China and Rome are not so different, nor as separate as you might believe."[33] Thus, in order to explain how Frank can be both Chinese and the demigod son of a Roman deity, the Chinese nation and the Roman Empire are casually compared with one another, erasing thousands of years of history and culture to make such a comparison. Likewise, Piper reflects on the similarities between the Greek afterlife and the Cherokee afterlife: "The more Piper learned about being a demigod, the more convinced she was that Cherokee legends and Greek myths weren't so different."[34] Again, in order to explain having a character who is both Cherokee and a child of a Greek goddess, Riordan erases these two cultures' distinctive histories, beliefs, and customs. Conflating Greek culture with the Chinese and Cherokee cultures also reinforces messages of assimilation because it attempts to justify the emphasis on the Western tradition through false comparisons.

Conclusion: Where Do We Go from Here?

Instead of relying on the Western worldview to shape the narratives of the next generation, perhaps exploring and adapting otherworld mythologies is the key to both creating characters minorities can identify with and allowing children to become empathetic and culturally sensitive to others. One potential partial solution to this issue of both the lack of diversity in young adult literature and the issue of white authors using mythological adaptations to recolonize minority children could be in the adaptation of various worldwide mythologies written by authors from those cultures. Although some may say that there is not a market for diverse young adult literature in general, the evidence indicates the exact opposite: for example, Angie Thomas's *The Hate U Give*, a contemporary young adult novel about police brutality and #BlackLivesMatter, has, at the time of this writing, spent 97 weeks on *The New York Times* bestseller list.[35] Rick Riordan himself is helping, in part, to fill this gap by using his ethos as an adapter of mythology for young readers through his new publishing imprint, Rick Riordan Presents. Rick Riordan Presents is an imprint of Disney-Hyperion Publishing and publishes middle-grade novels adapted from mythologies from around the world. More specifically, Riordan describes the aims of the imprint in this way:

> Our goal is to publish great middle grade authors from underrepresented cultures and backgrounds, to let them tell their own stories inspired by the mythology and folklore of their own heritage. Over the years, I've gotten many questions from my fans about whether I might write about various world mythologies, but in most cases I knew I wasn't the best person to write those books. Much better, I thought, to use my experience and my platform at Disney to put the spotlight on other great

writers who are actually from those cultures and know the mythologies better than I do. Let them tell their own stories, and I would do whatever I could to help those books find a wide audience![36]

In this way, Riordan is actually using his privilege to amplify the voices of authors whose works may not have found their audience otherwise. Currently, Rick Riordan Presents has published an adaptation of Indian mythology, *Aru Shah and the End of Time* by Roshani Chokshi; an adaptation of Mayan mythology, *The Storm Runner* by J. C. Cervantes; and an adaptation of Korean folklore, *The Dragon Pearl* by Yoon Ha Lee. This imprint and Riordan's use of his ethos to support authors of color introduce new complexities into readings of his *Percy Jackson and the Olympians* and *Heroes of Olympus* series. Though seemingly good-intentioned, it is impossible to ignore the messages of assimilation present throughout his Greek and Roman mythological adaptations. However, the new imprint and the titles it is publishing allow minority children to see themselves and their cultures represented in ways that they probably have not seen before.

One complication that arises from studying young adult literature and the interpretative choices made on behalf of young adults is that the audience of these books is not always comprised of just teenagers. Formative years are extending well into peoples' twenties and thirties—what has traditionally been considered "adulthood." More and more adults are turning to young adult literature, including Greek mythological adaptations. The themes Greek mythological adaptations address, then, must be at least in some way relevant to the lives of adults as well as young adults. This consumption of young adult literature by adults may correspond to the lengthening of adolescence; for various economic and social reasons, many adults are not able to become independent until well into their twenties. Mavis Reimer and Heather Snell write, "Perhaps writers and readers of YA texts have abandoned the long-standing premise that adulthood is or ought to be a stable condition of knowledge, identity, or authority."[37] Adulthood is not a fixed point; the process of identity formation and coming of age is still relevant to so-called adults in contemporary society, meaning that issues of culture and diversity in regard to identity formation are still relevant.

In the subheading for this conclusion, I asked: Where do we go from here? My answers are not new, but they bear repeating. As scholars, we need to critically examine diverse and multicultural literature published for young adult readers and point out problematic messages or interpretations when we find them. As educators, we need to choose books or point our students to books that represent minority characters positively, whatever that may mean, or, if we choose books with problematic representation, we need to be willing to have those difficult conversations with our students about imperialism, assimilation, and institutionalized racism. Publishers need to publish more books by authors of color and hire more people of color, and white people already working in publishing need to be aware of their own privilege and use it to amplify minorities when choosing books to publish or when hiring for their companies. Authors in privileged subject positions writing about marginalized characters also need to learn how to recognize and avoid stereotypes. There will never be an unproblematic book because people themselves are problematic; life is a series of learning and unlearning. But, by taking these steps, we can move toward a brighter future for children of color in young adult literature.

Notes

1. I would like to thank Dr. Gretchen Busl from Texas Woman's University for looking over earlier drafts of this chapter.
2. Geerts, "Continuity and Change," 19.
3. Although Riordan is the main focus of this chapter, there are many other authors who have written Greek mythological adaptations for young adults. Some examples of such books include Madeleine Miller's *Song of Achilles*, Michelle Maddow's *Elementals* series, Josephine Angelini's *Starcrossed* series, Aimee Carter's *Goddess Test* series, and Meg Cabot's *Abandon* series.
4. Campbell, *The Masks of God*, 609, 611, 621, and 623.
5. Leighton, "Rediscovering Mythology," 63.
6. Sanders, *Adaptation and Appropriation*, 24.
7. Ibid., 23.
8. Hutcheon, *A Theory of Adaptation*, 20.
9. Leighton, "Rediscovering Mythology," 62.
10. Morey and Nelson, "A God Buys Us Cheeseburgers," 249–50.
11. Buchbinder, "From 'Wizard' to 'Wicked,'" 136.
12. Ibid.
13. Sanders, *Adaptation and Appropriation*, 126.
14. Walker, "Young People's Mental Health," 82.
15. Myers, "Where Are the People of Color in Children's Books?"
16. Flood, "'Dire Statistics' Show YA Fiction is Becoming Less Diverse."
17. Rose, *The Case for Peter Pan*, 26.
18. Nodelman, "The Other," 29.
19. Ibid., 30.
20. Nodelman, *The Hidden Adult*, 164.
21. Suhr-Sytsma, "Jeanette Armstrong's Slash," 29.
22. Nodelman, *The Hidden Adult*, 164.
23. Bradford, "The Case of Children's Literature," 274.
24. Yoon, Simpson, and Haag, "Assimilation Ideology," 112.
25. Riordan, *The Lightning Thief*, 72–3.
26. Morey and Nelson, "'A God Buys Us Cheeseburgers,'" 248.
27. Buchbinder, "From 'Wizard' to 'Wicked,'" 136.
28. Riordan, *The Lost Hero*, 5.
29. Riordan, *The Son of Neptune*, 70.
30. Ibid., 74.
31. Ibid., 117 and 119.
32. Ford, "'Creative Cussing,'" 21.
33. Riordan, *The Son of Neptune*, 121.
34. Riordan, *The Mark of Athena*, 144.
35. "Young Adult Hardcover."

36 "Rick Riordan Presents."
37 Reimer and Snell, "YA Narratives: Reading One's Age," 8.

Bibliography

Bradford, Clare. "The Case of Children's Literature: Colonial or Anti-Colonial?" *Global Studies of Childhood* 1, no. 4 (2011): 271–9.

Buchbinder, David. "From 'Wizard' to 'Wicked': Adaptation Theory and Young Adult Fiction." In *Contemporary Children's Literature and Film: Engaging with Theory*, edited by Kerry Mallan and Clare Bradford, 127–36. New York: Red Globe Press, 2011.

Campbell, Joseph. *The Masks of God: Creative Mythology*. New York: Penguin Compass, 1991.

Flood, Alison. "'Dire Statistics' Show YA Fiction is Becoming Less Diverse, Warns Report." *The Guardian*, July 27, 2018. www.theguardian.com/books/2018/jul/27/dire-statistics-show-ya-fiction-becoming-less-diverse-warns-report. Accessed January 10, 2019.

Ford, Genevieve Larson. "'Creative Cussing': The Sacred and the Profane in Rick Riordan's Mythical Middle Grade Novels." *The ALAN Review* 43, no. 2 (2016): 20–33.

Geerts, Sylvie. "Continuity and Change in the Treatment of Frightening Subject Matter: Contemporary Retellings of Classical Mythology for Children in the Low Countries." *International Research in Children's Literature* 7, no. 1 (2014): 18–36.

Hutcheon, Linda. *A Theory of Adaptation*, 2nd ed. Abingdon: Routledge, 2013.

Leighton, Alexander. "Rediscovering Mythology: Adaptation and Appropriation in the Percy Jackson and the Olympians Saga." *Mousaion* 32, no. 2 (2014): 60–73. www.hdl.handle.net/10520/EJC166207. Accessed December 20, 2018.

Morey, Anne, and Claudia Nelson. "'A God Buys Us Cheeseburgers': Rick Riordan's Percy Jackson Series and America's Culture Wars." *The Lion and the Unicorn* 39, no. 3 (2015): 235–53. www.muse.jhu.edu/article/608038. Accessed August 30, 2018.

Myers, Walter Dean. "Where Are the People of Color in Children's Books?" *New York Times*, March 15, 2014. Accessed February 20, 2019. www.nytimes.com/2014/03/16/opinion/sunday/where-are-the-people-of-color-in-childrens-books.html. Accessed December 3, 2015.

Nodelman, Perry. *The Hidden Adult: Defining Children's Literature*. Baltimore: John's Hopkins University Press, 2008.

Nodelman, Perry. "The Other: Orientalism, Colonialism, and Children's Literature." *Children's Literature Association Quarterly* 17, no. 1 (1992): 29–35. www.muse.jhu.edu/article/249281. Accessed December 20, 2018.

Reimer, Mavis, and Heather Snell. "YA Narratives: Reading One's Age." *Jeunesse: Young People, Texts, Cultures* 7, no. 1 (2015): 1–17. www.muse.jhu.edu/article/588650. Accessed November 2, 2015.

"Rick Riordan Presents," *Rick Riordan*, www.rickriordan.com/rick-riordan-presents/. Accessed January 16, 2019.

Riordan, Rick. *The Lightning Thief*. New York: Hyperion Books for Children, 2005.

Riordan, Rick. *The Lost Hero*. New York: Hyperion Books, 2010.

Riordan, Rick. *The Mark of Athena*. New York: Disney Hyperion Books, 2012.

Riordan, Rick. *The Son of Neptune*. New York: Hyperion Books, 2011.

Rose, Jacqueline. *The Case for Peter Pan, or the Impossibility of Children's Fiction*. Philadelphia: University of Pennsylvania, 1993.

Sanders, Julie. *Adaptation and Appropriation*, 2nd ed. Abingdon: Routledge, 2016.

Suhr-Sytsma, Mandy. "Jeanette Armstrong's Slash and the Indigenous Reinvention of Young Adult Literature." *Studies in American Indian Literatures* 28, no. 4 (2016): 25–52. www.muse.jhu.edu/article/649877. Accessed December 20, 2018.

Walker, Steven. "Young People's Mental Health: The Spiritual Power of Fairy Stories, Myths and Legends." *Mental Health, Religion & Culture* 13, no. 1 (2010): 81–92.

Yoon, Bogum, Anne Simpson, and Claudia Haag. "Assimilation Ideology: Critically Examining Underlying Messages in Multicultural Literature." *Journal of Adolescent and Adult Literacy* 54, no. 2 (2010): 109–18. www.jstor.org/stable/20775366. Accessed December 20, 2018.

"Young Adult Hardcover," *New York Times*. January 20, 2019. www.nytimes.com/books/best-sellers/young-adult-hardcover/. Accessed January 16, 2019.

Part Two

Literature and Popular Culture

6

Jane Eyre in Space: Adapting Brontë's Novel for Young Adult Fans of Sci-Fi and Fantasy

Tara Moore

One of Jane Eyre's strengths is her ability to adapt to new and stark environments. Charlotte Brontë's character survives not only a girls' school organized around a starvation diet but also an oppressive gothic manor house prone to fires and exposure on a desolate moor. A cast of modern Janes has turned up in new, speculative locales that also require survival tactics and the same intense determination associated with Brontë's heroine. Readers can now find Jane aboard spaceships, on a faerie-cursed battlefield, and deep within the headquarters of a ghost relocation society. It seems that the novelty of situating Jane in unusual, sci-fi/fantasy settings tickles young adult adapters' penchant for irony. The iconic Jane travels well. Once young adult adapters figure out what to keep and what to shave from her story, Jane is able to retain her message about power and equality even in these startling, new environments.

    This chapter will not be arguing the value of the adaptations versus the original *Jane Eyre*. Previous critics have considered the worth and placement of later hypertexts.[1] David Buchbinder, like others before him, recommends judging any adaptation based "on the merit of what it sets out to do as a text in its own right."[2] With this excellent advice in mind, I will be assessing how three speculative novels have adapted the *Jane Eyre* narrative for young adult audiences and what the adaptive choices say about the demands of the modern young adult market. While finding similarities, or fidelity, in the adaptations makes for a pleasing encounter, analyzing why adapters needed to change the original story actually reveals more about this text's place in the modern young adult market. Garry R. Bortolotti and Linda Hutcheon argue: "By revealing lineages of descent, not similarities of form alone, we can understand how a specific narrative changes over time."[3] This, then, is the basis of my analysis of the *Jane Eyre* hypertexts: how Brontë's story has developed for the modern young adult audience in the second decade of the twenty-first century. The main questions I wish to pursue are: (1) In what ways do authors alter the values of the original text to suit a modern young adult market? and (2) What is it about Brontë's original work that still beats at the heart of these renderings?

Just as biology celebrates adaptation as streamlining an original product—DNA—to be more successful, so too, Bortolotti and Hutcheon argue, should critics admire the continuing development of a narrative in flux.[4] Modern young adult adaptations, particularly those within the speculative fiction category, have responded to the cultural shifts or "cultural selection" in Brontë's plot. My focal texts include *Ironskin* (2012) by Tina Connolly; *Brightly Burning* (2018) by Alexa Donne; and *My Plain Jane* (2018) by Cynthia Hand, Brodi Ashton, and Jodi Meadows. To emphasize that shared hypotext and to enhance this present argument's clarity, I will frequently introduce the young adult protagonists as Stella/Jane or Rochart/Rochester to underscore the role of each new, adapted character as it relates to Brontë's original narrative.

The Trappings of Jane's New Worlds

In *Film Adaptation and Its Discontents: From* Gone with the Wind *to* The Passion of the Christ, Thomas Leitch develops a new grammar of adaptation intended for film adaptations of novels, one that can be usefully applied here to identify the careful deviations in these *Jane Eyre*-inspired texts. Leitch's grammar includes the designation of "updating," in which beloved characters demonstrate "a distinctly modernist sensibility."[5] Another relevant category is the "analogue," in which the adaptation "invokes" rather than retells the hypotext. This chapter focuses on three speculative novels: it contains one steampunk version set shortly after the Great War, one alternate Victorian universe prone to hauntings, and one decidedly sci-fi novel. This last, Alexa Donne's *Brightly Burning*, presents an analogue adaptation that sets Jane's story in space. A past climatic apocalypse sent a few thousand lucky humans into space to orbit Earth until the thaw. Now, two hundred years later, humanity continues to wait out the ice age. Engineer Stella/Jane has an opportunity to leave her malnourished life aboard one derelict starship to work aboard the *Rochester*, a well-equipped ship with a small and mysterious crew. Stella begins tutoring a young girl on the *Rochester*, but the governess is distracted by her attraction to her pupil's older brother, Hugo Fairfax/Rochester, and the maniacal laughter she sometimes hears aboard their starship. It turns out that *Rochester* holds secrets: a history of concocting biological weapons used to winnow the orbiting human population and Hugo's psychotic mother. Stella exposes a plot to cull the poor of the fleet, and her strategizing eventually convinces most of the remaining human population to "deorbit" and return to earth's surface.

Tina Connolly's novel, *Ironskin*, is also an analogue adaptation, this one a high fantasy. *Ironskin* invokes *Jane Eyre* in the story of Jane Elliot, a young governess and survivor of the recent Faerie War. She bears an unhealable facial wound from a faerie attack, a wound that leaks a curse of intense rage if Jane does not bind it with faerie-stopping iron. Once installed in a remote manor house, Jane Elliot learns that her new charge has fey abilities, which make sense when she later discovers her employer's secret: the Faerie Queen, the enemy of all mankind, possessed Mr. Rochart/Rochester and is in some magical way the mother to the human child Dorie/Adele. Rochart, who was a prisoner of the faerie court for decades, has returned to humankind but is still partially possessed by his fey captors. They have given him fey artistic gifts to make women impossibly beautiful. Only Jane realizes that his surgical procedure is actually a fey process that will allow fey soldiers to take over the bodies of the affected women. In the climax, Jane and an awakened Rochart battle the Faerie Queen and destroy her.

Only one of these novels retains a Victorian setting. *My Plain Jane*, by Brodi Ashton, Cynthia Hand, and Jodi Meadows, adds a speculative bent, since in this world some people can see and communicate with ghosts. This adaptation updates the hypotext even as it conflates the Brontë siblings' biographies with *Jane Eyre*'s narrative. Sixteen-year-old Charlotte Brontë and her surviving sisters attend school not only with the character Jane Eyre but also with the ghosts of Lowood, whom only Jane can see. When Jane leaves for Thornfield Hall, Helen Burns (a ghost) comes with her. Meanwhile, Charlotte escapes starvation at Lowood by joining her clumsy brother, Branwell, who has started a job with the Society for the Relocation of Wayward Spirits. Both Brontë siblings want to impress the top agent, Alexander Blackwood, but their task includes recruiting a reluctant seer: Jane. The plucky team of teenagers discovers that Mr. Rochester has been possessed by an evil ghost at the behest of the Duke of Wellington, the head of their Society, and the duke plans to take over Great Britain. The teens react by planning a coup. In the end, Jane recognizes her power over ghosts, and Charlotte finagles her way out of Lowood and into the Society, but only to provide fodder for her writing plans. The novel ends with married couple Edward and Bertha Rochester happily reunited, and romance budding between Charlotte Brontë and the ghost-busting agent, Alexander Blackwood.

All of the novels under consideration here express more assertively feminist ideology for Jane than the original novel did. While the adapting authors clearly love Brontë's work enough to pull it apart and replicate its structure, they also use their adaptations to react to the oppression Jane's story represents for modern readers. According to Anne Morey and Claudia Nelson, "one of the most marked features of neo-Victorian fictions is aggression toward the content of nineteenth-century fictions."[6] Victorian critics resented Jane's self-assertion, but the new Janes aggressively enact far greater self-assertion in a defense of Jane's rights and selfhood. These new Janes show great agency, even violent action, to claim what they want from the world.[7]

The Trouble with Mr. Rochester

In 2011, when *The Independent* ran a review of all previous screen adaptations of Brontë's novel, one main point the author developed was the casting directors' reluctance to choose actors with a 17-year age gap in the romantic leads. After all, Brontë depicts an 18-year-old Jane meeting an approximately 35- to 40-year-old Rochester on the lane near Thornfield in her 1847 novel. While Hollywood did not initially shy away from casting older actors with young female leads, producers of *Jane Eyre* adaptations did; at some point the visual of such an age gap had come to be seen as "indecent."[8] Data does not support that such an age difference would have been entirely normal, even in 1847. Estimates put the age at first marriage for women around 23 to 26, and for men from age 25 to 30, "with ages rising as one rose in class status."⁹ Widowers like Rochester often married women of a similar age, if perhaps 2-to-5 years younger.

A 17-year age gap does not quite constitute the type of May–December marriage that Victorians would have read about in works by Charles Dickens and George Eliot. Kay Heath points out that, with a succession of older suitors in Dickens's novels, it is only in *Little Dorrit* that an older "forty-ish suitor, after many misgivings, win[s] his quest."¹⁰ A large gap does seem out of the norm for the nineteenth century. Mrs. Fairfax shows that, even in Brontë's storyworld, the age difference grates on righteous sensibilities: "there are twenty years of difference in your ages. He might almost be your father."¹¹ Society supports an alliance between a genteel but impoverished Miss Ingram, aged 25, and Rochester, but even this is called "unequal"—by Jane herself.¹² The Victorian press too took up this issue when it descried the crassness of the Victorian marriage market.¹³ A financially vulnerable woman might be willing to sell her youth and fecundity to a rich man, even an older man, to secure economic stability; however, this did not mean that her action was sanctioned by the developing ideas of romance in marriage.

Unlike Victorian authors, authors of young adult texts have a special, though unspoken, charge to represent healthy choices for their young readers, especially relating to relationships. Young adult authors take the influence they have on the molding of the romantic ideal seriously. To keep their books shelved in the popular young adult section, authors must create female protagonists aged 18 at the oldest. How, then, do the young adult authors balance romance with the necessary warning against lecherous, older men? Adapters of *Jane Eyre* have approached the age issue in a number of ways. They have slightly lessened the age gap between the lovers (*Ironskin*), removed it altogether (*Brightly Burning*), or, most dramatically, eviscerated the romance plot between such unsuited people (*My Plain Jane*). This last one warrants the most attention for its creative circumvention of the child-bride scenario.

My Plain Jane's authors do narrate Jane's budding love for a much older Rochester, but the romance comes to a crashing halt. It turns out Rochester's body has been possessed by his evil, dead older brother Rowland, and it is Rowland's ghost who wants to marry Jane. Once Edward Fairfax Rochester is in possession of his body again, the story shows his dedication to his age-appropriate wife, Bertha. Jane, meanwhile, acknowledges that her fascination for Rochester is "not healthy" mostly because of the age difference.¹⁴ Once she rejects the romance plot for herself, Jane's biggest love interest is the platonic one for her best friend, the ghost-girl Helen Burns. Friendship reigns as this new Jane's defining relationship. The novel does end with Jane meeting a teenaged Edward Rochester Jr., an appropriately aged love interest, but only after Jane has established platonic friendships at the center of her life.

Mrs. Rochester Poses a Problem

Twenty-first-century readers may be familiar with the moral balance of a story, how a character pays in some way if he or she acts selfishly, especially at the cost of others' happiness. Criticism of *Jane Eyre* famously acknowledges Rochester's own literary punishment: the physical effects of the accident on his limbs and his eyesight. However, with today's cultural values, no such punishment would purify a romantic character from the charge of imprisoning a woman for over a decade. Taken literally, this reads as a crime against women and a human rights violation. In the same way that young adult authors cannot condone teenagers conducting affairs with men in their thirties or forties, they must also carefully craft the situation of Mrs. Rochester's "crimes" and imprisonment to maintain a moral balance that does not destroy reader empathy for Jane or Rochester. In each of these three speculative *Jane Eyre* adaptions, the authors find ways to exonerate Rochester from the crime of abusing Bertha. *My Plain Jane* completely disassociates the crime of imprisonment from Rochester. His evil brother possesses his body and keeps Bertha Rochester caged for 15 years. This adaptive twist allows full punishment to fall on Bertha's long-time abuser.[15]

Critics like Adrienne Rich and Sandra Gilbert have argued that Brontë's Bertha Rochester serves as "Jane's alter ego"; Annette Federico, meanwhile, has criticized this approach, saying that emphasizing this duality reduces Bertha "to little more than a facet of Jane's mind."[16] Indeed, when young adult adaptations give Bertha more agency, it becomes harder to see her as an extension of Jane's "madness." Such is the case in at least one of the adaptations—*My Plain Jane*—in which Bertha is a coherent prisoner with ghost-controlling powers of her own. Here Bertha has agency enough to work with Jane to attack their enemies, and we see her reestablishing a healthy relationship with her husband once he is exorcised.

In *Brightly Burning*, the "madwoman in the attic" is Hugo/Rochester's mother, not only a victim of her husband's medical testing but also a fugitive from the law. Hugo was supposed to execute his mother for her crimes: after becoming psychotic, she murdered her husband. Instead, Hugo hides his mother aboard his spaceship in defiance of the law. The plotline exonerates Hugo from any crimes against his mother and instead sets him up as her protector. Even Jane empathizes with his choices. This "Bertha" is the only incoherent and uncontrollable Mrs. Rochester in the lineup, and she feels like a plot point rather than an alter ego.

The Victorian Context Asserted

Neo-Victorian writing has been called "double natured" and possessed of a "dual vision."[17] In this position, it acknowledges the past, perhaps even teaching readers the societal norms of the Victorian past, while crafting a twenty-first-century conflict. Such is the case with *My Plain Jane*, which takes place in an alternate Victorian reality. The novel uses its position as neo-Victorian to present readers with training in how to read a Victorian novel. Chapters commonly contain norming insight into the rules of Victorian society that novices may not yet grasp. For example, readers learn that "young women like Jane didn't belong in pubs."[18] Readers also receive training on what a single man and woman can and cannot do together according to Victorian sexual niceties. The book presumes that a portion of their readers will require help negotiating the limitations placed on Jane and Charlotte as Victorian women. The authors present the training glibly, entertaining readers already aware of the historical facts, as in this example: "young women of this time period felt faint regularly. Because corsets."[19]

As that last line indicates, the adapters not only translate Jane's historical situation but also modify Brontë's writing style. When I led a *Jane Eyre* discussion class at my local library, the students, all retired adults, commented frequently on the imposing language of Brontë's original text. Her vocabulary was precise, dense, and entirely entrenched in the speech patterns of her own day.[20] These committed readers explained that it was taking them longer to read the novel because they were looking up so many of the words ostensibly penned by an 18-year-old journaling protagonist. "Is this speech representative? Did they really talk like this?" my book group wondered. Clearly, there is a market for more accessible versions of *Jane Eyre*, since the publisher Readable Classics has included this title in its list of works that it has "gently" edited while "retaining the original authors' voices."[21] The periodic sentences and poignant but challenging vocabulary in Brontë's work means that retellings are welcome.

The authors of *My Plain Jane* have a unique opportunity to build upon Charlotte Brontë's original idea of the narrator speaking directly to the reader. Christan Monin calls this "direct address" and ties it to the epistolary history of early novels.[22] Plenty of first-person narrations exist, but Brontë's "Reader, I married him" rests upon a meta-textual assertion, that the tale Brontë tells is unapologetically one in book form intended for entertainment. Adapters embrace this famous phrase, not only echoing Brontë but also building on this upfront focalization, one that reads as very modern. Taken from a twenty-first-century perspective, this "Reader, I married him" resembles the act of breaking the fourth wall. The technique has been part of performances for a long time, but it feels particularly modern today because of the reliance on it in snarky twentieth- and twenty-first-century films. Readers know that the young adult authors are imitating Brontë but adding an edgy, modern twist at the same time when they write brief lines like "Reader, it smelled like fire."[23]

My Plain Jane relies on an upbeat, tongue-in-cheek tone that feels deeply ironic when laid overtop the original frame of the hypotext. This seems to be a trend in adaptations of nineteenth-century novels, since, as David Buchbinder argues, this same treatment has been given to the adaptation *Pride and Prejudice and Zombies*.[24] Moreover, Buchbinder calls Seth Grahame-Smith's zombie attack on Jane Austen's novel a "sampling."[25] *Kirkus Review* labels *My Plain Jane* a "supernatural mashup."[26] Like *Rosencrantz and Guildenstern Are Dead*, these two novels pause sometimes to quote the hypotext's original dialogue. Overall, the adaptations retell the *Jane Eyre* story with a very modern, trendy vernacular. Based on speedy banter found in blockbuster movies like *Deadpool* (2016) and the Thor franchise (2011–17), and even the lovable but far-fetched teen conversation in John Green's novels, young readers of this current moment enjoy and even expect rapid-fire quips and fan-friendly cultural references.

Like these other pop texts, *My Plain Jane* blends late-twentieth- and early-twenty-first-century cultural associations into Jane's world. While Brontë made reference to the tropes of her day—the Byronic hero, the powerless governess, the austere and selfless missionary—such cultural references do not transition well into today's young adult fiction. Though the hypertext novels call the Rochester character "brooding," none reference his origins in the Byronic character due to Byron's fall from favor and his lack of relevance among young adult readers. Instead, the authors have brought in cultural references that a reading audience who is also willing to pick up a book about ghost-busting might also understand and enjoy. Hand, Ashton, and Meadows ease readers into cultural and, especially, sci-fi references early when their characters drop frequently memed lines from movies like *Ghostbusters* ("when there's something strange in your neighborhood, you could, um, write the Society a letter") and *Sixth Sense* ("I see dead people").[27] By the end of the novel, readers will have encountered references to *The Hobbit*, *Princess Bride*, Harry Potter, and recurring references to a steamy Mr. Darcy from *Pride and Prejudice*, clearly a text readers are expected to have experienced in the original or via a cinematic adaptation.

These cultural references to current franchises work to anchor *My Plain Jane* to the present, but, altogether, they also affect the telling of Brontë's story. They break down "the barrier between the past and present," infusing a tale that is largely Brontë's—her characters, a similar historical setting—with the equivalent of video game Easter eggs of modern cultural meaning.[28] Putting these ideas into Brontë's characters' mouths makes them feel relevant, flexible, and less ostentatious. The fact that *Jane Eyre* is often taught in high school literature curriculum, perhaps as the only representation of the Victorian novel American students ever read, means that teenagers have been taught to put Brontë's novel on an intellectual pedestal. Putting contemporary references into the characters' mouths pulls down that pedestal.

Body Image and the Adapted *Jane Eyre*

The hypertexts' approach to beauty also marks them as part of the current cultural moment. Brontë's original narrative foregrounded Jane's poor looks, as voiced by Bessie when she visits the adult Jane: "you look like a lady, and it is as much as ever I expected of you: you were no beauty as a child."[29] Logical Jane still feels disappointment about how society views her body, and she "is not quite indifferent" to Bessie's poor assessment of her looks.[30] A more searching description enters Jane's narration when she prepares for her new job at Thornfield: "I sometimes regretted that I was not handsomer: I sometimes wished to have rosy cheeks, a straight nose, and small cherry mouth; I desired to be tall, stately, and finely developed in figure; I felt it a misfortune that I was so little, so pale, and had features so irregular and so marked."[31] Jane dresses herself like a Quaker to match her estimation of her own physical appearance.

Later Jane sketches her plain features alongside an ivory miniature of what she imagines Blanche Ingram to look like. The exercise, a punishment for her infatuation with Rochester, is not only an expression of her self-control but also an expression of her self-loathing. Poor Jane represents the two images in different media, chalk vs. the "freshest, finest, clearest tints."[32] Jane uses the two media to express the class difference between herself and her imagined rival. Like today's youth, she compares the reality of her face alongside the unattainable beauty of a fantasy, combined with media enhancement.

The trope of being concerned with one's looks and fitting in is perfectly in keeping with today's young adult market. Consider the host of young adult novels concerned with body image, including Julie Murphy's *Dumplin'*, Laurie Halse Anderson's *Wintergirls*, Rainbow Rowell's *Eleanor & Park*, and the Brontë-inspired graphic novel, *Jane, the Fox and Me*, by Fanny Britt. The 2018 Netflix movie, *Sierra Burgess Is a Loser*, covers this theme with depth and complexity. The spunky and talented protagonist must overcome a conundrum: while she knows her appearance should not matter, she must also acknowledge that it does influence how the world sees her and interacts with her.

Brightly Burning does not emphasize Jane's plainness at all. In fact, we first meet her gearing up for a party among her teenage cohort, and she receives many compliments. Readers do encounter one half-hearted attempt at establishing Jane's plainness—"I am ordinary. My face is at least"—but Stella/Jane's general confidence undermines any depth to that Brontë-esque theme.[33] Instead, Stella's "plainness" comes in the form of her socioeconomic status. Because she can empathize with poverty, she involves herself in a rebellion plot. She works to protect the poor among the Starfleet population, especially after she learns that the poor are being culled to protect the remaining resources.

The other two adaptations I have included in this analysis do cause their adapted Janes to be othered by their looks. While the adapted Jane is indeed plain in *My Plain Jane*, the novel's ghost characters think Jane is gorgeous, a result of her unique status as a ghost "Beacon."[34] Ghosts treat Jane as an otherworldly beauty, a stark contrast to the treatment she expects from her human contacts. The greater lesson comes from the character Charlotte Brontë, who continues to use spectacles hung around her neck so that her face is not constantly "disfigured" by her disability. In a simple reversal worthy of any after-school special, Charlotte finally prioritizes her vision over her appearance in the conclusion when she starts wearing regular spectacles fulltime. The character's choice privileges a woman's profession and capability above her appearance.

In *Ironside*, Jane's facial wound others her and makes her self-conscious. Her peers see her as dangerously disfigured. She wishes to be beautiful, but the plot's message chastises the quest for beauty. Rochert/Rochester makes rich women beautiful through his fey powers, but by dabbling with unearthly beauty, they become the pawns of the enemy fey. By developing a theme of dangerous beauty that imperils a woman's agency, the novel adds a subtle instructive subtext. Jane Elliot learns this lesson firsthand when she temporarily wears an exquisite fey mask; eventually she relinquishes the power of this ill-gotten beauty when she recognizes her own internal strength. These adaptations tackle the body image issue more directly than Brontë did, creating resolutions that celebrate women who can reject the hollow demands of beauty.

The Powers of Jane

A dismissal of standardized beauty is partly a victory for characters who start to recognize feminist values. By naming their landmark text *The Madwoman in the Attic*,

Gilbert and Gubar cast *Jane Eyre* as a touchstone text of Victorian proto-feminism. This same important critical work analyzes the limitations Victorian culture placed on women and the ways that authors, especially women authors, voiced these exasperating conditions in their writing. Gilbert's foundational essay, "A Dialogue of Self and Soul: Plain Jane's Progress," offers key ideas that continue to resonate in the recent young adult adaptations. For example, Gilbert claims that Jane's oppression—because of her poverty, but moreover, because of her gender—causes her to "rage even to madness."[35] Brontë creates a character who has epic self-control, but who chooses to burst out at strategic moments to voice the inequalities that threaten to destroy her. Today, readers love Jane for her passion, but this quality antagonized some among her earliest audiences. According to Gilbert, "what horrified the Victorians was Jane's anger."[36]

Brontë's earliest critics did not appreciate the way Jane questioned her circumstances and paraded an "ungodly discontent."[37] Brontë's Jane mostly contains her frustration, only rarely bursting into eloquent expression. She has "fiery" words for her Aunt Reed when she is only 10 and passionate self-assertive words for Rochester eight years later: "Do you think, because I am poor, obscure, plain, and little, I am soulless and heartless? You think wrong! I have as much soul as you!"[38] Today's readers have been taught that Jane does indeed have a reason to be angry. Gilbert argues that Jane's passionate outrage is what kindles the fire that eventually burns down Thornfield Hall.[39] Modern audiences embrace Jane's anger, and recent adapters have found ways to give new expression to it. In *Ironskin*, Jane's new power is tied to her fey wound and the rage it exudes. This steampunk Jane learns to become comfortable with her rage, but she can also stop it from becoming all-consuming, channeling it into her battles against her attackers. This transition into a freely raging Jane feels like a feminist release from the burden of culture that bound Brontë's heroine.

Adapters have relished imbuing their Janes with greater levels of agency and the freedom to act on that agency. Diana Dominguez identifies Jane's attractiveness for modern readers even after 170 years in print:

> Jane resonates with readers because they feel a sense of kinship and commonality; at their core, her experiences are their experiences, ... The longing to belong, to be loved, to be accepted on an equal footing, to be self-sufficient, to be allowed to make one's own decisions, to choose one's own path: these are universal human desires and emotions.[40]

Modern Janes are unfettered by Victorian expectations about a woman's place in the domestic sphere. The adapted heroines can fight new battles and rage against specific injustices: the psychologically crippling demands of beauty expectations (*Ironskin*) or socioeconomic injustices (*Brightly Burning*). And then, there's the ongoing work to be done about gender roles—*My Plain Jane* recasts that theme in humorous and meaningful ways.

Adapters work carefully to create a Jane who struggles against a power hierarchy no matter her setting. *Brightly Burning* takes *Jane Eyre* on a dystopian journey in which the protagonist has an opportunity to expand on Brontë's original charge of equality: "it is my spirit that addresses your spirit" she says to Rochester, "just as if both had passed through the grave, and we stood at God's feet, equal—as we are!"[41] *Brightly Burning*'s heroine takes this call beyond her romantic relationship as she sparks a rebellion. This protagonist's insistence on equality brings about a new stage in human society. The Epilogue shows Stella in a powerful position within her society, planning deorbiting strategies with starship captains and having a say in the choice to destroy all remaining chemical weapons. This adaptation focuses on social inequalities, and Stella becomes a champion for the poor. Neither is she a domestic Jane; instead, Stella is an influencer and a leader, despite being only 18.

As Hutcheon explains, there is a complex relationship between the hypotext and its hypertexts, especially when cultural distance makes cultural representations in the hypotext uncomfortable for the modern reader: "the urge to consume and erase the memory of the adapted text or to call it into question is as likely as the desire to pay tribute by copying."[42] While these young adult novels in question do not work like *Wide Sargasso Sea* (1966) to "erase" Brontë's text in favor of a more diverse one, they do call plenty of Brontë's gender-based suppositions into question while also honoring Brontë's early, proto-feminist voice. These adaptations of *Jane Eyre* are not "vampiric" since they do not "draw the life-blood from [their] source and leave it dying or dead, nor [are they] paler than the adapted work. [They] may, on the contrary, keep that prior work alive, giving it an afterlife it would never have had otherwise."[43] *Jane Eyre* will live on as a beloved classic, but these published versions of Brontë's story serve as publisher-endorsed fan-fiction that attests to the enduring nature of the original characters while also bringing them into a twenty-first-century value system.

Ironside blends the *Jane Eyre* plot with other young adult categories: the warrior girl story and the high fantasy tale. The Faerie Queen character draws from high fantasy. As Lloyd Alexander explains, she is a "conventional character[r]—[a] personae of myth and fairy tale, … gorgeously costumed and caparisoned."[44] The Faerie Queen brings her own rules to a story laid over Brontë's plot structure, rules about fey-stolen children, and gifts that come with a high price. Readers who already enjoy young adult novels like Holly Black's *Tithe* (2002) and Melissa Marr's *Wicked Lovely* (2007) would recognize the marks of faerie on this story and make sense of it within that category even if they had not already experienced *Jane Eyre*. Additionally, the fighting girl has gathered a following in young adult literature, with noticeably more actively violent heroines like *Hunger Games*'s Katniss Everdeen, *Red Queen*'s Mare Barrow, and the Razorland series' Deuce.[45]

So, to update *Jane Eyre*, Tina Connolly has blended Brontë with categories of literature beloved by the current young adult readership. The result is a more powerful Jane, a warrior Jane whose decision at the end of the novel is not to enslave herself to domestic contentment hidden away at Ferndean but to combat the remaining fey and free other women from their clutches: "[It was a] race between Jane and the dead Queen's followers. It was a mission. It was her purpose. This Jane was meant to fight."[46] That final phrase, nearly the last of the entire book, feels like a reaction against Brontë's conclusion, one that critics like Parley have found "problematical" because Brontë's

Jane "conform[s] to the norm."[47] Connolly's finale uses repetition to emphasize the possibilities for a modern Jane: "She would always be this Jane…This Jane who had fought the fey and survived, this Jane who was taking their power for herself … This Jane was meant to fight."[48] The emphasis on "this Jane" resonates as a contrast between Brontë's Victorian Jane and the possibility of Jane in the twenty-first century.

Armelle Parley crafts the difference between the hypotext and its adaptations into an analysis of the contemporary moment of writing: "rewritings are in fact testimonies to the contemporary world whose preoccupations often find their way into the new texts" and "rewritings are also undeniably informative about our present times and literature."[49] So, in what ways do these new Janes inform critics about our present times and tastes? One point they raise is the insufficiency of the romance. Recently young adult narratives have turned away from placing the romantic relationship on a pedestal. Now they highlight the importance of the female protagonist's friend group, especially the importance of her female network. *Jane Eyre* is not permitted to be a love story any longer: there is not enough sustaining meat on that story for the modern reader. Instead, the narrative must be a composite of several narratives—quest, high fantasy, dystopia—to garner the respect of the young adult market.

But the young adult novels that build on Brontë's story certainly do not erase her work, nor do they condemn her work to the dust heap of history. Instead, they give it new life. According to Mark Llewellyn, "as the neo-Victorian text writes back to something in the nineteenth century, it does so in a manner that often aims to re-fresh and re-vitalise the importance of that earlier text to the here and now."[50] Readers who adore Brontë can relish the familiar and thrill to the ironies in the innumerable possibilities of *Jane Eyre* and modern blends of genre categories. If this is a reader's first exposure to Brontë's character, he or she might well use this as a space to learn about Victorian cultural restrictions, even when they are portrayed through the synthesis of a spaceship's etiquette. Enjoyment of Jane in new forms of literature might send youthful readers to meet her on her own terms, burdened as she is by her time but with still so much to say.

Notes

1 Margot Blankier explains Gerard Genette's ideas about hypotexts and hypertexts: "Adaptations, particularly of canonical works, are also informed by and engage in dialogue with previous adaptations, to form a network of hypertexts that link to one another. Though these hypertexts share links with others, however, each hypertext is essentially a descendant of a single hypotext." See Blankier, "Adapting and Transforming 'Cinderella,'" 109.
2 Buchbinder, "From 'Wizard' to 'Wicked,'" 136.
3 Bortolotti and Hutcheon, "On the Origin of Adaptations," 445.
4 Ibid., 445–6.
5 Leitch, *Film Adaptations and its Discontents*, 100.
6 Morey and Nelson, "The Secret Sharer," 3.
7 Creating a feminist adaptation of a Victorian classic has become a trend, almost a default of any recent retelling. In 2018, the same year that two of these *Jane Eyre*

adaptations appeared, a BBC miniseries introduced audiences in the UK to a feminist version of *The Woman in White* and playwright Michael McKeever staged his feminist play *Dracula*.

8 "Jane Eyre—Readers, She's Marrying Him Again."
9 Phegley, *Courtship and Marriage*, 14.
10 Heath, *Aging by the Book*, 42.
11 Brontë, *Jane Eyre*, 220.
12 Ibid., 136.
13 Phegley, *Courtship and Marriage*, 15.
14 Hand, Ashton, and Meadows, *My Plain Jane*, 414.
15 The evil older Mr. Rochester is ousted from his brother's body and trapped in a talisman, an object that serves as a prison for unruly ghosts.
16 Rich, "Jane Eyre," 475; Gilbert, "A Dialogue of Self and Soul," 487; Federico, *Gilbert and Gubar's The Madwoman in the Attic after Thirty Years*, 31.
17 Madsen, "Double Narratives," 83–4.
18 Hand, Ashton, and Meadows, *My Plain Jane*, 14.
19 Ibid., 11.
20 Modern readers are unlikely to grasp all of the syntactical and symbolic references to the King James Bible which Patsy Stoneman has identified in *Jane Eyre*'s original language. See Stoneman, "A Poem in a Foreign Language?" 313.
21 *Jane Eyre* (Readable Classics).
22 Monin, "Addressing the Reader," 2.
23 Hand, Ashton, and Meadows, *My Plain Jane*, 140.
24 Buchbinder, "From 'Wizard' to 'Wicked,'" 134. *Jane Eyre* inspired its own paranormal sampling with Sheri Browning Erwin's 2010 novel, *Jane Slayre: The Literary Classic with a Blood-Sucking Twist*.
25 Ibid., 144.
26 Review of *My Plain Jane*.
27 Hand, Ashton, and Meadows, *My Plain Jane*, xi; 97.
28 Lee and King, "From Text, to Myth, to Meme."
29 Brontë, *Jane Eyre*, 78.
30 Ibid., 78.
31 Ibid., 84.
32 Ibid., 137.
33 Donne, *Brightly Burning*, 340.
34 Hand, Ashton, and Meadows, *My Plain Jane*, 91.
35 Gilbert, "A Dialogue," 336.
36 Ibid., 338.
37 Rigby, Review of *Jane Eyre*, 452.
38 Gilbert, "A Dialogue," 343; Brontë, *Jane Eyre*, 216.
39 Ibid., 343.
40 Dominguez, "Nevertheless, She Persisted," 36.
41 Brontë, *Jane Eyre*, 216.
42 Hutcheon, *A Theory of Adaptation*, 7.
43 Ibid., 176.
44 Alexander, "High Fantasy and Heroic Romance."
45 Moore, "Violent Girls," 130.
46 Connolly, *Ironskin*, 302.

47 Parley, "Jane Eyre, Past and Present."
48 Connolly, *Ironskin*, 302.
49 Parley, "Jane Eyre."
50 Llewellyn, "What Is Neo-Victorian Studies?" 170–1.

Bibliography

Alexander, Lloyd. "High Fantasy and Heroic Romance." *The Horn Book*, December 16, 1971. https://www.hbook.com/1971/12/choosing-books/horn-book-magazine/high-fantasy-and-heroic-romance/. Accessed February 27, 2020.

Blankier, Margot. "Adapting and Transforming 'Cinderella': Fairy-Tale Adaptations and the Limits of Existing Adaptation Theory." *Interdisciplinary Humanities* 31, no. 3 (2014): 108–23.

Bortolotti, Gary R., and Linda Hutcheon. "On the Origin of Adaptations: Rethinking Fidelity Discourse and 'Success'—Biologically." *New Literary History* 38, no. 3 (2007): 443–58.

Brontë, Charlotte. *Jane Eyre*. New York: W.W. Norton, 2001.

Buchbinder, David. "From 'Wizard' to 'Wicked': Adaptation Theory and Young Adult Fiction." In *Contemporary Children's Literature and Film: Engaging with Theory*, edited by Kerry Mallan and Clare Bradford, 127–46. New York: Palgrave Macmillan, 2011.

Connolly, Tina. *Ironskin*. New York: Tor Books, 2013.

Dominguez, Diana. "Nevertheless, She Persisted: Jane Eyre at 170." *Journal of South Texas English Studies* 7, no. 1 (2018): 37–41.

Donne, Alexa. *Brightly Burning*. New York: Houghton Mifflin Harcourt, 2018.

Federico, Annette. *Gilbert and Gubar's The Madwoman in the Attic after Thirty Years*. Columbia: University of Missouri, 2009.

Gilbert, Sandra. "A Dialogue of Self and Soul: Plain Jane's Progress." In *The Madwoman in the Attic*, edited by Sandra Gilbert and Susan Gubar, 336–71. New Haven, CT: Yale University Press, 2000.

Hand, Cynthia, Brodi Ashton, and Jodi Meadows. *My Plain Jane*. New York: Harper Teen, 2018.

Heath, Kay. *Aging by the Book: The Emergence of Midlife in Victorian Britain*. Albany: SUNY Press, 2009.

Hutcheon, Linda. *A Theory of Adaptation*. New York: Routledge, [2006] 2013.

Jane Eyre (Readable Classics) Kindle Edition. Amazon. https://www.amazon.com/Jane-Readable-Classics-Charlotte-Bronte-ebook/dp/B00332EWAQ. Accessed October 3, 2018.

"Jane Eyre—Readers, She's Marrying Him Again." *The Independent*, September 2, 2011. https://www.independent.co.uk.

Lee, Alison, and Frederick D. King. "From Text, to Myth, to Meme: *Penny Dreadful* and Adaptation." *New Perspectives on Film Adaptations of 19th–Century Novels and Short Stories* 82 (2015). https://journals.openedition.org/cve/2343.

Leitch, Thomas. *Film Adaptations and Its Discontents: From* Gone with the Wind *to* The Passion of the Christ. Baltimore: Johns Hopkins University Press, 2007.

Llewellyn, Mark. "What Is Neo-Victorian Studies?" *Neo-Victorian Studies* 1, no. 1 (2008): 164–85. http://neovictorianstudies.com/past_issues/Autumn2008/NVS%201-1%20M-Llewellyn.pdf. Accessed March 22, 2020.

Madsen, Lea Heiberg. "Double Narratives, *Struwweipeter* and (Mis)Reading Misbehaviour." *Neo-Victorian Studies* 10, no. 1 (2017): 83–109.

Monin, Christan. "Addressing the Reader in Charlotte Brontë's Novels: *Jane Eyre, Villette, and The Professor*." Masters Thesis. The College at Brockport, 2010. https://digitalcommons.brockport.edu/eng_theses/26/. Accessed March 22, 2020.

Moore, Tara. "Violent Girls: Power, Predation, and the Use of Weapons in Young Adult Fantasy Narratives." In *Handmaids, Tributes, and Carers: Dystopian Females' Roles and Goals*, edited by Myrna Santos, 114–30. Newcastle upon Tyne: Cambridge Scholars Press, 2018.

Morey, Anne, and Claudia Nelson. "The Secret Sharer: The Child in Neo-Victorian Fiction." *Neo-Victorian Studies* 5, no. 1 (2012): 1–13.

Parey, Armelle. "Jane Eyre, Past and Present." *Revue LISA* 4, no. 4 (2006). https://journals.openedition.org/lisa/1741. Accessed November 14, 2019.

Phegley, Jennifer. *Courtship and Marriage in Victorian England*. Santa Barbara: Praeger, 2012.

Review of *My Plain Jane*, by Cynthia Hand, Brodi Ashton, and Jodi Meadows. *Kirkus Review*, March 20, 2018. https://www.kirkusreviews.com/book-reviews/cynthia-hand/my-plain-jane/. Accessed October 2, 2018.

Rich, Adrienne. "Jane Eyre: The Temptations of a Motherless Woman." In *Jane Eyre: A Norton Critical Edition*, edited by Richard J. Dunn, 469–83. New York: W.W. Norton, 2001.

Rigby, Elizabeth. Review of *Jane Eyre. The Quarterly Review* (1848). In *Jane Eyre: The Norton Critical Edition*, edited by Richard J. Dunne, 451–3. New York: W.W. Norton, 2001.

Stoneman, Patsy. "'A Poem in a Foreign Language?': *Jane Eyre*, the King James Bible and the Modern Reader." *Brontë Studies* 37, no. 4 (2013): 312–17. doi: 10.1179/1474893212 Z.00000000037.

7

Megan Shepherd's The Madwoman Trilogy and the Female Voice: The Twenty-First-Century Young Adult Adaptation of *Frankenstein* and the *Frankenstein* Franchise

Melanie A. Marotta

Introduction

When Juliet Moreau first meets Elizabeth von Stein's son, Hemsley, in Megan Shepherd's adaptation of *Frankenstein*—*A Cold Legacy* (2016)—she notices that his mannerisms differ from those of other people. During the Twelfth Night bonfire celebration, Hemsley unemotionally informs Elizabeth that he "had an accident" after a tree branch tore through his body, an injury that would have killed a mortal being.[1] Over the course of the next few days, Elizabeth repairs Hemsley's body while explaining to Juliet that the experiments documented in Victor Frankenstein's Origin Journals make Hemsley's existence possible. As Elizabeth explains the few ways that Hemsley can die—like by fire—Elizabeth tells Juliet, "Everything else I can stitch back together and he's good as new."[2] The amalgamation of Victor Frankenstein and Elizabeth Lavenza, reimagined as the "new" character of Elizabeth von Stein, is, like Hemsley, "stitch[ed] … together," creating something new. Shepherd has reconceptualized the Gothic novel for a postmodern reader in *A Cold Legacy*. Postmodern adaptation allows for female characters to be placed at the forefront of novels that were historically male-centric.

In her examination of the postmodern in children's literature, Stephanie Yearwood asserts that young adult literature in particular "has fully embraced the postmodern mode," enabling works thought to be on the periphery to be accepted into the "mainstream."[3] American author Shepherd has adapted three iconic British novels from the Romantic (Gothic) and Victorian periods, so that she may create the stunning Madwoman Trilogy: *Madman's Daughter* (*The Island of Dr. Moreau*), *Her Dark Curiosity* (*Dr. Jekyll and Mr. Hyde*), and *A Cold Legacy* (*Frankenstein*). Within this trilogy, Shepherd effectively captures three science fiction texts integral to the genre, specifically those that showcase nineteenth-century advancements in science and technology. In his examination of *Frankenstein*, Brian Stableford notes that it has a well-known structure—"the Frankenstein formula"—one which has been recreated repeatedly in other texts. He asserts that this structure features the "unruly and unfortunate artefact bringing about the downfall of its creator."[4] Further, Stableford identifies *Frankenstein* and *The Last Man* as works that "became formative templates heading powerful traditions of imaginative fiction."[5]

In her trilogy, Shepherd depicts the transformation of Juliet from the professor's adolescent daughter (Juliet and other characters repeatedly refer to Moreau and Frankenstein as the "mad scientist" character) to a young adult asserting her own identity. Yearwood defines what she calls a "recipe" for postmodern young adult literature: "They create realms of intertextual reference where multiple stories affect/reflect/interact as the past is questioned, prodded, retold, recovered, or remade."[6] In order to create *A Cold Legacy*, Shepherd has not only adapted the journey of Frankenstein, namely his creation of the creature and his relationship with Elizabeth, but also, in the name of intertextuality, added elements of others' famed works. For example, Juliet's best friend is named Lucy Radcliffe (invoking Shakespeare, Anne Radcliffe, and *Dracula*) and Elizabeth is related to the Ballantyne family (alluding to the Scottish young adult writer, R. M. Ballantyne). Shepherd has also altered Shelley's novel so that the creature may still live and Frankenstein and Elizabeth never marry. By revising Shelley's novel, Shepherd creates a character in Juliet who is relatable in both contemporary and Gothic periods. Juliet narrates her story, offering commentary for her readers about her societal positioning with regard to gender and class. The protagonist is consistently surrounded by adult and young men telling her who she is; she also repeatedly rises and falls in the social hierarchy. Unfortunately, while Shepherd's portrayal of Juliet is progressive, the adapter elects to retain stereotypes regarding ethnic minorities and people with disabilities (reflected in the Ajax and Balthazar characters).[7] In her postmodern adaptation of *Frankenstein*, Shepherd places the adolescent female voice at the forefront of the journey to self-awareness and autonomy, one that concludes with freedom of self for Juliet.

Cinematic Adaptations of Shelley's Novel and of the Author's Life

When Shelley's novel, *Frankenstein*, was published, the writer's gender was debated. In early-nineteenth-century Britain, it was generally unthinkable that a woman in her twenties had the ability to create a text that would become the start of the science fiction genre. The novel, published anonymously, still spurs debate over authorship, with some still preferring to believe that Percy Bysshe Shelley was its creator. Notably, upon the novel's 200th anniversary in 2018, David Barnett, in an article for the UK's *The Independent*, questions why, in this genre that Shelley has created, do fewer women than men receive fame? Why, when female writers are recognized, must their popularity—their worth—be subsequently justified? Barnett's article (written upon the brink of the #MeToo and Time's Up movements, which call attention to abuse and exploitation of women) thoughtfully documents glaring differences in Shelley's introductions, namely those preceding the 1818 and 1831 editions. In the preface to the 1818 edition, one which J. Paul Hunter has cited as being written by Shelley's partner, Percy Bysshe,[8] the Shelley persona offers her reasoning for her completion of the contest. According to this preface, the other male writers preferred to immerse themselves in preoccupations of the Romantic Movement, namely the Alps' natural environment, while she remained behind to finish her famed novel. Percy portrays Shelley as hardworking but disloyal to the Romantic Movement as she does not embrace the precepts as the men do. Examining this preface, Barnett observes, "It's curious because it's very self-deprecating."[9] In the introduction to the 1831 edition, which Shelley wrote, she begins by explaining to her readers the reasoning behind its inclusion and is apologetic for doing so. She attempts to excuse her act by explaining that her publisher has requested it. Shelley explains, "I am the more willing to comply, because I shall thus give a general answer to the question, so very frequently asked me—'How I, then a young girl, came to think of, and to dilate upon, so very hideous an idea.'"[10] The gender politics that Shelley faced in the nineteenth century were oppressive—that point has been well-established in critical analyses of the literary and historical period. Further, the preface from 1818 captures the gender politics active in this group of friends, in Shelley's marriage, and in British society. In order for Shelley's work to be accepted by her audience, Percy's preface was added, subjugating her voice and casting aspersions over the authorship of the novel.

Conflicting views regarding Shelley's behavior are captured in James Whale's film, *The Bride of Frankenstein* (1935). The film's introduction acts as an envisioning of Shelley's creative process, specifically that of *Frankenstein*. In the scene, Shelley is sitting in the parlor working on her needlepoint while conversing with Percy and Lord Byron. As Byron waxes poetic about the storm and himself, he compliments Percy's literary skills while belittling Shelley's. Linda Hutcheon observes, "Part of both the pleasure and the frustration of experiencing an adaptation is the familiarity bred through repetition and memory."[11] As viewers experience the sequel to Whale's *Frankenstein* (1931) and the beginnings of a franchise, they also take part in the continuation of his reimagining of Shelley's story. Notably, Whale (along with Boris Karloff) is responsible for the iconic image of the creature. Shepherd attempts to reclaim Shelley's image of the creature with her characterization of the undead, namely, Hemsley and Edward. In the sequel to Whale's film, the audience is reminded not only of Shelley's original story but also of Whale's first adaptation and, fundamental for this examination, the behavioral expectations of women during the Romantic period. While viewing *The Bride*'s opening, the audience sees Shelley's forced duality, an attribute added to Shepherd's characterization of Juliet. In effect, contained within *Frankenstein*'s two introductions and in Whale's film are two versions of Shelley: one that conforms to societal norms regarding women's conduct and a dissenter "behind the scenes." After Byron celebrates the writing prowess of Percy and himself, Percy questions Shelley's exclusion from this group. Even though it appears that Byron enjoys Shelley's novel, he expresses his skepticism that Shelley with her "bland and lovely brow conceived of *Frankenstein*."[12] Shelley appeases Byron—the symbol of Romantic masculinity—yet unsettles the gender hierarchy in her response. She mocks Byron's work while simultaneously asserting that she is only writing horror so that she may fulfill the desires of the audience. Whale's depiction of Shelley channels the duality that women in the early nineteenth century faced—their inner and outer selves, respectively—and also shows viewers the demands placed on women to conform to societal constructs while struggling to meet their own needs.

Writer Charlotte Gordon, in her introduction to Penguin's release of Shelley's 1818 edition, observes the gender politics at work in the novel: "Where are the powerful female characters? With the exception of Margaret Saville, the women are unable to exert any influence over the men in the story … When women are not allowed to have a voice, Mary implies, loss ensues."[13] In order for Shelley to publish one of the greatest literary works of all time, she had to appease the public by hiding her name, allowing Percy's introduction, and publishing with a company that had a reputation for releasing second-rate work.[14] In the twenty-first century, readers comprehend that these acts should not have been necessary and may even be angered at their occurrence, because "the end justifies the means" does not sit well with this audience. So that Shelley may navigate her gendered society, she published her novel under the aforementioned terms. Even though Shelley may have remained in the background, by writing her groundbreaking work and fighting for its release, she demanded to be seen and used her publication to do so. *Frankenstein*'s female characters may lack power, but ultimately Shelley's "voice" is victorious. Nevertheless, it remains that Shelley, because of her gender identity, had disadvantages, some of which in spite of everything remain in place. Barnett gets to the crux of the issue for women writers, one which is still relevant in the twenty-first century, namely that women continue to lack visibility in the arts.

Adaptation, Video Games, and the *Frankenstein* Franchise

In *A Theory of Adaptation*, Linda Hutcheon delineates the many motivations behind the art of adaptation. Referring to modes, Hutcheon differentiates between "telling, showing, and interacting" as adapters' methods of communication with their audience.[15] Specifically, "telling" refers to literary modes, "showing" indicates two-dimensional visual work, and "interacting" denotes the immersive experience of video games. For adaptations of Shelley's famous novel, the audience has numerous choices if they wish to experience a version of her vision. For example, Nintendo released three video game adaptations of Shelley's novel in the early 1990s: *Frankenstein: The Monster Returns* (1991; Nintendo Entertainment System); *The Adventures of Dr. Franken* (1993: Super Nintendo Entertainment System [SNES]) or *Dr. Franken* (1992; GameBoy); and *Mary Shelley's Frankenstein* (SNES; an adaptation of Kenneth Branaugh's 1994 film). While these video games are not the only immersive releases that exist, they are significant to this chapter's argument because of their platform and intended audience. Nintendo has been known to offer video games specifically for children and adolescents, rather than to an adult audience (as many tend to be). In fact, the NES was called the Family

Computer (Famcom) in Japan, later renamed for US consumers.[16] According to *The Economist*, "By 1990 American children were more familiar with Mario than with Mickey Mouse," thereby highlighting the NES's target audience: children.[17] Since this chapter concerns a young adult readership and places emphasis on the female character and writer, Nintendo's immersive experience with regard to these criteria has been noted here in particular.

Dr. Franken is a decidedly damaging adaptation of Shelley's work. The goal in both GameBoy and SNES[18] versions of this single-player game is to collect the remains of Franky's female, aptly named Bitsy. In *Dr. Franken*, Franky traverses the castle, fighting monsters by shooting lightning bolts, all the while aiming to reform Bitsy in Dr. Frankenbone's machine. By remaking the female, the game's designers continue to perpetuate the damsel in distress stereotype that is common in video games during the late twentieth century and persists in twenty-first-century video games. It is this stereotype that Shepherd attempts to discontinue with her trilogy, thereby offering readers a positive take on Shelley's novel. Referencing cinematic adaptations of other films, Hutcheon asserts the awareness of the viewer not only to the novel as source text but also to other films. What is in question is how the source texts and subsequent adaptations are going to affect the reader: "For audiences, such adaptations are obviously 'multilaminated'; they are directly and openly connected to recognizable other works, and that connection is part of their formal identity, but also of what we might call their hermeneutic identity."[19] This final term Hutcheon defines by referencing Stephen Hinds, stating that "This is what keeps under control the 'background noise.'"[20] Essentially, the audience needs to be mindful that vague associations to other media are possible, but they are not the primary materials in question. Thus, *Dr. Franken*'s varied influences—other video games and Whale's films—need to be controlled by Shelley's novel, thereby becoming the game's "'background noise.'" This is what has aided Shepherd's *A Cold Legacy* in becoming a forward-thinking adaptation of *Frankenstein*. Even though Shepherd's series includes numerous references to other literary works and popular culture motifs, the three source texts act as a proverbial white noise machine drowning out other influences, including that of Whale's films. One problem with *Dr. Franken* and with other adaptations is that during the process of adaptation, the voice of the female writer has been removed from view and thus has been diminished in effectiveness as a result.

The damsel in distress motif has been consistently problematic, and when this sexist view of the woman is marketed to children and young adults, it is disturbing. The audience witnesses a rendition of Shelley's novel that places the male in focus while relegating the female to object status. As Hutcheon asserts, "there are significant differences between being told a story and being shown a story, and especially between both of these and the physical act of participating in a story's world."[21] In each of the three types of adaptations—literary, cinematic, and gaming—the creator controls the audience's focus. What happens when the female voice is removed and the remainder is a cannibalized source text? Zach Waggoner cites Athomas Goldberg and Laetitia Wilson, observing that when a player uses a character called the "agent," the player is directed by the designers' story and has no options when playing.[22] As *Dr. Franken* was developed in the 1990s, when many games included the agent character, it may be subjected to the same criticism. The user encounters a static male character on a fixed quest; therefore, it is the game designers that direct the players. The player is immersed in an experience that promotes the passivity and inferiority of women.

Dr. Franken's developers fuse Shelley's Victor Frankenstein and Whale's characterization of the creature in order to create their vision. As a result, the developers objectify the female creature, perpetuate emphasis on the male experience, and overwhelm Shelley's voice and the female experience. The player utilizing the agent sees through male eyes a woman without agency rather than experiencing Shelley's vocalizations. As the storyteller working through her characters, thereby making sure her voice is experienced, Shelley prods the reader to a specific directionality. In effect, if adaptation is enacted in a case like Shelley's, does the adapter have a responsibility to the source text and the new audience? How close to the source does the adapter need to be? Through the use of her three male foils, Shelley cautions the reader about male hubris in relation to her characters' actions while simultaneously emphasizing the same in relation to gender constructs in her society. In reference to the method of adaptation—Hutcheon's "telling, showing, interacting"—and the amount of imaginative control the audience is permitted, does responsibility to the source text increase or decrease? Should the adaptation be considered a new creative work and, therefore, no responsibility is warranted? As Hutcheon explains, "When we play a first-person shooter videogame and become an active character in a narrative world and viscerally experience the action, our response is different again" from that garnered from text-based or visual sources.[23] In *Dr. Franken*, the gamer has no option but to be the cartoonish (big-headed, sunglass-wearing, orange t-shirt and purple shorts sporting) Franky who, if the initial gameplay is successful, picks up Bitsy's arm. *Dr. Franken* is unmistakably told from a male point of view, one that asserts that a woman has no control over her body and that it exists within the purview of men. Franky treats Bitsy as a doll—one that he rebuilds—thereby having control over her body. Shelley's novel, however, is decidedly influenced by Mary Wollstonecraft's plight for equal rights for women.[24]

It is in the literary form through the use of the reader's imagination that the audience is able to assert more control—in other words, make more choices. Hutcheon asserts that "In the telling mode—in narrative literature, for example—our engagement begins in the realm of imagination, which is simultaneously controlled by the selected, directing words of the text and liberated—that is, unconstrained by the limits of the visual or aural."[25] The authority remains with the author, who expertly maneuvers the reader in the direction desired. The reader is left, however, to use the skills of the imagination to fill in any blanks, to create one's own visual to complement the text. In Shepherd's *A Cold Legacy*, the author takes elements of the original source text, weaving a female-centric plot around them. Shelley had to use restraint in her creation; even though her father allowed her to learn about science, centering a text on a female scientist during the nineteenth century, and one that was directed to an adult audience, would have been laughable. Although gender equality still does not exist in the twenty-first century, Shepherd has more creative control than Shelley had in the nineteenth century. The question regarding responsibility to her reader remains: Does Shepherd have any obligations to the source text and to her early-twenty-first-century young adult audience to present a strong female character? The burden that Shelley had to bear as a child of activists ensured that Shelley, as storyteller, offered her readers a scathing critique of her male-centric society. Shepherd, in writing from 2013 to 2016, has elected to tell her story through the adolescent Juliet who has a less-than-idyllic family life and is on her way to becoming a scientist. As a writer during the first wave of feminism, Shelley's responsibility is to assert the need for equal rights for women and men and the abolition of gendered roles. Shepherd's responsibility during the fourth wave of feminism is the same as Shelley's, but now she has more latitude to do so. In her Madwoman trilogy, Shepherd does what Shelley could not: she not only places an adolescent woman in the role of scientist and narrator, but she also allows her to choose her own fate.

The Need for Twenty-First-Century Adaptations: The Female Character as Daughter and Scientist

Like Shelley, Shepherd writes her trilogy using first-person narration, representing the voice of Juliet Moreau. Whereas Shelley funnels information from the scientist, Frankenstein, through the fame-seeking yet moral Walton, Shepherd makes her protagonist the narrator so that the reader may experience events firsthand. In reference to young adult literature and the figures of parents within, Roberta Seelinger Trites discusses dominance and submission: "Writers are another source of authority within adolescent literature as an institution. Investigating the ways that they employ aspects of narrative structure to manipulate the reader reveals much about the adolescent reader's potential empowerment and repression."[26] When readers encounter Shelley's plot (or that of Shepherd's other sources, H. G. Wells and Robert Louis Stevenson), a male character tells the story to the audience. In Shelley's case, a young woman's portrayal of society is presented showing adult readers that (a) society values male voices; however, (b) there exists the possibility for change for women, and it is she who stands as the example. Director and writer Haifaa Al-Mansour and writer Emma Jensen eloquently capture Mary Shelley's spirit in the cinematic release aptly titled *Mary Shelley* (2018). In the film, William Godwin says to Mary, "Rid yourself of the thoughts and words of other people, Mary. Find your own voice."[27] In other words, Godwin is instructing Shelley to separate herself from others' desires, instead placing her stylistic requirements above all others and leaving the emotional baggage behind. Shelley's parents greatly impacted *Frankenstein* and it is this aspect that Shepherd has expertly depicted in her adaptations.

As the reader progresses though the trilogy, Shepherd shows that Juliet has scientific leanings. However, the reasoning behind her interest in the scientific arts is key to understanding this character. In the traditions of adolescent literature, the figure of the parent (or parents) is fundamental to the plot, which centrally focuses on the maturation of the adolescent protagonist. As Trites states, "Parents of teenagers constitute a more problematic presence in the adolescent novel because parent-figures in YA novels usually serve more as sources of conflict than as sources of support. They are more likely to repress than to empower."[28] In reference to Shepherd's trilogy, adaptation enables Shepherd to change the emphasis to female characters instead of the three male characters while retaining the tumultuous parent–child relationship as portrayed in Shelley's novel. By adapting popular canonical texts, Shepherd has these undeniable reputations looming, which can be burdensome to a new writer,[29] as well as issues pertaining to the Gothic and Victorian novels. Shepherd chooses to honor her source texts' literary periods, while simultaneously reflecting contemporary concerns relevant to young women in both spaces (i.e., the threat of sexual assault). What overshadows Juliet's life and her future is the figure of the absentee parent, namely, her father.

As a working-class young woman, Juliet has few rights and options available to her. As *The Madman's Daughter* opens, Juliet works cleaning a lab in King's College, London. Juliet recalls her past, specifically how she and her family previously belonged to the upper class. Brian Attebery documents the movement in children's literature cited by Anne Scott MacLeod, notably "sentimental formulas and from 'the late nineteenth-century idealization of childhood.'"[30] There is no ideal family in Shepherd's novels. Juliet dispels this myth while simultaneously documenting the dangers for women in nineteenth-century England. Juliet's mother turned to sex work not to retain their lavish lifestyle, which is partially preserved, but to ensure that they had a place to live. Shepherd provides her reader with the character of Juliet through which she reveals the lack of choices that women have.

Shepherd highlights the vulnerability of adolescents both in the past and in contemporary society. Upon her mother's death due to consumption, 14-year-old Juliet is left with little money and no residence. Since Juliet's father has fled, she is orphaned. When Trites documents the varied parental figures in adolescent literature, she focuses on three groupings, one of which she calls the "involved parents."[31] As her example of this parent type, Trites offers Marmee from *Little Women*, who "works diligently to help her daughters become socially indoctrinated 'little women.'"[32] Juliet's mother teaches her how to be a fantasy—the ideal upper-class woman. Juliet's mother has been objectified by the patriarchal system; in turn, she passes this objectification on to her daughter, thereby making her a living doll—an embodiment of the patriarchy. A version of the "sentimental family"—the ideal family—that Attebery defines is found in Juliet's mother. Even though they have lost their reputations, their community standing, and their money, Juliet's mother attempts to ensure that her daughter may be prepared to marry well and retain her former "respectable" place in society. Regrettably, Juliet's mother teaches her to live in an illusion rather than reality. Juliet's mother's lifestyle—one that Shepherd accurately recreates—offers no depth and no authentic opportunities for women. Shelley implies that Victor's mother, Caroline, would have been consumed by society had his father not stepped in and "saved her" upon her father's demise. It sounds much like the construct of the hero saving the princess, but there is an element of truth to the story.

In twenty-first-century young adult literature, the issue of surveillance appears in reference to technology; however, it may be interpreted in a different form here. Juliet is fired from her job as a maid because she successfully fights back when her employer attempts to rape her. Dr. Hastings tells Juliet that she has no other option but to be sexually assaulted, that if she does not resist, he will pay her, and that she will not lose her job. Dr. Hastings has been constantly harassing her as she works; Juliet has no parental supervision and the lack of it is problematic. As Dr. Hastings threatens to violently rape Juliet, she contemplates her options: either be raped and fired or resist and be fired. Shepherd effectively captures situations relevant in both nineteenth and twenty-first centuries and to both young and adult women. In a no-win situation, Juliet is taking back her power. For Juliet, resistance, and even death, is preferable to violation. During the conversation in the lab where Dr. Hastings repeatedly threatens Juliet, she verbally insults him, and while she envisions physically attacking Hastings, she also dreams of Montgomery saving her. During the nineteenth century two types of works were seen: those that featured the orphan girl and those that contained women who are violently victimized—rape chosen over death.

As an orphan—her father abandons her after he is accused of performing unnatural experiments (this character is based on Wells's Dr. Moreau) and Juliet and her mother lose everything—the protagonist has no male protector figure. Mrs. Bell, her female employer, acts as a surrogate mother to Juliet, revealing to her the realities that women of all classes face. Trapped in the lab with Hastings, Juliet realizes first that her parent, Mrs. Bell, is not there to save her and then her mind turns to the male character of Montgomery, later her husband in the third novel. Shepherd's novels do not contain the happy families of the sentimental novels that Attebery describes, nor are happy outcomes available to Juliet.[33] Rather, Shepherd incorporates the vulnerability and the underlying strength of the young adult dystopian novel heroine. Once Juliet realizes that she has no one to depend on other than herself, she weighs the options available to her and cuts the tendon in Hastings's hand, one that will ensure he is never again capable of performing surgery, thereby ending his career. Shepherd provides adolescent readers with a female protagonist who has the scientific knowledge and mental strength to care for herself; no male savior is needed to protect her from Hastings. There is no functioning familial unit for Juliet; she must locate a surrogate. In twenty-first-century science fiction, the community is a desirable unit as it offers safety and enables survival for its protagonists. Rather than being made of blood relations, the community is a patchwork of like-minded people who see relations with others as a necessity for continuity of life. As arrest for Juliet's assault of Hastings is imminent, Mrs. Bell gives Juliet her bag and money, and her best friend, Lucy, offers her money as well. Notably, Lucy is a constant in Juliet's life and it is partially for her that she brings Edward, her former love interest and one of her father's creations, back to life after his death in *A Cold Legacy*.

Juliet shows that the reason behind her cutting Hastings is not only because she may physically escape but also because she desires to cause him pain. Her rage is a response to the treatment of women by men in her England and from her father's abandonment of the family. During her trip to see the father who abandoned her, Juliet ponders her feelings for Montgomery and asserts, "The crush I'd had on him then seemed silly now that I knew how the world worked. Servant boys didn't grow up and marry their masters' daughters. Instead, women fell from privilege and sold themselves on the street … the fairytale was gone."[34] On the ship venturing toward Moreau's secret island, Juliet puts forward the notion that illusions regarding societal constructs for her have been shattered. While Juliet's acceptance of sexism and classism is possible, she refuses to come to terms with her father's abandonment of her family and lack of love.

Juliet ventures to the island in search of her father because she refuses to accept that his acts as a scientist are immoral and because she has nowhere else to go. In *The Madman's Daughter*, Juliet reminisces about her relationship with Moreau, clearly recollecting his cruelties to animals—he drowned the family dog—and his neglect of his daughter, Juliet. Juliet Just critiques parental figures in young adult novels, writing, "Afflicted by anomie, sitting down to another dismal meal or rushing out the door to a meeting, the hapless parents of Y.A. fiction are slightly ridiculous. They put in an appearance at the stove and behind the wheel of the car, but you can see right through them."[35] The Madwoman trilogy's parents may be rather "ridiculous" to its adolescent characters, but isn't that what makes them realistic? Sixteen-year-old Juliet and her friend, Lucy, have authentic problems, relatable issues with which to deal. Lucy's parents do not wish her to spend time with Juliet as her family has been disgraced: Juliet takes on the position of the adolescent "bad-influence." In *A Cold Legacy*, the authorities who seek Juliet and her friends (her surrogate family) find them at Elizabeth's castle, Ballantyne, because Lucy's father places an article in a newspaper seeking their whereabouts. In the article, Radcliffe appears repentant for his part in the King's College secret society, but it is farcical as he only desires to cover his indiscretions by ending the lives of Juliet and her friends. Like Victor and Henry in *Frankenstein*, both Juliet and Lucy struggle with the dominance of their fathers. The women have abusive fathers, a fact revealed throughout the novels, and it is through the revelations of their fathers' depravity that the young women transition into adults.

In the trilogy, in order for her character to evolve, Juliet must also reject the notion that she and her father are alike—ensuring that if she becomes a scientist she will not become as immoral as he. She, too, must come to terms with the fact that a woman may become a scientist, a position that the twenty-first-century adaptation permits. When the group flees London in *A Cold Legacy*, seeking refuge with Elizabeth, Juliet notices that Montgomery's hands resemble that of a surgeon and not a servant. Once they are ensconced in the castle and he discovers that Elizabeth has been utilizing Frankenstein's research so that she may reanimate the dead, Montgomery tells her to emulate her mother, not her father. In *Her Dark Curiosity*, so that she may save her friends and herself, Juliet animates some of her father's creations which, in turn, kill almost all of the secret society. Juliet's actions cause her father's death, but they do not lessen her feelings of inadequacy and shame. Trites discusses the absentee parent and the substitute parent, referring to this figure as *in loco parentis*.[36] In her analysis of the novel *Daddy Long Legs*, Trites states that "Over and over, Judy rebels against the lack of knowledge she has about her benefactor … she seeks information about him to equalize the imbalance that comes from his knowing everything about her and her knowing nothing about him."[37] Juliet is repeatedly kept ignorant about her father and her guardians, Elizabeth and Professor Von Stein. Once she literally rids herself of her father, she must symbolically decide that she can be a scientist who does not have to follow either in his path or Elizabeth's. Trites continues, "The power imbalance exists entirely within the Symbolic Order, for Judy knows that although she is actual to him, he can never be more than symbolic for her."[38] Von Stein and Elizabeth have identified Juliet as the ideal heir for Frankenstein's journals, therefore protecting their secrets and ensuring that the science contained within is used wisely, if at all. Unfortunately for Juliet, this fact is kept from her until after Hemsley's accident. Justifiably, Juliet feels betrayed not only by her biological father but also by her surrogate parents. After the Origin journals are introduced to Juliet, she vows to Elizabeth that she will not use them to reanimate the dead.

In order for Juliet to accept that she may become a scientist if she desires or that she may choose her fate, Juliet must obtain her own power. Juliet must compensate for the knowledge that she lacks; she does so by following her father's and her surrogate mother's paths before maturing and choosing uncertainty. In the second novel, *Her Dark Curiosity*, Juliet brings her father's creatures to life so that they may kill those who threaten the lives of her friends—her chosen family. As the novel closes, Juliet meets with Elizabeth, learning that her family name is Frankenstein and that Victor is her great-great uncle. Edward is dying from poison and Juliet asserts she wishes to use Frankenstein's research to ensure Edward's mortality. To this Elizabeth responds, "Think hard Juliet. It's only a handful of scientists who are ever even faced with this decision. The smart ones turn back. Only the mad push forward."[39] As Frankenstein does with Walton in Shelley's novel, Elizabeth attempts to teach Juliet the dangers of ambition combined with hubris. Elizabeth teaches Juliet about Frankenstein's work so that she may protect it from being immorally used and so that she will continue her work with amputees. Both Moreau and Elizabeth are involved with the immoral use of science: science for personal gain. Furthermore, if Juliet is to develop her own sense of self, she must reject Moreau's and Elizabeth's ideology.

Wosk documents the reoccurrence in the literary and visual arts of men making dolls to resemble women. In her analysis of George Bernard Shaw's dramatic adaptation of Ovid's *Pygmalion*, Julie Wosk identifies Ovid's story as the origin of "men's enduring fantasy about fabricating an ideal female."[40] Both Shelley's Frankenstein and Wells's Moreau have been identified as attempting to play god with their respective creations. Moreau creates a species from humans and animals, ensuring that his beings have a code of conduct to follow, which places him in a position of superiority. Shelley's novel, however, shows the creation of a human being due to Frankenstein's loneliness and feelings of inferiority stemming from his relationship with his father. Wosk asserts, "Mary Shelley in *Frankenstein* saw the horrors of dismemberment and reconstruction."[41] Regarding the doll figure, the norm in popular culture leans toward the construction of female dolls by male characters, rather than those of the same sex. Frankenstein's obsession for superiority leads him to create a male doll; it is telling of male gender constructs in the nineteenth century that Frankenstein is unable to control his physically strong creation. In her discussion of men dressing their dolls, which are actually real women, Wosk reveals, "The men view the 'dolls' as commodities—not real women with feelings or modesty but just insensate beings."[42] Frankenstein figuratively murders his female creation once he realizes that she will, like his first creation, be able to think for herself.

Once he realizes that she will have free will, he dissembles her. In *A Cold Legacy*, Juliet must channel Walton rather than Frankenstein. At the close of Shelley's novel, Walton chooses to be heroic and save the crew's lives instead of going forth with his desires. He makes the ultimate sacrifice that enables his maturation as a character. Juliet cannot follow either Frankenstein's or Elizabeth's path. Both ensure that Hemsley's death is not permanent. Because she wants to make her friend happy after Edward's death and, more importantly, she wants to squash her feelings of inadequacy, Juliet brings Edward back to life. At the conclusion of Shepherd's trilogy, Edward must banish himself from "normal" society. He leaves to seek the whereabouts of Frankenstein's creation because he—and Shepherd channels Shelley here—asserts that he must be with someone who is like him. Juliet makes the ultimate sacrifice like Walton; she refuses to reanimate Lucy when she dies. She understands that by making this choice she causes anguish for Lucy's loved ones, including herself. Juliet makes the moral choice, an act that reveals her maturity.

Conclusion: Possibilities

In director Al-Mansour's cinematic biopic, Polidori shows Mary an image of a body. As she gazes upon it, the character states, "Is this possible? Reanimation?"[43] Shelley's novel and Shepherd's trilogy are about what Shelley's persona expresses in the film: possibilities. Through her adaptation of three canonical texts, Shepherd offers her readers a notable contribution to the twenty-first-century young adult genre. As the daughter of activists, Shelley may have felt a sense of duty regarding her parents' societal viewpoints. As a result, she writes a novel that replicates the gender roles of nineteenth-century Britain. Shelley places the male storylines forefront while intermittently adding Elizabeth's experiences and subjugation. Shepherd reimagines Victor Frankenstein as part of Elizabeth's history and, as with Juliet's father, Victor's history attempts to overshadow and influence Elizabeth's life. While the trilogy is imperfect, Shepherd's lead female character is impressive due to her agency. Shepherd does not portray Juliet as a doll, a material object manipulated by the patriarchy. Rather, she is capable of independently choosing her life's path. When the Shelley adaptation concludes, like Shelley's original work, Shepherd leaves it open-ended. There is hope for change regarding constructed gender roles for women. Juliet closes the novel with choices regarding her professional and personal life. In the question that plagues women in the twenty-first century and offers great uncertainty, yes, women may have it all if they wish it. Shepherd does not alter Shelley's voice; instead, she preserves her assertion about the capabilities of women for future generations.

Notes

1 Shepherd, *A Cold Legacy*, chapter 8.
2 Ibid., chapter 12.
3 Yearwood, "Popular Postmodernism for Young Adult Readers," 50.

4   Stableford, "Science Fiction before the Genre," 19.
5   Ibid.
6   Yearwood, "Popular Postmodernism for Young Adult Readers," 50.
7   I would be remiss if I did not mention that while Shepherd portrays Juliet as a modern adolescent, her novels are overwhelmingly monochromatic. Characters that differ from the nineteenth-century norm, namely people of disability, are Othered as stereotypes are recreated.
8   Shelley, "Preface," 5. See Hunter's footnote for information regarding authorship.
9   Barnett, "Women in Science Fiction."
10 Shelley, "Introduction to *Frankenstein*," 165.
11 Hutcheon, *A Theory of Adaptation*, 21.
12 *The Bride of Frankenstein*.
13 Gordon, "Introduction," xxi.
14 Ibid., xviii.
15 Hutcheon, *A Theory of Adaptation*, xvi.
16 "How Super Mario Because a Global Cultural Icon."
17 Ibid.
18 *The Adventures of Dr. Franken* has a sequel, thereby showing the popularity of the game. Super Nintendo Entertainment System (SNES) is one of the platforms for the *Dr. Franken* game.
19 Hutcheon, *A Theory of Adaptation*, xvi.
20 Ibid.
21 Ibid., xvii.
22 Waggoner, *My Avatar, My Self*, 9.
23 Hutcheon, *A Theory of Adaptation*, 27.
24 Mary Shelley's mother, Mary Wollstonecraft, wrote *A Vindication of the Rights of Women* (1782) about the desire for gender equality in her society.
25 Hutcheon, *A Theory of Adaptation*, 23.
26 Trites, *Disturbing the Universe*, 55.
27 *Mary Shelley*. Directed by Haifaa Al-Mansour.
28 Trites, *Disturbing the Universe*, 56.
29 Regarding the trilogy's reception, the first novel has been awarded the North Carolina Young Adult Book Award for 2013 and it has been optioned by Paramount. See Megan Shepherd, *MeganShepherd.com*, http://meganshepherd.com/new-page/.
30 Attebury, "Elizabeth Enright and the Family Story," 120.
31 Trites, *Disturbing the Universe*, 58.
32 Ibid.
33 Attebury, "Elizabeth Enright and the Family Story," 123.
34 Shepherd, *The Madman's Daughter*, chapter 6.
35 Just, "The Parent Problem in Young Adult Lit."
36 Trites, *Disturbing the Universe*, 60.
37 Ibid., 63.
38 Ibid.
39 Shepherd, *Her Dark Curiosity*, chapter 45.
40 Wosk, *My Fair Ladies*, 9.
41 Ibid., 109.
42 Ibid., 67.
43 *Mary Shelley*. IFC Films, 2018.

Bibliography

The Adventures of Dr. Franken. MotiveTime, 1993.

Attebery, Brian. "Elizabeth Enright and the Family Story." *Children's Literature* 37 (2009): 114–36.

Barnett, David. "Women in Science Fiction: If Mary Shelley Invented the Genre Why Are So Few Female Sci-Fi Writers Household Names?" *The Independent*, January 25, 2018. https://www.independent.co.uk/news/long_reads/women-science-fiction-authors-mary-shelley-frankenstein-200-ursula-k-le-guin-sci-fi-writers-female-a8177556.html. Accessed November 28, 2019.

The Bride of Frankenstein. Directed by James Whale. Performed by Boris Karloff, Colin Clive, and Valerie Hobson. Universal Studios, 1935.

Cunningham, Joel. "Read N.K. Jemisin's Historic Hugo Speech." *B&N Sci-Fi and Fantasy Blog*, August 20, 2018. https://www.barnesandnoble.com/blog/sci-fi-fantasy/read-n-k-jemisins-historic-hugo-speech/a.

Gordon, Charlotte. Introduction. *Frankenstein: The 1818 Text*. New York: Penguin, 2018.

"How Super Mario Because a Global Cultural Icon—It's a Me." *The Economist*, December 24, 2016. https://www.economist.com/christmas-specials/2016/12/24/how-super-mario-became-a-global-cultural-icon. Accessed November 2, 2019.

Hutcheon, Linda. *A Theory of Adaptation*, 2nd ed. London: Routledge, 2013.

Just, Juliet. "The Parent Problem in Young Adult Lit." *New York Times*, April 1, 2010. https://www.nytimes.com/2010/04/04/books/review/Just-t.html. Accessed March 3, 2019.

Mary Shelley. Directed by Haifaa Al-Mansour. Performed by Elle Fanning, Douglass Booth, and Stephen Dillane. IFC Films, 2018.

Shelley, Mary. "Frankenstein; or, the Modern Prometheus." In *Frankenstein*, edited by J. Paul Hunter, 1–161. London: W.W. Norton, [1818] 2012.

Shelley, Mary. "Introduction to *Frankenstein*, Third Edition (1831)." *Frankenstein*, edited by J. Paul Hunter, 2nd ed., 165–9. New York: W.W. Norton, 2012.

Shepherd, Megan. *A Cold Legacy*. Balzer + Bray, 2016. Kindle.

Shepherd, Megan. *Her Dark Curiosity*. Balzer + Bray, 2014. Kindle.

Shepherd, Megan. *The Madman's Daughter*. Balzer + Bray, 2013. Kindle.

Shepherd, Megan. *MeganShepherd.com*, http://meganshepherd.com/new-page/.

Stableford, Brian. "Science Fiction before the Genre." In *The Cambridge Companion to Science Fiction*, edited by Farah Mendlesohn and Edward James, 15–31. Cambridge: Cambridge University Press, [2003] 2009.

Trites, Roberta Seelinger. *Disturbing the Universe: Power and Repression in Adolescent Literature*. Iowa City, IA: University of Iowa Press, 2000.

Waggoner, Zach. *My Avatar, My Self: Identity in Video Role-Playing Games*. Jefferson, NC: McFarland, 2009.

Wosk, Julie. *My Fair Ladies: Female Robots, Androids, and Artificial Eves*. New Brunswick, NJ: Rutgers University Press, 2015.

Yearwood, Stephanie. "Popular Postmodernism for Young Adult Readers: Walk Two Moons, Holes, and Monster." *The Alan Review* 29, no. 3 (2002): 50–3.

8

Austen, Wollstonecraft, and Zombies: Female Autonomy in Jane Austen's Popular Canon

Eileen Totter

While the approach to young adult dystopian heroines in novels varies in goals and approaches, one does not often include Seth Grahame-Smith's *Pride and Prejudice and Zombies*, and the franchise built around his text that followed, into this group. This is at least partly because the series began with Seth Grahame-Smith inserting gore and sexier scenes in the hopes of attracting male readers to drive sales, as multiple scholars have noted. Rebecca Soares rejects the text for trying to make a book written by the female Jane Austen about women's lives a text for men.[1] Tim Lanzendörfer's "'So Many Unmentionables About': Parody, *Pride and Prejudice and Zombies*, and the Politics of Mash-up Fiction"[2] and David Buchbinder's "From 'Wizard' to 'Wicked': Adaptation Theory and Young Adult Fiction"[3] are comparatively gentler with their criticism, but they concur with Soares. While Grahame-Smith's male gaze in his adaptation problematizes the *Pride and Prejudice and Zombies* franchise, it is still a world where Grahame-Smith uses the zombies as an obvious metaphor for how an unhappy marriage drains the life out of women, while the only truly independent woman in the text is Elizabeth Bennet, now a grizzled zombie-hunting veteran.

Grahame-Smith uses the dystopian world he adapts from Austen's narrative to question both marriage and the upper class's ability to ignore the suffering of anyone poorer than they are. Illustrating this point is Charlotte Lucas, who marries in the hopes that the wealthy Mr. Collins will grant her a respectable death after she is bitten by a zombie; instead she slowly decays while her wealthy family does not even notice. Social critique is typically the point of dystopian novels, which Isabel Santalauria defines as texts "that concentrate on the protagonists' struggles to fight apparently utopian societies which are nonetheless controlled by totalitarian forces; to undermine openly despotic systems; or to survive apocalypse after alien attacks, lethal plagues or natural cataclysms."[4] Lanzendörfer cements the idea of the *Pride and Prejudice and Zombies* franchise as purposefully using its outlandish premise to explore "the literal break-in of those aptly named 'unmentionables'—described in a tone of haughty detachment—into the lives of the upper classes, causing much havoc before finally being repelled."[5] Thus, the text interrogates power structures even as it does its best to shock its audience.

The sequel to Grahame-Smith's text, Steve Hockensmith's *Dreadfully Ever After* is more transparent in attempts to refashion Austen and even Grahame-Smith's work into a young adult dystopian work, ending with an Elizabeth Bennet who is both happily married (Grahame-Smith has her retire to marry) and powerful as a zombie hunter. Indeed, Hockensmith uses the components of Grahame-Smith's adaptation that exist chiefly for gore (e.g., Lady Catherine's endless supply of ninjas) and instead examines how this affects race and class in Regency England, following Santaularia's contention that dystopian worlds mirror the concerns of our own.[6] There are problematic aspects in Hockensmith's work as well: even as he tries to recreate a more diverse Austen canon through the young adult dystopian world and heroine formulas, his focus is still on the thoughts and concerns of white women. Yet through these adaptations and revisions, the *Pride and Prejudice and Zombies* franchise not only examines the fears of upper-class corruption and women forsaking independence for the security of marriage through the zombie apocalypse but also proposes a solution to these problems because of the zombie gore, not despite it.

The *Pride and Prejudice and Zombies* Series and the Young Adult Genre

In order to understand how Grahame-Smith and Hockensmith incorporate the young adult dystopian heroine into their respective texts, a basic understanding of the genre and the heroine is required. Santaularia contends that the young adult dystopian genre serves as a means to "reflect on serious global concerns."[7] Miranda A. Green-Barteet argues that such settings "empower [female protagonists] to redefine what it means to be a young woman" and allow them "to be strong, active young women who willingly challenge authority and even confront injustice when they feel compelled to do so."[8] The young adult dystopian heroine rejecting traditional femininity is an idea Grahame-Smith and Hockensmith explore, but their reasons behind that exploration differ as each writer has separate goals in their respective adaptations of Austen's canon into the young adult dystopian genre. David Buchbinder's "From 'Wizard' to 'Wicked': Adaptation Theory and Young Adult Fiction" discusses how contemporary adaptations are frowned upon,[9] concluding that Grahame-Smith's insertion of violence into an otherwise unchanged text "suggest[s] the novel is in fact an appropriation,"[10] focused only on attracting male readers.[11] Rebecca Soares in "Morbid Curiosity and Monstrous (Re)Visions: Zombies, Sea Monsters, and Readers (Re)Writing Jane Austen" concurs with Buchbinder, arguing that Grahame-Smith destroys Austen's narrative to appeal to male readers.[12]

However, such a reading ignores how Grahame-Smith casts Elizabeth as a woman who desires agency in a world that wishes to confine her. As Elizabeth's foil, Grahame-Smith's Mr. Collins is a buffoon that nearly faints during a zombie hunt,[13] but also reminds Elizabeth that she must become a traditional wife if she accepts his proposal. This rare nonviolent deviation from Austen's text establishes Elizabeth as not just violent or sexualized but also unwilling to sacrifice her independence for the comfortable conformity of marriage.[14] In contrast, Hockensmith's work is a sequel, not an adaptation or appropriation; thus, he is freer to create a world that is more closely aligned with the young adult dystopian genre. Elizabeth's fear of childbirth is symbolized through imagining Jane's infant as a zombie sucking the life out of her,[15] and the climax involves imperial England stealing the lifeblood of brown foreigners to keep their monarchy alive.[16] While Grahame-Smith's text is dependent on adding shock values to Austen's original narrative, Hockensmith transforms Austen's canon into a young adult dystopia, critiquing how society restricts gender, class, and race.

Grahame-Smith's Zombification of Marriage

Grahame-Smith is unapologetic in his use of often-sexualized gore in his adaptation. Indeed, in his introduction to the hardcover edition of *Pride and Prejudice and Zombies*, he details how hyper-focused he was on placing violence into Austen's novel of manners,[17] implying the violent additions are solely for shock value to generate sales. However, his bombastic adaptation rewrites Elizabeth as a dystopian heroine in her own right. While he jokes about vomit and zombies in both the novel and the paratext, Grahame-Smith asks his readers to consider the zombies as a metaphor for marriage: "an endless curse that sucks the life out of you and won't die."[18] This linking of marriage to death is furthered in the narrative. The most obvious example is Charlotte Lucas: she is the one character who marries for comfort rather than love or passion, later dying a slow death.[19] Meanwhile, Elizabeth, a heroine who opposes such strict gender roles, kicks Darcy across the room after his first marriage proposal[20] and survives. Elizabeth assumes the young adult dystopian heroine's role of actively resisting unjust authority through her newfound violent nature.[21] While Grahame-Smith makes no attempts to pretend his adaptation was not a commercial endeavor, his presentation of society's obsession with making sure women are in respectable marriages in a world that has more pressing needs reflects Santaularia's assertion that young adult dystopian fiction serves as a way to analyze our own concerns about the world we live in.[22]

Yet I contend that it is through his masculinized adaptation that Grahame-Smith, intentionally or not, establishes Elizabeth as a young adult dystopian heroine. Soares[23] and Buchbinder note how Elizabeth is sexualized to appeal further to male readers. Their arguments are confirmed when Grahame-Smith revises the text to focus on Elizabeth lifting her skirt to kick Darcy when he disrespects her while proposing to her for the first time.[24] Additionally, Soares notes Elizabeth bests her male counterparts in both battle and sexuality with her newfound abilities as she "penetrates" and "consumes"[25] male opponents. The male gaze cannot be ignored, but Elizabeth's dynamic/sexualized body also Others her in a way that causes men to attempt to make her conform: once, when Mr. Collins (unsuccessfully) proposes, and again when Mr. Darcy eventually convinces her to become a traditionally feminine wife at the novel's end.

Sara K. Day's "Docile Bodies, Dangerous Bodies: Sexual Awakening and Social Resistance in Young Adult Dystopian Novels" proposes the following:

Western culture has largely taken to portray young women as simultaneously desirable and dangerous, presenting them as creatures whose sexuality must be controlled by implicit or explicit rules and regulations ... literary representations of adolescent womanhood have long been fraught with warnings that seek to restrict young women's explorations of their own physical agency and desire.[26]

Grahame-Smith incorporates the idea of the beautiful but deadly heroine. Elizabeth is not only desirable but also cruel, scolding her sisters for crying at the sight of their dead friends.[27] Thus, when Elizabeth is Othered into a sexual, dangerous young adult dystopian heroine, her resistance against marriage underscores the global concerns[28] that dystopian fiction reflects. While the Bennet sisters have an avenue of securing an independent life,[29] Mrs. Bennet still wants them to enter traditional marriages.[30] When Mr. Collins proposes to Elizabeth, he reminds her she will need to give up her role of hunter to become a proper wife.[31] Elizabeth refuses because her identity as a warrior is more important to her than marriage, keeping her agency in a world that seeks to curtail it.[32] Her aversion to marriage and romance is reflected in her relationship with her sisters as well, when she scolds Jane for letting her feelings for Mr. Bingley "soften the instincts bestowed by our Oriental masters."[33] Elizabeth views marriage, and the expected deference to masculine authority in marriage, as something that is detrimental to herself and her sisters. This revised Elizabeth is a heroine who actively rebels against marriage, and anything that would fall into traditionally feminine traits like tears and love, seeing independence as preferable to conforming to society's expectations.

Thus, it is perplexing that after multiple examples of how marriage erodes a woman's agency, Grahame-Smith would conclude his text with Elizabeth, Jane, and Lydia all retiring from zombie hunting after their respective marriages. Lanzendörfer argues that Grahame-Smith deliberately complicates the text with these marriages.[34] Instead of ending with the upper and middle classes of England intermingling, it ends with Elizabeth becoming a static wife rather than a zombie hunter.[35] Yet how and why Grahame-Smith seemingly abandons the young adult dystopian heroine in the conclusion intentionally problematizes the text. Day discusses how young adult heroines lose their subversive voice because of society's belief that heterosexuality is the default for young women.[36] When Elizabeth enters a heterosexual union, she gives up her sword without a word of protest, affirming Grahame-Smith's thesis that marriage is harmful for women. Grahame-Smith's sudden deference to Austen's ending is his final critique of how marriage limits women, as the heroine Elizabeth has to forsake the identity and independence she values to marry Darcy.

Hockensmith and the New England

Whereas Grahame-Smith adapts Austen's work to the point of appropriation,[37] Hockensmith writes an original text based off of both Austen's and Grahame-Smith's works. Thus, Hockensmith's approach in adapting Elizabeth Bennet as a young adult dystopian heroine is grounded in creating a bleak world that allows him to examine gender and racial concerns of the twentieth century.[38] While Grahame-Smith admits to simply inserting violence into the original text,[39] Hockensmith draws from Austen's cultural context, specifically Mary Wollstonecraft's plea for educating women in *A Vindication of the Rights of Women* (1792), which inspires Mary Bennet. While Grahame-Smith leaves Mary unaltered in his adaptation, Hockensmith refashions her into a young adult dystopian heroine alongside Elizabeth. While Elizabeth is famous for her brains and willingness to correct her mistakes, her sisters are often presented as foils to highlight Elizabeth's strengths. Mr. Bennet praises Elizabeth's quick wits at the novel's beginning, unlike her sisters, who are "silly and ignorant like other girls,"[40] making Elizabeth the Regency equivalent of "not like other girls." The elevation of Elizabeth over her sisters is most obvious with Mary Bennet, the sister who seeks mental improvement, but falls short: "'What say you, Mary? for you are a young lady of deep reflection I know, and read great books, and make extracts.' Mary wished to say something very sensible, but knew not how."[41] Of the Bennet sisters, Mary is the closest to being formally educated. But when she has a chance to prove herself, she has no voice. While Austen ridicules the impossible ideal for women, Elizabeth herself represents an ideal that not even the angelic Jane, and definitely not the cerebral Mary, can ever hope to reach.

However, Hockensmith's Mary Bennet exists in a world created to confront and critique how women are encouraged to forsake independence in favor of marriage, allowing her to become more active—and protective of her new agency—following the young adult dystopian heroine formula. Even as a veteran zombie hunter, Elizabeth is too lively to advocate for the more philosophical Wollstonecraft, but Mary's intellectual nature is ideal for introducing Wollstonecraft's proto feminism to twenty-first-century readers. When Mary scolds Kitty for her frivolity, she argues that Wollstonecraft understands the human condition better than any of Kitty's "wretched novels."[42] Mary is the most esoteric Bennet sister, and the one least likely to marry—indeed, *Pride and Prejudice* ends with Mary living with her mother rather than a husband.[43] But Mary's "little shake"[44] of Wollstonecraft's text at Kitty frames the scene as more than Mary burying her nose in a book to appear smart: she applies her knowledge to critique the society that pressurizes her to conform to a strictly gendered marriage. Lanzendörfer notes that unlike the previous texts, Mary openly discusses women's roles in their society.[45] Additionally, Megan McDonough and Katherine A. Wagner observe that Mary's protest reflects a trend in young adult fiction where the heroine asserts her agency based on "her unique personality."[46] Indeed, Mary's severe nature sets her apart from her sisters in all versions of Austen's text. Adapting Mary into a Wollstonecraft-inspired proto-feminist not only emphasizes her individuality[47] but also allows Hockensmith to interrogate gendered assumptions for women that exist even today.

Mary's adventures as an intellectual zombie hunter illustrate for modern readers how intellectual women were seen in Austen's lifetime. When Mary asks for a copy of *A Vindication of the Rights of Woman*, the shopkeeper responds, "But wouldn't the lady prefer a nice frothy novel, instead?"[48] In response to the passively sexist shopkeeper,

Mary counters that she is buying the text so the shopkeeper can "give it to the next young lady looking for a nice frothy novel,"[49] demonstrating a desire to help other women empower themselves through reading. Her actions still reflect the holier-than-thou Mary in *Pride and Prejudice*: she sees her opinion as best. But she now seeks to undo the damage of the strictly gendered world she lives in through resistance. Hockensmith's Mary is a girl who stands apart intellectually from her peers and her family, and she asserts her own independence and individuality to help other women gain agency, demonstrating the heroic desire for independence despite society's disapproval.

Hockensmith does not erase Mary's priggish nature, emphasizing how Mary does not fit into mainstream society, though she still wishes to better the world she lives in. Mary admits that unlike her more active sisters, her "specialty … was noting the errors of others."[50] Because of her exposure to Wollstonecraft's treatise, Mary becomes a more realized character. Lanzendörfer notes that Mary's rebellion, inspired by Wollstonecraft, succeeds while Elizabeth's more traditional plan of working within high society to find the cure for Darcy implodes.[51] However, Lanzendörfer fails to note how Mary's vulnerabilities also subvert the young adult dystopian heroine's expected role. As McDonough and Wagner explain, the dystopian novel often relies on "gender binaries,"[52] in this case female emotion versus male logic. As a logical woman, Mary is even accused by her own father of being too masculine. When Kitty describes Mr. Darcy as "a male Mary," Mr. Bennet replies, "Mary's like a male Mary."[53] The twenty-first century ostensibly embraces independent women, so another Elizabeth Bennet-styled heroine does little to examine how women are shunned for nonconformity. Thus, he turns to Mary, who is still an outsider because of her intellectual nature, and her refusal to hide her abilities and discernment. This earns her scorn from her society and even her father, but it does not deter Mary from becoming instrumental in saving Darcy, and eventually England, from zombification. Hockensmith fully cements Mary as a young adult dystopian heroine when she decides to act to better her world not through feeling ashamed by her family's comments or the shopkeeper's reaction to her purchase of *A Vindication of the Rights of Woman*, but due to her own realization that if she wants to help herself become genuinely independent, she must seize her own agency. Hockensmith completes his transformation of Mary Bennet into a young adult dystopian heroine when Mary informs Elizabeth that she will actively seek positive change, something which Lanzendörfer argues leads to her asserting her own agency despite how her family and her society see her.[54] The difference in Grahame-Smith's and Hockensmith's values concerning the young adult dystopian genre is most apparent in Mary's growth. Since Mary is not a character who lends herself to gore or shock value, Grahame-Smith invests little time in her. Hockensmith, however, moves her to the foreground, thus creating a dystopia where more than one heroine can exist.

While the unmarried Mary's outsider status allows her to enjoy adventures as a young adult dystopian heroine, her elder sister, Elizabeth Bennet, ends her career as a zombie slayer in order to become Mrs. Fitzwilliam Darcy. As such, she must endure verbal abuse from those in Derbyshire who cannot accept a woman who not only once slayed zombies on a regular basis but also dared to marry above her class.[55]

The aristocratic disdain for the active woman—even if she conforms—remains. The difference lies in how the authors contextualize the aforementioned disdain. After Darcy is bitten by a zombie, Darcy's doctor is rude to Elizabeth.[56] Hockensmith uses the violent descriptions associated with horror fiction to his advantage. While Elizabeth has no choice as a wife but to defer to societal pressure, she wishes to "bend the mulish old fool"[57] for his rudeness. Hockensmith uses the violent descriptions associated with horror fiction to his advantage. The revenge fantasy is as violent as one would expect from a zombie novel, but the conflict Elizabeth faces is real: the only socially proper choice, of course, is to please the doctor until he agrees to keep the zombie attack on Darcy—and the bite he suffers—a secret. Elizabeth forsakes her agency through marriage. Whereas marriage empowers Austen's Elizabeth, contemporary audiences live in a world where this idea of proper wifehood has been critiqued; Hockensmith does the same in his text, showing a formerly independent Elizabeth under strain when conforming to her wifely role.

Elizabeth's sexual conflicts concerning her marriage are another part in Hockensmith's attempt to return her to the young adult dystopian heroine role, even after her marriage. While Jane and Lydia are sidelined as mothers, Elizabeth's aversion to childbirth sets her apart sexually from the more traditional Jane. Indeed, in contrast to *Pride and Prejudice* and *Pride and Prejudice and Zombies*, *Dreadfully Ever After* begins with Elizabeth as a married woman, one aware of the societal expectations to have a child. The conflict between killing zombies and motherhood is introduced early in the novel, as Elizabeth and Darcy visit Jane and Charles Bingley. Jane is absent from the text, leaving Bingley to tell his child that mothers do not fight zombies because it is not part of their narrow identity: "Mumsy is mumsy."[58] After Jane forsakes her warrior identity to become a mother, it becomes the focal point of her existence and negates her previous identity of a warrior—the few mentions of Jane in the text are about her children or her state of pregnancy—she does not speak to Elizabeth at all in the text. Hockensmith illustrates how society places wives and mothers—even the few that have the skill to combat the zombie menace in England—strictly in the domestic sphere, a pressure that Elizabeth is beginning to feel herself.

Darcy assumes that Elizabeth is upset because she is not yet a mother.[59] Darcy plays the role of the devoted husband. Indeed, his concern for Elizabeth, along with the long walks that Darcy and Elizabeth are mentioned sharing, can be seen as the happy ending to the walking scene in *Pride and Prejudice*, when Elizabeth, frustrated with Darcy's snobbish ways, leaves him behind.[60] Though Hockensmith critiques marriage, *Dreadfully Ever After*'s Elizabeth and Darcy's marriage is as equal as it can be in their time. However, Darcy also assumes that Elizabeth wants to be a mother, something that is so ingrained in society that Elizabeth is ashamed to discuss her feelings on the matter. She explains that rather than feeling maternal anticipation when she visits Jane Bingley, she equates the baby to a zombie "sucking life from the living."[61] Hockensmith uses the violent language associated with masculine texts to highlight a major concern, especially in Austen's lifetime: Elizabeth is aware of the high mortality rate for mothers, and while it may not be the same as dying in combat, it is a bloody death nonetheless. Her disdain for the societal ideal of marriage is so strong that she equates the act of breastfeeding as equivalent with the infant cannibalizing the mother. She is also aware of how repugnant her stance is to conservative England; even though Darcy is her soul mate, she still prepares herself as if for battle, showing that women who exist outside the sphere of pleasing wife are in battle with conservative values. Hockensmith turns the expectations for violent imagery around in this passage. The zombies and violence are part of Hockensmith's narrative. Unlike Grahame-Smith, however, Hockensmith uses these elements to explore the very real fear of childbirth and loss of agency in becoming a traditional mother. Again, Hockensmith is using violence not to attract male readers, but employs the gruesome environment to emphasize his heroine's grievances with her narrow social role as a wife.

With Mary and, eventually, Elizabeth fulfilling the role of the unique, resisting heroine who seeks to change her dystopian society for the better, including Kitty Bennet in his work seems like an odd choice. After all, in both the original text and Grahame-Smith's mash-up, Kitty is a peripheral character at best. Yet *Dreadfully Every After* begins at a point when Elizabeth has reached *Pride and Prejudice*'s narrative conclusion: marriage to Darcy. While Hockensmith presumably could not move assumed protagonist Elizabeth to the background like he does with the now married Jane and Lydia, he does use this revision as an opportunity to focus on Kitty Bennet. Kitty's narrative arc begins similarly to the preceding versions in Austen and Grahame-Smith's respective texts. Indeed, one of Kitty's first thoughts involves her wishing that her "warrior's clothes"[62] were more fashionable. Her thoughts become more nuanced as she continues to assist Elizabeth and Mr. Bennet in seeking a cure for Darcy's condition. Indeed, Kitty becomes upset when her father implies that she is ignorant.[63] Whereas in Austen's original text (and Grahame-Smith's zombification of the original text), Kitty's involvement in the narrative would end after her emotional display—the best example is when she breaks down when Mr. Bennet threatens to never let her attend balls again[64]—in Hockensmith's sequel Kitty is upset with her family's expectations that she will never grow past her silliness. Now that Elizabeth can no longer assume the role of the young adult dystopian heroine due to her marriage, Hockensmith positions Kitty into that role as the character who struggles with how she is seen in society and her own desires. She grows to resent the narrowness of her current role and seeks to find her own sense of independence in a world that wants her to eventually enter a strict role defined by her gender, confirming the defining quality for young adult dystopian heroines: rejecting mainstream beliefs to further her own independence.

Kitty's willingness to break away and better the dystopia she lives in is manifested in her relationship with Nezu, a ninja in Lady Catherine's employ who plans to kill Elizabeth to avenge his father's death. In many ways, Nezu (and Hockensmith's writing for the ninjas and servants in general) invests with agency Grahame-Smith's problematic creation of faceless minions for Lady Catherine. Before, the servants and ninjas were there to create a higher body count. While there are still many deaths in Hockensmith's sequel, he sincerely attempts to humanize the Japanese servants in Lady Catherine's employ. While preparing to kill the Bennets, a few ninjas have a conversation with Nezu, including Momoko, who complains about Kitty's obnoxiousness.[65] This is a brief scene, but they are named and have some personality—a far cry from *Pride and*

Prejudice and Zombies. While all of these characters, save for Nezu, suffer the grisly fate one might expect from a franchise titled *Pride and Prejudice and Zombies*, they demonstrate some personality and frustration with their positions, becoming more developed as Hockensmith rewrites Grahame-Smith's work as a crushing critique of heterosexual marriage and its oppression of women.

Nezu has no qualms with critiquing Kitty's behavior. Eventually, he realizes that despite the aspects of Kitty's character he finds grating, he loves her for her vitality.[66] However, there are conflicts between their families: It is revealed that one of the many ninjas Elizabeth killed in *Pride and Prejudice and Zombies* when Lady Catherine attacked her was Nezu's father—and he has sworn vengeance against Elizabeth as a result.[67] While Nezu and Kitty do not marry in the text, it is clear that they are on their way. The parallels between the Elizabeth and Darcy of *Pride and Prejudice* are apparent, but there are complications here as well. Hockensmith acknowledges the racial tensions when Kitty notes that she "was English; [Nezu] was Other."[68] Kitty is the white heroine synonymous with dystopian fiction, while the Japanese servant, Nezu, is a character rarely seen in the genre. The inclusion of Nezu is particularly noteworthy because, as Mary J. Couzelis explains, young adult fiction often avoids "the complexity of racial identity."[69] However, the resolution and Nezu's redemption are brief at best.

Hockensmith follows roughly the same formula for Elizabeth's role in bettering the world, as Elizabeth rescues and adopts the Indian children on whom and on their deceased parents Dr. Sir Angus MacFarquar, the king's personal physician, has conducted ghastly experiments.[70] Once again, Hockensmith's dystopia incorporates both gore and the more subtle hideousness of Austen's England. Jane Austen's unfinished novel, *Sanditon*, introduces Miss Lambe, a heiress that Sarah Salih describes as Austen's "only 'brown' character,"[71] who clearly influenced Hockensmith's exploration of race in his *Dreadfully Ever After*. Though she is not white, Miss Lambe is a wealthy heiress who, as Salih notes, has an extraordinary amount of freedom in her lifetime.[72] Austen meant for her to be one of the most financially powerful characters in the book, but as the white denizens of Sanditon plot and plan how to use her resources for their own means, it becomes clear that while they want the resources the brown woman can provide them, they have no interest in her humanity.

Hockensmith addresses Austen's treatment of race in his novel, proposing a solution to England's exploitation of brown children through the relationship between Gurdaya and Elizabeth. While attempting to find a cure for Darcy, Elizabeth learns that the English nobility has kidnapped and performed grisly experiments on people of color in order to develop a serum that slows the zombie virus—a cure intended only for wealthy nobles.[73] Even readers with only peripheral knowledge of Regency England can understand the parallels between imperial England oppressing the nations these young people come from for material gain and zombie-ridden England literally stealing the lifeblood from these same people to slow the zombie virus. Unlike the more bombastic violence seen in this franchise, the victims' youth and pitiable state are meant to draw sympathy from the reader, as well as anger at the society that would hurt children to maintain the power of old white men—King George III has been infected, and his "madness" has been abated enough for him to resume his duties as king, thanks to the serum. What Austen implies in *Sanditon*—that England sees people of color as commodities rather than humans—reaches its grim conclusion in *Dreadfully Ever After*.

The "Miss Lambe" of Hockensmith's text is the Indian orphan Gurdaya. Like Miss Lambe, Gurdaya is a brown character dehumanized by English society, but unlike Miss Lambe she actually appears in the text, and readers learn the specifics of her torture in fine detail. The solution Hockensmith proposes to this problem allows Elizabeth to remove power from the patriarchy and even exhibit maternal characteristics, thus redefining the role of wife and mother. She inspects the orphaned Gurdaya's wounds: her arms are covered in scars inflicted by her captors in attempts to find a cure for the zombie virus.[74] Elizabeth's horrified reaction to the violence, relatively minor compared to the other acts in the text, is the maternal instinct that she could not feel about Jane's children. Elizabeth's desire to rescue and protect Gurdaya allows Elizabeth to fulfill the maternal role on her terms, remaining active as a zombie fighter and helping others who have been hurt because of English imperialism.

Hockensmith's ideas are apparent in Gurdaya's rescue: Elizabeth ends Regency imperialism not just through hyper-violence but by finding motherhood on her own terms as well. However, this twist problematizes Hockensmith's attempts to create a more inclusive England. The celebration of a white woman (Elizabeth) saving a brown girl (Gurdaya) is not a new scenario in Western cultures. Twentieth- and twenty-first-century scholars have noted how people of color are often used to empower white women in media, rather than media addressing people of color's concerns.[75] Hockensmith fails to subvert this problem, making Gurdaya's peril the catalyst for Elizabeth's growth. Gurdaya's presence allows Elizabeth to express compassion, and even motherly feelings, with none of her fears of pregnancy and death in childbirth. However, Gurdaya is suspiciously silent through the majority of her appearances in *Dreadfully Ever After*. She states her name and how long she has been a prisoner,[76] but the narrative quickly shifts to Elizabeth's rediscovered heroism. Some readers may argue that this passage is similar to how Miss Lambe is framed in *Sanditon*—however, her presumed exploitation of the Sanditon citizens is framed as negative, while Gurdaya's silent suffering is meant to ennoble the white Elizabeth Bennet.

While Hockensmith's attempts to create a racially inclusive variation of Austen's canon are flawed, his novel concludes with a finale that is meant only to create an inclusive sphere. Grahame-Smith never examines the racial conflicts introduced in *Pride and Prejudice and Zombies*, and Austen could only allude to the tensions in her own lifetime in *Sanditon*. Hockensmith directly addresses the concerns not through a physical battle but during Mr. and Mrs. Bennet's argument as their surrogate grandchildren—the Indian children Elizabeth rescued—are playing. The old-fashioned Mrs. Bennet has trouble reconciling her view of England with the idea of Elizabeth fighting zombies while married[77] and Kitty's relationship with ninja Nezu.[78] Mrs. Bennet struggles to understand that life in England—both culturally and personally—is becoming less white. She herself muses that she is still adjusting to her surrogate grandchildren being "[s]o brown."[79] Mr. Bennet gently corrects his wife, informing her that the children are not only foreigners but also English.[80] Though flawed, Hockensmith's conclusion ultimately demonstrates his proposed solution to a decaying society: inclusion and diversity over the stagnant Regency, led by warriors that accept everyone, regardless of race or gender. Thus, the young adult dystopian heroines help to forge a better world by not forsaking their independence to follow strict gender roles, creating a fuller message than Grahame-Smith's "zombie attack" on marriage.

Ultimately, Hockensmith proposes that a dying England will find new life not in strict gender roles or by sustaining the nobility at the cost of people of color, but rather in becoming a country that recognizes strength in diversity, and that even characters as obtuse as Mrs. Bennet will eventually see that as well.[81] The parallels to *Pride and Prejudice* are apparent, but the inclusion of two Indian grandchildren and a daughter who slays zombies as an equal with her spouse stresses that England is becoming more inclusive for both race and gender.

Conclusion

Grahame-Smith and Hockensmith reimagine *Pride and Prejudice* as a young adult dystopian novel—and rewrite Elizabeth (and Kitty) as synonymous with that genre—with different goals in mind. Grahame-Smith shocks and horrifies, emphasizing the horrors of women's loss of power through marriage. Whereas Grahame-Smith seeks to subvert Austen through appropriation,[82] Hockensmith draws upon Austen's world, and the gendered and racial tensions. The execution is imperfect: Even as Hockensmith tries to create a more racially diverse world for the dystopian heroine, Gurdaya and Nezu serve as foils for the white Elizabeth and Kitty. At the same time, Hockensmith's conclusion featuring warrior wives, Indian children playing in the English countryside, and at least two interracial relationships[83] is presented as a pathway to happiness. Hockensmith reimagines the zombie/classical literature mash-up, creating a text as subversive as Austen's *Pride and Prejudice* was when it was first written.

Notes

1 Soares, "Morbid Curiosity and Monstrous (Re)Visions," 430.
2 Lanzendörfer, "So Many Unmentionables about," 93.
3 Buchbinder, "From 'Wizard' to 'Wicked,'" 134.
4 Santaularia, "Typescript of the Second Origin," 2.
5 Lanzendörfer, "So Many Unmentionables," 110.
6 Santaularia, "Typescript of the Second Origin," 1.
7 Ibid.
8 Green-Barteet. "I'm Beginning to Know Who I Am," 35.
9 Buchbinder, "Adaptation Theory," 128.
10 Ibid., 133.
11 Ibid.
12 Soares, "Morbid Curiosity and Monstrous (Re)Visions," 430.

13 Austen and Grahame-Smith. *Pride and Prejudice and Zombies*, 57. (Hereafter, *PPZ*.)
14 Ibid., 85.
15 Hockensmith, *Dreadfully Ever After*, 14. (Hereafter, *DEA*.)
16 Hockensmith, *DEA*, 297.
17 Grahame-Smith, Introduction to *Pride and Prejudice and Zombies: The Deluxe Heirloom Edition*, 9.
18 Austen and Grahame-Smith, *PPZ*, 319.
19 Ibid., 237.
20 Ibid., 151.
21 Lanzendörfer, "So Many Unmentionables," 98.
22 Santaularia, "Prefiguring the Female Hero," 4.
23 Soares, "Morbid Curiosity and Monstrous (Re)Visions," 433; Buchbinder, "So Many Unmentionables," 133.
24 Austen and Grahame-Smith, *PPZ*, 115.
25 Soares, "Morbid Curiosity and Monstrous (Re)Visions," 435.
26 Day, "Docile Bodies, Dangerous Bodies," 75.
27 Austen and Grahame-Smith, *PPZ*, 58.
28 Santaularia, "Prefiguring the Female Hero," 1.
29 Lanzendörfer, "So Many Unmentionables," 99.
30 Austen and Grahame-Smith, *PPZ*, 9.
31 Lanzendörfer, "So Many Unmentionables," 101.
32 Austen and Grahame-Smith, *PPZ*, 85.
33 Ibid., 95.
34 Lanzendörfer, "So Many Unmentionables," 103.
35 Austen and Grahame-Smith, *PPZ*, 102.
36 Day, "Docile Bodies," 76.
37 Buchbinder, "Adaptation Theory," 134.
38 Santaularia, "Prefiguring the Female Hero," 1.
39 Austen and Grahame-Smith, *PPZ*, 9.
40 Austen, *Pride and Prejudice*, 9. (Hereafter, P&P.)
41 Austen, *P&P*, 9.
42 Hockensmith, *DEA*, 41.
43 Austen, *P&P*, 326.
44 Hockensmith, *DEA*, 41.
45 Lanzendörfer, "So Many Unmentionables," 103.
46 McDonough and Wagner, "Rebellious Natures," 165.
47 Hockensmith, *DEA*, 165.
48 Ibid., 124.
49 Ibid.
50 Ibid., 135.
51 Lanzendörfer, "So Many Unmentionables," 104.
52 McDonough and Wagner, "Rebellious Natures," 167.
53 Hockensmith, *DEA*, 158.
54 Lanzendörfer, "So Many Unmentionables," 103.
55 Hockensmith, *DEA*, 21.
56 Ibid.
57 Ibid., 22.
58 Ibid, 11.

59 Ibid., *DEA*, 13.
60 Austen, *P&P*, 39–40.
61 Hockensmith, *DEA*, 13.
62 Ibid., 50.
63 Ibid., 55.
64 Austen, *P&P*, 255.
65 Hockensmith, *DEA*, 264.
66 Ibid., 213.
67 Ibid., 263.
68 Ibid., 208.
69 Couzelis, "The Future is Pale," 14.1.
70 Hockensmith, *DEA*, 256.
71 Salih, "The Silence of Miss Lambe," 330.
72 Ibid., 350.
73 Hockensmith, *DEA*, 257.
74 Ibid., 258.
75 Couzelis, "The Future is Pale," 131.
76 Hockensmith, *DEA*, 257–8.
77 Ibid., 283.
78 Ibid.
79 Ibid., 284.
80 Ibid., 285.
81 Ibid., 286–7.
82 Buchbinder, "Adaptation Theory," 134.
83 Kitty and Nezu are the major interracial pairing in the text, but Mrs. Bennet notes that Georgiana Darcy has become romantically involved with a ninja (Hockensmith, *DEA*, 283–4).

Bibliography

Austen, Jane. *Pride and Prejudice*. London: Pearson Education, [1813] 2003.
Austen, Jane, and Seth Grahame-Smith. *Pride and Prejudice and Zombies*. Philadelphia: Quirk Books, 2009.
Buchbinder, David. "From 'Wizard' to 'Wicked': Adaptation Theory and Young Adult Fiction." In *Contemporary Children's Literature and Film: Engaging with Theory*, edited by Kerry Mallan and Claire Bradford, 127–46. New York: Palgrave Macmillan, 2011.
Couzelis, Mary. "The Future Is Pale: Race in Contemporary Young Adult Dystopian Novels." In *Contemporary Dystopian Fiction for Young Adults*, edited by Balaka Basu, Katherine R. Broad, and Carrie Hintz, 131–44. London: Routledge, 2013.
Day, Sara K. "Docile Bodies, Dangerous Bodies: Sexual Awakening and Social Resistance in Young Adult Dystopian Novels." In *Female Rebellion in Young Adult Dystopian Fiction*, edited by Sara K. Day, Miranda A. Green-Barteet, and Amy L. Montz, 75–92. London: Routledge, 2014.
Grahame-Smith, Seth. Introduction to *Pride and Prejudice and Zombies: The Deluxe Heirloom Edition*, by Jane Austen and Seth Grahame-Smith, 9–11. Philadelphia: Quirk Books, 2009.

Green-Barteet, Miranda A. "'I'm Beginning to Know Who I Am': The Rebellious Subjectivities of Katniss Everdeen and Tris Prior." In *Female Rebellion in Young Adult Dystopian Fiction*, edited by Sara K. Day, Miranda A. Green-Barteet, and Amy L. Montz, 34–49. London: Routledge, 2014.

Hockensmith, Steve. *Dreadfully Ever After*. Philadelphia: Quirk Books, 2011.

Lanzendörfer, Tim. "'So Many Unmentionables about': Parody, *Pride and Prejudice and Zombies*, and the Politics of Mash-up Fiction.'" In *Books of the Dead: Reading the Zombie in Contemporary Literature*, edited by Tim Lanzendörfer, 92–125. Jackson: University of Mississippi Press, 2018.

McDonough, Mary, and Katherine Wagner. "Rebellious Natures: The Role of Nature in Young Adult Dystopian Female Protagonists' Awakenings and Agency." In *Female Rebellion in Young Adult Dystopian Fiction*, edited by Sara K. Day, Miranda Green-Barteet, and Amy L. Montz, 157–70. London: Routledge, 2014.

Salih, Sara. "The Silence of Miss Lambe: Sanditon and Fictions of 'Race' in the Abolition Era." *Eighteenth-Century Fiction* 18, no. 3 (Spring 2006): 1–25. Accessed December 20, 2018. doi: 10.1353/ecf.2006.0049.

Santaularia, Isabel. "'Typescript of the Second Origin' and Current YA Dystopian and Post- Apocalypse Fiction in English: Prefiguring the Female Hero." *Alambique: Revista Académica de Ciencia Ficción y Fantasia / Jornal Acadêmico de Ficção Científica e Fantasía* (2017). Accessed September 1, 2019. doi: 10.5038/2167-6577.4.2.5.

Soares, Rebecca "Morbid Curiosity and Monstrous (Re)Visions: Zombies, Sea Monsters, and Readers (Re)Writing Jane Austen." *Women's Writing* 25, no. 4 (November 2018): 429–42. Accessed January 1, 2019. doi: 10.1080/09699082.2018.1510078.

9

A Twist in Time or a Break in Narrative: Adapting the Disney Classic Canon for a Young Adult Audience

Michelle Anya Anjirbag and Madeleine Hunter

In 2017, Penguin Random House published *Phasma*, a tie-in novel written by Delilah S. Dawson that explores the history of Captain Phasma, an original character introduced in Disney's *The Force Awakens* (2017). That same year, licensed books accounted for twelve percent of all book sales and twenty-eight percent of all children's book sales, with book industry analysts declaring licensed publishing "one of the hottest areas in publishing to watch."[1] As publishers continue to announce lists of best-selling and critically acclaimed authors, including Jason Reynolds, Leigh Bardugo, Marie Lu, Sarah J. Maas, Matt de la Peña, Mackenzi Lee, and N. K. Jemisin, who have been signed to write tie-in novels for young adult audiences, it appears that tie-in novels no longer occupy "the very lowest rung on the literary ladder."[2] What happened to precipitate this transformation of one of the most maligned products in the publishing industry? This chapter focuses on one specific manifestation of the current boom in licensed publishing—The Walt Disney Company's *Twisted Tales* novels (2015–present)—in order to explore one of adaptation studies' most neglected forms, as well as the way understandings of adolescence function within and inform the contemporary adaptation industry.[3]

Narrative Novelties

Books that emerge as a product of licensed publishing are best approached through the lens of novelization, defined as "novels based on previous and normally 'original' filmic texts."[4] Novelizations as understood today rose alongside the "New Hollywood" blockbuster in the late 1960s.[5] Most offer prose reworkings of filmic narratives written by ghostwriters. The innately commercial nature of a novelization's production conflicts with "idealized notion[s] of literature according to which a work of art is only a work of art if the motivation for creating it comes from the author himself or herself"[6] and are often cast as "mere accessories" and "worthless by-products"[7] of the contemporary culture industry's pursuit of profit. These texts, however, have much to offer adaptation scholars, particularly those interested in how adaptation functions within contemporary media ecologies. Novelizations are a form of tie-in merchandise: commodities that are produced for the purpose of generating additional income and increasing the brand recognition of a larger media franchise in the process. If we avoid the inclination to view these media products as a result of "crass commercialism"[8] and instead approach them as products of "an economic as well as semiotic and aesthetic mode of adaptation,"[9] we can learn much about the fundamental oscillation between familiarity and novelty that defines adaptation and its pleasures.

As described by Linda Hutcheon, "adaptation is repetition, but repetition without replication"[10] that emerges from "a creative and an interpretive act of appropriation/salvaging,"[11] through which a text is transposed from one media object into a new, different media object. Adaptation studies' early focus on fidelity has obscured the role that difference plays in defining adaptation's ontology. The very status of a text as an adaptation is a license for divergence; the specific pleasure of "experiencing adaptations *as adaptations*" lies in tracing these divergences.[12] Thus, Elliott argues, "tie-in merchandise must be unfaithful in order to flow across the widest possible range of platforms and attract the greatest possible number of consumers."[13]

This need for content differentiation has driven the diversification of the licensed publishing market and its outputs, with franchises looking to move beyond straightforward models of novelization. The *Star Wars* and *Star Trek* franchises, for example, began experimenting in the 1970s with what Baetens describes as "'continuative' novelizations—novelizations that, rather than trying to reproduce the content and the flavour of a movie, reuse its characters and fictional universe in order to multiply and broaden its content matter."[14] Now an established and proliferate form of tie-in merchandise—particularly for television series—continuative novelizations act as what Henry Jenkins terms "extensions."[15] Extensions are best conceptualized as the "optional" elements of a transmedia story. They add to audience enjoyment, expanding the narratives of the texts from which they are adapted by extending the timeline over which the narrative takes place, exploring character backgrounds and motivations, and/or developing and expanding the fictional world of the original narrative. They are not, therefore, essential for understanding other entries within the larger story, especially those that form the core of the franchise. An audience member who does engage with these extension media, however, is rewarded with the pleasures that accompany their newly expanded insight into the story and its world. This viewer becomes able to spot references and allusions, make connections between narrative events, and discern new meanings concomitantly implied to be "hidden" from the average viewer. It is for this reason that Thomas Van Parys argues that extension media performs a "mythologizing" function.[16] Their differentiations only have meaning if apprehended in relation to the text from which they are adapted, thus encouraging a return to the newly reified original.

In this light, our case study is faced with a categorization problem. This discussion is framed in terms of novelization, but Disney's *Twisted Tales* cannot technically be classified as novelizations. As of 2019, the series consists of nine novels by three authors, with each book retelling the narrative of a classic Disney animated feature with a narrative twist. The first novel in the series, *A Whole New World* (2015) by Liz Braswell, offers a retelling of the narrative of Disney's *Aladdin* (1992) in which the sorcerer Jafar succeeds in his plan to use Aladdin to acquire the magic lamp. The *Twisted Tales* are not Braswell's first time working with the Walt Disney Company. Her *The Nine Lives of Chloe King* series (2004–2005) was adapted into a television series of the same name by the Disney–ABC Television Group channel ABC Family in 2011. To date, Braswell has authored four other *Twisted Tales*. *Once Upon a Dream* (2016) presents a version of *Sleeping Beauty* (1959) where the prince's kiss fails to wake Aurora. In *As Old as Time* (2016), the otherwise absent figure of Belle's mother is cast as the Enchantress responsible for the Beast's curse in a reimagining of *Beauty and the Beast* (1991). *Part of Your World* (2019) asks the reader to imagine a version of *The Little Mermaid* (1989) where the film's climactic battle is won by the sea witch, Ursula. Additionally, Braswell will write *Straight on Till Morning* (2020), a reimagining of *Peter Pan* (1953). *Reflection* (2018), an adaptation of *Mulan* (1998), is authored by up-and-coming fantasist Elizabeth Lim, who will also write the forthcoming *So This Is Love* (2020)—an adaptation of *Cinderella* (1950) where Cinderella never tries on the slipper. *Reflection* sends Mulan on an Orpheus-like quest to the underworld to save Captain Li Shang after he suffers a fatal injury from a blow that in the film is intended for her. *Mirror, Mirror* (2019) and *Let It Go* (also titled, *Conceal, Don't Feel*) (2019) are by Jen Calonita, an experienced middle-grade and young adult author best known for the *Fairy Tale Reform School* series (2016–19). In *Mirror, Mirror*, it is the prince rather than Snow White who succumbs to an enchanted sleep, while *Let It Go* asks readers to imagine a version of *Frozen* where Anna and Elsa were raised apart from each other as children.

These narrative twists not only disqualify these novels from being regarded as straight novelizations but also disqualify them from being classified as extensions. For a text to be an extension of another text, it must "operate in a shared world."[17] The *Twisted Tales* narratives exist in a continuity that is explicitly presented as divergent from that of the animated films they adapt; they cannot extend the story because they are not part of it. In order to describe the precise nature of the mythologizing that these texts perform, we repurpose Clare Parody's concept of the "multitext." While Parody employs the term to describe the sum total of the "vast quantities of interlinked media products and merchandise"[18] on which a franchise is built, we suggest that the term "multitext" might be better employed to describe the deliberately multiple texts that emerge from contemporary practices of media franchising. In a multitext, iterations exist laterally rather than vertiginously; their disparate continuities do not exist to replace or overwrite one another, because their multiplicity is integral to their hermeneutic identity. By presenting an "alternate universe" retelling of the texts that they adapt, the *Twisted Tales* novels participate in the construction of a multitext, their deliberate construction of difference reaffirming the "classic" status of the Disney animated films they retell.

The current licensed publishing boom is most dynamic in young adult fiction, and this is part of what makes Disney's intervention into the form so interesting. It should surprise no one to learn that The Walt Disney Company—one of the world's largest transnational media conglomerates and largest producer of children's and family media—has a pioneering history when it comes to tie-in merchandise.[19] The company prides itself on "its legacy of creating world-class stories and experiences for every member of the family."[20] Of course, this vision of the family has very much been comprised of parents with young children. How does one incorporate—or, "tie-in"— the adolescent to the Disney brand?

Narratives for Novices

The Walt Disney Company has long sought to construct its animated features as children's classics. Prior to the possibility of home release, Walt Disney Studios periodically rereleased its films in cinemas, not only allowing audiences to see them again but also ensuring that viewing experience became common to multiple generations of children. Disney thus constructed its films as "cherished legacies from previous generations and gifts of love to the next"[21]—a defining characteristic of children's classics. In the twenty-first-century era of cross-media ownership and conglomeration, however, the dispersion of content across multiple media platforms is not only desirable but also imperative, and so the Walt Disney Company has moved away from a strategy focused on intergenerational transmission to one that focuses on maintaining relevance over the course of the individual's lifespan. Disney's foray into the world of young adult publishing via Disney Publishing Worldwide forms part of this pursuit of the lifelong consumer.

The young adult publishing market has expanded exponentially as we enter the second decade of the boom that began with the appearance of a certain British boy wizard in 1998, and which was aged up with the help of some sparkly vampires.[22] When tracking an industrial history of the form, one finds that different subgenres move in and out of ascendency—in 2019, dystopia is dead and vampires are out; feminism, activism, and rom-coms are in[23]—endowing the category with a reputation for mutability. Young adult literature is a literature of change, an understanding tied to understandings of adolescence and the adolescent as constituting a liminal state,[24] the space between, "a period when individuals are neither institutionalized as children nor accepted into adult roles and society fully ... also conceptualized as a series of rites of passage."[25] In young adult fiction, this process of personal transformation is often projected outward, with many works of young adult literature constructing a "powerful metaphoric connection between a troubled inner life and the injustices and cruelties of wider society."[26] Roberta Seelinger Trites asserts that it is "the very determined way that young adult novels tend to interrogate social constructions, foregrounding the relationship between the society and the individual"[27] that constitutes the defining characteristic of literature for adolescent readers. For Trites, this interrogation is largely performative, a tool of institutional regulation through which readers learn to reconcile themselves to existing structures of power and oppression. However, others argue for young adult literature as a literature of "breaking away and becoming,"[28] a literature in which adolescents are represented and mobilized as agents of social change and transformation. This contradiction underpins Disney's *Twisted Tales*, which engage the idea of the adolescent as a site of transformative energy that licenses the creation of new commodities, thus incorporating the adolescent into the Disney brand.

The ties between Disney animated films and literary traditions are long-established via Disney's use of the storybook as a framing device in its early animated films. The *Twisted Tales* series sees Disney step away from this more established story-telling tradition and instead assert its own story-telling legacy. The ever-changing, liminal nature of the market and readership has made young adult publishing a niche in which media companies like Disney can experiment with multitextuality. The *Twisted Tales* seize upon medial difference as a license for narrative difference, distinct from the adapted animated classics. As texts addressed to a young adult audience, the overt and explicit act of divergence upon which the *Twisted Tales* novels are predicated reaffirms a narrative of disjunction between childhood and adolescence as temporally situated categories. How the *Twisted Tales* perform this disjunction will be the focus of the remainder of this chapter.

From Ur-stories to Your-stories

To experience an adaptation as an adaptation is to engage in what Catherine Grant describes as an act of recall. Building on the work of scholars such as John Ellis,[29] Grant suggests that the most important act that adaptations "need to perform in order to communicate unequivocally their status as adaptation is to (make their audiences) *recall* the adapted work, or the cultural memory of it."[30] Engagement in the performance of recall afforded by an adaptation as product requires partaking in what Hutcheon describes as "a conceptual flipping back and forth between the work we know and the work we are experiencing,"[31] an oscillation between past and present that takes on a particular resonance in the case of adaptations that transpose their adapted text across age categories. Because the experience of recall is a temporally situated phenomena, the flipping back and forth between texts that Hutcheon describes has the potential to afford a flipping back and forth between selves. In the case of the *Twisted Tales*, the adolescent reader is invited to recall what they knew of the narrative as a child experiencing the designated "classic" animated film in simultaneity with the new narrative proffered by the novel. In bringing the two temporalities into contact, the *Twisted Tales* in turn makes visible the interval separating them.

Each novel's paratext plays a crucial role in initiating this process of comparative reception. The paratext signals a text's relationship to the adapted property that it both extends and references, making tie-in novels "rare cases of literature in which, from a business point of view, the paratext … has as much importance as the text itself if not more."[32] Each *Twisted Tale* signals its complex relationship to its source text through its cover, which makes clear that it is "the Disney Version"[33] of each fairy tale that has preeminence and not older fairy-tale cultures. Disney released two different editions of the *Twisted Tales* novels, through Disney Press in the United States and Autumn

Publishing in the UK. Both editions take recognizable iconography from the relevant animated film and recontextualize it to reveal a darker undertone. The Disney Press editions combine lurid color schemes with a dark silhouette of a character from the narrative that peers out at the reader through blank, glowing eyes over gothic-inspired fonts to create an aesthetic effect reminiscent of mid-twentieth-century pulp fiction and film. The Autumn editions opt for a more contemporary aesthetic, with images of characters and settings emerging against a black backdrop from amid a cloud of pale smoke, underneath a title font with spindly curves and dips that recalls Tim Burton's pop-Gothic aesthetics. The title of each book is a reference to an iconic song or phrase from the adapted film. Decontextualized, these lyric fragments take on a new resonance. *A Whole New World*, for example, refers to the iconic love ballad from *Aladdin*. In the film, this phrase is used as an uplifting metaphor for a change in perspective and opportunity offered by new romance. In the context of the *Twisted Tales*, the phrase transforms into a sinister omen of the dystopia to come. "As Old as Time" experiences a comparable transmutation from a statement on the enduring nature of the fairy tale itself to a hint of an ancient menace yet to be unleashed. Additionally, each cover signals the specific act of divergence the novel will perform by asking a "what if" question to the reader, positioned near the title itself. By asking, "What if the sleeping beauty never woke up?" the cover of *Once Upon a Dream* invites the reader to experience a different iteration of the story they think they know. These paratextual questions demand reader engagement with a doubled temporality, where the memory of the narrative experienced in childhood is read in dialogue with the narrative presented by the *Twisted Tales*. The reader thus participates in a tracing of similarity and difference that requires the reader to read the text, and through it, themselves, in terms of who they are now and who they have been, a reflective process integral to the condition of adolescence.

Young adult fiction's focus on the adolescent coming to terms with society and its institutions necessitates a transformation of the time-spaces in which the narratives of the *Twisted Tales* unfold from that of their source texts. Disney films are often set in timeless, perfect, quasi-medieval, heavily European-inflected lands. Any world-building rooted in a sense or awareness of time, in any capacity, automatically complicates the timelessness associated with Disney's reproductions of fairy tales. This complication is represented most forcefully in *Reflection* and *As Old as Time*, both of which add locations and dimensions to their preexisting time-spaces. These new locations are rooted in specific historical periods or mythic locations that exist external to Disney's fairy-tale kingdoms and thereby complicate the temporal structure of the narrative through their inclusion. In *Reflection*, Diyu, the Chinese Underworld, becomes an addition to the fabric of the animated film. Mulan's journey there facilitates the narrative twist and adds to the texture of cultural authenticity sought by the filmmakers in the aesthetic creation of the film.[34] Diyu itself feels fully constructed, simultaneously in dialogue with Chinese mythologies and the Disney film. In comparison, Belle's world is very explicitly meant to be eighteenth-century France, albeit in a universe where magic is normal and the Beast's kingdom has been forgotten as a result of that magic. The world-building in *As Old as Time* draws on quasi-historical positioning, seen when Belle reflects on her father's treatment by the Beast, referencing the law of the land: "This was the eighteenth century. The age of reason ... This was about breaking the laws of France. Even if the little magical castle was hidden far from the worlds of Paris and Versailles."[35] The rigid positioning of the setting in a particular historical and geographic location emphasizes the difference between the novel and the film and solidifies the idea that in *this* narrative, time exists, and therefore so do consequences. These worlds preexist the narratives unfolding and will continue beyond their conclusion. This sense of temporality, specifically of being bound by time and thereby subject to growth and change, reinforces that these are adolescent narratives patterned by the change and relative instability associated with the adolescent experience, as opposed to the relative stability, safety, and ability to return to an unchanged home that forms one of the dominant patterns of children's fiction.[36]

Exchanging the fairy-tale time-space of "once upon a time" for the more expansive time-space of fantasy fiction results in the representation of kingdoms beset by a culture and politics implied to have been censored from the films. This political authorization, combined with the shift in age-group of the audience addressed, allows the authors of the *Twisted Tales* novels to make use of their audience's increased capacity for internal focalization and represent a more complex world than that with which the reader is familiar from the films. *A Whole New World*, for example, opens with an image of Agrabah by night, all "rose-flavoured ices and trinkets."[37] This image quickly gives way, however, to that of "a whole other Agrabah," one where "the streets were silent as shadow and black as death" and in which "thieves, beggars, murderers, and the poorest of the poor lived."[38] Aladdin's poverty and all that it entails is more starkly rendered. Both the condition and the causes of his poverty are treated as the outcome of systemic failings of Agrabah's political system, headed by a sultan "who still sat in his beautiful golden-domed palace, playing with his toys while his people starved on the streets."[39] This critique, which complicates readers' recall of the Agrabah of the film, spills into Aladdin's first conversation with Jasmine, who asks "why isn't anything being done about this?"[40]

Part of Your World performs a similar revision of its source text, constructing the merfolk kingdom of Atlantica as beautiful but ultimately frivolous, thereby deconstructing the film's assertion of an "under the sea" utopia. Braswell's underwater kingdom is one of "unimaginable dreamy splendour," populated by citizens who are "long-lived and content, with nothing but time and aesthetics on their minds."[41] Reframed as such, the novel invites the reader to reinterpret the film's formal concerts, impromptu jam sessions, and spontaneous serenades as the diversions of an untroubled and indolent populace. The novel also strays briefly into ecological critique as Ariel attempts her return to the shore in the hopes of rescuing her father, King Triton, from his imprisonment by a still-disguised Ursula. The film addresses fishing as a site of tension between the two species, but the ethics of the practice itself are left uninterrogated. *Part of Your World* instead represents a broader portrait of humans' environmental mismanagement of the ocean, an issue with contemporary relevance for readers. Ariel's journey to Eric's castle takes her through water that has "began to stink of organic matter, tar, things alien to the ocean,"[42] an obstacle course of trawling nets, raw sewage, and a mysterious bright yellow substance that burns Ariel's scales.[43] Human capacity for "waste" is critiqued on two levels: waste as detritus and as the act of being wasteful. Ursula's attempt to hurt Ariel by capturing Flounder prompts wasteful overfishing, causing Ariel to lament "the greed of Dry Worlders."[44] In *Once Upon a Dream*, concepts of filial obedience and the divine right of kings are interrogated. Throughout the novel, Aurora routinely questions her parent's decision to consign her to the care of the fairies Flora, Fauna, and Merryweather. As the novel reaches its conclusion, her frustration boils over, prompting her to explode: "What my parents wanted? Did they *show* any great insight or ability in *parenting*?"[45] This recrimination prompts her aunt Merryweather to respond "Well, *you* try being bound by human kings and human law .... We had to do what the king said. Your own rules, people."[46] No choice is as simple as it may have appeared in each novel's filmic precursor; no action is without consequence. Grappling with these consequences and incorporating them into one's understandings of the world is the challenge that each novel sets for its protagonists and, in turn, readers.

The *Twisted Tales* invite their readers to reexamine not only the story-worlds but also the characters themselves, through metatextual commentary. This might be achieved through as little as a throw-away line, such as when the Beast remarks to Belle, "You were my prisoner. Why *would* you listen to anything I said?"[47] The characters also reflect on their extratextual behavior in ways that make apparent possible consequences of their earlier actions, as seen when an encounter with General Li's spirt in Diyu prompts Mulan to remember her last conversation with her father before running away to take his place in the army—an event from the film that occurs prior to *Reflection*'s narrative scope: "She'd been so petulant, so angry ... she didn't regret going in his place. Only that she'd deceived her family."[48] Throughout *Part of Your World*, Ariel reconsiders the decisions she made "when she was an idiot minnow"[49] and reexamines the impact of her actions on others:

> For a dizzying moment Ariel saw things from her sister's—and her father's—perspective: countless humans swarming everywhere on the Dry World; only a tiny kingdom of mer below in the World Under the Sea. Losing a daughter to a human wasn't just tragic on a personal level; it also meant the loss of one of the dwindling mer to the ever-growing mass of humans.[50]

In this moment Braswell's novel requires that Ariel and, by extension, the reader reconsider a moment from the narrative and, through reflection, gain new insight. This is rearticulated at a metafictive level later in the novel as Ariel prepares for her final confrontation with Ursula, when Eric recalls the events of *The Little Mermaid*'s narrative as an aspiring composer and librettist. Hearing the story from a different angle allows Ariel to "mentally [replay] the scene of going to talk to Ursula about giving her legs, but from a different perspective—Ursula's."[51] This narrative repositioning allows her to see how foolish and self-centered, and open to exploitation and manipulation, she had been. *Once Upon a Dream*, conversely, recasts its heroine's fall into an enchanted slumber as a deliberate choice. Braswell reimagines Aurora's life as one characterized by loneliness and frustration. Faced with an embodiment of her own malaise and melancholy, Aurora confides to Phillip that the carefree young maiden dancing and singing her way through the woods that won his heart was an illusion, the product of a fleeting interlude of joy in the life of a "directionless, indecisive, despondent, sad, little girl."[52] Phillip's attempt to refute Aurora's narrative of self-loathing is met with her confession: "*I pricked my own finger!*"; "I knew I was going to die or sleep forever and I was completely fine with that!"[53] Other novels in the series are not as cutting in their appraisal of the adapted narratives; nevertheless they too depict their characters reevaluating and critiquing the choices made within the narrative of the "original" Disney film.

It is not only the narratives' order of events that the *Twisted Tales* transform, but the perception of events' duration. *Once Upon a Dream* opens with a transmediation of the scene in which Philip kills the dragon-formed Maleficent. These two minutes of animation become five pages of Philip's perspective, moving the reader from observing the scene from the outside to being directly embedded in the character's perspective of what has just occurred. A similar shift occurs in the opening of *Reflection*, where during the battle at the mountain pass, approximately two minutes of animation equates to five to six pages of text, capturing the reader with a familiar scene before transitioning through the narrative's breaking point, into the new story. Both instances exemplify one of the effects of transmediation from film to novel: events can be and are related over longer durations of exposition. As seen especially in the latter half of *Once Upon a Dream*, it might take several chapters to relate events that the narrative then iterates occurred within the span of two minutes of the overall narrative's time.[54] The way the novels play with time, stretching or compressing the sense of narrative movement, facilitates the dialogue between the adaptation and the source text as space is created for protagonist reflection. These reflective moments, like the novels' paratextual taglines, can take the form of "what ifs" that bring explicit attention to the doubled temporalities at play, creating a reading experience in which the text is constantly being reevaluated in terms of the underlying temporality. Aladdin's inner monologue upon meeting the Genie in *A Whole New World* is indicative: "In a different time, he could almost see the two of them become friends. Or at least talking, or … Aladdin shook his head. Another time, another place."[55] Such longings highlight the texts' status as divergent adaptations, reinforcing the reader's awareness of the narratives that exist extra-diegetically but constantly in relation to the *Twisted Tales*.

And yet, even as they encourage a reactivation of childhood memory through their overt and self-referential performances of intertextuality, the *Twisted Tales* often seek to render explicit the futility of returning to childhood and its symbolic idyll. Returning to childhood is always impossible: Ariel's onshore adventures have disrupted Atlantica's peaceful eternity; Belle cannot relive her childhood now that she knows her mother; and as queen, Aurora cannot "visit childhood haunts."[56] Indeed, *Once Upon a Dream* takes this thematic conceit further, offering its young adult audience a narrative motivated by fighting against timelessness, as this novel features a teenager being driven mad by stasis. She *seeks* time, in a sense, for her right to grow, change, and reclaim her life and her autonomy over it—a far cry from sleeping for one hundred years and waking with a kiss to "happily ever after."

Endings and Futures

The *Twisted Tales* explore how adolescence and the change it embodies can be incorporated into a corporation with a brand identity built upon a foundation of childhood. These books are complicated precisely because of the conflict between their identity as young adult texts and the demands of the Disney brand. Through the novels' attempts to reconcile these disparate things we see that childhood and adolescence do not seamlessly combine. In essence, the tale must be *twisted* so that form itself—whether the Disney form or the fairy-tale form—can be eclipsed, opening the narrative to new possibilities. However, the divergence actually curtails the potential complexities to be unlocked in the original narratives, even as it exposes them. By framing these as divergences and not extensions, the Walt Disney Company tacitly indicates that these narratives "don't belong here."

The liminality of young adult fiction—the ephemeral nature of the market and readership—has made young adult publishing a niche in which media companies like Disney can experiment with multitextuality. By collaborating with established authors to create "original" narratives that exist alongside the narrative of the property being adapted, these narratives are legitimized by a creative energy that is deployed to curtail actual transformation and development. Despite their divergent paths, the novels end in inevitably familiar places, albeit with the "happily ever after" mitigated or deferred: Aurora wakes and meets Philip outside of the dream world, but their assumed marriage becomes a conscious choice; Shang grapples with the truth about Mulan's identity before the army marches to the Imperial City; Belle and the Beast are united but the curse is not fully broken; Aladdin and Jasmine defeat Jafar to start building Agrabah anew; and Ariel and Eric reunite, defeat Ursula, and restore Triton to Atlantica. The narratives arrive at an expected place along a divergent path. Such divergence takes readers further from the source narratives and calls into question what constitutes hope, or a happy ending, in these stories. All of the *Twisted Tales* ultimately defer closure; the trials that the characters face are frequently just the first step in a longer adventure, one that is implied to wait just beyond the confines of the novel itself.

This complication of a happy ending is less of a "tie-in" and more of an untying of a brand foundationally built on childhood and the notion of "happily ever after." That is the crux of adapting the Disney animated film for a young adult audience; ultimately the needs of the audience have changed. Through that lens, then, the deeper, unknown story is actually about the readers, not the characters. It is not only the narratives that become twisted, but the readers' expectations, which should no longer be about waiting for a happy ending. Things might not be perfect, but it is possible to find contentment.

And yet, the adolescent can have neither the fairy tale nor the space defined by contentment; both narratives are impossibilities. By being diversions from the known narrative, solidified through the reader's awareness of the differences between the two narratives, the *Twisted Tales* become annexed into another branch of the multitext. What adolescents have instead from viewing the twisting of the expected story is a sense of what might have been. The acquisition of new knowledge does not bring them closer to a realistic possibility, just another "might have been." But the ultimate gain in knowledge of what "might have been" comes from the exploration of the protagonists' interior lives, who they become as a result of the narrative's corruption, or, better yet, how they were better able to understand themselves. Whether exploration was focalized on truths about the people and places they ruled, about their families, or those about themselves, these young adult adaptations are defined by self-discovery and growth that can only occur through the passage of time in imperfect worlds.

Ultimately, the *Twisted Tales* are an example of what Elliott refers to as "corporate intertextuality,"[57] an attempt to capitalize on the practices that constitute convergence culture.[58] In the age of the media franchise, to capitalize on the growth industry that is licensed publishing, Disney has to deliberately disrupt their franchise in order to maintain their relevance. By breaking and twisting the narratives, Disney can reassemble them to be more in dialogue with narratives outside of the company's properties. Across the series, the protagonists are called on to right past wrongs and fix the mistakes of previous generations; yet, these are not stories about revolution or radical upheaval. These narratives are slower. They are about change that will be arduous and, above all, time-consuming. Truly, there is no happily ever after; the resolution of each novel is just that—a resolution, a statement of intent, and a hope that maybe, someday, things *might* be better. That this in itself is a message incorporated into but deliberately kept separate from the cultural DNA of the Walt Disney Company as a corporation bears further examination. As the series continues, this kind of adaptation remains worth considering, both in terms of what possibilities are left open to contemporary readers and the broader cultural purpose of stories to help us make sense of our realities.

Notes

1 "Licensed Books Gain Popularity in the U.S."
2 Murray, *The Adaptation Industry*, 25.
3 Murray, *The Adaptation Industry*.
4 Baetens, "From Screen to Text," 226.
5 Ibid., 230.
6 Mahlknecht, "The Hollywood Novelization," 150.
7 Ibid., 139.
8 Thompson, *The Frodo Franchise*, 6.
9 Elliott, "Tie-Intertextuality," 195.
10 Hutcheon, *A Theory of Adaptation*, 7.
11 Ibid., 8.
12 Ibid., 114.
13 Elliott, "Tie-Intertextuality," 202.

14 Baetens, "From Text to Screen," 231.
15 Jenkins, "Adaptation, Extension, Transmedia."
16 Van Parys, "Another Time, Another Canon," 74.
17 Jenkins, "Adaptation, Extension, Transmedia."
18 Parody, "Adaptation Essay Prize Winner," 211.
19 Elliott, "Tie-Intertextuality," 195; Thompson, *The Frodo Franchise*, 4.
20 "About—Leadership, Management Team, Global, History, Awards, Corporate Responsibility."
21 Stevenson, "Classics and Canons," 113.
22 Corbett, "YA Comes of Age."
23 Corbett, "New Trends in YA"; Corbett, "Bologna 2019: New Ventures, Milestones, and Trends."
24 Coats, "Young Adult Literature," 33.
25 Waller, *Constructing Adolescence*, 32.
26 Hilton and Nikolajeva, "Introduction," 7–8.
27 Trites, *Disturbing the Universe*, 20.
28 Reynolds, *Radical Children's Literature*, 79.
29 Ellis, "The Literary Adaptation."
30 Grant, "Recognizing Billy Budd in Beau Travail," 57.
31 Hutcheon, *A Theory of Adaptation*, 139.
32 Mahlknecht, "The Hollywood Novelization," 149.
33 Schickel, *The Disney Version*.
34 See Anjirbag, "Mulan and Moana"; Lan Dong, *Mulan's Legend and Legacy*.
35 Braswell, *As Old as Time*, 118.
36 See Nikolajeva, *From Mythic to Linear*.
37 Braswell, *A Whole New World*, 1.
38 Ibid.
39 Ibid., 19.
40 Ibid., 41.
41 Braswell, *Part of Your World*, 31.
42 Ibid., 79.
43 Ibid., 79–80.
44 Ibid., 374.
45 Braswell, *Once Upon a Dream*, 434.
46 Ibid., 435.
47 Braswell, *Tale as Old as Time*, 197.
48 Lim, *Reflection*, 102.
49 Braswell, *Part of Your World*, 386.
50 Ibid., 261.
51 Ibid., 380.
52 Braswell, *Once Upon a Dream*, 303.
53 Ibid., 307, 308.
54 Ibid., 250–88.
55 Braswell, *A Whole a New World*, 193.
56 Braswell, *Once Upon a Dream*, 350.
57 Elliott, "Tie-Intertextuality," 193.
58 See Jenkins, *Convergence Culture*.

Bibliography

"About—Leadership, Management Team, Global, History, Awards, Corporate Responsibility." *The Walt Disney Company*, https://www.thewaltdisneycompany.com/about/. Accessed October 11, 2019.

Anjirbag, Michelle Anya. "Mulan and Moana: Embedded Coloniality and the Search for Authenticity in Disney Animated Film." *Social Sciences* 7, no. 11, (November 2018): 230. doi:10.3390/socsci7110230.

Baetens, Jan. "From Screen to Text: Novelization, the Hidden Continent." In *The Cambridge Companion to Literature on Screen*, edited by Deborah Cartmell and Imelda Whelehan, 226–3. Cambridge: Cambridge University Press, 2007.

Braswell, Liz. *A Whole New World: A Twisted Tale*. Los Angeles, CA: Disney Press, 2015.

Braswell, Liz. *As Old as Time*. Los Angeles, CA: Disney Press, 2016.

Braswell, Liz. *Once Upon a Dream*. Los Angeles, CA: Disney Press, 2016.

Braswell, Liz. *Part of Your World: A Twisted Tale*. Los Angeles, CA: Disney Press, 2018.

Calonita, Jen. *Mirror, Mirror: A Twisted Tale*. Los Angeles, CA: Disney Press, 2019.

Coats, Karen. "Young Adult Literature: Growing Up in Theory." *Handbook of Research on Children's and Young Adult Literature*, edited by Shelby Anne Wolf, Karen Coats, Patricia Enciso, and Christine Jenkins, 315–29. New York: Routledge, 2011.

Corbett, Sue. "Bologna 2019: New Ventures, Milestones, and Trends." *Publishers Weekly*. April 2, 2019. https://www.publishersweekly.com/pw/by-topic/childrens/childrens-industry-news/article/79699-bologna-2019-new-ventures-milestones-and-trends.html. Accessed October 11, 2019.

Corbett, Sue. "New Trends in YA: The Agents' Perspective." *Publishers Weekly*. September 27, 2013. https://www.publishersweekly.com/pw/by-topic/childrens/childrens-industry-news/article/59297-new-trends-in-ya-the-agents-perspective.html. Accessed October 11, 2019.

Corbett, Sue. "YA Comes of Age." *Publishers Weekly*. September 30, 2011. https://www.publishersweekly.com/pw/by-topic/childrens/childrens-industry-news/article/48916-ya-comes-of-age.html. Accessed October 11, 2019.

Dong, Lan. *Mulan's Legend and Legacy in China and the United States*. Philadelphia: Temple University Press, 2011.

Elliott, Kamilla. "Tie-Intertextuality, Or, Intertextuality as Incorporation in the Tie-in Merchandise to Disney's Alice in Wonderland (2010)." *Adaptation* 7, no. 2 (August 2014): 191–211.

Ellis, John. "The Literary Adaptation." *Screen* 23, no. 1 (May 1982): 3–5. https://doi.org/10.1093/screen/23.1.3. Accessed September 3, 2019.

Grant, Catherine. "Recognizing Billy Budd in Beau Travail: Epistemology and Hermeneutics of an Auteurist 'Free' Adaptation." *Screen* 43, no. 1 (March 1, 2002): 57–73. https://doi.org/10.1093/screen/43.1.57. Accessed September 3, 2019.

Hilton, Mary, and Maria Nikolajeva (eds.). "Introduction: Time of Turmoil." In *Contemporary Adolescent Literature and Culture: The Emergent Adult*, 1–16. Burlington, VT: Ashgate, 2012.

Hutcheon, Linda. *A Theory of Adaptation*, 2nd ed. London: Routledge, 2013.

Jenkins, Henry. "Adaptation, Extension, Transmedia." *Literature/Film Quarterly* 45, no. 2 (Spring 2017). https://lfq.salisbury.edu/_issues/first/adaptation_extension_transmedia.html. Accessed September 3, 2019.

Jenkins, Henry. *Convergence Culture: Where Old and New Media Collide*. New York: New York University Press, 2006.

"Licensed Books Gain Popularity in the U.S." *License Global*, March 26, 2018. https://www.licenseglobal.com/retail-trends/licensed-books-gain-popularity-us. Accessed February 14, 2019.

Mahlknecht, Johannes. "The Hollywood Novelization: Film as Literature or Literature as Film Promotion?" *Poetics Today* 33, no. 2 (June 2012): 137–68.

Murray, Simone. *The Adaptation Industry: The Cultural Economy of Contemporary Literary Adaptation*. New York: Routledge, 2012.

Parody, Clare. "Adaptation Essay Prize Winner: Franchising/Adaptation." *Adaptation* 4, no. 2 (September 2011): 210–18.

Reynolds, Kimberley. *Radical Children's Literature: Future Visions and Aesthetic Transformations in Juvenile Fiction*. Basingstoke: Palgrave Macmillan, 2010.

Schickel, Richard. *The Disney Version: The Life, Times, Art, and Commerce of Walt Disney*, 3rd ed. Chicago, IL: Ivan R. Dee, 1997.

Stevenson, Deborah. "Classics and Canons." In *The Cambridge Companion to Children's Literature*, edited by M. O. Grenby and Andrea Immel, 108–23. Cambridge: Cambridge University Press, 2010.

Thompson, Kristin. *The Frodo Franchise: The Lord of the Rings and Modern Hollywood*. Berkeley: University of California Press, 2007.

Trites, Roberta Seelinger. *Disturbing the Universe: Power and Repression in Adolescent Literature*. Iowa City: University of Iowa Press, 2000.

Van Parys, Thomas. "Another Canon, Another Time the Novelizations of the Star Wars Films." In *Star Wars and the History of Transmedia Storytelling*, edited by Sean Guynes and Dan Hassler-Forest, 73–85. Amsterdam: Amsterdam University Press, 2017.

Waller, Alison. *Constructing Adolescence in Fantastic Realism*. London: Routledge, 2009.

Part Three

Making the Past Present

10

Rewriting Nineteenth-Century New York City for the Modern Teen

Amy L. Montz

At the end of her novel set in 1920s New York City, Libba Bray provides an Author's Note that begins, "A lot of research went into creating the world of *The Diviners*," and then she proceeds to discuss the type of research she conducted to faithfully portray the time, the place, and the subject of her paranormal mystery. She concludes that "There are some dynamite resources out there if you're interested in further research about the time period. A full bibliography can be found on the *Diviners* website: TheDivinersSeries. com. Happy creepy reading."[1] Reading this after concluding Bray's excellent novel led me to an academic quandary: *why*? Why rewrite, so faithfully, historical New York City for contemporary teenagers? Why include bibliographies and authorial notes that describe the painstaking process of researching the text?

This question haunted me throughout my participation in a 2017 National Endowment for the Humanities Institute on Material Culture in Nineteenth-Century New York City.[2] I originally intended to research pieces of material culture in young adult novels set in nineteenth-century New York—fashion, jewelry, furniture[3]—but as the Institute used New York City as our classroom, I became fascinated with the material culture of the city itself, especially the few preserved spaces of nineteenth-century material culture: the Tenement Museum, the Merchant House Museum, and the Metropolitan Museum of Art. I began exploring young adult novels set during the nineteenth century, in New York City, and discovered that it was not as prolific a genre as I had hoped. Not many novels attempted to explore the New York City of the nineteenth century. Of course, I wondered why.

My answer came in exploring those spaces left from that century: there just is not a lot of nineteenth-century New York *left*. While the three museums give accurate and authentic creations and recreations of the living spaces of their nineteenth-century denizens, so much else has been destroyed, built over, and repurposed. But still, these authors, like Libba Bray, faithfully researched not only books and tracts but, most importantly, *spaces*.

I argue that because these authors are using it as such, nineteenth-century New York City is a canonical text, faithfully represented in documents, historical tracts, and the buildings of the time. While the majority of historical young adult novels actually prefer the Roaring Twenties as their focus in New York City—Libba Bray's The Diviners series, for example, or Anna Godbersen's *Bright Young Things*—and while children's literature prefers the New York of the contemporary era—*Harriet the Spy* (1960s) and *From the Mixed-Up Files of Mrs. Basil E. Frankweiler* (1970s)—young adult novels set in nineteenth-century New York explore several of the same issues seen in these texts (agency, freedom of movement, gender dynamics) while at the same time positioning our characters in the real spaces (now museums) left from that century.[4] Through an exploration of the Merchant House Museum, the Tenement Museum, and the New York Historical Society, I argue that these spaces are canonical texts rewritten for the twenty-first-century young adult reader, carefully researched and preserved in text by the authors. Further, by using historical documents mentioned in the novels, the bibliographies, and the authors' notes, I explore how history has influenced the scripting of young adult novels, for an audience seemingly hungry for historical accuracy.

Why New York City? Introducing the Big Apple to the Reader

New York is always presented as a defiant place, a space of hope and freedom for the heroines, in particular. In their introduction to their collection, *Children's Literature and New York City*, Keith O'Sullivan and Pádraic Whyte offer an explanation as to why New York is so popular a setting for these texts for young readers: "In fact, it is as much an imagined space as it is a real place; yet, there is an inextricable link between the imagined and the real. The mythology of New York has helped maintain its resilience and survival in reality."[5] It is here, in that "inextricable link between the imagined and the real," that I see these novels I discuss today existing. Nineteenth-century New York is both real and imagined: real, because it existed, and we have the historical record for it, and imagined, because so many of these spaces and places are gone, lost to skyscrapers and pop-ups and new construction. O'Sullivan and Whyte note that "The identity of New York ... is not static; it is a city that is constantly reinventing and remaking itself, both in its urban landscape and in its population."[6] Like the dynamic character of the city itself, these adaptations function as dynamic reinventings and remakings. The authors see the fading landscape of nineteenth-century New York City and turn it into a living and breathing space for their readers. This reinvention and dynamic character of the city is, ultimately, the purpose of adapting a city from a previous century.

Further, New York, past and present, offers freedom of travel for the young character who, by basis of age, may not have that freedom to start with. In "'New York is a Great Place': Urban Mobility in Twentieth-Century Children's Literature," Sonya Sawyer Fritz argues that for the novels she studies, "far from casting New York as a treacherous or exclusive place, the novels represent the city as a place without boundaries, a place that can belong to the child regardless of racial identity or socioeconomic status."[7] Fritz even notes that the city becomes "Portrayed as the child's friend, complicit in the young person's independent navigation of its spaces."[8] Fritz looks at texts written in their historical moment of publication, like *Harriet the Spy*. What we see with nineteenth-century-set adaptations is the progression of New York City from treacherous to welcoming because the teenager is gaining agency. Both novels I will discuss feature female teen protagonists, and both novels offer different presentations of the restrictions placed on teenaged girls in the nineteenth century. For the most part, the wealth belonging to the girls' families not only places them in positions of privilege but also restricts their movements the most. With historical accuracy, these novels present the wealthier characters, especially girls, as restricted in movement both in the city and in society, while working-class characters—usually represented by boys in these texts—are allowed freedom of movement because (a) they are boys and (b) they are poor.[9] Part of the novels' plots involve the attempt to gain freedom of movement within the city, and the female protagonists go through elaborate lengths to disguise, escape, sneak out, or explore their city with their male accomplices.

This freedom of movement is, for Eric L. Tribunella, instrumental to the figure of the flâneur within children's narratives. His article, "Children's Literature and the Child Flâneur," argues that the figure of the flâneur, the "idle wanderer or man about town, defined primarily by two activities: strolling and looking,"[10] can also be seen through the figure of the child: "By placing the child in the city, and often imbuing the protagonist of urban fiction with both a critical gaze and a sense of wonder, children's literature both confirms the possibility of the child flâneur and makes use of this figure to contend with the ramifications of modernity."[11] For these heroines, they contain both "a critical gaze and a sense of wonder" as they explore the city before them, with the freedom not usually allotted to girls of their class or status. Yet while their male counterparts freely exhibit flâneur characteristics, the girls learn, and learn quickly, how to navigate the streets in order to, in no small part, escape the oppressive life they lead.

Even the concept of New York City in literature is offered as a structured escape for children. The 2003 *Storied City: A Children's Book Walking-Tour Guide to New York City* explores famous places as seen through the eyes of fictionalized children in well-known novels. Leonard S. Marcus organizes his guide according to neighborhood, with *James and the Giant Peach* for Midtown Manhattan[12] and *From the Mixed-Up Files* for Central Park.[13] Marcus begins his walking-tour guide by noting, "As a city of superlatives where people have long come to follow their dreams, New York was bound to lodge itself in the world's imagination and to become a favorite setting for literature."[14] He also concludes his work with a Bibliography, each book marked with its corresponding age group.[15] This guidebook, marketed to and written for children, emphasizes the importance of accuracy and impact for an adolescent audience. *Storied City*'s publication argues for an adolescent audience that desires literary tourism but, specifically, tourism that applies to their age group. In no small way, the Bibliographies and Acknowledgments of the two novels I examine, as well as Libba Bray's, offer the same aspect of literary tourism for the young adult reader. These are real spaces influencing fictional texts and allowing for a realistic setting in a fictional novel. By giving the young adult reader something to look for—a painting in the Merchant

House, a room in a tenement—these novels argue that young adults are as invested in space and setting as they are in characters and plot.

Why History? Introducing Historical Moments to Teen Audiences

It is important to note that these bibliographies, intense details of setting, and acknowledgments listing museums and archival materials are not for the classroom but for teen readers themselves. The question of course then becomes, why? Why give teen readers this level of detail about the writing process and introduce them to the rather disintegrating nineteenth-century history of New York City? Myra Zarnowski's "History Writing That's 'Good to Think With': *The Great Fire, Blizzard!* and *An American Plague*" argues that for younger readers, past and present often offer recognizable patterns and extreme differences, and "[t]his means seeing the past in terms of both continuity and change."[16] But this seems a didactic approach, and these novels and their research histories are anything but. While it is important that young adult readers see "the past in terms of both continuity and change," much of that is lost in writing about nineteenth-century New York City. Outside of the three museums—the Tenement, the Merchant House, and the Met—the New York City of these novels is practically unrecognizable in today's Manhattan. Progress is often at the price of the past, but there are no declarations of villainy. New York is *defined* by progress; these novels encourage it.

In *The Cambridge Companion to the Literature of New York*, Cyrus R. K. Patell writes that "Arising from the rich variety of experiences to be found on the streets and in the neighborhoods of the city, New York writing dramatizes the ways in which difference—whether it is based on culture, ethnicity, race, gender, sexuality, or class—is not a problem to be solved, but rather an opportunity for individual and cultural growth."[17] This Companion text is rich with discussions of known and rather unknown texts of New York, ranging from Whitman and Wharton to working-class observations and penny papers' investigative journalism of the nineteenth century. Patell argues for a "cosmopolitanism" in New York that "arises from the points of contact among its different neighborhoods and among the cultures and subcultures they represent."[18] This cosmopolitanism of New York is, perhaps, the commonality these novels strive for between past and present. New York City then and now is the true melting pot of America and seems to have always offered the "opportunity for individual and cultural growth." This fact flies in the face of more conservative critics who see the movement toward diversity in young adult literature to be pandering. Chandra L. Power's "Challenging the Pluralism of Our Past: Presentism and the Selective Tradition in Historical Fiction Written for Young People" asserts that "By challenging works of historical fiction that present minority perspectives and experience critics raise the issue of presentism," defined by Power as "writing about historical events from a modern vantage point."[19] This accusation that some critics face is due to the inclusion of nonwhite, nonheteronormative, nonmale voices in historical young adult fiction. While writers of historical young adult fiction are including these voices because they are authentic, they face backlash from those who try to keep history white and heteronormative. Inclusion of research in these texts is, I argue, one way to keep naysayers at bay. The historical narrative proves a diverse and thriving historical record, one often silenced by the louder voices of social norms. One way to approach this disconnect is through presenting a wealthy white protagonist exploring historical spaces that she would not normally have access to in a usual narrative.

These Shallow Graves and the Tenement Museum

Andrew S. Dolkart, in *Biography of a Tenement House: An Architectural History of 97 Orchard Street*, calls the Tenement Museum "an extraordinary survivor from the first major wave of tenement construction in New York City in the 1860s and 1870s."[20] He further notes that "the fact that 97 Orchard Street retains much of its historic fabric provides a unique opportunity to document, analyze, and interpret the housing conditions in which the urban poor lived from the mid-nineteenth century to the early decades of the twentieth century."[21] I quote this Introduction at length because I think the language Dolkart uses—"extraordinary," "survivor," "unique"—is what is truly at stake with the Tenement Museum and for much of what remains of nineteenth-century New York. Updates and changes in regulations, adding breeze windows, for example, in the apartments, or regulating the amount of people who could live in one space, changed the face of 97 Orchard Street, almost forever. To truly see how the poor lived, one must actually *see*; this is the argument made by the very existence of the Tenement Museum.

In *These Shallow Graves*, Jennifer Donnelly offers heroine Jo the chance to explore all aspects of New York City life, from the gilded houses of Gramercy Square to the treacherous waterfronts and poverty-stricken tenements. She travels on a ferry to Brooklyn, strides across the Brooklyn Bridge, walks through a multifamily tenement where her love interest, Eddie, grew up in desperate poverty, and finally ends at the *Tribune*, where Jo fulfills her dream of becoming a newspaper reporter, despite her upper-class upbringing. Much of the novel has Jo challenging her conventional, upper-class heritage, and she struggles against the restraints of class and gender until the end of the novel. Eddie helps her escape some of these confines, not only because he is a boy but also because he is poor. In Donnelly's novel, boys are free to move about the city, but so, too, are poor girls. Fay is an Artful Dodger in the novel, a quick pickpocket and friend of Eddie's from when he still lived in the tenements. When Jo goes to Brooklyn to do some investigative work of her own, she misses the ferry back to Manhattan and almost takes a fatal trip with two murderers when Fay saves her. Jo tells her, "I'm glad you happened to be on Fulton Street" and that she "had the feeling someone was watching me. It was you, wasn't it?"[22] Fay tells her that not only did she notice Jo but so did a pickpocket as well as the two murderers. Jo's distracted nature—so focused on the death of her father and solving his murder—and her inability to blend into her surroundings make her an easy mark for the City's more troubled side. Fay takes her home across the Brooklyn Bridge that Jo declares is "exciting!" because "Papa said it isn't safe for young ladies to stroll across."[23] Fay, flabbergasted, asks, "How is a long walk across a boring old bridge exciting? Tell me, Jo Montfort, are all rich people insane?" to which Jo replies, "Walking *anywhere* on my own is exciting."[24] One of the parts of life Jo craves the most is freedom of movement, which Fay, as a working-class woman, has. She takes Jo on what Jo sees as an adventure, not to give her an adventure but simply to bring her home and keep her out of danger. Jo's insistence on traveling alone while investigating her father's mysterious death culminates in many troubles, but her ultimate trouble comes from home, from her Uncle, rather than the city's ne'er-do-wells. Donnelly portrays many spaces of homes, including Jo's house, as potentially dangerous, because they are easily infiltrated.

When Jo visits the tenements with Eddie, she is unprepared for the intense poverty she encounters and that she learns Eddie lived in. Eddie tells Jo that they lived in "one room of an apartment," and when Jo says she wants to go inside, Eddie tells her that she doesn't. She refuses to listen. She

> walked up to the stoop and pushed the door open. The smell was eye-watering—unwashed bodies, urine, and smoke. A small gas lamp sputtered in the dark, airless hallway, illuminating the crumbling walls. A man was sprawled on the dirty staircase in a drunken stupor. Two filthy children sat on a step above him, prodding him with a stick and laughing.[25]

Jo, sympathetic, thinks that she "had never seen poverty like this, or people so helpless against it. She turned and walked out of the house, grieved to know that Eddie had suffered such poverty himself, amazed that he'd survived it."[26] Donnelly calls attention to the concerns of Gilded-Age New York City and the extremes of richness (Jo's life) and poverty (Eddie's life) that exist in the city. This direct comparison calls to mind other extremes of wealth for current readers, who while in New York City encounter degrees of rich and poor on every street.

Jennifer Donnelly, in her Acknowledgments, calls the Tenement Museum "the most awesome time machine ever."[27] And it is, because Donnelly's description of this tenement is a direct comparison to the physical space of the Tenement Museum: the crumbling walls; the ill-lit gas lamp, now electric, but dim; and the small spaces in which multiple bodies were crammed, desperate for a home. Further, in the novel, Jacob Riis's *How the Other Half Lives: Studies among the Tenements of New York* (1890) features prominently, published the same year the novel is set. Both Jo and Eddie have read it and discuss it as one of the reasons they both went into journalism. Donnelly not only mentions this book but also includes it in a bibliography at the back of the novel, for which Donnelly tells us, "The following works provided information and inspiration and I would like to acknowledge my debt to their authors."[28] In it are a handful of books about tenements in New York.

In July 2017, I had the privilege of a special tour of the Tenement Museum. Because of the fragility of the space, and the Herculean efforts to maintain it, most tours get to see only parts of the museum. Too many bodies in too many spaces all at the same time could damage the already-damaged building. However, because we were with the NEH group, we got to see all of the floors, explore several of the rooms on our own and with the guide, and, in my case, either get bitten by bedbugs or have an allergic reaction to the wallpaper (it's still unclear). It has no air-conditioning, of course, and several of the rooms are left in the manner in which they were found. There are displays, most notably one on clothing to demonstrate how people worked from home, and we were to imagine the amount of bodies filling just one of these apartments. Large immigrant families, plus boarders.

I cannot fully explain what it is like to read about a place and then explore that place in person, except to say that when I researched an article on literary tourism on the lives of Jane Austen and Elizabeth Gaskell, I felt the same way.[29] This trip became not just a historical trip for me but a site of literary tourism, which in and of itself is both beautiful and problematic. For the novel, it opens Jo's eyes to the poverty she's never had to experience firsthand, only read about in books. But further, she enters a living space without permission, walking into people's homes without invitation, becoming a poverty tourist. It becomes a call to action for Jo, and she forgoes a life of leisure for a life of freedom and journalism, writing about the very people she's seen in her travels through New York, but it will always be with privileged eyes; despite her fall from socioeconomic grace, Jo remains upper class in her breeding, her blood, and her ideology. I, too, have my privileged twenty-first-century white eyes, as I look at these once-private, now-public spaces. How does the site of life, especially of poverty-stricken life, become a site of tourism? I felt not only excited to explore this space because of the history it contained but also guilty, ashamed almost, of spying on such abject poverty. It reminded me, in no small part, of the post–Hurricane Katrina tours of the devastated Ninth Ward.[30]

Jack Kugelmass has similar thoughts in "Turfing the Slum: New York City's Tenement Museum and the Politics of Heritage." He asks,

> If the Tenement Museum is about the preservation of cultural memory and therefore, about the inclusion of individuals who might otherwise have been marginalized, then who precisely are the people whose experiences the museum intends to legitimize? The answer has much less to do with actual people who lived in 97 Orchard Street—some 10,000 people since it was built, most of them Jews, according to the research of the museum's consulting genealogist—than with the complex politics and agendas of the museum's creators.[31]

He later argues that "Whatever its intention, the Tenement Museum is organically connected to American Jews and to what may remain the *uniqueness* of their immigrant experience" (203). The museum's attempts to remain true to the reality of the tenement are admirable, and it offers different tours inspired by people who lived and worked in the tenement. But at the end of the day, it still becomes poverty tourism if it is not approached as a moment for education, rather than mere observation.

Donnelly's book offers the same sort of education to her young adult readers without becoming didactic. When Jo returns from the building, Eddie asks her, "Have a good look?" and one can imagine the "edge that had crept back into his voice" that Jo "ignored."[32] A smart reader is asked to think through a few things in this moment. One, whether Jo is "slumming" in poverty tourism for a boy she likes or if she's really affected. Donnelly writes that "Jo realized she had tears in her eyes. She blinked them back, not wanting Eddie to see them. He was proud and would think they were tears of pity, not sorrow."[33] Eddie's story of growing up in poverty changes her and, it can, in turn, change a reader. Eddie tells her that he wanted to become a reporter "to tell the stories of the people in that house. ... The ones that never get told. I want to tell the world that these people exist. Nellie Bly's doing it. Riis and Chambers are doing it. They're changing things. I want to change things, too."[34] These experiences inspire Jo to leave a life of privilege and to work with Eddie at the *New York Tribune*. The novel tells us that "That girl was gone. And so were the illusions she had carried."[35] Even Eddie sees this change in her. He compares her to Nellie Bly, the undercover journalist who published *Ten Days in a Madhouse* after going undercover on Blackwell's Island in the lunatic asylum. In no small way, Eddie sees the comparisons because like Bly, Jo is subjected to an insane asylum when she was falsely admitted to cover up the murders committed by her uncle.

Jennifer Donnelly ends her book with hope: hope for a possible romantic future between Eddie and Jo; hope for Jo's future in journalism; hope for change because of the hard work of investigative journalism. But further, she ends her book with an Author's Note, in which she names the real-life inspirations for Jo and her story, an Acknowledgments, in which she thanks the many historical museums that inspired her, and a Bibliography, for further reading. She inspires her young audience to find the true stories of nineteenth-century New York City through the pages of her novel and beyond, through the places, spaces, and voices of nineteenth-century New York.

The Appearance of Annie Van Sinderen and the New York Historical Sites

Katherine Howe concludes her novel about the intersections of the nineteenth century and the twenty-first century with acknowledgments to "A number of institutions and scholars [who] made the historical aspects of this book possible" and refers directly to the Merchant House Museum, of which she points out that its "meticulously preserved 1830s interior allowed me a clear imagination of the inside of Annie's house, and I'm grateful to them for working to preserve the rare heritage of nineteenth-century architecture in New York City."[36] One of the ways the Museum preserves its space is through donations, house tours, and, a few times a month, ghost tours. In July 2017, I had the unique opportunity in unbearable heat—the Merchant House registered 94 degrees on the second floor at 7:00 at night!—to attend a ghost tour at this unique and well-preserved space. This was a delight for me, of course, not only because I am interested in these types of spaces but also because it came so soon after reading Howe's novel about ghosts themselves (although to be fair, as Howe reminds us, it's a ghost story that never uses the word "ghost").

This space is gorgeous because it's preserved; unique because it's been preserved since the nineteenth century; and historical because the surviving daughter did very little to change the house, so much of the original furniture, decorations, and interior spaces remain intact. The ghost tour I attended was in fact my third visit to the Merchant House and my second with the NEH Institute. An historian colleague from the Institute and I decided to attend the ghost tour for research purposes (we also attended a walking ghost tour through Greenwich Village, where the Merchant House is located, so in fact, I had three visits to it in July 2017), and I felt the place come alive in ways I had not before, no pun intended. We began in the lower floor with a short video about the ghostly encounters in the house over the years and then went through the rest of the house by candlelight. While we saw no ghosts (that we are aware of), we saw the house as it would have been seen in its original nineteenth century: darkened, with candlelight its only illumination.

In Howe's novel, the Merchant House inspires the house where Annie, the nineteenth-century ghost, lives during her time period and where the male main character, Wes, finds her in the twenty-first century. She is out of place and out of time, flashing in and out of view first at a séance in what we come to learn was a bedroom in her family home and then sitting on the steps outside of the house. She appears in the pizza parlor that has taken over the first floor of her house, and she is unable to distinguish between the bells of the door and those that chime to call her to dinner. Past and present begin to converge for Annie and she is caught between two centuries: both at her house in the nineteenth century and at the pizza parlor and apartments for rent it has become in the twenty-first. "I can't see anyone," she says. "I'm alone, but somehow I'm surrounded by people and smells and I can hear a bell jangling, but I can't tell if it's the bell Mother uses to summon us for meals or if it's something different."[37]

The novel begins with Wes's point of view, and then after Wes and Annie have a few odd encounters, the narration switches to Annatje, her full name, though she prefers Annie. When she first appears back home, she finds herself in "Mother's bedroom. In our house on First and the Bowery, not my aunt's in Hudson Square where we all went to be safe after the …"[38]—a trailing off that we later discover is a physical threat against her father for political leanings. The sampler on her mother's wall from Daniel 12:2 is rather ominous for a girl who finds herself skipping through centuries: "*And many of them that sleep in the dust of the earth shall awake, some to everlasting life, and some to shame and everlasting contempt.*"[39] But also among the sampler are other artifacts of the nineteenth century, which Annie describes for the reader:

> The room looks the same as when we fled a week ago. Lottie's left sand on the floor, which will make Mother wild. She hates to see residue of cleaning. The coverlet is pulled up over the bed, white knotted lace stretched all the way up over the bolster. Lottie's left the key in the bed frame, too, because Mother's always after her to tighten the ropes. Enamel bowl and pitcher on the washstand, empty. Knotted lace doily on the dressing table. On the doily, a pair of gloves, a silver hairbrush, and a cut-glass bottle of perfume.[40]

Some of the details seem to come straight from the Merchant House Museum itself, as seen in person and on their website. The house has been featured many times in various different media to sell its preservation mission and its ghost story. It seems only fitting that such a house would inspire this novel as well. Howe's details of a nineteenth-century bedroom, down to the sand used as cleaner on the floor, walks the young adult reader back through time. Even the reference to the key to make the ropes "tighten" offers a glimpse into the common saying, "sleep tight."

Annie finds herself skipping through time and bedrooms and wakes completely in her own bedroom, shared with her sister. She tells us,

> The room that Beatrice and I share is on the third floor, with two tall windows looking over the kitchen garden and privy at the rear of the house, windows dressed in dark wool hangings now that the weather's turned cool. Mother is still choosing the furniture for the drawing and dining rooms, but she's already appointed her and Papa's rooms. Their beds are as heavily carved and draped as old Spanish galleons, topped with plumes of ostrich feather.[41]

Other clues to the time period—a sampler on the wall, a washstand in the corner, a sewing basket by the rocking chair—are all inspired by items found in the Merchant House itself, because the Merchant House is, like the Tenement Museum, a "time capsule" to the past. Offering these details is instructing young adult readers in a way that is not didactic. Simply informative. What they choose to do with this information is up to them. These details let readers enjoy the books and not feel lectured to and offer them space for further inquiry, should they desire. A more didactic text with a set agenda will turn off young readers who approach the novels for "fun" reading rather than schoolwork.

Annie's explorations of both centuries of New York take her far afield, to a private cemetery, the Bowery, and The New York Historical Society, as she navigates the reasons why she is unable to find rest in death.[42] Partly this is due to the missing cameo ring given to her by her forbidden working-class Jewish lover, Herschel. It is a "red shell cameo ring."[43] We later discover she is the ancestor of the freegan urban survivalist Maddie, who is the daughter of old New York money. They recognize it in a painting hanging in Maddie's home and also see evidence of the cameo ring on Annie's brother's fingers. Maddie recalls that the ring is most likely at the New York Historical Society,[44] adding another layer of research to this novel. Maddie arrives to find her family's heirlooms, and we discover the reason Maddie has shunned their money: they come from a heritage of "slavemongers."[45] At the Historical Society, the ring falls out of its box and comes to land at Annie's phantom toes:

> The gold band is dented and crushed into almost an oval shape, and a thick layer of grime lines the setting that holds the red sliver of shell in place. The carving is less fine than I remember, the white form of Persephone dulled and chipped in places. The shell-red background has faded to a burnished oaken brown.[46]

There is only one cameo ring in the New York Historical Society database, but there is also a brooch, accession number 1950.296, dated 1780–1880. It is made of shell and gold and described as: "Oval cameo brooch, once belonging to Arabella Ludlow Lewis, descendant of Francis Lewis and Gabriel Ludlow, depicting profile female bust with flowers in hair (perhaps the goddess Ceres/Demeter) carved in shell; 3-dimensional gold frame around cameo depicting twining lilies, pin attachment."[47] Most importantly, the gallery note tells us that "This cameo brooch belonged to Arabella Ludlow Lewis (ancestor of the donor), a descendant of Francis Lewis, a signer of the Declaration of Independence, and Gabriel Ludlow."[48] What the Historical Society does, and what its role in this novel tells us it does, is to preserve New York City's history through objects. Objects are of importance, as are places and homes, and the role of the cameo ring in the novel is significant both because it helps Annie return to her time and death and because it calls for preservation of historical artifacts.

The Appearance of Annie Van Sinderen ends with both an Author's Note that discusses her own encounters with ghosts and haunted places and Acknowledgments, which give thanks to the people and places that made this book possible. It is in these liminal spaces that I truly wish to walk. To return to this chapter's initial question of "why," I'd like to pose it again. Why such an Author's Note that offers personal insight into the author's life and, indeed, her home? Why is it necessary to tell teenage readers that the Merchant House Museum was the inspiration for Annie's home? Part of it is, of course, citation. Authors, whether creative or academic, should give credit where credit is due. Yet there is something more important happening here: an insistence of reading these texts for their historical turn. These final notes, in Howe's and Donnelly's books, and others put history in the hands of the young adult readers.

Calls to Arms

On the Merchant House Museum website, at the time of this writing, there is a page entitled "A CALL TO ARMS!" On it, the trust discusses in detail how neighboring construction projects are jeopardizing the house and would cause irrevocable damage to the building, its ornamental plasters, and its preservation. The website informs us that

> Studies undertaken by several of the city's top engineering firms have concluded that construction next door is absolutely guaranteed to cause irreversible damage, possibly catastrophic, to our 1832 landmark building. And we know from experience: the museum has a decades-long history of damage from construction at adjoining and nearby properties, making the building that much more vulnerable.
> At particular risk is the museum's original plaster work—the ornamental elements (considered by experts to be the "finest surviving" from the period) as well as the plaster walls and ceilings. Engineering studies show that the vibrations from adjacent demolition, excavation, and construction would cause the fragile 187-year-old plaster to crumble. Vibration can also cause the nails that fasten the

ceiling laths to the framing to "back out," causing catastrophic failure of the ceiling support system.

Even the most advanced, state-of-the-art monitoring systems can only track the damage—*after* the damage has been done.[49]

I quote this at length because it represents why preservation of nineteenth-century New York is so hard: new construction can cause damage not only when restoring or renovating buildings on property but, further, on adjacent properties or even properties within the block. In a city that never sleeps, construction never ends. Housing is a necessity in New York City, and so many of the older homes have been converted into multifamily living spaces. I end this piece with the note that began it: there just isn't that much of nineteenth-century New York City *left*. And that which is left is in constant danger of being destroyed.

Young adult literature is a market that has bloomed in the last ten years. And while many academics and critics discount the importance of young adult literature—I look to my own colleague who once asked me, upon hearing I had initiated and begun to teach a young adult class, "When are kids going to read real books?"—we can see that the *authors* are not discounting the intelligence and hunger for information their audiences have. A bibliography in the back of a book suggests to the young adult reader that she can continue the conversation of the novel, if she so wishes. A recognition of space in Acknowledgments offers the young adult reader an opportunity to explore the very real spaces of the literature that he has enjoyed. The young adult reader, in short, is expected to further their reading and explore the world around them, because their favorite characters have done so. *From the Mixed-Up Files of Mrs. Basil E. Frankweiler*, a classic New York exploration text, made me, as a young child, want to visit the Metropolitan Museum of Art and *live* there. And I see further evidence that authors recognize their readers' desires to invest in the worlds of their books. The Harry Potter Experience, Platform 9 3/4, all of these spaces have become literary reality. And the places that are reality have become literary. We must, like our authors, trust in the intelligence and curiosity of young adult readers to know *more*. In a world in which Education and Labor Departments may become merged, where the Liberal Arts and Humanities are discounted, where screens take the place of books, we must encourage, above all else, that intelligence and curiosity. It leads to action.

Notes

1 Bray, *The Diviners*, 581.
2 I am grateful to Catherine Whalen and Kasey Grier for their leadership of the National Endowment for the Humanities Summer Institute, American Material Culture: Nineteenth-Century New York in July 2017, and all of my cohort who participated in the Institute. It was a joyous experience. Further, I want to thank the College of Liberal Arts at the University of Southern Indiana for the generous LARA (Liberal Arts Research Award) that provided me with a course release to work on this chapter and the collection as a whole.

3 My interest is still in these things, but more on how they appear within the pages of descriptions of nineteenth-century New York City.
4 Anna Godbersen's Luxe series is set in late-nineteenth-century New York City, and I considered using the series in this chapter. However, her research is limited, and her Acknowledgments of the time researching are limited to the following: "I am also indebted to all of the insanely knowledgeable librarians at the New-York Historical Society" (n.p.). I decided to focus instead on specific settings of the novels, that is, the Tenements and the Merchant House Museum.
5 O'Sullivan and Whyte, "Introduction," 1.
6 Ibid., 3.
7 Fritz, "New York Is a Great Place," 86.
8 Ibid.
9 And, in the case of *The Appearance of Annie Van Sinderen*, the male teen protagonist is allowed freedom of movement because he's a contemporary character. The novel involves elaborate time jumps from past to present.
10 Tribunella, "Children's Literature and the Child Flâneur," 64.
11 Ibid., 67.
12 Marcus, *Storied City*, 48.
13 Ibid., 62.
14 Ibid., v.
15 Ibid., 132–40.
16 Zarnowski, "History Writing That's 'Good to Think with,'" 253.
17 Patell, "Introduction," 3.
18 Ibid., 4.
19 Power, "Challenging the Pluralism of Our Past," 426.
20 Dolkart, *Biography of a Tenement House*, 3.
21 Ibid.
22 Donnelly, *These Shallow Graves*, 282.
23 Ibid., 284.
24 Ibid.
25 Ibid., 209–10.
26 Ibid., 210.
27 Ibid., n.p.
28 Ibid.
29 Montz, "The Personal Is Pilgrimage."
30 As a New Orleans native, I felt these were in particularly bad taste. It made me wonder how ancestors of those who lived in the tenements would feel.
31 Kugelmass, "Turfing the Slum," 186.
32 Donnelly, *These Shallow Graves*, 210.
33 Ibid.
34 Ibid.
35 Ibid., 482.
36 Howe, *The Appearance of Annie Van Sinderen*, n.p.
37 Ibid., 134.
38 Ibid., 113.
39 Ibid., 114, emphasis original.
40 Ibid.
41 Ibid., 121–2.

42 There are other references to nineteenth-century New York City, including references to Seneca Village, a mostly African and Black community destroyed to create Central Park. Annie also references the Broncks' farm, which later becomes the Bronx.
43 Howe, *The Appearance of Annie Van Sinderen*, 116.
44 Ibid., 312.
45 Ibid., 333.
46 Ibid., 340.
47 "Brooch-Cameo."
48 Ibid.
49 The Merchant House Museum Website.

Bibliography

Bray, Libba. *The Diviners*. New York: Little, Brown, 2013.
"Brooch-Cameo." The New York Historical Society. https://www.nyhistory.org/exhibit/brooch-cameo. Accessed January 14, 2019.
Dolkart, Andrew S. *Biography of a Tenement House: An Architectural History of 97 Orchard Street*, 2nd ed. Chicago: Center for American Places at Columbia College, 2012.
Donnelly, Jennifer, *These Shallow Graves*. New York: Ember, 2015.
Fritz, Sonya Sawyer. "'New York Is a Great Place': Urban Mobility in Twentieth-Century Children's Literature." In *Children's Literature and New York City*, edited by O'Sullivan and Whyte, 85–96. New York: Routledge, 1997.
Howe, Katherine. *The Appearance of Annie Van Sinderen*. New York: G.P. Putnam's Sons, 2015.
Kugelmass, Jack. "Turfing the Slum: New York City's Tenement Museum and the Politics of Heritage." In *Remembering the Lower East Side: American Jewish Reflections*, edited by Hasia R. Diner, Jeffrey Shandler, and Beth S. Wenger, 179–211. Bloomington: Indiana University Press, 2000.
Marcus, Leonard S. *Storied City: A Children's Book Walking-Tour Guide to New York City*. New York: Dutton Children's Books, 2003.
The Merchant House Museum Website. http://merchantshouse.org/calltoarms/. Accessed January 14, 2019.
O'Sullivan, Keith, and Pádraic Whyte (eds.). *Children's Literature and New York City*. New York: Routledge, 2014.
Patell, Cyrus R. K. "Introduction." In *The Cambridge Companion to the Literature of New York*, edited by Cyrus R. K. Patell and Bryan Waterman, 1–9. New York: Cambridge University Press, 2010.
Power, Chandra L. "Challenging the Pluralism of Our Past: Presentism and the Selective Tradition in Historical Fiction Written for Young People." *Research in the Teaching of English* 37, no. 4 (May 2003): 425–66.
Tenement Museum Website. https://www.tenement.org/. Accessed January 14, 2019.
Tribunella, Eric L. "Children's Literature and the Child Flâneur." *Children's Literature* 38 (2010): 64–91.
Zarnowski, Myra. "History Writing That's 'Good to Think with': *The Great Fire, Blizzard!* and *An American Plague*." *Children's Literature in Education* 40 (2009): 250–62.

11

Find Our Past Voice: Reimagining the Nineteenth-Century Feminist in Young Adult Literature

Brett Carol Young

Sheridan Blau argues, "it is the distinct capacity of literature, among the varieties of discourse, to enable us imaginatively to have lively, emotionally moving, and intellectually transformative experiences."[1] He further explains that classic archetypes within literature have become the basis for almost all forms of storytelling, so much so that it has become the tendency to describe one text as another: that is, any story of star-crossed love or tragic deaths or even just young love is described as a *Romeo and Juliet* story. For Blau, as with many critics, what makes a text canonical is the broad-reaching and relatable themes, but for many modern readers—especially inexperienced young adult readers—these canonical texts are not nearly as attainable as Blau presents them. While the stories may be considered universal in theme and therefore "classic," for the untrained reader they are often clouded by the simultaneously solemn and flowery language, and unfamiliar customs and social restrictions. For inexperienced readers, the language and presentation of canonical texts make the "emotionally moving, and intellectually transformative experiences" inaccessible and, ultimately, unread.

It is perhaps to some surprise that while young adults often deem canonical literature as too old, boring, or stuffy, they simultaneously gorge themselves on adaptations and reimagined classics. As Jennifer Miskec astutely observes in her article on incorporating young adult adaptations of classics in the classroom as companion or introductory texts, the problem with classical or canonical literature and a strictly young adult audience is that they "occupy different cultural spaces,"[2] although in different cultural spaces, the themes and elements of canonical literature remain distinct features in young adult literature, even if the structure has been whittled away to create one more easily devoured by the younger and less-experienced audience. And for multiple teen-driven novels the plot is not merely derived from the themes of canonical literature, but is either directly borrowed from the canon or presents characters who are obsessed with classics. Both formats unashamedly remind the audience that all they have read has been written before, and with a small nudge and wink that suggests the reader should place the original next on their list. Consider the immensely popular *Twilight*

Saga (2005–8): Bella is first enthralled with the pale Edward, who reminds her of Heathcliff from her favorite book, *Wuthering Heights* (1847). She refers to the text often and in *Eclipse* (2007), as she is torn between Edward and Jacob, Bella not-so-subtly compares their loves to the love triangle of Heathcliff–Cathy–Linton. The influence of Emily Brontë and William Shakespeare on Meyer's saga is so prevalent throughout that Little, Brown and Company started repackaging those classics with similar stark black covers and the now-iconic *Twilight* images in white and red, resulting in an increase in sales, especially among teens.

While adaptations and reimagined texts open a doorway into canonical literature for many readers, the door does not always stay open for long. Without the modern guide that adaptations provide, many canonical texts return to being just as inaccessible as they were before. As Guy Bland explains, regarding teaching classical literature to students, "most of the classics offer few of what John Steinbeck called 'points of contact'—that is tangible, meaningful experiences and themes students can fit into their lives. These connections are crucial to get students to read. Without them teachers must try to sell literature that is essentially meaningless."[3] Bland further questions the need to read canonical literature if other literature—especially adaptations—can present readers with the same themes, but in a manner they can relate to and enjoy. While this argument is hotly debated among anyone who loves or hates what has been deemed classic, the concept is still relevant: many adaptations are well-written pieces of literature that present the same themes but through stories that modern readers can relate to regardless of their reading experience. The relatability, or points of contact, for many is what draws experienced and inexperienced readers alike to particular "favorite" novels. As Bland exemplifies, the texts that we fall in love with are not necessarily the best written, but they are the stories that touch our souls the most. And while canonical literature may have universal themes, an inexperienced reader is not going to read it if they cannot connect with it.

What allows the themes of literature to connect with its audience is not by whom or when it was written, but that the reader can see themselves within the text.[4] Because of this, what is often most problematic to a modern audience whose world views are more multicultural and liberal than almost any of the "classics" is the lack of the marginalized voice, even with an abundance of "universal" themes relating to love, hate, war, and death. For the modern audience and the inexperienced reader—and especially young adult readers—marginalized voices often have a stronger impact by resonating with the reader's world better. By adding stronger female or other underrepresented voices, adaptations recognize that these voices are the audiences' voices; recognition of these voices is needed to provide Steinbeck's "points of contact" to these readers by establishing a sense of modern connection within the often alienating world of the past.[5] Adaptations that emphasize voices that are traditionally muted in canonical texts allow modern audiences to connect with the nuances that are often overlooked by unskilled readers approaching the canon for the first time. Recreating the original text by presenting more modern characteristics and ideals, these types of adaptations act as a more encompassing bridge between the historical restrictions of the original text and the liberties of the modern reader. For the marginalized voice to shine within these adaptations, it is essential that the themes of the original text remain preserved no matter how extensively the characters—and occasionally even plot—are altered. Representing the marginalized voice within the canonical "universal" theme allows those who cannot find themselves represented in classic literature to reimagine how they might fit into the original text.

In this chapter, I argue that the use of embedded modern voices in canonical adaptations allows for a broader and easier understanding of the complicated obstacles that canonical literature often has with inexperienced, young adult readers. Revamping old characters or embedding new characters into canonical texts allows an adaptation to guide its readers through a cultural period and to present a better understanding of the shifts between the canonical text and the modern age. In turn these adaptations allow for voices that are traditionally unheard in canonical literature to present commentary on and within the original text. In other words, adaptations create a connection between the modern reader and the canon by demonstrating how they should interpret and understand the text. It is these connections between reader and canon that make adaptations vital to the inexperienced reader. While there are several different types of adaptations, I further argue that the embedded adaptation works best for making such connections between readers and the canon, as demonstrated in Megan Shepherd's *The Madman's Daughter* (2013).

Embedded Adaptations in Young Adult Literature

Adaptations of canonical characters or texts are not a particularly new concept in literature; literature has been borrowing, stealing, and adapting older texts since the beginning. However, with the ever-increasing awareness of fan fiction through various internet-sharing sites, the presence of these reenvisioned and parallel texts has become more and more popular, especially in young adult literature.[6] The use of reenvisioned and parallel literature can be traced as far back as Dante's *Divine Comedy* (1320)—a reenvisioned presentation of basic Catholic doctrine—or Milton's *Paradise Lost* (1667)—a parallel text of *The Book of Genesis*. When discussing reenvisioned and parallel adaptations it is vital to note the subtle but distinct separation between the two: while parallel adaptations are always reenvisioning, few reenvisioned adaptations can simultaneously be defined as parallel. The primary distinction is that reenvisioned adaptations relocate the source text's plot and characters in a new setting, while parallel texts reimagine the story from an alternative, yet simultaneous perspective. For example, Jane Smiley's *A Thousand Acres* (1991) is a reenvisioned novel of Shakespeare's *King Lear*, whereas Jean Rhys's *Wide Sargasso Sea* (1966) is a parallel novel to Charlotte Brontë's *Jane Eyre* (1847).[7] At its worst, reenvisioned and parallel adaptations are nothing more than a brand: a shell of the story type they have modelled. At their best, they provide an alternative construction that allows the modern, inexperienced reader a chance to understand the constructs and implications of the original text through a lens they are more familiar and comfortable with.

The use of parallel adaptations is fairly uncommon in young adult literature, compared to the reenvisioned novel. What makes the parallel adaptation problematic for a young adult audience—or really any audience—is the reliance of the parallel work on the original text. In other words, readers must have an intimate understanding of the canonical text or time period of the text before being able to understand the relationship between the parallel and the original. The heavy reliance of parallel novels on the canon often makes the text less accessible to inexperienced readers, especially if they have not read or do not know the original plot. However, this is not to say there are none of these adaptations or that they cannot be done in a way that allows them to stand alone from the canon and time. Terry Pratchett's parallel novel, *Dodger* (2012), presents the world of Charles Dickens's *Oliver Twist* from a young Artful Dodger's perspective and life. And while Pratchett presents his Dodger in a truly fun and ingenious manner that does not require too much knowledge of *Twist*, it is still riddled with allusions to Dickensian London as well as other Victorian nuisances.[8] Such a reliance on any subject—text, time period, and so on—can create an overwhelming burden for both the author and their audience when determining what needs to be explained and what can be assumed prior or common knowledge. Doing so requires an understanding of the cultural space that is shared between the canonical, the parallel, and the audience. For parallel adaptations, these shared spaces are generally too reliant on one another for inexperienced readers, whereas in reenvisioned adaptations the space can be more open to present a broader spectrum for interpretation.

Unlike the parallel adaptation, the reenvisioned adaptation is more common in young adult literature because it is more accessible. While the reenvisioned adaptation relies heavily on the original canonical text for plot, characters, and themes, these adaptations allow for transformation of the basic elements from the original text within a new cultural space that is more relatable to teen and modern readers. In other words, while the basic structure of the text might be easily recognized as a specific story to an experienced reader, the elements of that story might be altered: *Romeo and Juliet* is still Romeo and Juliet, but they are no longer emblazed within a star-crossed love affair in Verona; instead they are from two culturally different backgrounds in the gang-ridden streets of Cincinnati—however, they get to remain star-crossed and doomed. This reenvisioned transformation allows for the cultural privilege that has formed around the language and structure of the canonical text to be reapproached and redesigned for the inexperienced and intrinsically melodramatic life of the average teenager. In other words, by retelling the same story—with the same plot, basic characters, and themes—but in a more "modern" language with elements that are culturally relatable to a modern audience, the reenvisioned adaptation allows the reader to experience the basic concept of the canonical text before encountering it.

Alongside parallel and reenvisioned adaptations, embedded adaptation has become more and more popular in young adult literature. Reenvisioned and parallel adaptations work in a structure that is very rarely within the construction of the original text. In these texts, the adaptation is altered in such a fashion that it is distinctly removed from the original text. In contrast, the embedded adaptation inserts a modern-thinking character within the original narrative to create a broader understanding of the social constructs. Through this new commentary, the "modern" character acts as a guide and helps the inexperienced reader navigate the plot and characters who remain firmly within the novel's original setting and time period. The primary distinction between the parallel and reenvisioned embedded adaptations is how the original text is used. For the embedded adaptation to work properly, the entirety of the original plot and structure must remain true. In other words, if the additional plot or characters were removed, the story would remain the same as it originally was, albeit through a more modern style of writing. To do so, embedded adaptation uses the basic plot, original characters, and setting to create a classical feel but with a distinctly modern tone allowing for a modern—and perhaps more importantly, inexperienced—audience to experience the thematic constructs and metaphoric depictions of a canonical text but through the language, presentation, and metaphors that are familiar to them. It presents the canon in an accessible manner.

While the embedded adaptation allows for canonical texts to become more accessible to inexperienced readers, it also acts as a guide to understanding the social constructions of canonical literature. By remaining within the confines of the canonical text, the embedded adaptation must be able to present those alien elements to a modern audience in a way that is both familiar and can be believably structured within the already existing plot. In addition to creating a modernized element—generally a new character with modern ideals—the embedded adaptation presents the opportunity to add to the social commentary on the original text. The plot itself remains relatively congruent with the original text with the exception of moments needed to follow or understand the new character in relationship to the original plot. In doing so, the embedded adaptation is almost a reversal of Miskec's description of the reenvisioned adaptation as using the canonical to "earn value." For Miskec, by using a classical plot the author has earned the value already previously connected to the original. I argue the opposite happens in embedded adaptations: rather than earning value from the original text, they provide value to the original by adding content that ultimately presents a more in-depth understanding of the original author's commentary, or in some cases lack of commentary. This can be an expansion on what is already there, or it can fill in the missing gaps. These missing gaps are not necessarily gaps the original author or readership were aware of, but rather gaps that a modern audience might notice, such as the role of marginalized characters or themes. The overwhelming purpose of the embedded adaptation, then, is to provide insight and understanding of the customs from the period of the original text in relationship to how the reader views the modern world.

A Modern Voice among the Past

Megan Shepherd's *The Madman's Daughter* is an embedded adaptation. The voice of Juliet Moreau acts in several different manners as a twenty-first-century guide embedded within an adaptation of H. G. Wells's *The Island of Dr. Moreau* (1896). Wells's novel is, perhaps, the perfect choice for the canonical text of a young-adult-marketed, embedded adaptation that focuses on the social and sexual presence of a modernized, fin de siècle young woman, strictly because there are no female characters in the original text, per se. I argue "per se" because technically in *The Island of Dr. Moreau* there is the wolf-woman and swine-woman who are barely mentioned; the fox-bear woman who is strictly concerned with the law but looked at unfavorably by the narrator for no defined reason; and the half-finished puma-woman who is unable to endure the pain and in her half-finished state wreaks havoc on Dr. Moreau's island and its inhabitants. The puma-woman is arguably the only female character of any consideration; however, the consideration in which she is mentioned looks only at her inability to become more "man"-like. The lack of true female characters draws even more attention to the monstrousness of the half-beast women as they attempt to act within their half-human form. The relative lack of female characters, or a feminist-driven plot, allows Shepherd to develop an embedded adaptation that presents a bridge into the Wellsian world for an inexperienced reader. More importantly, it allows Shepherd to present the voice of a modern woman rather than manipulate a modern character around the nuances of early feminism. In other words, Shepherd provides her readers with a guide through both the expectations and a modern commentary of the period.

In the most basic of ways, Juliet guides readers through Wells's original text and commentary before presenting her own commentary and telling her own story. Shepherd introduces Juliet as Dr. Moreau's daughter before inserting her into Wells's opening scenes, allowing readers to become accustomed to the juxtaposition between Juliet as proper young Victorian woman and her modern independence and intelligence. Once placed firmly in both worlds—her nineteenth-century setting and her twenty-first-century politics—Juliet enters into Wells's novel by leaving England with Montgomery, Dr. Moreau's assistant in both novels, to find her father, who fled London years ago after horrible speculations were made about the exact nature of his surgical practices, again similar in both novels. Juliet is determined to prove that the speculations about her father are false, so her life can return to what it once was. As in Wells's novel, on the voyage to the island, Montgomery saves a shipwrecked man—Edward Prendick in the original, Edward Prince in Shepherd's adaptation—and agrees to bring him along to the island. In both novels, Prince and Juliet slowly discover and experience first-hand the truths about Dr. Moreau and the horrific advances he has made through vivisection.[9]

In Wells's novel, Prendick's narrative of the creatures of the island and Dr. Moreau's madness is quite clearly a disturbed commentary on the threat of man's desire to play God through developments in science and medicine. By giving voice to Juliet, rather than Edward, Shepherd offers her own commentary on the nineteenth century. Shepherd remains true to the nature of the embedded adaptation and does not undermine Wells's original fears; however, the purpose of the embedded adaptation is to add new commentary to the already existing structure in order to provide an understanding between the modern reader and the original text and time period. So, while ever present, the discussion on the horrors of medicine and science takes a back seat to the presentation of Juliet's interest and obvious talents in science and medicine in relationship to her roles and obligations as a woman in the nineteenth century.

Through the presence of Juliet, Shepherd is able to demonstrate the rigid confines of what was acceptable and unacceptable for a woman to feel, think, do, and know and, more importantly, perhaps, demonstrate the influence of nineteenth-century feminism upon twenty-first-century feminist movements.

Juliet's interest in medicine, and her overwhelming desire to be in control of her life and decisions, allows Shepherd to skillfully manipulate Juliet through the limitations of a woman during the nineteenth century while maintaining a modern voice readers are familiar with. The modernity of Juliet's voice and actions is often presented in juxtaposition with the "proper" role of a young, nineteenth-century woman. Shepherd takes the discussion a step further into the twentieth century with the role and presence of intelligent women as equals in mind and substance to their male counterparts, focusing specifically on Juliet's very capable scientific and medical mind. Shepherd is quick to inform her readers within the first chapter that Juliet's medical knowledge is not only unusual for a woman but also viewed as inappropriate. At a party, Juliet corrects two of the male medical students who do not know the correct number of bones in the human body. Annoyed that she is right, he asks:

"And how would a girl know such things?"
I straightened. "Whether I'm right or wrong has nothing to do with gender."
I paused. "Also, I'm right."
Adam smirked. "Girls don't study science."[10]

In three lines of dialogue Shepherd has set up the precedent for Juliet within the novel: Women can be just as intelligent as men in the sciences, even if it was not deemed proper in the nineteenth century.

This quick scene, one that has no comparison in Wells's text, which takes place almost completely on the island, is important within the constructs of the embedded adaptation because of how it demonstrates the connection between a twenty-first-century voice within a nineteenth-century world. Shepherd uses the men in the scene to represent nineteenth-century expectations of gender roles: Juliet, as a woman, should not have a scientific mind or knowledge. Furthermore, Juliet's friend, Lucy, counters Juliet in this scene, flippantly responding to questions by batting "her pretty lashes. 'Well, I'm sure *I* don't know.'"[11] Lucy is there for one thing: to find husbands for herself and Juliet. Lucy reflects how a modern audience might expect a proper, young Victorian woman to act. However, Lucy really isn't a proper Victorian young woman at all, which for many inexperienced readers would go unnoticed. In many ways she's just as much a twenty-first-century teenager as Juliet: she's snuck out of her house to meet her best friend and go to an unsupervised party with a bunch of men, drink whiskey, and play risqué parlor games. She is really anything *but* a proper Victorian woman. However, she does reflect what many modern readers, especially young adults, consider Victorian-like. To further promote the idea that Lucy is a better representation of the Victorian woman, Shepherd has Juliet look toward Lucy's actions for all her social cues. This suggests that while it is clear that Juliet is not "proper," Lucy is more aligned with how the Victorian period is perceived.

By working with these assumptions, embedded adaptations are able to work against them and begin to demonstrate the restraints and possibilities of the time through a modern lens. In the case of Juliet and Lucy, a trained Victorianist would note that both characters are acting in irrational and risqué manners and are more neo-Victorian than truly Victorian. However, for the average teenage reader in the twenty-first century their actions appear relatively normal for a typical teen party, or at least what they might imagine a party might be like in nineteenth-century London. Juliet's narration of her uncertainty, her wish to be more like Lucy and her heightened awareness that "men like these don't marry girls like me [a maid],"[12] eases readers into understanding the general idea of Victorian England and literature. Furthermore, Juliet's narration sets Lucy up as being a proper young Victorian woman and herself as the outsider.

Embedded adaptations are not meant to simply reconstruct the original text with a modern, often marginalized, character; they must also recreate the social and political climates of the original text in a manner that becomes easier for the modern reader to comprehend without any significant knowledge of the time period the original canonical text was written. Or more simply stated, embedded adaptations work within and depend on the stereotypes and assumptions teen readings already have about the social and political climate of the period of the original text.

Canonical literature can be isolating to modern readers, especially teenagers, because they feel like an outsider to the world within the text. Victorian canonical literature, I argue, can be one of the most alienating forms of literature to inexperienced readers. What makes Victorian canonical texts particularly off-putting for many modern readers—aside from sheer length—is its familiarity simultaneously paired with its unfamiliarity. Unlike Shakespeare, Chaucer, or Wordsworth, whose language needs a significant amount of unpacking and upfront knowledge to even understand the basic concepts, the language of Victorian novels feels familiar. When Jane Eyre explains in the final chapter, "Reader, I married him,"[13] there is little ambiguity. The familiarity of the language creates for many young readers a false sense of readability: I know these words; therefore, I must be able to understand the meaning of the text. What is unfamiliar is the societal and political context of the text. This creates a constant push–pull of the known and unknown when reading, which is problematic to many inexperienced readers because they recognize the world that is presented, but are unable to navigate the social customs and constructs that are very rarely explained. This inability to navigate often leaves readers frustrated, unsure, and dismissive of the canon.

From this frustration, the inexperienced reader begins to make their own sweeping commentary on actions and period of the canonized literature. Their commentary is usually a mixture of what they might already know of the time period and how they perceive that theme in their own lives, with a large side of speculation. For instance, even the most inexperienced reader has preconceived notions regarding the Victorian period, women, and feminism of the time. However, these notions are rarely formulated around what Victorian feminism was, but rather an ill-informed, fantastically dreamed, radical Victorian woman. These modern visions of women in hoop dresses, fighting against the patriarchy for the rights to their own life are hardly what feminism looked like in the Victorian period, but is often what inexperienced readers bring to canonical texts labeled as early feminist writing. And this confusion is distinctly marked by readers who are unaware that the small actions against societal norms are more than just small acts of rebellion.

The embedded adaptation helps to unpack these moments for inexperienced readers. By presenting the societal norm through the lens of a modern narrator, the Victorian trope can be acknowledged and understood. Consider again the comparisons Juliet makes between herself and Lucy in the opening scenes of *The Madman's Daughter*: Juliet is clearly marked as the modern embedded audience (intelligent, knowledgeable, and stubborn), and Lucy is the preconceived idea of the Victorian woman (docile with bouncing curls, flirtatious but safely feminine). The two interact in a pseudo-Victorian construct that is on the verge of stereotypical—neither Victorian nor modern in nature—that allows the inexperienced reader to begin to learn the social norms needed to understand canonical texts while making it easier to identify the changes between Victorian and modern settings.

In *The Madman's Daughter* this understanding is guided through Juliet, who equally presents the social restraints of the Victorian woman and an independent, modern, scientific mind. In doing so, the embedded adaptation fills the void that many inexperienced readers have with canonical Victorian texts: an intelligent woman with a voice that is distinctly her own who must still succumb to the regulations of society at that time. To further ease the inexperienced reader into the realm of Victorian canonical texts, Shepherd creates a pull between the modern narrating voice of Juliet and those of her Victorian parents. Although Juliet's mother is dead long before the novel begins, Juliet's thoughts continually return to her mother and what she would have deemed proper or improper for her to do as a young lady. While this imagined motherly advice gives readers some idea of how a young woman should act in Victorian society, Juliet's concerns don't move beyond proper dress and the improper display of affections toward Montgomery and Prince. It is Dr. Moreau that presents a clearer image of the expectations of an unwed young Victorian woman. Moreau is continually reprimanding and scolding Juliet's curiosity and interests in his scientific endeavors, proclaiming shortly after her arrival on the island: "A girl interested in science. How *modern* of you [Shepherd's italics]. I suggest you find more appropriate interests. Montgomery, we've an old needlepoint set, haven't we? … you'd only be in the way. Science is best left to men. Women have too delicate a constitution."[14] Uninterested in the potential of Juliet's mind, Dr. Moreau treats her with near constant mockery and continues to remind her of her place in his life, on the island, and in society. Instead of focusing on Juliet's intelligence and awareness of what is happening around the island—something he acutely ignores—Moreau is more concerned with the possibility of marrying her off to Prince, who is at least "of proper breeding."[15] For Moreau, Juliet is another part of his property that should and will act as he sees best.

The social restrictions placed upon Juliet, both through her father's perception of her and her own memory of her mother, further reminds readers that while Juliet's actions and thoughts might be very modern, she is still an embedded character within an adapted Victorian text. As the embedded character, Juliet's narration and modern voice guide the inexperienced reader through the social constructions of the historical setting of the adapted canonical text. In other words, the reader doesn't need to understand all the nuances of the period or what was considered radical and what was traditional. Instead, the reader only needs to be able to determine the differences between the embedded character's perspective and the text's Victorian setting.

This new creation mixed within the old social structure creates within itself a commentary for the inexperienced reader to use as an introduction when beginning to navigate and understand the complicated obstacles and nuances of the marginalized voices in the nineteenth century. The intelligence of Juliet as a neo-Victorian character gives readers the chance to see the struggles and apprehensions of women in canonical texts. For the inexperienced reader, this connection between the original structures of the literature and the modern embedded characters creates fully functioning and relatable aspects that in turn can lead to appreciation and understanding of their various roles in the original text. Juliet describes secretly reading and studying anatomy, hidden "in the laboratory closet during [Montgomery's] lessons."[16] As her story continues, her knowledge of science and medicine is clearly more than simply knowing the placement of a few bones and ligaments. But Juliet is also her father's daughter, as she continually reminds her audience and herself: "My father's blood flowed in my veins, too."[17] While Juliet's concept of her father's blood is more in connection to his scientific experiments and her role in them, it is also a constant reminder that no matter how modern she appears, thinks, or acts, Juliet must still function within the time period of the novel: Victorian England. Because of Juliet's distinctly modern voice set against a strictly Victorian landscape of customs and expectations, each time she thinks or says or acts in a way that is comfortable to a modern reader she must explain away her impropriety. These explanations act as constant reminders to the reader that no matter how familiar the narrator feels or appears, the text is not wholly modern and must be interpreted as such. These neo-Victorian explanations entwined with modern expectations allows for a commentary that is neither Victorian nor modern, but rather a precariously dangled bridge between the two, ever demonstrating how one leads to the other and the other is reflected in the previous.

Creating the Connection: A Conclusion

Although the undertones of nineteenth-century female voices within modern, embedded characters may be unfamiliar to inexperienced readers, the importance of being aware of how these marginalized voices changed and grew toward acceptance should not be. In order for readers to grasp the concepts of relevancy of canonical texts, these types of adaptations are crucial in leading inexperienced readers through the meaningful experiences they may find in canonical literature, by first presenting them with a familiar voice. This familiar voice is vital for the inexperienced reader who is keen on navigating out of the known in modern texts and into the unfamiliar of many canonical texts. Various adaptations, but especially embedded adaptations, act as important place-markers designed to help young adult readers when reading canonical texts. *The Madman's Daughter* demonstrates the restrictions women fought against and how even the slightest rebellion was an action of progress.

Each type of adaptation demonstrates a different but crucial element in understanding canonical texts, but for the young adult reader perhaps the trend of embedded adaptations is the most critical for connecting a new, modern readership with canonical literature. The embedded adaptation doesn't just help build Steinbeck's concept of "points of contact"; it carves out footholds for its readers. *The Madman's Daughter* still presents the monstrosities of Moreau's island, but through Juliet's modern voice, readers can begin to understand and wade through the restrictions of the Victorian period. While other adaptations attempt to explain or connect to the canon through direct modernization or parallel structures, the embedded adaptation forces readers to approach the juxtapositions and similarities between modernity and the past head-on by entering the text itself. Through the embedded, modern voice, inexperienced readers are better able to navigate the unknown because they have a guide.

To state it simply: adaptations create connections, the connections needed between readers and texts. They allow readers to understand the time period, the characters, the plot. By filling in the spaces that are not always easily or clearly seen by inexperienced readers, adaptations begin to demonstrate why and how we have the characters we love and adore in literature today, by making those of the past more easily accessible. The voices of the past might not be easily understood by inexperienced readers who cannot see their own image among the canonical texts, but voices like Juliet's have led readers to understand that while not exactly the same, their voice may be akin to those of the past. And through these similarities, inexperienced readers can begin to make the connections between the past and today.

Notes

1 Blau, "Literary Competence and the Experience of Literature," 42.
2 Miskec, "Young Adult Literary Adaptations of the Canon," 75.
3 Bland, "Speaking My Mind," 21.
4 Ibid., 22.
5 Ibid.
6 While fan fiction is decidedly a heavy presence in many adolescent literary circles and in the concept of adaptations, this chapter will not discuss the practice of writing fan fiction as a connection to canonical literature, even as an unpublished reenvisioned construct. However, it should still be stated that the majority of fan fiction uses some form of reenvisioned texts as its basic platform, usually in a manipulation aspect of the parallel text. In these manipulation aspects the overall plot of the text becomes world-canon and the reenvisioned elements are scenes that either happened "off-screen" or have been added on as side stories to the original plot, though, as anyone who has even the smallest experience in fan fiction knows, the most predominant manipulation aspect of fan fiction is romantic partners, wherein whole canonical plotlines are ignored to fit the new "ship" of two previously unconnected characters.

Moreover, fan fiction is generally written as adaptations of more modern texts, that is, canonical texts. While fan fiction is a truly complicated and intricate aspect within reenvisioned literature and deserves a thorough discussion, this chapter does not have the space or time to indulge in the implications of that form.

7   Winner of the 1992 Pulitzer Prize for Fiction, Jane Smile's *A Thousand Acres* is a modernized, Midwestern version of Shakespeare's *King Lear*. Set on a thousand-acre farm in the heart of Iowa, owned by a farmer with three daughters, the story is told through the point of view of the eldest daughter, Ginny. As in *King Lear*, Smiley's novel focuses around the hidden truths that arise when an aging man wants to divide his "kingdom" among his three daughters: Ginny (Goneril), Rose (Regan), and Caroline (Cordelia). In addition to the use of similar characters and roles within the novel that mirror the play, Smiley also relies on critical moments within the play—such as the storm—to propel her novel, while also manipulating the various themes of madness, appearances, familial conflict, and ownership. It is the clear mapping between Shakespeare and Smiley that marks *A Thousand Acres* as a reenvisioned adaptation.

    Unlike Smiley's novel, Jean Rhys's *Wide Sargasso Sea* is a parallel novel to Charlotte Brontë's *Jane Eyre*. Rhys uses the same characters from Brontë, but in an alternative structure. Rhys poses and answers the questions: Who was the woman in the attic, before Mr. Rochester? And how did she come to be locked in an attic in England? And is she truly crazy? None of these answers are fully given, or reliably within Jane Eyre, but Rhys provides a possible answer. In three short parts, Rhys presents Antoinette Cosway—later renamed Bertha by an unnamed gentleman, presumed by those familiar with *Jane Eyre* to be Mr. Rochester—in her native home in Jamaica: from her childhood through to the setting of the Thornfield Hall on fire. While most of Rhys's novel is wholly separate from Brontë's, the third and shortest part does overlap with what is presented of Bertha or Antoinette in *Jane Eyre*, and the backstory that Rochester provides in explanation to Jane is easily recognized as similar to Rhys's parallel suggestion of what might have happened. It is these distinct connections, alignments, and overlapping moments between Rhys and Brontë that mark the novel as parallel rather than reenvisioned.

8   For instance, fairly early in Pratchett's novel, Dodger encounters the Barber of Fleet Street. While nothing happens to Dodger—else it'd be a rather short novel—an aware audience is waiting for the murderous barber to attack. Instead, this leads Dodger to meet up with the journalist, Charlie, a young representation of the very Baz himself. While Dickensian in style and structure, overall Pratchett uses very little of Dicken's canonical text to support his resculpted presentation of Dodger, but he does overload the novel with Victorian subtleties until it is almost a literary guide of who's who in Victorian culture and literature. However, it is equally enjoyable for the non-Victorian scholar to read and even for the child who might know the Artful Dodger from *Oliver Twist* but also might not.

9   At the time of Wells's publication, vivisection, or the act of using surgery to dissect a living animal—generally without anesthetics—in order to understand or observe the living internal structure, was a heated discussion in Europe and America in regard to its moral implications. In 1875, the National Anti-Vivisection Society was formed in attempts to draw awareness to and end the practice of vivisection. Wells's novel drew even further awareness to the horrors, while also questioning the purpose of and degree to which science may advance, which ultimately resulted in the British Union

for the Abolition of Vivisection two years later in 1898. A year later, Mark Twain, an animal rights activist before such a concept was ever formally developed, presented his support for the London Anti-Vivisection Society, arguing that any results from vivisection that prove "profitable to the [human] race would not remove my hostility to it. The pains which it inflicts upon unconsenting animals is the basis of my enmity towards it, and it is to me sufficient justification of the enmity without looking further" (Fishkin 26).

10 Shepherd, *The Madman's Daughter*, 10.
11 Ibid., 8.
12 Ibid., 7.
13 Brontë, *Jane Eyre*, 429.
14 Shepherd, *Madman's*, 156.
15 Ibid., 269.
16 Ibid., 10.
17 Ibid., 203.

Bibliography

Bland, Guy. "Speaking My Mind: Out with the Old, in with the (Not so) New." *The English Journal* 90, no. 3 (January 2001): 20–2.
Blau, Sheridan. "Literary Competence and the Experience of Literature." *Style* 48, no. 1 (Spring 2014): 42–7.
Brontë, Charlotte. *Jane Eyre*. New York: Bantam, 2003.
Brontë, Emily. *Wuthering Heights*. New York: Penguin, 2003.
Dante, Alighieri. *Divine Comedy*. Translated by Mark Musa. New York: Penguin, 2003.
Dickens, Charles. *Oliver Twist*. New York: Penguin, 2003.
Draper, Susan. *Romiette and Julio*. New York: Atheneum Books for Young Readers, 1999.
Fishkin, Shelley Fisher. "Introduction." In *Mark Twain's Book of Animals by Mark Twain*, edited by Shelley Fisher Fishkin, 1–34. Oakland: University of California Press, 2011.
Hardy, Thomas. *Jude the Obscure*. New York: Penguin. 1998.
Meyer, Stephanie. *Eclipse (Twilight Sagas)*. New York: Little, Brown Books for Young Readers, 2009.
Milton, John. *Paradise Lost*. Edited by Gordon Teskey. New York: Norton, 1993.
Miskec, Jennifer. "Young Adult Literary Adaptations of the Canon." *The ALAN Review* (Summer 2013): 75–85.
Pratchett, Terry. *Dodger*. New York: Harper Collins, 2013.
Rhys, Jean. *Wide Sargasso Sea*. New York: Penguin, 2011.
Shakespeare, William. "King Lear." In *The Norton Shakespeare*, edited by Stephen Greenblatt, Walter Cohen, Jean E. Howard, and Katharine Eisaman Maus, 2318–478. New York: W.W. Norton, 1997.
Shakespeare, William. "Romeo and Juliet." In *The Norton Shakespeare*, edited by Stephen Greenblatt, Walter Cohen, Jean E. Howard, and Katharine Eisaman Maus, 872–939. New York: W.W. Norton, 1997.
Shepherd, Megan. *The Madman's Daughter*. New York: Blazer & Bray, 2013.
Smiley, Jane. *A Thousand Acres*. New York: Anchor, 2003.
Wells, H. G. *The Island of Dr. Moreau*. New York: Penguin, 2005.

12

A Tale of Two Women: Representing Femininity in Charles Dickens's *A Tale of Two Cities* and Sarah Rees Brennan's *Tell the Wind and Fire*

Maya Zakrzewska-Pim

Introduction

The representation of women in novels has changed drastically between the Victorian era and the modern day, due to the altered position that women occupy in society. Feminist movements from the late-nineteenth century onward have granted women more political, economic, and social power. The battle for equality, however, has not yet been won; there are more similarities between how Victorian and contemporary women are represented than one might expect. This chapter will discuss the representation of women in Charles Dickens's *A Tale of Two Cities* (1859) and Sarah Rees Brennan's young adult adaptation of it, *Tell the Wind and Fire* (2016). An analysis of a Victorian novel that has been adapted for a modern audience is one way to clearly draw attention to these similarities, since having the same premise of a narrative makes a comparative analysis clearer. This chapter will show how Victorian ideas about femininity have influenced modern representations of women, which argues that Victorian novels like *A Tale of Two Cities* are more relevant to modern audiences than their publishing dates suggest.

Victorian women were often presented as embodying either an "angel" or a "monster."[1] Female purity in the nineteenth century was usually represented by "an angel in the house,"[2] that is, the sort of woman depicted in conduct books since the eighteenth century: submissive, modest, and selfless. However, "the fact that the angel woman manipulates her domestic mystical sphere to ensure the well-being of those entrusted to her care reveals that she *can* manipulate; she can scheme; she can plot–stories as well as strategies"[3] suggests an underlying potential for complexity of character typical of modern narratives, even if it is only ever implied in Victorian novels. Frequently, though, for every angel in the house there exists a monster, endowed with such masculine characteristics as assertiveness or aggressiveness, which are typical of a male life of "significant action," and thus women who display such traits are monstrous because they are unfeminine.[4] *A Tale of Two Cities*, which depicts an angelic Lucie Manette and monstrous Madame Defarge, is a perfect example of representing women in such opposition to each other.

Associating specific character traits with one or the other gender has not gone out of fashion. June Pulliam, in her analysis of Suzanne Collins's *The Hunger Games* trilogy, draws upon the feminist psychoanalytic work of Nancy Chodorow to examine contemporary constructions of gender. Chodorow argues that empathy is central to girls' definition of self,[5] and Pulliam views Katniss's seemingly masculine behavior as being motivated by a desire to protect others, rather than as an act of defiance.[6] Where modern narratives are unlikely to represent characters (male or female) as unequivocally angelic or monstrous, at least in their actions, there persists an idea of there being a "right" and "wrong" way of thinking, and more and less appropriate motivations for women to act on. This is visible in Brennan's twenty-first-century incarnation of Lucie Manette, since she is the narrator of her own story, which provides insight into the complexity of her decision-making process. Lucie's actions almost always reflect how she thinks others want her to act and what they want her to represent based on their ideas of what a woman should be like: pure, innocent, and with limited agency. Her thoughts, however, reveal that her actions are a mask, under which is an independent woman perfectly capable of taking care of herself as well as the people in her life: a woman who does not need to be saved, but tries to be, in fact, the savior—of herself and of others.

In *A Tale of Two Cities*, Lucie is important because she is often the reason for which the men around her make the decisions they do; nevertheless, she is rarely party to the decision-making process itself. Most of the scenes she appears in are focalized through male characters; she has no voice or agency of her own. In contrast to Dickens's novel, Brennan places women, and the contemporary debates surrounding them, at the forefront of her novel. This begins with her choice of title, continuing with her casting of Lucie as narrator, which allows Brennan to bring to light the very relevant discussions of the representations and (mis)interpretations of women in the media, and conversations surrounding the issue of consent. The retelling creates an illusion of women having power and agency, which is only dispelled upon a closer reading. Lucie is not only subject to others' authority because she is a teenager; it is also because she is a woman and thus must conform to the expectations of her family and the society at large. Even her Aunt Leila, who leads the Rebellion and overthrows the Council, must maintain her own good opinion among the rebels so as not to lose power.

A Tale of Two Cities is particularly well suited to be adapted for a teenage audience, with its backdrop of the excitement of a revolution, a love triangle, and its emphasis on self-discovery. Roberta Seelinger Trites observes that young adult novels are concerned with how individuals exist in society, rather than just focusing on self and self-discovery, as children's literature does.[7] This is one of the preoccupations of *A Tale of Two Cities*, and so many of its adaptations, as well. A frequent criticism leveled at Dickens for the text is that it does not concern itself enough with history and historical accuracy to be a novel about the French Revolution.[8] This is only true, though, if we demand that Dickens's historicism be classed as referential (focusing on specific historical figures and events) instead of seeing it as conceptual (a novel engaged with concepts of agency, individuality, and the representativeness available in a historical event).[9] It is this conceptual perspective that makes the novel so well suited to young adult adaptations.

The Significance of Titles

The title of an adaptation is often the first sign the reader is given of the adaptation's relationship with an earlier text. The title of Brennan's novel, *Tell the Wind and Fire*, is a direct quote from Dickens's novel, in which the words are originally uttered by Madame Defarge: "Tell the wind and fire where to stop ... but don't tell me."[10] The title itself may not be enough for readers to connect Brennan's novel to Dickens's text, as it is a subtle connection relying on in-depth knowledge of the original text, which young readers are unlikely to have. Adaptations for young audiences are, after all, often created in the hopes of introducing their audiences to, and encouraging interaction with, the sources. The order in which the texts are encountered is (in most cases) flipped, and it is the adaptation that exists in the reader's mind as the original, while the original is the text that is compared to a "previous" one. Adaptations thus must stand on their own, independent of their predecessors. Nevertheless, adaptations are usually "announced and extensive transposition[s] of a particular work,"[11] and by forging such explicit links with their sources they claim the cultural currency held by canonical texts. However, even if the reader fails to pinpoint the exact source of the quotation, there is a nod toward Dickens in Brennan's biographical note on the inside flap, mentioning her "shocking" sin of reading a first edition of one of his books in the bathtub. The link to *A Tale of Two Cities* solidifies when the reader opens the book, though, to find the novel dedicated to "C.D" (presumably Charles Dickens), and the full quote that inspired the title, with Dickens's full name and the title of his novel on the following page.

The use of this quotation is important because it brings women to the foreground, having been first uttered by a woman. Madame Defarge uses it to express her desire for revenge; she is unstoppable—a force of nature stronger than wind or fire—because of the strength of her hatred for the nobility, particularly the Evrémondes. The Evrémonde brothers raped and killed Madame Defarge's sister and killed her brother. Madame Defarge is one of the strongest characters in *A Tale of Two Cities* because of her unwavering convictions, which result in single-minded action, concerning the undeserved status the nobility hold in society. These words evoke a woman's conviction, strength, and action, and by using them for a title, Brennan is announcing that this is the sort of character her audience may expect to find in her novel. This implication is underscored by the blurb, which ends with: "With both halves of the city burning, and mercy nowhere to be found, can Lucie save either boy—or herself?" This question firmly places Lucie in the position of active protagonist, even to a reader unable to recognize the implications of the title. However, when the words are first used in Brennan's novel by Lucie's grandmother, they convey her determination to save the man she loves.[12] The quote appears again later, but Lucie takes issue with her aunt's misuse of the quote: "She should have remembered that my grandmother was the first to say those words, when people said she could not save the man she loved. She should have remembered that she had taught me to be unstoppable too."[13] Lucie and her grandmother are placed in opposition to Aunt Leila because of the opposing motivations that drive them: love and hatred. Since Lucie is the novel's heroine, and Aunt Leila is depicted as misguided at best, a villain at worst, the implication here is that being an unstoppable woman is only acceptable if such force of character is displayed for the right reasons.

(Un)Acceptable Motivations: Love versus Hatred

In *A Tale of Two Cities*, Lucie is always represented as the perfect daughter (helping to rescue her father from prison, taking care of him in England) and the perfect wife (keeping a home for Darnay and then following him to France and appearing outside his prison daily to keep up his spirits as she stayed there with their daughter Lucie, waiting for her husband to be released). When other characters talk about her, it is always in her role as daughter, wife (or love interest), or mother. The novel gives no sense of her identity outside of her relationship to others, giving the impression that her entire life consists of the roles she occupies. At first glance, Lucie in *Tell the Wind and Fire* seems to represent the same feminine characteristics as her Victorian counterpart, that is, the ideal of love and devotion to family, which is a key element in the ideology of the Victorian middle-class family.[14] For instance, others see her taking care of her father—but they do not see how guilty she feels for having lied about her mother to save him, since that would have implicated him in working against the laws of the Council. In this, she may have been the "perfect" daughter to her father, but she failed to honor her mother's memory by claiming no relation to her.[15] Like her Victorian counterpart, the modern Lucie almost always represents herself in relation to her familial and romantic relationships, but the added insight into these bonds provided by Lucie as the narrator of her story reveals she does not fulfill her role in them as perfectly as it may seem from the outside.

Lucie's motivation is always love for those close to her. It is based on the belief that "love is when you save someone no matter what the cost."[16] Lucie's literal interpretation of this doctrine becomes obvious early in the narrative, when Lucie tells Mark, Ethan's uncle and the leader of the Light Council, that the guards who stopped them at the train station discovered Carwyn's identity as Ethan's doppelganger. This implicates the Stryker family, since creating doppelgangers is illegal. Lucie knows, even as she divulges this information, that she "was signing the guards' death warrant. But they had tried to kill Ethan. It was Ethan or them."[17] Brennan thus presents a female character far more ruthless than her predecessor and far less likely to fit into the perfect feminine mold (so "gentle and pure"[18]) that many of Dickens's female characters fall into: Lucie from *A Tale of Two Cities*, Florence from *Dombey and Son* (1846–8), and Agnes from

David Copperfield (1850). Of course, it is impossible to know what the Victorian Lucie would have done were she presented with such a choice, but the men in her life never ask for her opinion, and thus she is spared any potential stain on her character that making such a decision may have made. Her strength lies in being a support for her husband. When she hears her husband's death sentence, she collapses, "but so strong was the voice within her, representing that it was she of all the world who must uphold him in his misery and not augment it, that it quickly raised her."[19] Though both Lucies are driven by love, they are represented differently because modern narratives favor active protagonists; the modern Lucie must make choices about whom she should be loving and devoted to, choices the Victorian Lucie is never given. Since she makes no complicated choices, the Victorian Lucie is not represented as flawed in the same way as her modern counterpart, and there is no chance to question whether or not she is doing the right thing.

While love is clearly represented as a defendable reason for morally ambiguous decisions, a desire for revenge, expressed by Madame Defarge and Aunt Leila, is not. Both women are willing to sacrifice others for their political cause, which has become intertwined with their personal desire for retribution. Madame Defarge seeks revenge against the Evrémondes' rape of her sister and their responsibility for both her siblings' deaths, while Aunt Leila wants the Strykers to pay for having her sister killed when she discovered the identity of Carwyn, Ethan's doppelganger; they both refuse to stop "until every drop of his blood has answered for mine."[20] They do not seek to punish only the people responsible, but their entire families. Madame Defarge dismisses her husband's hesitation about sacrificing Charles Darnay because, as Daniel Stout observes, "who the revolution thinks you are is not a matter of what you have or haven't done";[21] it is about where you come from and what you represent, and as such she can avoid any inconsistency that sympathy might prompt, because she is not ruling on individuals. It is convenient for both women that their political views push them to punish those they have personal grudges against, though; neither is acting purely on ideological conviction.

By prioritizing a political cause, Madame Defarge and Aunt Leila cease to see people as individuals and, consequently, are willing to sacrifice others for what they believe. Aunt Leila is willing to risk sacrificing a child to ensure she can kill Ethan Stryker, which is represented as the ultimate villainous act. Killing a child requires a woman to go against her so-called maternal instincts, after all, and Lucie's absolute and immediate refusal to contemplate such an act, even if it means losing Ethan, strongly suggests that these instincts are desirable in the modern woman, just as they were in the nineteenth century. In both novels, then, there seems to be the Victorian binary of an angelic and monstrous femininity presented, but the modern Lucie's willingness to sacrifice others suggests more complexity. She draws the reader's attention to the danger of simplifying people's characters to brand them as heroes or villains; she sees that if she had stayed in the Dark city, "revenge might have been all I wanted as well,"[22] thus representing herself as simultaneously an angel and a monster.

The modern Lucie cannot embrace her "monstrous" femininity in its entirety. Her actions at the end of the novel, when she is prepared to sacrifice Ethan to save Marie, suggest that ultimately, Victorian notions about womanhood persist. Lucie's choice is surprising since her motivation throughout the novel has been love specifically for Ethan. Of course, Marie is also one of her loved ones, so wanting to save her is consistent with Lucie's desire to protect those she loves. However, the lack of hesitation on her part calls into question her love for Ethan, which she spends most of the novel reiterating. During her conversation with Aunt Leila after the ball, when Leila wants Lucie to join their committee, Lucie realizes that she does not want to do that, "Not even to save Ethan. [She] was so tired of compromises and cowardice."[23] This is a pivotal point of the novel, when Lucie allows all pretense to drop. Her exasperation and exhaustion is understandable, but it draws attention to her unreliability as a narrator. Based on how she presents herself in the first three-quarters of the novel, protecting Ethan is her absolute priority, so her sudden shift comes across as inconsistent characterization.

By choosing Marie, a child, over Ethan, she embraces the feminine characteristics associated with motherhood. It must be remembered that "actions or experiences are not in themselves inherently transgressive, alienating or conformist. Rather, they are defined as such in relation to existing social codes and structures, these codes being subject to social and historical chance."[24] We cannot take this book out of its context, and the fact that these views are what they are (and that maternal instincts unquestionably trump romantic love) points to the Victorian legacy underlying modern representations of women. As Robyn McCallum points out, "Adolescent fiction ... functions within a dominant humanist and liberal paradigm of personal maturation which valorizes intersubjective responsibility. Thus, the representation of transgressive behavior frequently has a conservative social function."[25] The ending of Brennan's novel seems to support this claim. I am by no means saying that Lucie should not have saved the child given the choice. Choosing Ethan over Marie would have made a more consistent and interesting character, though, especially since it feels as if this decision were made at least in part to remain faithful to the source's ending; Carwyn cannot be saved if he is to embrace Sydney Carton's fate. Read from this perspective, Lucie and Brennan indeed have no choice.

Becoming a Woman in the Twenty-First Century

McCallum discusses the formation of adolescent identities in young adult literature and how this often happens in relation to the social structures and institutions around young adults. The modern Lucie's dilemmas and difficulties in navigating her world all illustrate how she attempts to become who she wants to be in response (positive or negative) to external stimuli. For most of the novel, Lucie feels as if she must act a part to be accepted, and this emphasis on appearances draws attention to how restrictive the performance of hegemonic femininity can be.[26] Judith Butler's work on performance of gender, that is, gender as an effect that is produced by the "stylization of the body and, hence, must be understood as the mundane way in which bodily gestures, movements, and styles of various kinds constitute the illusion of an abiding gendered self,"[27] is a useful way of viewing Lucie's actions to better understand her motivations.

She is frustrated and exhausted by playing a role, by trying to "be everything to him, to [Ethan], to the council, to be so much and never be anything objectionable ... it's effortless because it's supposed to be effortless."[28] She is trying to form her identity in relation to her environment, "in dialogue with the social discourses, practices and ideologies constituting the culture which an individual inhabits,"[29] a dialogue that is rebellious and transgressive. Lucie becomes the character she is at the end of the narrative because she resists those around her; her sense of identity is based in opposition.

McCallum describes transgressive behavior as being premised on the "existence of social, ideological, legal or cultural codes and conventions which constitute boundaries and constraints upon a person's actions, speech, thoughts and sense of identity."[30] Lucie's very act of saving Ethan—refusing to accept the *sans-merci's* verdict, standing vigil outside of his tower, and, on the last day, dressing differently, the choice of clothing itself an act of insubordination—is transgressive. Lucie dresses not like a woman but "like a soldier, and my long, loose, fair hair made me look like fairy-tale damsel."[31] Her description suggests that soldiers are not expected to be women, and a soldier's clothing with her otherwise feminine appearance is a jarring sight. This is precisely her intention, though: "If people found that incongruous, if they did not know what to make of me, I had not known what to make of myself either. They could learn."[32] Throughout the novel, Lucie tries to conform to society's expectations but finds she cannot, as she is constantly disagreeing with and fighting against them, feeling as if she is playing a part instead of being herself. In a final desperate expression of desire to be what others want her to be so she can save those she loves, Lucie wishes that she were less human and instead "a puppet, could be some smiling, dancing thing that would make all the right moves."[33] But she is human, a human girl trying to figure out how to fit into the patriarchal society she finds herself in, without losing herself along the way. And she does this by rebelling against the expectations this society places upon her.

The modern Lucie scoffs at the traditional gender roles she feels everyone around is attempting to enforce, including Ethan. She accuses him of acting as if she were "a piece of china to be kept in a glass case. Maybe you want me to be breakable, so you can shield me. But I'm not. How can I be fragile and do everything I have to do?"[34] However, in attempting to subvert them, Lucie appropriates those same behaviors she finds most worthy of criticism; after all, as Ethan accurately points out, she treats him as if he were the helpless one.[35] This desire to protect is her main motivation throughout the narrative; she sees him as "a golden boy in every sense of the word, untouched by darkness or suffering."[36] But she also sees him as naïve and does not understand his refusal to perform for society, to use his charm and smile to bend people to his will, something she is too afraid to not do for most of the novel. It is this refusal to manipulate others that draws her to him in the first place; she falls in love with him because he is the only one to give her a choice, who does not insist on her being someone else[37] because he himself refuses to be anyone other than who he is. Even though she accuses him of exhausting her because she must act a part for him, as she does for others, this is never something he imposes on her. If she pretends to be someone other than herself with Ethan it is because she chooses to, to protect him. It is not to meet his expectations but to meet her own. This decision on her part reveals just how much her expectations for herself are based on her assumptions of what others think she should be and how much she cannot escape the pressure of these expectations even as she rages against them.

The Victorian Lucie is far less active in Darnay's rescue, and she does not try to defend her individuality at any point in the novel. She does keep watch outside his prison, but this is to raise his spirits, so that he might see her; she has no intention or ability to break him out or to protect him in any way. She is described as changing the way she dresses, choosing gowns resembling mourning clothes, but it is emphasized that throughout the fifteen months of Darnay's imprisonment she remains comely and pretty.[38] In *A Tale of Two Cities*, Lucie is not the one to save Darnay when he's on trial: the first time, it is Dr. Manette, and the second time it is Sydney Carton. In *Tell the Wind and Fire*, Dr. Manette appears by Ethan's prison essentially to raise his daughter's spirits and stand beside her; he is not the driving force behind the operation, unlike in Dickens's novel. In *A Tale of Two Cities*, before she brings out the letter in court to condemn Charles Darnay once and for all, Madame Defarge meets Lucie, who implores her "sister-woman," as a "wife and mother"[39] to spare her husband. Lucie identifies herself as the roles she occupies in relation to others, rather than perceiving herself to be an independent being. Furthermore, various male characters talk about her as if she were an object rather than a person, usually in the context of whether they should marry her (Stryver and Carton[40] or Stryver and Lorry[41]). Even Carton, when he confesses his hopeless love for her, foresees a happy future for Lucie in which she forges new ties that will "bind" her ever more strongly to the "home" she "adorn[s]."[42] His vision presents Lucie as occupying an entirely decorative position that she is tied to and cannot leave as a daughter, wife, and mother; she is nothing except for the roles she plays in relation to the men in her life. The Victorian Lucie is shown to accept the limitations placed on her by others and to accept these as her defining characteristics, in a way that the modern Lucie is not.

Even if it is more acceptable for women to be active agents in their own lives, though, that does not mean it is easy for women to act, due to the persisting ideas about women. The modern Lucie's difficulties in making others see her as an individual is a good example of this. The *sans-merci*, with Aunt Leila at the head, make Lucie into a symbol of their political resistance. The modern Lucie points out, "An icon didn't do anything of its own volition. A symbol didn't act of its own accord. Both cities projected what they wanted onto me, and wanted me to stay still as they did it."[43] She cannot be a symbol and individual simultaneously, and as the narrative progresses she grows increasingly angry at having her sense of self constantly redefined by others. Nobody cares that she wants to be neither; society continues to project its desires onto her: "The Light saw me as someone the laws existed to protect. The Dark saw me as someone who proved that the laws could be broken."[44] First as a child, then as an adolescent, and always as a woman, Lucie constantly finds herself disempowered.

Lucie explicitly articulates the problems with peoples' attitudes toward young girls at the ball before the *sans-merci* attack: "Consider this ... When a girl sits and smiles and is silent, you can decide you know her, but that does not mean you do. Don't read into my silences or my smiles. Don't assume you know a thing about me."[45] Her words draw attention to people's tendencies to project what they want to on others, especially young girls, taking away whatever power they may have left in this patriarchal society. Not only does she battle sexism, but she also must defend her status as an adolescent against adults like her Aunt Leila, who refuses to treat her as an equal because of her age. Leila even tries to take credit for Lucie's rescue of her father because she was the one to instruct her how to behave—she treats Lucie like a puppet and projects her own desires onto her. Aunt Leila appeals to what she imagines must be Lucie's desire for power by telling Lucie to think of how much of it she has as a symbol, not understanding Lucie's sarcastic response: "It's unlucky that I'm a person too, isn't it?"[46] Of course, Lucie belongs in the minority of young women placed in the public eye (although, with the increased popularity of social media in the last decade, increasingly more young girls are scrutinized by the public), but whether famous or not, all young girls are seen and judged by those around them, and they all must find a way to develop their own identities in the face of the opinions of the majority.

Navigating Society as a Woman: Performing Femininity

Though for most of the text she rebels against the behavior society thrusts upon her, the modern Lucie does not entirely renounce how she has been taught to act to get what she wants. She manipulates the public to ensure Ethan's release from the tower, just as she did when she rescued her father, following Aunt Leila's plan, when she first discovered how to gain people's sympathy. Lucie wants "everyone talking about [her]" and "everyone watching."[47] The difference between her actions here and when she saved her father is that she does not lie to ensure Ethan's release; she is "only" very selective about when she reveals the truth, whereas to save her father she denied her mother and her family.

Every part of Aunt Leila's scheme to save Dr. Manette is planned. Lucie goes to the cages in the evenings (to attract the biggest crowd), and she wears and says what Aunt Leila tells her to.[48] Lucie transforms the tragedy of dozens of families who watch their loved ones suffer in the cages, "racked with misery ... crouched around their pain ... cracked voices sounded like birds,"[49] into the tragic story of a child about to be orphaned, as she appears in the cemetery day by day, soothing peoples' pain. The public's sympathy forces the Light Council to pardon Dr. Manette as it struggles to maintain its image as merciful and fair. It is society's opinion here that is clearly a crucial factor in the Council's decision-making process, and so ensuring they are on Lucie's side is essential to securing Dr. Manette's release.

All this planning is intended to give people what they want, so that in turn they will give Lucie the support she needs. And they want entertainment, pain like "death on a stage: beautiful, bloodless."[50] Otherwise, they would look away, and she would have no chance of saving her father. The crowd would be unwilling to feel the guilt that would inevitably accompany any display of real suffering on Lucie's part, since it would implicate the viewers in participating in the creation of this suffering. After all, if people refused to watch, refused to come to the cages, there would be no point in the Light Council keeping them, and such public suffering would stop. But people keep coming, playing their part in maintaining this system of punishment. She needs them to sympathize with her, and Leila convinces her that she cannot rely on honesty to achieve this. It is a live performance, like the one she gives in the studio with Ethan, and live performances are important, because people trust them more, rarely considering how carefully these, too, are scripted.[51] And Lucie's performance in front of Ethan's tower is improvised and scripted in equal parts. She allows herself to break down, to feel and express her emotions, to be "an ugly mess, no artifice and no dignity left, and people I did not know were watching me with sympathy. Not everyone had turned away. Not every heart had to be won by trickery."[52] She allows herself to express more emotion, and people are not afraid of it, which makes her in turn less afraid, too. Lucie still needs people to see her and to sympathize with her, though, so she times her visits to gain their support.

The importance that timing has on manipulating a crowd into supporting one's causes is demonstrated in *A Tale of Two Cities*, when Madame Defarge chooses to share Dr. Manette's letter at Darnay's trial. As Darnay is condemned for the second time, the narrator describes the "wild excitement, patriotic fervor, not a touch of human sympathy"[53] that pervades the room as the jurymen vote unanimously to convict him. Madame Defarge chose her moment to procure Dr. Manette's letter condemning the Evrémondes as well, knowing this would incite the courtroom to sentence Darnay and that the people would encourage each other until they would be unstoppable, blind to reason. Manipulating people based on when to share information with them is what modern Lucie does in her attempt to save Ethan. By speaking the truth outside of Ethan's tower, Lucie is taking ammunition away from Aunt Leila, as her aunt cannot use the truth against her since she would incriminate herself in doing so. Lucie uses it to her advantage against Aunt Leila in their stand-off outside Ethan's prison: "Aunt Leila had taught me how to appear in front of the media and the crowds. I had to believe that she cared more about how things looked than I did."[54] Aunt Leila needs the public's support to remain in power, and a thirst for power (to allow her to get her revenge) is what drives her.

Part of appealing to the crowd, of performing the femininity others expect to see from her, is ensuring her appearance, especially her choice of clothing, and it emphasizes the impression Lucie attempts to make when she appears in public. The instance when she dresses as a soldier to make a stance against these expectations is one example. Earlier in the novel, though, Lucie dresses (or is dressed by others) to fit the ideas about femininity created by others. She appears by her imprisoned father as an innocent child dressed in white to emphasize her purity, soothing the pain of others as she walks to give the impression of goodwill.[55] She "looked like the symbol of what all Light magic should be … an angel … a golden-haired child with a sweet, sad face … the Golden Thread in the Dark."[56] When Mark Stryker wants to reignite this sympathy to gain the public's support after Ethan is accused of plotting with the *sans-merci*, he has Lucie dress in white for a television interview she attends with Ethan, to remind the public of her previous (successful) performance. However, she notices that "draped white on a child made her seem pure ... Audiences believed children's words. They did not believe the words of women. Just having this body made me suspect. Putting it on display was even worse."[57] Sara K. Day points out the liminal space adolescence occupies between childhood and adulthood and argues that the adolescent body is unsettling because it blurs the boundaries between gender roles and romantic relationships: "Western culture has largely taken to portray young adults of young women as simultaneously desirable and dangerous, presenting them as creatures whose sexuality must be controlled by implicit or explicit rules and regulations."[58] This is exactly what happens here: "A child, a daughter, could be innocent in a way a woman—and a woman with her man—could not be."[59] Once again, there is a clear link drawn between how a woman is perceived based on her relationship to men, a link that similarly encumbers the Victorian Lucie. Madame Defarge wants her to die, after all,[60] because of her association with Darnay, even though Lucie has no noble blood; her marriage is enough to condemn her. In the adaptation, Lucie's public image is always based on her relationships with men—first as a daughter saving her father, then as Ethan's girlfriend. This latter relationship is viewed by others as false, either because the public fears she is being used or is the one using Ethan.[61] This makes her either the helpless victim that both cities seem to want to make of her, using her as their symbol, or an example of the monstrous kind of femininity they fear, that is, an active woman who does not conform to their expectations.

Conclusion

In *Tell the Wind and Fire*, Lucie spends much of her time fighting the expectations others place on her, expectations that clearly have their roots in Victorian perceptions about femininity. The very fact Lucie is represented as rebelling against these traditional notions is a significant difference between the adaptation and its source, which underscores the impact that feminism has made on women's position and power in society. By the end of Brennan's novel, Lucie exemplifies the characteristics traditionally associated with women, thus confirming McCallum's (1999) claim about young adult novels often having conservative conclusions, whereby the narrative strategies of a text "are frequently assimilated into an ideologically inscribed model of maturation which values socially cooperative forms of intersubjectivity."[62] However, there are certain challenges the modern woman faces, which *Tell the Wind and Fire* highlights and which are not swept under the carpet by its otherwise underlying conservatism.

Specifically, I am referring to how the adaptation deals with consent. Both the source and adaptation condemn men forcing themselves on women in any way; however, in Dickens's novel, this occurs in the background. Madame Defarge wants revenge on the Evrémondes because her sister was raped and killed by them and her brother died defending her. The violation here has occurred to a background character. Though there is no rape in Brennan's novel, there are multiple scenes where Carwyn regularly violates Lucie's personal space. Carwyn uses public situations to touch or kiss her because she cannot refuse, since everyone else thinks he is Ethan. Lucie realizes how wrong this is when Marie comes home and proudly announces that her teacher told her she protested for feminism and established autonomy over her own body[63] because she refused to let a boy kiss her and bit him when he failed to listen. Lucie confronts Carwyn about her anger at his behavior at the ball, where, once again, he puts her in a situation she does not want to be in: "Do you think it's funny to touch me without my permission, when you know I don't want you to? Does it make you feel good about yourself?"[64] At no point does Lucie give in to Carwyn's advances, or begin to have feelings for him, nor is she confused about him and Ethan. Part of the reason might be Brennan's fidelity to the source; after all, Dickens's Lucie never wavers in her love for Charles, either. But it is refreshing to see a heroine who chooses the boy who gives her a choice, and not the one who tries to force her affection.

The novels reflect situations in which consent is an issue in different ways because of the context and time they are set in. Conversations about the small actions that violate a woman's space are a modern phenomenon, and it is only in the last decade that the world has seen a massive increase in conversations about consent, and raising young people's awareness of its importance in high schools and universities has become commonplace. The #MeToo Movement emphasizes the relevance of this issue to today's audience, and exploring it in the way Brennan has done offers readers the chance to consider their own relationships and interactions with people. Dickens, just like Brennan, is critical of a man's unsolicited attentions to a woman, but the way his novel represents this differs because what kind of behavior was unacceptable has evolved. The "smaller" violations Brennan's novel represents are no less significant, though; they are indicative of an ongoing struggle that women in twenty-first-century societies face, a struggle they have had to face since before the nineteenth century. Perceived from this angle, Victorian novels such as *A Tale of Two Cities* are relevant for the modern reader, showing both how things used to be and have changed, as well as how many things remain the same.

Notes

1 Gilbert and Gubar, *The Madwoman in the Attic*, 20.
2 Ibid.
3 Ibid., 26.
4 Ibid., 28.
5 Chodorow, *The Reproduction of Motherhood*, 167.
6 Pulliam, "Real or Not Real," 176.
7 Trites, *Disturbing the Universe*, 19–20.
8 Alter, "The Demons of History," 137; Rignall, "Dickens and the Catastrophic Continuum," 575.
9 Stout, "Nothing Personal," 31.
10 Dickens, *A Tale of Two Cities*, 334.
11 Hutcheon, *A Theory of Adaptation*, 8,
12 Brennan, *Tell the Wind and Fire*, 51.

13 Ibid., 314.
14 Waters, "Gender, Family, and Domestic Ideology," 121.
15 Brennan, *Tell the Wind and Fire*, 54–5.
16 Ibid., 62.
17 Ibid., 30
18 Beckwith, "Introduction," 7.
19 Dickens, *David Copperfield*, 327.
20 Brennan, *Tell the Wind and Fire*, 311.
21 Stout, "Nothing Personal," 241.
22 Brennan, *Tell the Wind and Fire*, 311.
23 Ibid.
24 McCallum, *Ideologies of Identity*, 128,
25 Ibid., 122.
26 Pulliam, "Real or Not Real," 174.
27 Butler, *Gender Trouble*, 179.
28 Brennan, *Tell the Wind and Fire*, 190.
29 McCallum, *Ideologies of Identity*, 4.
30 Ibid., 118.
31 Brennan, *Tell the Wind and Fire*, 326.
32 Ibid.
33 Ibid., 151.
34 Ibid., 190.
35 Ibid., 191.
36 Ibid., 64.
37 Ibid., 60.
38 Dickens, *A Tale of Two Cities*, 273.
39 Ibid., 266.
40 Ibid., 142–5.
41 Ibid., 147–51.
42 Ibid., 156.
43 Brennan, *Tell the Wind and Fire*, 83.
44 Ibid., 82.
45 Ibid., 230.
46 Ibid., 341.
47 Ibid., 323.
48 Ibid., 54.
49 Ibid., 52.
50 Ibid., 56.
51 Ibid., 145.
52 Ibid., 320.
53 Dickens, *A Tale of Two Cities*, 319.
54 Brennan, *Tell the Wind and Fire*, 334.
55 Ibid., 53.
56 Ibid., 56.
57 Ibid., 146.
58 Day, "Docile Bodies," 75.
59 Brennan, *Tell the Wind and Fire*, 153.
60 Dickens, *A Tale of Two Cities*, 324.

61 Brennan, *Tell the Wind and Fire*, 153.
62 McCallum, *Ideologies of Identity*, 128.
63 Brennan, *Tell the Wind and Fire*, 113.
64 Ibid., 248–9.

Bibliography

Alter, Robert. 1969. "The Demons of History in Dickens' 'Tale.'" *NOVEL: A Forum on Fiction* 2, no. 2 (Winter): 135–42.
Beckwith, Charles E. "Introduction." In *Twentieth Century Interpretations of a Tale of Two Cities*, edited by Charles E. Beckwith, 1–18. Eastwood Cliffs, NJ: Prentice-Hall, 1972.
Brennan, Sara Rees. *Tell the Wind and Fire*. Boston, MA: Clarion Books, 2016.
Butler, Judith. *Gender Trouble: Feminism and the Subversion of Identity*. London: Routledge, [1990] 1999.
Chodorow, Nancy. *The Reproduction of Mothering: Psychoanalysis and the Sociology of Gender*. Berkeley: University of California Press, [1978] 1999.
Day, Sara K. "Docile Bodies, Dangerous Bodies: Sexual Awakening and Social Resistance in Young Adult Dystopian Novels." In *Female Rebellion in Young Adult Dystopian Fiction*, edited by Sara K. Day, Miranda A. Green-Barteet, and Amy L. Montz, 75–94. Farnham: Ashgate, 2014.
Dickens, Charles. *Dombey and Son*. Oxford: Oxford University Press, [1846–8] 2008.
Dickens, Charles. *David Copperfield*. Oxford: Oxford University Press, [1849–50] 2008.
Dickens, Charles. *A Tale of Two Cities*. Oxford: Oxford University Press, [1859] 1999.
Gilbert, Sandra M., and Gubar, Susan. 1980. *The Madwoman in the Attic: The Woman Writer and the Nineteenth-Century Literary Imagination*. London: Yale University Press, 1980.
Hutcheon, Linda. *A Theory of Adaptation*. London: Routledge, 2006.
McCallum, Robyn. *Ideologies of Identity in Adolescent Fiction: The Dialogic Construction of Subjectivity*. New York: Garland, 1999.
Pulliam, June. 2014. "Real or Not Real—Katniss Everdeen Loves Peeta Melark: The Lingering Effects of Discipline in the 'Hunger Games' Trilogy." In *Female Rebellion in Young Adult Dystopian Fiction*, edited by Sara K. Day, Miranda A. Green-Barteet, and Amy L. Montz, 187–202. Farnham: Ashgate, 2014.
Rignall, John M. "Dickens and the Catastrophic Continuum of History in *A Tale of Two Cities*." *ELH* 51, no. 3 (Autumn 1984): 575–87.
Stout, Daniel. "Nothing Personal: The Decapitation of Character in 'A Tale of Two Cities.'" *Novel: A Forum on Fiction* 41, no. 1 (Fall 2007): 29–52.
Trites, Roberta Seelinger. *Disturbing the Universe: Power and Repression in Adolescent Literature*. Iowa City. University of Iowa Press, 2000.
Waters, Catherine. "Gender, Family, and Domestic Ideology." In *The Cambridge Companion to Charles Dickens*, edited by John Jordan, 120–35. Cambridge: Cambridge University Press, 2001.

13

"In fair Verona, where we lay our scene": Adaptation, Literary Tourism, and Locating Juliet

Dana E. Lawrence

Romeo and Juliet has long been viewed as particularly relevant to adolescents because of its depiction of two teenagers, and it is often the first Shakespearean play read in school by young adults.[1] Academic Shakespeare feeds the popular Shakespeare machine, providing what Douglas Lanier describes as "ready-made cultural prestige" and a built-in market for Shakespeare in mass media.[2] The play's omnipresence in school curricula and popular culture has inspired countless adaptations in nearly all forms of media. In fact, the tale of Shakespeare's "star-crossed lovers" is so ubiquitous that one need not have read the play in order to know its story and characters. Historically, adaptations of Shakespeare's plays for children and young adults have been intended as an introduction to the "real thing"—with the hope that the adaptation will inspire the young reader to seek out the "originals." Young adult novel adaptations are offered by publishers and educators as supplementary texts that will make the plays more accessible and more relevant to teenagers. However, Jennifer Hulbert, Kevin J. Wetmore, Jr., and Robert L. York argue, "By linking Shakespeare so firmly to education, we firmly ensconce him within the world of youth culture, but in a dualistic role, at once both adversarial to youth and wholly recognizable to them."[3] In other words, a contemporary adaptation of *Romeo and Juliet* is still marked by the cultural status of Shakespeare and may not achieve the goal of inspiring resistant young adult readers to return to the source text on their own.

Within the plentiful and varied young adult novel adaptations of *Romeo and Juliet*, I identify three broad types: (1) parallel novels from the perspective of secondary characters in the play; (2) revisions of the play set in an entirely different time/place/ and so on; and (3) meta-retellings in which the protagonist directly engages with the play in some way—either through studying or performing (usually for school or other educational activity, but not always)—even as she (the protagonist is usually a girl) participates in her own version of the story. In this third category, Shakespeare's cultural authority is often the point, and the play's personal relevance to the novel's characters is established as they work their way through the text. The protagonist in meta-retellings of *Romeo and Juliet* is almost always a headstrong teenage girl who, like Juliet, is caught between wanting to please her parents and wanting to assert her individual desires.

In these novels, the play is, at first, a source of conflict, and the female protagonist's increasing engagement with the text ultimately leads her to a clearer understanding of who she is and who she wants to be. Inevitably, the protagonist finds herself identifying with Juliet and her problems, and Shakespeare's play becomes a therapeutic text that helps her deal with her own personal struggles.

A subset of *Romeo and Juliet* meta-retellings adds a layer of textual engagement by incorporating yet another intertext: literary tourism. Like most meta-retellings of *Romeo and Juliet*, Verona's tourism narrative enacts a connection between individual and text, quoting Shakespeare while also encouraging the visitor to rewrite the narrative through their interactions with the tourist sites. Because of the blurred boundaries between Verona's actual history and its Romeo and Juliet fiction, tourists can easily imagine that they are "walking in the footsteps of" Shakespeare's lovers *and* that they can pretend to *be* (Romeo and) Juliet. In Suzanne Harper's 2008 novel, *The Juliet Club*, 17-year-old Kate Sanderson wins an essay contest and is invited to participate in a month-long seminar to study the play in its setting so that she might "embod[y] the spirit of the plays" and "channe[l] the spirit of Shakespeare's most romantic characters," according to the eclectic Professora Marchese.[4] In meta-retellings featuring tourism, the protagonists have a detached familiarity with the text of *Romeo and Juliet*, almost to a fault, and their journey to Verona challenges what they think they know about the play while also empowering them to make the narrative their own. Nicola Watson connects the experience of tourists with that of readers, noting, "In visiting the real place, the tourist seeks to verify what he or she has learned from prior representation. The reality of the experience, however, is generated by the tourist, not the place, and so is not dissimilar to the experience of reading."[5] Kate's seminar roommate, Lucy, is consumed by the romance of "standing on the very spot where Juliet stood when she first met Romeo,"[6] while Kate is unmoved by her visit to Juliet's house. Observing tourists in the courtyard and on the balcony, Kate notes, "Not one person . . . was reading the informational signs helpfully posted nearby, or even thumbing through a guidebook."[7] Kate assumes that the guidebooks will somehow jolt enamored tourists back to reality, but, historically, that has not been their intent. Whereas Kate performs a strict reading of *Romeo and Juliet*, annoyed by Lucy's claim that the story is romantic, Lucy connects to the text on a more personal level. She explains to Kate: "Well, I know the ending is a downer, but I just stop reading before Juliet takes that sleeping pill."[8] Lucy's interpretation of the play is inaccurate, but accuracy isn't the point. Lucy's interactions with the text are rooted in pleasure and fantasy, much like tourists' interactions with literary tourism sites.

In this chapter, I will examine Suzanne Selfors's 2008 meta-retelling, *Saving Juliet*, through the lens of literary tourism. The novel's narrator, Mimi Wallingford, like Kate, has been immersed in Shakespeare since she was a small child. As the novel begins, Mimi is playing the role of Juliet, though she feels no particular connection to the character, but her performance of the role is causing debilitating anxiety. Mimi is "descended from the clan that has graced the American stage since the early twentieth century," and her duty to her family's legacy is the primary source of conflict in the novel.⁹ Ultimately, Mimi must travel to Verona to understand *Romeo and Juliet* beyond the script; however, unlike Kate, Mimi finds herself in Verona by accident—and by magic. Selfors's novel blends literary tourism and time travel to allow Mimi to *literally* walk the streets of Romeo and Juliet's Verona. As tourists visiting the sites of *Romeo and Juliet*, the protagonists of both *Saving Juliet* and *The Juliet Club* immerse themselves in the play—minimizing the distance between the fictional reader and Shakespeare's characters. However, in *Saving Juliet*, the play and its setting are inextricably bound, emphasizing the liminal boundary between fantasy and reality in literary tourism. While contemporary adaptations of *Romeo and Juliet* often make the play more relevant to young adult readers, the addition of literary tourism demonstrates the ways in which meaning is created by the participants. Rather than simply identifying with and learning from Juliet and other Shakespearean characters, Mimi reclaims and rewrites the tragic heroine, usurping Shakespeare's authority and asserting her own over the text and over her own life. Young adult readers are thus invited to do the same, and Shakespeare's *Romeo and Juliet* is reinterpreted not as an assignment that must be overcome but as a living, malleable text that places readers in the role of collaborator.

"They're Fictional Characters!":[10] Adaptation and Shakespeare Tourism

Shakespeare tourism, like all literary tourism, shares with young adult novel adaptations a general dismissal of its content as frivolous, inauthentic, and unworthy of scholarly attention. It is only relatively recently, through the work of Nicola Watson, that literary tourism has been analyzed as a cultural phenomenon within the field of literary studies.[11] In general, popular adaptations of Shakespeare—whether in the form of films, tourism, or children's texts—have been defined in opposition to scholarly treatments of Shakespeare and his works. Both young adult adaptations and literary tourism are criticized as inauthentic because they are assumed to misappropriate the authority of Shakespeare in the service of mass market appeal and fail to accurately represent the plays. However, questions of fidelity and authenticity are irrelevant when the adaptations themselves seek not to replicate but rather to interrogate the source texts and their cultural caché. In fact, Shakespeare is often absent from or sidelined both in young adult adaptations and in tourism; instead, the reader/tourist is invested with authority and ownership over the narrative. And while this narrative is certainly informed by an individual's familiarity (or lack thereof) with an author or source, it is not dependent upon direct knowledge of the text. As in all forms of adaptation, the audience's experience is shaped by innumerable factors that are sometimes shared and sometimes unique to the individual, which means that each visitor and each reader participates in creating meaning—yet another layer in the palimpsest that is adaptation. William Shakespeare's name may be invoked, but his authority extends beyond the text of his plays only because of the continued engagement of scholars, artists, readers, audiences, and adapters.

Since the nineteenth century, prose retellings have been the preferred genre for children's Shakespeare. While the Lambs and subsequent authors of children's Shakespeare present their retellings as objective preparatory reading for the real thing, Amy Scott-Douglass posits that the adapters knew that they were presenting their own interpretations of the plays, which would influence the way readers understand and experience Shakespeare even before they encountered his works.[12] In fact, Laura Tosi credits the Lambs with introducing the voice of the narrator to adaptations of Shakespeare, leaving "no ambiguities for the reader."[13] Alison H. Prindle argues that the very act of adapting drama to narrative—even when the goal is to make the text more understandable—"creates an observer's role for the child, rather than the collaborative, interactive role offered by … drama."[14] In addition to changing the reader's experience, such adaptations, according to Howard Marchitello, erase Shakespeare and his text, becoming the story of Shakespeare rather than of the play.[15] The result is an inauthentic understanding of both the playwright and his work. Paradoxically, though, authentic Shakespeare is a fiction in itself—a fiction that has made it possible to create Shakespeare the Myth, which Graham Holderness identifies as "an atmosphere of unscrupulous opportunism, commercial exploitation and gross imposture; the laissez-faire environment of a cultural industry in which the free play of market forces determines all values."[16] Shakespeare adaptations and Shakespeare tourism undoubtedly uphold the playwright's mythological and canonical status, though not in the deceitful way Holderness describes. Both developed in response to not only consumer demand but also out of genuine respect for Shakespeare's texts and his cultural significance.

Like children's adaptations of Shakespeare's plays, literary tourism invites audience engagement, presenting a re-vision of an old narrative and allowing visitors to create meaning based on their prior knowledge and their connection to the text/space. Juliette Wells explains that literary tourism is rooted in "the desire [of readers] to extend their emotional connection with a beloved text into real-world places, which offer the opportunity to relate to an author and her world in a different—and potentially closer or more satisfying—way than through reading alone."[17] Travelers' imaginations are shaped by the stories told by site managers, and these stories create what Athinodoros Chronis identifies as "tourism imaginaries," which are composed of "both 'real' and 'imagined' aspects of tourism places"[18] and "transform an otherwise inconspicuous space into an attractive tourism destination."[19] Tourists have an integral role in making meaning from these narratives through acts of "performative authenticity," in which, Yujie Zhu explains, "meanings and feelings are embodied through the ongoing interaction between individual agency and the external world."[20] In other words, a site's authenticity is created not through facts or evidence but through an individual's "integration of personal memory, meanings, and physical settings."[21] Though the physical sites of literary tourism are "real," in the sense that they exist, the significance of these sites depends upon a combination of imposed narrative and visitor imagination.

While the Bard's hometown of Stratford-upon-Avon has built an industry around Shakespeare the man,[22] Verona, Italy, brands itself the "City of Love" based not on the many Italian versions of the Romeo and Juliet story[23] but on Shakespeare's dramatic tale of the "star-crossed lovers." Today, Juliet's house is the principal Shakespeare site in Verona, and tourists flock there by the thousands to gaze up at the balcony, have their photo taken with the bronze statue of Juliet in the courtyard, and leave messages of love on the wall or deposit a letter in Juliet's mailbox. Tourists are invited to imagine Shakespeare's characters strolling around Verona, even if none of the stories are true. Like young adult adaptations, Verona's Romeo and Juliet tourism industry positions itself as both a surrogate for and an homage to Shakespeare's text, even as the primary sites and less conspicuous markers around the city invite visitors not only to follow in the doomed lovers' footsteps but also to participate in a communal performance of the play. And where is Shakespeare in Verona? He is everywhere and nowhere. Shakespeare is given credit for the play that shapes Verona's narrative; however, he performs a supporting role. Verona is Juliet's city, and this fictional heroine is reimagined as "real"—even as everyone knows and acknowledges that, in fact, she isn't. In *Saving Juliet*, however, Juliet is quite real, and Mimi's friendship with Shakespeare's heroine results in new identities and new narratives for both.

"Two daughters, both alike in dignity":[24] Shakespeare for Girls

Beginning in the early-nineteenth century, Shakespeare's heroines were presented as exemplary for girls and women—to whom Shakespeare was thought to have a special connection.[25] The Lambs and subsequent nineteenth-century adapters of Shakespeare for children sanitized Shakespeare's bawdy and controversial plays by excising plots and characters deemed inappropriate for young readers and, as Erica Hateley has noted, by appropriating the reader's interpretive power to "designate and disseminate that which they perceive as being valuable."[26] Early adaptations present their retellings as objective, preparatory reading for the real thing, even as their editorial choices and textual commentary define what is "valuable" in Shakespeare, which, for girls, is limited to the lessons that may be learned from the plays. These lessons, Ariane Balizet observes, were "rules of gendered decorum and expectations for girls' inherent weakness and failure."[27] More than one hundred years later, we can see a continuation of this girl-centric approach to Shakespeare adaptation in teen films and young adult novels. In the late 1990s and early 2000s, there was an explosion of "teenpic"[28] adaptations of Shakespeare's plays—all of which engaged the plays featuring complicated heroines: *Othello*, *Taming of the Shrew*, *Twelfth Night*, *Hamlet*, and, of course, *Romeo and Juliet*. Though *William Shakespeare's Romeo + Juliet* (1996), *10 Things I Hate About You* (1999), *Hamlet* (2000), *O* (2001), and *She's the Man* (2006) emphasize the characters' resistance to social constraints, these updated versions of Shakespeare's heroines, like those of nineteenth-century adapters, maintain the status quo, "perpetuating idealized representations of race, class, and gender."[29] All of these teen Shakespeare films feature economically advantaged, conventionally beautiful, heterosexual white girls, and their identities are largely defined by their relationships to their fathers, brothers, and boyfriends. As in Shakespeare's plays, the girls who ultimately conform to gendered expectations of behavior have happy endings, while those who do not meet tragic ends.

Significantly, all Shakespeare "teenpics" released since the 1990s have had girls as their target audience. Even the film adaptations of male-driven plays like Othello and Hamlet ultimately highlight the teen girl character, suggesting that, in contemporary popular culture, as in the nineteenth century, Shakespeare adaptations are for girls. Young adult novels exhibit a similar trend. According to Elizabeth Bullen, Kim Toffoletti, and Liz Parsons, "From 1995 to 2004 sales [of young adult novels] increased 86.9% to $444.4 million, of which series fiction for girls made up a significant proportion."[30] Adaptations of Shakespeare in young adult fiction, as in teen films, often feature teen girl protagonists and follow conventions of teen romance. This combination, dubbed "Chick Lit Jr." by Joanna Webb Johnson, is thus doubly marginalized and dismissed as frivolous, because it targets girl readers. Johnson positions this genre within "a feminist children's literary tradition," noting that the "novels address classic issues of YA novels: coming of age, identity, sexuality, and material culture."[31] Examples of Shakespeare adaptations within this genre abound,[32] but *Romeo and Juliet* is the only play with a specific concern for the experiences of teenagers. Thomas Moisan describes the young lovers as "the embodiments of the need adolescents have to differentiate themselves, and their sense of 'self,' from the sense of self imposed by culture and society."[33] Juliet, in particular, is restrained by the parent/child hierarchy, in which, Diane Elizabeth Dreher explains, "fathers prize their daughters as valuable possessions, failing to see them as individuals" and withholding girls' "freedom to develop into mature women."[34]

Of the major "universal" themes that define *Romeo and Juliet*, the one that makes its way into young adult adaptations of the play most often is that of parent/child conflict. This is unsurprising, since, as Roberta Seelinger Trites has noted, "The conflict with parent-as-authority-figure seems to be one of the most pervasive patterns in adolescent literature."[35] Paradoxically, rather than affirming the implied reader's adolescent identity, such narratives often "delegitimize adolescents" by "conveying frequently to the readers the ideological message that they need to grow up, to give up the subject position culturally marked 'adolescent.'"[36] So, in narratives ostensibly about a teen character's desire to assert independence, the protagonist—and, by extension, the young adult reader—is still beholden to an adult authority figure. As a result, according to Trites, literature for adolescents teaches them "that authority is not and should not be theirs" and that their desires "must be repressed for the greater good" until they reach adulthood.[37] In *Saving Juliet*, Mimi—like Shakespeare's Juliet—wrestles with her parents' expectations of her, her desire to pursue her own interests, and her attempts to connect with peers. Mimi is 17 years old, placing her firmly on the cusp of adulthood, though she is not sure how to assume that role in the midst of parental demands and personal uncertainties. However, the adult authority figures in *Saving Juliet* are neither helpful guides nor models of maturity, and Mimi instead grows and learns from her peers. The adults are certainly still "in charge" and figures against whom the characters rebel, but the adolescent characters are invested with agency and "gain insights from each other rather than from some sort of omniscient adult. The ideology affirms teenagers' power, especially when it functions in community."[38] In Shakespeare's play and in its young adult adaptations, Juliet must assert her independence from her parents as part of the coming-of-age plot. Whereas Shakespeare's Juliet is ultimately punished for her transgressions, contemporary young adult adaptations celebrate her agency, reflecting chick lit jr.'s characteristically "approachable path to understanding the challenges associated with leaving childhood and accepting adult responsibility."[39] For modern teenage girls like Mimi, Juliet serves as a guide—not a model—during their own coming of age.

"Romeo and Juliet Land": Temporal Tourism and Rewriting Shakespeare in *Saving Juliet*

Mimi Wallingford's adventure begins when she finds herself magically transported to the Verona of *Romeo and Juliet*, participating in what Rüdiger Hienze terms "temporal tourism." In literature, temporal tourism takes the form of time-travel narratives, which have "the question of 'what would have happened if' " at their core.[40] Such "counterfactual" narratives mirror the experience of literary tourism, in which imagination transcends reality: "Logic is not the primary purpose; rather, history, legend, and myth are shown to be close together, and notions of temporal stability and progression as well as a naturalistic world view are undermined."[41] Throughout today's Verona, the presence of Romeo and Juliet is simultaneously real and imaginary, thanks to physical structures and expert mythologizing. The narrative of *Saving Juliet* likewise blurs boundaries, combining the fantasy of time travel with Mimi's direct addresses to readers, assuring them that her story is true: "I warned you in the beginning that you might not believe the story I was about to tell, so you've probably anticipated this moment."[42]

William Shakespeare and his play are raked over the coals, so to speak, by Mimi and her onstage Romeo, Troy. Troy complains to Mimi, "I'm totally sick of Shakespeare. Can't understand a single word."[43] Mimi, while annoyed with Troy's superficiality, privately agrees: "Shakespeare was a genius, but ever hear of overkill? If I could go somewhere and never again hear a single, solitary Shakespearean word, I'd be a happy camper."[44] Here, Mimi and Troy echo the complaints of many young readers who are introduced to Shakespeare in school. Adaptations often address questions of relevance and accessibility, and *Saving Juliet* asks and answers them, creating distance between source text and author. Mimi hates the play's tragic conclusion: "What kind of ending is that anyway? I'd totally write a different ending."[45] Troy questions the play's realism: "What guy would poison himself over a girl he had known only for a few days?"[46] Of course, Troy fails to understand the play, in general, as Mimi observes: "Romeo is supposed to begin the play in a deep state of melancholy. . . . Troy never quite got the fact that a depressed person wouldn't strut onto the stage."[47] But the truth is that Troy doesn't care about the play: "I only did this because my agent thinks Romeo is the perfect role for a sex symbol."[48] Though Mimi is critical of

Troy's inauthentic performance as Romeo, she, too, is unable to connect with *Romeo and Juliet* or her lead role onstage; instead, it is a souvenir necklace, purchased by Mimi's aunt in Stratford, that provides the opportunity for Mimi to immerse herself in Shakespeare's narrative.

Alongside questions of Shakespeare's authority, conflict over parental authority is at the heart of *Saving Juliet*'s parallel storylines. Mimi, the last descendent of her great theater family, takes the stage out of a sense of obligation—all but forced upon her by her mother. Mimi constantly feels the burden of her family legacy, and she longs to take control of her own future—which is looming in the form of college acceptance letters. "Wishing that her life could be completely different,"[49] Mimi sees college as her "chance to get away."[50] Like Mimi, Selfors's Juliet resents her domineering mother and the constant reminders that the "family's reputation rests on your shoulders."[51] Though, at 13, Juliet is much younger than 17-year-old Mimi, she is also on the cusp of adulthood, thanks to her impending arranged marriage. After meeting Lady Capulet and Juliet, Mimi immediately recognizes their similarities: "Two daughters, both alike in dignity, forced down paths of their mothers' choosing."[52] Before her journey to Verona, Mimi repeatedly expresses a wish to be more rebellious, but she limits herself to silent rebellion: telling people off in her head.[53] When Mimi discovers that her mother has been using her trust fund—money that Mimi had earned as an actor over many years—to fund the failing Wallingford Theater, all of the frustration she had swallowed down for so long explodes out of her. It is this moment that leads to Mimi's sudden journey back in time.

As a meta-retelling, *Saving Juliet* not only engages Shakespeare's play but also examines teen Shakespeare trends. In an attempt to attract a younger audience to the theater, the Board of Directors of the Wallingford Theater decided to produce *Romeo and Juliet*, starring teen heartthrob, Troy Summer. Upon approaching the stage door, Mimi notices the resulting change in patron demographics: "this was not the crowd of retirees who usually came to the Wallingford to watch classical renditions of Shakespeare's plays. Teenagers formed the line, girls to be exact."[54] The scene reflects the general cultural divide over Shakespeare as serious literature and Shakespeare as mass entertainment. The theater's "classical renditions" appealed to traditionalists who have no interest in making the plays "relevant," but such an audience cannot sustain a modern theater. Even Mimi, a teenage girl, is dismissive of the young playgoers, whom she views as silly fangirls who are only interested in seeing their famous crush. Teen Shakespeare onstage is dismissed as frivolous as readily as films and novels targeting teen audiences. Such adaptations are viewed as gimmicks that cannot represent "authentic" Shakespeare—even though such a thing doesn't exist. In keeping with Mimi's (and purists') assumptions about attempts to appeal to young audiences, the teen fans only have eyes for the famous "Romeo." Observing the girls' reaction to Troy's arrival, Mimi notes, "They tried to take bits of him, anything they could manage, artifacts to carry around tucked in bras or enshrined in lockets."[55]

This desire to possess a piece of Troy echoes eighteenth-century tourists' practice of cutting away chunks of bark from the mulberry tree that Shakespeare himself had allegedly planted in the garden of New Place, the home in which he died in

Stratford-upon-Avon. In Verona, visitors to Juliet's tomb frequently chipped away bits of the heroine's marble sarcophagus to take with them.[56] In both cases, tourists attempted to create a physical connection to the author and character by taking these souvenirs via vandalism. Again, in both cases, clever merchants seized upon the demand and sold various objects made of "genuine" mulberry bark or red marble. In her work on souvenirs, Susan Stewart asserts that such an object "represents not the lived experience of its maker but the 'secondhand' experience of its possessor/owner."[57] Like adaptation, a souvenir is "an allusion and not a model; it comes after the fact and remains both partial to and more expansive than the fact."[58] Stewart continues, "It will not function without supplementary narrative discourse that both attaches it to its origins and creates a myth with regard to those origins."[59] In meta-retellings like *Saving Juliet*, the narrative is similarly tied to its source while actively creating a new story through the protagonist's interactions with Shakespeare's play.

Mimi's Aunt Mary serves as the real-life counterpoint to the play's Nurse character, and she is Mimi's closest confidant and role model. In a gesture of support as Mimi wraps up the production of *Romeo and Juliet*, Mary gifts her a necklace, which she purchased at an antique store years earlier: "The owner said it was rare but I suspect it's just a tourist trinket."[60] Packaged with the necklace is a notecard offering background information about the piece. According to the card, in 1890, a merchant planned to auction off his collection of William Shakespeare's "writing implements," but his house burned down before the sale:

> Being a merchant of clever mind, Mr. Burtrand scooped up the ashes of the burned implements and poured them into small bottles. He claimed that he had captured the genius that had traveled from Shakespeare's hand through his favorite quills. This is one of those very bottles. Whether the ashes came from the quill that wrote *Hamlet*, *Twelfth Night*, or *Romeo and Juliet*, they are certain to influence your destiny.[61]

The legend behind the necklace alludes to the deliberate destruction of New Place by its occupant, Reverend Francis Gastrell, due to his frustration with the numerous tourists trespassing on his property to access the famous mulberry tree.[62] Prior to burning down the house, Gastrell had cut down the tree, but, apparently, that wasn't enough to deter Shakespeare's fans. The necklace's history also places it within the long tradition of selling "genuine" Shakespeare artifacts to gullible (or hopeful) tourists. Mimi is not so gullible, assuming that the contents of the necklace's bottle are "[p]robably ashes from someone's fireplace."[63] The significance of the necklace for Mimi is the giver—Aunt Mary—not Shakespeare.

Mimi attaches no site-specific meaning to the necklace, because she was never in Stratford-upon-Avon. Without memories attached to it, Stewart maintains, the souvenir is nothing but a trinket:

> The souvenir as bibelot or curiosity has little if any value attached to its materiality. Furthermore, the souvenir is often attached to locations and experiences that are

not for sale. The substituting power of the souvenir operates within the following analogy: as experience is to an imagined point of authenticity, so narrative is to the souvenir. The souvenir displaces the point of authenticity as it itself becomes the point of origin for narrative. Such a narrative cannot be generalized to encompass the experience of anyone; it pertains only to the possessor of the object.[64]

Mimi does not have a narrative to attach to the necklace—not yet, anyway—so any claims of authenticity are meaningless. Significantly, it is the necklace's *lack* of authenticity that leads to the discovery of its magical powers. Preparing to go onstage for her final performance as Juliet, Mimi wears the gift from her aunt as a source of comfort. When her mother sees the new piece of jewelry, she tells Mimi that she cannot wear it, because it is "not a period piece" and "not part of the costume."[65] Though the production of *Romeo and Juliet* is marketed as an update, Mimi's mother will not completely relinquish her hold on the family theater's classical roots. The concern with authenticity shared by young adult Shakespeare, adaptation, and literary tourism is captured here in the fight over the necklace, which turns physical as Mimi's mother tries to remove it. Though Mimi manages to hold onto the bottle, she ends up breaking it. With the ashes cupped in her hand, Mimi steps outside with Troy, a gust of wind blows the ashes into both of their faces—and suddenly they are in 1594 Verona.

Anyone interested in authenticity will note that *Romeo and Juliet* is thought to have been written around 1594, though the play's setting is far less specific. However, authenticity is not the goal in *Saving Juliet*. The Verona that Mimi and Troy experience is not the "real" sixteenth-century city but Shakespeare's Verona. It is also Mimi's Verona, it seems, because everyone they encounter speaks American English—a fact that Mimi finds both strange and a relief. In fact, other than the characters identifying the city as Verona, there are no specific landmarks or descriptions that suggest anything more than popular representations of sixteenth-century Europe in any period film: crowded public squares, the presence of livestock, stinking streets, and so on. Both Mimi and Troy remark upon this generic version of Verona when they compare it to a "Renaissance Fair"—an evaluation based entirely on what people are wearing.[66] Throughout *Saving Juliet*, in fact, "Verona" is defined by its characters. The city, in Mimi's words, is "Romeo and Juliet land,"[67] peopled with Shakespeare's characters and their contemporaries. At the same time, Mimi is fully aware that this is the Verona of *Romeo and Juliet*—a product of Shakespeare's imagination. Shakespeare doesn't exist in this Verona, because he *created* it. When Mimi encounters something that is not in the play, she notes that her "subconscious had changed the story."[68] She repeatedly explains to the reader what happens in the play, comparing her experiences with the characters to what she thinks she knows about them. As Mimi's expectations are upended and she gets to know Shakespeare's characters as real people, she begins to reject Shakespeare's version of the story. Having already established that she dislikes the play's tragic ending, Mimi gradually moves from complaining about Shakespeare's choices as a writer to deciding to usurp the Bard's authority and "write" the story *she* wants by interfering with the expected plot points: "Shakespeare may have created this predicament but I was the one who could change it."[69] From the beginning, Mimi's experience of the world of the play reveals that all of her assumptions about reading or performing Shakespeare "correctly" were wrong, and this realization empowers her to make the story her own.

While *Saving Juliet*'s Verona may be fake, Romeo and Juliet are real. As a professional actor, Mimi struggles to connect with the character of Juliet, who seems like "just a lovesick girl who made the really bad choice of committing suicide."[70] And, thanks to "hindsight," she attributes her stage fright to her inability to look "beyond Juliet's surface or imagin[e] a life for her beyond the script."[71] Once Mimi meets Juliet, however, she is immediately drawn to the girl's "realness": "She wasn't like [the make-up artist's] Juliet—full-lipped and perfect. Nor was she like Hollywood's Juliet—graceful and angelic. She looked *real*, the way a girl is supposed to look."[72] When Mimi first encounters Romeo, he is her "dream Romeo": a lovesick boy moping about Rosaline.[73] As she draws near him, she notices, "He smelled sweaty, but in a nice way" and he "looked boyish and cute."[74] Mimi resists the urge to tell Romeo his own story, but she can't help but reassure him: "You'll fall in love again."[75] With this exchange—her first interaction with one of Shakespeare's characters—Mimi inadvertently prevents Romeo from meeting Juliet at the Capulet ball, all but erasing Shakespeare's story as she knows it. Before she realizes that she is in Verona by magic, Mimi is certain that everything she is experiencing is a fantasy of her making, and she wonders, "shouldn't I be able to control my own dream?"[76] It is within this "dream" that Mimi realizes that she can seize control over her own life.

After discovering that she really is *in* Shakespeare's play, Mimi takes ownership of her ability to usurp the Bard's authority. She explains to Troy, "Those ashes transported us into the story. But by being in it, we've changed it!"[77] Having identified the souvenir necklace as an enchanted talisman, Mimi and Troy set out to replicate its magical effects so they can return home. However, their queries about a "Shakespearean quill" are met with confusion, because, of course, no one knows who Shakespeare is in his Verona.[78] Without the hand (or quill) of *Romeo and Juliet*'s writer, Mimi must transition from revising the play through her actions to actually doing some writing of her own. Fearing that she won't be around to save Juliet, Mimi writes her a letter, explaining everything that happened and telling Juliet that "even if things go terribly wrong, she should never, ever consider suicide."[79] This moment is a reversal of the tourist and fan practice of writing letters to Juliet seeking advice—a tradition dating back to the 1930s. For decades, Juliet's "secretaries" have been collecting and responding to these letters, writing in the voice of Shakespeare's Juliet. Now, anyone can play the role of Juliet, dropping in to the Juliet Club to reply to letters as one of many tourist activities in Verona. It is noteworthy that Mimi never desires to *be* Juliet, even when she admires the young girl's rebellious nature. Instead of seeking advice, she offers advice based on her experiences and her knowledge of Shakespeare's play.

The role of Shakespeare in meta-retellings of *Romeo and Juliet* is to provide—through his play—an opportunity for the protagonist to find solutions to her own problems based on a deeper understanding of Shakespeare's narrative and characters. In *Saving Juliet*, Shakespeare's authority is questioned, critiqued, and, finally, diminished as Mimi goes from reciting to rewriting his words. When Mimi tells Troy of her plan to actively change the plot, he tells her that the story can't be different, "[b]ecause Shakespeare didn't write it different."[80] He adds, "Juliet's destiny is already mapped out."[81] As someone resisting the "destiny" ordained by her mother, Mimi finally finds her inner rebel, observing that, while Shakespeare may have created Romeo and Juliet "for a single purpose," "Shakespeare wasn't running this show."[82] So, Mimi sets out to change the star-crossed lovers' fate, helping them escape Verona and, especially, Juliet's mother. *Saving Juliet*'s resolution is reminiscent of *The Wizard of Oz*: "You've always had the power, my dear. You just had to learn it for yourself."[83] In Mimi's case, it is the friar who solves the problem: "You told me that someone else had authored Romeo and Juliet's story. But you are the one who helped Juliet find freedom and helped Romeo find love . . . . It would seem, my child, that God, in His wisdom, has made you the author of all our stories."[84] Mimi's quill—not Shakespeare's—is the magical charm they need to return to twenty-first-century New York. With Troy, she burns the quill, and they recreate the blown ashes that sparked their time travel. In the end, Mimi learns that no one gets what they want by waiting or wishing, and she advises her readers, "You have to pick up a quill and write your own damn story."[85]

Tourists in Verona today have the same opportunity to remember and rewrite *Romeo and Juliet* the way they want it to be, and the sites associated with the play invite visitors to do just that. Despite the presence of site markers explicitly acknowledging a building or an artifact as a replica or as an artistic interpretation, visitors to Juliet's House in Verona still wait in line to touch the bronze statue of Juliet in hopes of finding love or to stand on Juliet's balcony and recite Shakespeare's famous lines. As Mimi is quick to note, "Even if you haven't read *Romeo and Juliet*, you're probably familiar with the balcony scene—the most famous scene in the entire play."[86] Never mind that the word "balcony" never appears in the text of the play; one would be hard-pressed to find a production or adaptation that doesn't at least allude to some version of the structure. Adaptation allows writers, directors, readers, and audiences to create the Shakespeare of their imaginations. Authenticity is rarely the point in these creative works, and even a tourist with the most critical eye can't help but get caught up in the beauty and fantasy of Romeo and Juliet's Verona. While all meta-retellings of *Romeo and Juliet* may begin with Shakespeare's text, the critical engagement of the fictional reader is always tied to that individual's personal experiences. Tourists, likewise, create meaning for spaces based on individual knowledge and desires. By incorporating literary tourism into young adult meta-retellings of *Romeo and Juliet*, adapters encourage not only understanding but also active ownership of the text.

Notes

1 Garber, *Shakespeare and Modern Culture*, 46; According to a 1989 study by Arthur N. Applebee, approximately 90% of public school students in the United States had read *Romeo and Juliet* by the time they graduated high school (quoted in Balizet, "Shakespeare, Television, and Girl Culture," n.p.).
2 Lanier, *Shakespeare and Modern Popular Culture*, 105.

3   Hulbert, Wetmore, Jr., and York "Dude, Where's My Bard?" 15.
4   Harper, *The Juliet Club*, 122.
5   Watson, "Shakespeare," 223.
6   Harper, *The Juliet Club*, 49.
7   Ibid., 51.
8   Ibid., 47–8.
9   Selfors, *Saving Juliet*, 6.
10 I observed this exclamation scrawled by an anonymous visitor on a sign posted in the tunnel entrance to Juliet's House in Verona.
11 Watson, *The Literary Tourist*.
12 Scott-Douglass, "Shakespeare for Children," 364.
13 Tosi, "I Could a Tale Unfold," 129.
14 Prindle, "The Play's the Thing," 138.
15 Marchitello, "Descending Shakespeare," 184–5.
16 Holderness, "Bardolatry," 5.
17 Wells, *Everybody's Jane*, 106.
18 Chronis, "Between Place and Story," 1798.
19 Ibid., 1799.
20 Zhu, "Performing Heritage," 1498.
21 Ibid., 1500.
22 See Pringle, "The Rise of Stratford as Shakespeare's Town"; Thomas, "Bidding for the Bard"; and Holderness, "Bardolatry."
23 See Moore, *The Legend of Romeo and Juliet*.
24 Selfors, *Saving Juliet*, 82.
25 Bottoms, "Familiar Shakespeare," 14.
26 Hateley, *Shakespeare in Children's Literature*, 26.
27 Balizet, "Shakespeare, Television, and Girl Culture," n.p.
28 Balizet, "Teen Scenes."
29 Deitchman, "Shakespeare Stiles Style," 479.
30 Bullen, Toffoletti, and Parson, "Doing What Your Big Sister Does," 506.
31 Johnson, "Chick Lit Jr.," 141.
32 Laura Tosi examines the transformation of Ophelia, Jessica, and Portia into "resilient and rebellious" girls in young adult adaptations of *Othello* and *The Merchant of Venice*. Tosi, "Shakespeare for Girls," 23.
33 Moison, "O Any Thing, of Nothing First Create!," 115.
34 Dreher, *Domination and Defiance*, 48.
35 Trites, *Disturbing the Universe*, 54.
36 Ibid., 83.
37 Ibid.
38 Ibid., 70.
39 Johnson, "Chick Lit Jr.," 147.
40 Heinze, "Temporal Tourism," 213.
41 Ibid., 225.
42 Selfors, *Saving Juliet*, 47.
43 Ibid., 19.
44 Ibid., 20.
45 Ibid., 28.
46 Ibid., 22.

47 Ibid., 59.
48 Ibid., 20.
49 Ibid., 9.
50 Ibid., 18.
51 Ibid., 6.
52 Ibid., 82.
53 Ibid., 28.
54 Ibid., 4.
55 Ibid., 7.
56 See Watson, "At Juliet's Tomb."
57 Stewart, *On Longing*, 135.
58 Ibid., 136.
59 Ibid.
60 Selfors, *Saving Juliet*, 30.
61 Ibid., 31.
62 Holderness, "Bardolatry," 4.
63 Selfors, *Saving Juliet*, 31.
64 Stewart, *On Longing*, 136.
65 Selfors, *Saving Juliet*, 40.
66 Ibid., 47, 123.
67 Ibid., 55.
68 Ibid., 57.
69 Ibid., 87.
70 Ibid., 8.
71 Ibid.
72 Ibid., 81.
73 Ibid., 61.
74 Ibid.
75 Ibid., 62.
76 Ibid., 63.
77 Ibid., 130.
78 Ibid., 133.
79 Ibid., 147.
80 Ibid., 162.
81 Ibid.
82 Ibid., 183.
83 *The Wizard of Oz*.
84 Selfors, *Saving Juliet*, 230.
85 Ibid., 241.
86 Ibid., 203.

Bibliography

Applebee, Arthur N. *A Study of Book-Length Works Taught in High School English Courses.* Albany, NY: Center for the Learning and Teaching of Literature, 1989.

Balizet, Ariane M. "Shakespeare, Television, and Girl Culture." *Borrowers and Lenders: The Journal of Shakespeare and Appropriation* 9, no. 1 (Fall 2014): n.p. http://www.borrowers.uga.edu/. Accessed April 17, 2019.

Balizet, Ariane M. "Teen Scenes: Recognizing Shakespeare in Teen Film." In *Almost Shakespeare: Reinventing His Works for Cinema and Television*, edited by James R. Keller and Leslie Stratyner, 122–36. Jefferson, NC: McFarland, 2004.

Bigliazzi, Silvia and Lisanna Calvi. "Introduction." In *Shakespeare, Romeo and Juliet, and Civic Life: The Boundaries of Civic Space*, edited by Bigliazzi and Calvi, 1–34. New York: Routledge, 2016.

Bottoms, Janet. "'Familiar Shakespeare.'" In *Where Texts and Children Meet*, edited by Eve Bearne and Victor Watson, 11–25. New York: Routledge, 2000.

Bullen, Elizabeth, Kim Toffoletti, and Liz Parsons. "Doing What Your Big Sister Does: Sex, Postfeminism, and the YA Chick Lit Series." *Gender and Education* 23, no. 4 (2011): 497–511.

Chronis, Athinodoros. "Between Place and Story: Gettysburg as Tourism Imaginary." *Annals of Tourism Research* 39, no. 4 (2012): 1797–816.

Deitchman, Elizabeth A. "Shakespeare Stiles Style: Shakespeare, Julia Stiles, and American Girl Culture." In *A Companion to Shakespeare and Performance*, edited by Barbara Hodgdon and W. B. Worthen, 478–93. Malden, MA: John Wiley, 2008.

Dreher, Diane Elizabeth. *Domination and Defiance: Fathers and Daughters in Shakespeare*. Lexington: University Press of Kentucky, 1986.

Garber, Marjorie. *Shakespeare and Modern Culture*. New York: Pantheon Books, 2008.

Harper, Suzanne. *The Juliet Club*. New York: Walker, 2008.

Hateley, Erica. *Shakespeare in Children's Literature: Gender and Cultural Capital*. New York: Routledge, 2009.

Heinze, Rüdiger. "Temporal Tourism: Time Travel and Counterfactuality in Literature and Film." In *Counterfactual Thinking/Counterfactual Writing*, edited by Dorothee Birke, Michael Butter, and Tilmann Koppe, 212–26. Boston, MA: De Gruyter, 2011.

Holderness, Graham. "Bardolatry: Or, The Cultural Materialist's Guide to Stratford-upon-Avon." In *The Shakespeare Myth*, edited by Holderness, 2–15. Manchester: Manchester University Press, 1988.

Hulbert, Jennifer, Kevin J. Wetmore, Jr., and Robert L. York. "'Dude, Where's My Bard?': Reducing, Translating, and Referencing Shakespeare for Youth: An Introduction." *Shakespeare and Youth Culture*, edited by Hulbert, Wetmore, and York, 1–41. New York: Palgrave Macmillan, 2006.

Johnson, Joanna Webb. "Chick Lit Jr.: More Than Glitz and Glamour for Teens and Tweens." In *Chick Lit: The New Woman's Fiction*, edited by Suzanne Ferriss and Mallory Young, 141–57. New York: Routledge, 2006.

Lamb, Charles [and Mary Lamb]. *Tales from Shakespeare: Designed for the Use of Young Persons*, 4th ed., 2 vols. London: M.J. Godwin, 1822. Baldwin Library of Historical Children's Literature Digital Collection. Web. http://ufdc.ufl.edu/juv. Accessed October 5, 2014.

Lanier, Douglas. *Shakespeare and Modern Popular Culture*. Oxford: Oxford University Press, 2002.

Letters to Juliet. Directed by Gary Winick. USA: Summit Entertainment, 2010.

Marchitello, Howard. "Descending Shakespeare: Toward a Theory of Adaptation for Children." In *Reimagining Shakespeare for Children and Young Adults*, edited by Naomi J. Miller, 180–92. New York: Routledge, 2003.

Moison, Thomas. "'O Any Thing, of Nothing First Create!': Gender and Patriarchy and the Tragedy of *Romeo and Juliet*." In *In Another Country: Feminist Perspectives on*

Renaissance Drama, edited by Dorothea Kehler and Susan Baker, 113–36. Metuchen, NJ: Scarecrow Press, 1991.

Moore, Olin H. *The Legend of Romeo and Juliet*. Columbus: Ohio State University Press, 1950.

Prindle, Alison H. "'The Play's the Thing': Genre and Adaptations of Shakespeare for Children." In *Reimagining Shakespeare for Children and Young Adults*, edited by Naomi J. Miller, 138–46. New York: Routledge, 2003.

Pringle, Roger. "The Rise of Stratford as Shakespeare's Town." In *The History of an English Borough: Stratford-Upon-Avon, 1196–1996*, 160–74. Stroud, UK: Sutton/Shakespeare Birthplace Trust, 1997.

Scott-Douglass, Amy. "Shakespeare for Children." In *The Edinburgh Companion to Shakespeare and the Arts*, edited by Mark Thornton Burnett, Adrian Streete, and Ramona Wray, 348–76. Edinburgh: Edinburgh University Press, 2011.

Selfors, Suzanne. *Saving Juliet*. New York: Greenwillow Books, 2008.

Shakespeare, William. *Romeo and Juliet*. Edited by Barbara A. Mowat and Paul Werstine. Folger Shakespeare Library. New York: Simon and Schuster, 1992.

Stewart, Susan. *On Longing: Narratives of the Miniature, the Gigantic, the Souvenir, the Collection*. Baltimore: Johns Hopkins University Press, 1984.

The Wizard of Oz. Directed by Victor Fleming. USA: Metro-Goldwyn-Mayer, 1939.

Thomas, Julia. "Bidding for the Bard: Shakespeare, the Victorians, and the Auction of the Birthplace." *Nineteenth-Century Contexts* 30, no. 3 (2008): 215–28.

Tosi, Laura. "'I Could a Tale Unfold …': Adaptations of Shakespeare's Supernatural for Children, from the Lambs to Marcia Williams." *New Review of Children's Literature and Librarianship* 15, no. 2 (2010): 128–47.

Tosi, Laura. "Shakespeare for Girls: Victorian versus Contemporary Prose Versions of *Hamlet* and *The Merchant of Venice*." In *Adapting Canonical Texts in Children's Literature*, edited by Anja Müller, 9–26. London: Bloomsbury, 2013.

Trites, Roberta Seelinger. *Disturbing the Universe: Power and Repression in Adolescent Literature*. Iowa City: Iowa University Press, 2000.

Watson, Nicola J. "At Juliet's Tomb: Anglophone Travel-Writing and Shakespeare's Verona, 1814–1914." In *Shakespeare, Romeo and Juliet, and Civic Life: The Boundaries of Civic Space*, edited by Bigliazzi and Calvi, 224–37. New York: Routledge, 2016.

Watson, Nicola J. *The Literary Tourist: Readers and Places in Romantic and Victorian Britain*. New York: Palgrave Macmillan, 2006.

Watson, Nicola J. "Shakespeare on the Tourist Trail." In *The Cambridge Companion to Shakespeare and Popular Culture*, edited by Robert Shaughnessy, 199–226. Cambridge: Cambridge University Press, 2007.

Wells, Juliette. *Everybody's Jane: Austen in the Popular Imagination*. London: Continuum, 2011.

Zhu, Yujie. "Performing Heritage: Rethinking Authenticity in Tourism." *Annals of Tourism Research* 39, no. 3 (2012): 1495–513.

From Ancient to Modern Myth: Storytelling in Jesmyn Ward's *Salvage the Bones*

Madeleine Tulip

At the beginning of Jesmyn Ward's 2011 young adult novel *Salvage the Bones*, Esch, the narrator, negatively compares herself to "the women who kept me turning the pages: the trickster nymphs, the ruthless goddesses, the world-uprooting mothers. Io, who made a god's heart hot with love; Artemis, who turned a man into a deer and had her dogs tear him cartilage from bone; Demeter, who made time stop when her daughter was stolen."[1] Classical myths, full of magic, desire, upheaval, betrayal, and violence, keep a firm hold on her imagination and spring to her mind at key moments of the narrative. Throughout the plot, the characters fall in and out of mythological roles, adhering to and breaking out of the classical molds of ancient Medea, her brother Absyrtus, and her unfaithful lover Jason, molds that Ward lays out for them through repeated references to the moments of betrayal and revenge made famous in antiquity through works like Apollonius' epic poem *Argonautica* and Euripides' tragedy *Medea*. But while these comparisons heighten and universalize Esch's own story, the world of *Salvage* is not shaped in accordance with ancient myth. Bois Sauvage, the novel's location, is ruled by its own mystical qualities, and even without her frequent invocations of ancient heroines, Esch's story already ends in the kind of universal tragedy that will be remembered as vividly as classical myth: the devastation of Hurricane Katrina. As Ward's own authorial bildungsroman, Esch's story in *Salvage the Bones* is a coming-of-age narrative that turns her not into the modern equivalent of a mythical character but into the next storyteller in a long line of (classical) bards, poets, and novelists, able to convey both the myth and the reality of the events of August 2005.

From August 23 to 31, 2005, Hurricane Katrina, a Category 5 hurricane, made landfall in Florida and Louisiana and quickly became one of the deadliest and costliest recorded hurricanes to hit the United States.[2] Katrina turned into a major scandal both in America and around the world due to the government's inadequate and problematic response to the events, after which places like New Orleans turned into veritable "war zones."[3] *Salvage* is set in Mississippi during the week leading up to the hurricane, following Esch and her family as they slowly grow aware of the storm's impending danger. Katrina serves as the metaphorical climax to the characters' individual storylines: Esch's slighted love and the revelation of her teenage pregnancy; her brother

Skeetah's struggle to keep his newborn puppies alive; and her other brother Randall's futile attempts to obtain a basketball scholarship. But Katrina's role in the novel goes beyond that of a narrative structuring device or a metaphor. *Salvage* is a subtle but nonetheless potent commentary on the politics leading up to and shaping the response to Hurricane Katrina, which draws on the Medea myth to invoke the themes of devastation, rage, and vengeance familiar to us from antiquity. Placing her novel in a long line of adaptations of Medea as sociopolitical commentary, Ward tells a story of Katrina through *Salvage* that becomes a poignant counterpoint to the ancient myth through its implied critique of an established status quo that allowed the catastrophe to come to pass in the first place.

Salvage the Bones has been identified as a young adult novel in a number of studies[4] and in the classroom is often read alongside works like Jewel Parker Rhodes's *Ninth Ward*, as students are encouraged to explore narratives about life for black teenagers in the American South.[5] Nevertheless, the novel has seldom been explicitly analyzed within the framework of young adult literature, however, with Esch's coming-of-age story read as separate from the novel's intertextual play or sociopolitical connotations. In this chapter I argue, however, that *Salvage*'s status as a young adult novel is an important component of its main narrative arc, which turns Esch into a modern mythical storyteller, following not only Ward's own career trajectory but also the footsteps of storytellers such as Edith Hamilton, Euripides, and Apollonius. The protagonist is a modern Medea figure who, rather than killing her own children, grows into a young woman telling the tale of Katrina and of the systemic neglect that allowed the hurricane to become the disaster that it was. This is a coming-of-age story that deliberately overwrites the traditional ending of the Medea myth, whereby the act of rewriting is both facilitated and shaped by the novel's young adult framework.

The motivation behind writing *Salvage* was no doubt political for Ward, mirroring the conclusion that Esch reaches by the end of the novel: that she needs to tell the story of the hurricane and of its destructive motherhood and, therein, to return to the political impetus that has long been contained within the tale of Medea. Within the novel, Esch's narration implicitly parallels the death of Medea's children, brought about by the hands of their own mother, with the hurricane's devastation, that was allowed for, in part, by the systemic neglect of the US government. In her memoir, *Men We Reaped*, Ward lays out the political aim of her novel, describing how *Salvage* allowed her to explore "why this epidemic happened ... how the history of racism and income inequality and lapsed public and personal responsibility festered and soured and spread here."[6] "[D]issatisfied with the way [Katrina] had receded from public consciousness," she wrote a story that reminded people of the causes of the hurricane and that rectified a story she felt had been continuously misrepresented: "I was angry at the people who blamed survivors for staying and for choosing to return to the Mississippi Gulf Coast after the storm."[7] Although *Salvage* is never openly didactic, it intentionally humanizes the reasons and circumstances behind a family's decision to not evacuate during the hurricane. The state of public misinformation about people's decisions to stay in their homes, in many instances, is subtly addressed within the novel: the Batiste's family's financial inability to evacuate, for instance, parallels the fact that Katrina struck New

Orleans two days before pay, welfare, or disability checks, leaving many citizens unable to cover the transportation costs of evacuation.[8] The systemic racism that shaped both the effects of and responses to Katrina is thereby poignantly echoed not only within Ward's own novel but also within the reception history of the so-called "Black Medea," a reception history *Salvage* self-consciously references and becomes part of.

However, as politically significant as *Salvage* is, the narrative itself focuses less on the actual events of Hurricane Katrina than on Esch becoming a storyteller able to understand and retell the destructiveness of Katrina as a "terrible mother," as a Medea in a long line of Medeas. The hurricane itself takes place only during the second to last day of the narrative, with the last day dedicated to assessing its damages. The novel's main body is preoccupied with Esch undergoing the kind of coming-of-age narrative that allows her to write about her individual experiences and the destruction of Katrina through the same mythical lens, and its ending looks to an uncertain future rather than one that promises radical change. *Salvage*'s classical allusions are a way to help Esch understand her own identity as a young mother finding herself in a comparable position to ancient Medea, while the sociopolitical charge of the myth's reception history underlines the marginalization that has Esch and her family end up in such a vulnerable position during the hurricane's impact.[9] The devastation caused by the storm, Medea's wrath incarnate, thereby frames three narrative layers: as a unique and local event, it irrevocably shapes the coming-of-age narrative of the novel's protagonist; as both an environmental and a sociopolitical disaster, it warily looks toward the future of America; as a universal story of oppression, it is bound to repeat itself as Medea is reborn elsewhere.

A Collection of Intertexts

Salvage draws on a number of literary intertexts, from William Faulkner's *As I Lay Dying*,[10] John Steinbeck's *Grapes of Wrath*,[11] to various other influences including Toni Morrison and Alice Walker.[12] Interestingly enough, when asked about her literary influences in an interview with Anna Hartnell, Ward names a number of authors but does not reference Edith Hamilton's *Mythology*, which she used as a reference when writing *Salvage*,[13] nor any other versions of the Medea myth except for a brief mention of Toni Morrison. As this lack of references implies, *Salvage* is not influenced by or rewriting any specific version of the Medea myth, but rather draws on Medea's experiences as they are remembered as an almost universally resonant narrative across the Western literary and cultural canon. And it is not only Medea's story that echoes through the narrative; unlike the Colchian Medea, Esch becomes "bold as a Greek"[14] and assumes the roles of both Eurydice, Psyche, and Daphne,[15] while her brother Junior becomes the Patroclus to Randall's Achilles.[16] Her mother Rose becomes a wanderer through the underworld, a Dante or Aeneas watching the devastation of hell as "the newly dead and the old dead littered the beaches, the streets, the woods."[17] And in his review of *Salvage*, Andy Johnson names Randall "a basketball court Hector,"[18] Daddy "a wounded Menelaus,"[19] and Skeetah an "off course ... Odysseus."[20] Classical mythology is a universal tongue in *Salvage*, and the fragmented and decontextualized allusions to the ancient stories help to heighten as well as to position the experiences of its characters.

Part of Ward's intention in including the classical allusions in her novel is a wish to reclaim something that has long been designated Western, European, and white. In a 2011 interview, Ward describes how:

> It infuriates me that the work of white American writers can be universal and lay claim to classic texts, while black and female authors are ghettoized as "other." I wanted to align Esch with that classic text, with the universal figure of Medea, the antihero, to claim that tradition as part of my Western literary heritage.[21]

It is surely no coincidence that Esch at some point forms an image of her baby as a "black Athena,"[22] referencing the famous strand of scholarship that attempts to show the Afroasiatic roots of classical civilization. Many of the classical references that accompany the main intertext, the Medea myth, are thus integrated so fluidly into the world of *Salvage* that they are barely recognizable as adaptations of or allusions to a separate sociocultural context. These references are disjointed, decontextualized, and, to the novel's young adult portion of the readership, largely unintroduced. These singular and intermixed allusions form part of a heightened, mythical language that is accompanied and reinforced by the novel's references to other mystical or fantastical traditions. For instance, when they first go to steal cow wormer from their white neighbors, Skeetah attempts to convince Junior to not follow them to their white neighbors' house by retelling the German fairy tale of Hänsel and Gretel.[23]

In her monograph on fairy tales in young adult literature, Anna Katrina Gutierrez, with reference to David Herman, describes how these kinds of intertextual references "foreground[] the way something global is made meaningful in a local context," often appearing in the guise of "schemas and scripts. These are generalized knowledge patterns ... through which we catalog the relationship between abstract models and their physical forms on the basis of their functions."[24] Based on their prominence in transcultural memoryspheres, Astrid Erll likewise describes classical myths as narrative schemata, as "powerful source[s] for premediation."[25] Indeed, classical myths and fairy tales alike appear schematically across *Salvage*, as knowledge structure more remembered than learned, a language assumed to be universal and flavoring the story more than shaping it. This has, first and foremost, a practical function in Ward's novel: for any member of the young adult portion of the readership not recognizing one of these referencing does not mean they lose out on the story's significance. Generally speaking, too, this schematization largely marked by a fragmentation and decontextualization of the ancient stories has allowed the classics to appear in all kinds of different guises, media, and contexts and has undoubtedly contributed to the perceived "democratic turn" in classical reception, the increased popularization of classical narratives, characters, and ideas.[26] More widespread and adaptable, perhaps, than ever before, the fluid shape in which classical schemata and references exist within our cultural memory across the West has, in this instance, allowed the signifier of "Medea" to go so far as to thematically connect the horrors of Hurricane Katrina to the growing pains of a young girl in the American South and has allowed Ward to reclaim the "universal figure of Medea" as her own.

Although references to classical antiquity are most common across *Salvage*, the story is not dominated by a purely Greco-Roman sense of mysticism but draws from a variety of sources, both preexisting and newly invented, to create a feeling akin to magical realism. In his book review of *Salvage*, Johnson not only summarizes the classical allusions he detects in the novel but also describes, for instance, Junior as "almost magical, elven."[27] Similarly, the lines between animals, as well as humans and animals are continuously blurred; the puppies of Skeetah's prizefighting dog China are "fluffy, downy balls [that] almost look like chicks" (21), leading Esch to wonder: "Would a human egg let itself be seen?"[28] All characters in the novel are, at some point or the other, compared to animals, usually small mammals such as squirrels, puppies, and monkeys,[29] while China is humanized and explicitly Americanized[30] throughout *Salvage*, frequently through comparisons with Esch's mother.[31] Emphasizing the subjectivity of Esch as a first-person narrator, the novel's language implicitly reflects the unique way in which she experiences the world: as a magical place filled with Ovidian shapeshifters and animal "familiar[s]," in which birds "wave them on" and in which dogs "lea[p] like a doe."[32]

Allusions to the classics and especially to Medea are invoked at key moments in the narrative, especially when Esch reflects on her relationships with Manny and Skeetah. But Bois Sauvage has its own magic and its own myths that are continuously related and invoked throughout the story, and the narrative is not restricted to a classical framework of reference. After the hurricane strikes and the Batiste family seeks refuge at Big Henry's house, they see how the house "was encircled by six of the trees that had stood in the yard but that now fenced the house in like a green gate. 'It's a miracle,' Big Henry said. 'All the trees fell away from the house.'"[33] Marking out the place that will serve as a communal hub for the people of Bois Sauvage to come together after the hurricane, the novel's environment follows its own rules.

As if to emphasize that *Salvage* is not merely a retelling of the classical storyline etched out for the characters in Euripides' or Apollonius' version of the Medea myth, Skeetah and China are invoked as a comparative point by Esch far more frequently than Medea and Jason. While Skeetah and China's narrative arc retells, in its own way, the relationship between the Greek hero and the Colchian princess, leading up to Jason's and Skeetah's betrayal, there are many moments in which the uniquely close relationship between Skeetah, as a dog owner, and China, as his fighting dog, becomes the dominant facet of the comparison.[34] Despite China undoubtedly embodying many aspects of Medea across the narrative, Skeetah and China exist as their own reference point, not representative of the Jason–Medea dynamic from antiquity but emblematic of a unique relationship of their own.

Meanwhile, the Greek myths Esch frequently invokes give her problematic, unrealistic, and idealized beliefs about her relationship with Manny. During one of the novel's sexual encounters between Esch and Manny amidst pine trees itself an allusion to the moment Medea and Jason first fell in love, standing "face to face without a word, as lofty pine trees when the wind is still"[35] Esch thinks herself "bold as a Greek I was making him hot with love, and Manny was loving me."[36] Initially caught up in the extremes of love she found in Hamilton's *Mythology*, Esch's coming-of-age narrative describes her gradual acceptance of a different, healthier reference point for a loving relationship. When she realizes that Manny will be neither the romantic partner nor the father she envisioned, Esch's thoughts return to Skeetah and China's relationship: "For some reason I see Skeetah when I blink, Skeetah kneeling next to China, always kneeling, always stroking and loving and knowing her. Skeetah's face when he stood across from Rico, when he told China, *Make them know*. I am on him like China."[37] Esch returns to Medea a few lines later, seeing herself as "Medea wielding the knife. This is Medea cutting."[38] At this point she understands that Skeetah and China's relationship runs parallel to the loving relationship between Medea and Jason she read of in the early parts of Hamilton's *Mythology*, while her own relationship with Manny has become more reflective of Medea's vengeance that inevitably follows. Medea's role, as realized in Esch, is no longer that of a lover but of a forceful avenger, foreshadowing the imminent impact of Katrina as a catalyst of a more universal rage yet. Although Medea's story and the classics remain a dominant framework all the way through the story, it is important both for the narrative construction of Bois Sauvage and for the thematic ending of *Salvage* that the classical myths are not invoked as an unchangeable framework. They exist as schematic references, used and discarded interchangeably with the magic already existing in Bois Sauvage, as ancient bones to be salvaged when the need occurs, but also to be buried again when the time comes.

A Black Medea

In his article on the allusions to classical Medea in *Salvage the Bones*, Benjamin Stevens lays the important groundwork for the way in which we may understand both the mode and the political stakes within Ward's reception of the Medea myth. Stevens focuses on the fact that, unlike her classical model Medea, Esch does not kill the child she carries, whereby "*Salvage* suggests that Esch like Ward has found in Greek myth a way of responding to such violence without perpetuating it. In this way the novel may be read as offering a model for classical reception as a kind of 'salvage' not only of materials from antiquity but also, no less importantly, what is left over from the wrack of modern life."[39] This is a vital recognition about the way in which reception operates in the world of *Salvage*—not as a straightforward narrative imposition of an intertext that shapes the story-world of *Salvage* according to its ancient mold but as a source of inspiration that is adapted in deconstructed and fluid form. Reception operates in schematic terms as Ward salvages only those connotations and story-points from antiquity that can be integrated into a world already shaped by its own rules and thematic concerns.

Stevens continues: "This critical, even political possibility brings us back to the image of reception as a kind of 'salvage' an act of recuperation after the fact that is at once richly creative and a reflection of impoverished necessity."[40] Here, Stevens alerts us to the sociopolitical implications of *Salvage*'s classical reception: Esch's decision to move away from the intertext of Medea at the story's close, growing into a narrator-figure of her own right, something Stevens calls "a transformative reception."[41] As a way to connect the idea of a transformative reception of the classical source-material to the "impoverished necessity" of Esch's sociopolitical context, Ward herself has drawn attention to the phonetic closeness between the words "salvage" and "savage" in an interview with the *Paris Review*, linking the process of salvaging after the hurricane to a form of savagery that is connoted positively as an ability to survive hardship.[42] The novel further develops this conceptional closeness of "savagery" Skeetah proudly compared the Batiste family to savages who manage to survive and thrive among the harshest of circumstances[43] and the idea of thriving through salvaging, schematically resurrecting both materials and ideas and stories from faraway and long ago. Stevens writes:

> In Ward's emphasis on necessity and pragmatism we may hear a distant echo of Medea's ancient status as outsider or barbarian: all who have been left behind after a storm are "savage," literally displaced and so figuratively considered out of (their, any) culture ... we who live in a world of storms are "savage" insofar as they themselves as we ourselves have been "salvaged," somehow left behind and saved. This state of affairs virtually requires cultivating a capacity for recovering what is useful from what has been lost. As such we are invited not only to consider but to practice the sort of classical reception necessary and yet potentially transformative embodied in the figure of Medea in Jesmyn Ward's *Salvage the Bones*.[44]

Along similar lines, Sinéad Moynihan speaks of Ward's rewriting as a "more politically engaged model ... that can more accurately be called 'recycling.'"[45] The sociopolitical disenfranchisement the characters find themselves in and the kind of schematic reception through which they resurrect the past not only can be described by phonetically similar words salvage and savage but are motivated by the same drive to restructure, refigure, and repurpose the(ir) past. These parallel impulses of refiguring salvaging and recycling classical myth and sociopolitical reality are embodied in the fluid shapes the Medea figure assumes in Ward's novel, becoming at once dog, storyteller, and hurricane.

As Esch draws on classical myth to understand the world and the relationships around her, the figure of Medea is configured into three different characters, reflecting the three main stages of the ancient sorceress's life. First, Medea fulfilled the role of "maiden,"[46] daughter of the Colchian king, then the role of Jason's lover, whose "great love for Jason made the loss of her family and her country seem to her a little thing."[47] Finally, she became the destructive mother, "carried ... away through the air out of his sight as he cursed her, never himself, for what had come to pass."[48] These three stages of Medea's life are, in part, reenacted in the stories of the three most significant "female" characters of the novel: Esch herself is initially the maiden described largely in Apollonius, experiencing her first love and wishing to flee from her father's court, while China enters the novel freshly a mother and willing to fight for the man she loves, Skeetah. Hurricane Katrina, explicitly designated female both through the storm's naming and through Claude's likening of storms with women,[49] becomes the embodiment of Medea's destructive power, paralleling the sorceress's escape on storm clouds with its own brutal train of destruction throughout the American South. These stages of Medea's life do, of course, intersect within the characters' representations, emphasizing, once more, the schematic manner of adaptation in Ward's novel.

Although she was largely demonized in antiquity, across its reception history the story of the Colchian sorceress and her infanticide has continuously been used as a framework to describe the experiences of marginalized women. From Christa Wolf's *Medea. Stimmen* to Marina Carr's *By the Bog of Cats*, playwrights have used the story of Medea as a way to illustrate the desperation of a woman who would choose to kill or, in Wolf's case, abandon her own children. Esch's environment living in extreme poverty and without a significant female role model who could guide her on questions of sexuality and motherhood drives her to consider attempting an abortion herself, a desperate measure that is perhaps not comparable to but evocative of Medea's decision to kill her children.[50] But while the world of *Salvage* is filled with the kind of sexism that leaves women in situations wherein a self-inflicted abortion seems like their only option,[51] equally to her sex it is Esch's racially coded poverty that leads her to consider such drastic measures. It forms one of the most politically potent points of connection to the Medea myth and its reception history and creates an ethical imperative in a novel Ward herself described as initially "not political enough."[52]

Although Bois Sauvage is a place that is marked by infrastructural and systemic poverty throughout,[53] there are clear delineations made between the "black heart of Bois Sauvage, and … the pale arteries."[54] The school in Bois Sauvage was only desegregated for the previous generation,[55] Esch and her family experience frequent racism from the white population of the town,[56] and there are differences in wealth illustrated by the fact that they attempt to steal from their white neighbors on two separate occasions during the novel. Esch and her family experience particularly stark poverty: Esch is unable to afford an abortion, her brother Randall relies on the money to be made from selling China's puppies to afford basketball camp,[57] and the children live on Ramen noodles, eggs, and at times even squirrels they hunt in the woods.[58] There is also a potential allusion to a lack of hurricane-proof infrastructure, leading to the flooding of the pit during Katrina, as Daddy describes how the water "'never came back here.' Daddy breathes. 'The damn creek.'"[59]

Although natural disasters such as hurricanes are still often perceived as so-called "acts of god," Hurricane Katrina is designated as a "non-natural disaster" in the scholarly literature, as a disaster "in which social factors contributed to increased vulnerability and inhibited recovery due to lack of socio-political and economic resources."[60] As Henry A. Giroux explains,

> after Hurricane Katrina hit the Gulf Coast, the consequences of the long legacy of attacking big government and bleeding the social and public service sectors of the state became glaringly evident … Hurricane Katrina made it abundantly clear that only the government had the power, resources, and authority to address complex

undertakings such as dealing with the totality of the economic, environmental, cultural and social destruction that impacted the Gulf Coast.[61]

Although for most of *Salvage* the father tries to prepare for the hurricane's impact "he would've told them he's fixing up for the hurricane,"[62] "Daddy's crazy, I think, obsessed with hurricanes this summer"[63] it is clear that he is powerless in the fact of the systematic neglect the Bush administration demonstrated when it came to the nation's most vulnerable bodies. What Giroux calls "the new biopolitics of disposability"[64] assumes a particularly tragic irony in the novel through Claude's foresight when it comes to Katrina, securing not only his own house to the best of his ability but also preparing a dump truck to rid the community of the accumulated rubble after the storm.[65]

The people depicted in *Salvage* the black working poor in the American South are among the population that were hit the hardest by Hurricane Katrina. Emily Chamlee-Wright and Virgil Henry Storr describe how "institutional racism played a role in the disappointing government response to the immediate crisis and continues to play a role in the slow pace at which recovery assistance is administered."[66] Following the tradition of the "Black Medea" and its common sociopolitical critiques, Ward's novel renders the hurricane as the embodiment of a modern Medea's wrath.

The Medea myth has a long history of being adapted to reflect themes of racism and marginalization, including works such as Hans Henny Jahnn's 1926 *Medea* and Steve Carter's 1990 *Pecong*. Among them are a number of adaptations in which Medea is turned into a more ambiguous, if not positive character, as her motivation to kill her children becomes her wish to save them from racial oppression. These works famously include Toni Morrison's *Beloved*, who is listed by Ward as an inspiration for *Salvage*, as well as Guy Butler's *Demea*, set in Apartheid South Africa.[67] Like Esch and China, Katrina is described as a mother throughout the narrative, but she is the embodiment of the final section of Medea's journey in which the sorceress chooses to murder her children:

> I will tie the glass and stone with string, hand the shards above my bed, so that they will flash in the dark and tell the story of Katrina, the mother that swept into the Gulf and slaughtered ... She was the murderous mother who cut us to the bone but left us alive, left us naked and bewildered as wrinkled newborn babies, as blind puppies, as sun-starved newly hatched baby snakes. She left us a dark Gulf and salt-burned land. She left us to learn to crawl. She left us to salvage. Katrina is the mother we will remember until the next mother with large, merciless hands, committed to blood, comes.[68]

Katrina becomes part of this ambiguous reception history of Medea, another murderous mother that swoops down on her children amidst continuing racial oppression and marginalization. Reading *Salvage* within the reception history of the "Black Medea," the novel's implication that the storm's impact is both a cause of and a response to systemic racism and neglect becomes evident. This connection further illuminates the sustained threat that exists for Esch and her family in an America shaped by what Hartnell calls "Katrina time," a time that offers a "disturbing glimpse of the unsustainability of a system that prioritizes profit over people, privatizes the public commons, and privileges an ideology of individualism at the expense of our collective futures."[69] Esch's reference to the next mother, coming "with large, merciless hands, committed to blood," is reflective of the reality of the post-Katrina environment, not only in the sense in which the government's response to the hurricane was emblematic and constitutive of an increasing racial divide but also referencing the landscape itself, open to the next threat. As a 2007 study on the Mississippi barrier islands concludes, Hurricane Katrina led to a 37 percent width increase between the islands, increasing the vulnerability of the Gulf Coast to further hurricane impacts.[70]

This is the story Esch must tell after the events of the novel have come to pass: a sociopolitical critique of systemic racism and sexism in modern America, filtered through her salvaging the myths and magic of classical antiquity, the fairy tales of her childhood, and the magical reality of Bois Sauvage itself. But although Esch initially identifies with the ancient sorceress she reads about in her school materials, as the novel proceeds both Esch's and China's ties to the ancient narrative loosen. Although China kills one of her puppies early in the novel, it is due to the puppies' infection with parvo, and she loses the others due to the storm and not by choice. Esch considers aborting her own child, but eventually chooses to raise it with the help of the "plenty daddies" Big Henry promises her.[71] Although the threat of other storms remains, and perhaps of a Medea-like rage overcoming Esch in the future, her choice at the end of the novel is to salvage from the ancient story rather than to stick to it word-for-word. She tries to finish "the entire mythology book, but I can't. I am stuck in the middle" (154).[72] Esch shuts the *Mythology* book and does not mark the page she stopped on, intending to write the end of her own story and to depart from the path Medea set out for her.

Shortly before this moment, the novel cautiously hints at the mode in which Esch's relationship with the past is constituted: through her memory, formative of the way in which she salvages both from her own history and from ancient mythology. Skeetah and Esch talk about the memories of their mother that pervade and shape much of the novel, memories that are often unclear and incomplete,[73] but nonetheless help Esch on her coming-of-age journey of turning into the novel's own narrator. The scene is filled with a sense of both recovery and loss as they attempt to reconstruct the past:

> "But I can't remember her voice," he [Skeetah] says. "I know the exact words she said, can see us sitting there by her lap, but all I can hear is my voice saying it, not hers." I want to say that I know her voice. I want to open my mouth and have her voice slide out of me like an impression, to speak Mama alive for him as I hear her. But I can't. "At least we got the memory," I say. "Junior don't have nothing."
>
> "You remember the last thing she said to you?" … "No," I say. "I don't remember."
>
> "I do," Skeetah says, and he props his chin on his fists. "She told us she loved us when she got into the truck. And then she told us to be good. To look after each other." "I don't remember that." I think Skeetah is imagining it.[74]

Despite Esch's doubts about the validity of Skeetah's recollections, she does not press him on and potentially destroy the version of their mother he remembers. Skeetah's memories provide comfort and strength to them as they survive the devastation of Katrina and provide Esch with a more constructive framework of motherhood than the one she relied on so far, that of Medea.[75] At the end of the novel Esch comes to fully understand the power of mnemonically salvaging, reshaping, and reconstructing the past out of whatever is available, even among the poverty that caused the death of her own mother and the sustained loss that will continue to surround her. Both decontextualized and fragmented classical stories from Hamilton's *Mythology* and the magic Esch experiences in Bois Sauvage help her to mnemonically reframe the story of Katrina as she renarrates it in *Salvage*. And even within the bleak sociopolitical reception history of the Medea myth, Esch manages to remember the ancient sorceress's story into a politically poignant tale of a community coming together after a catastrophe.

The journey of Esch as a young mother, initially with little agency, developing into the memory-driven, salvaging narrator of her own story, is the novel's central narrative arc, a coming-of-age story that defines *Salvage* as young adult fiction as well as shapes the novel's relationship with its classical intertext and the myth's sociopolitical implications. Esch's growing rejection of Medea as a model for motherhood is allegorical for the novel's increased distance from the Medea myth as a way to define its sociopolitical environment. While in the ancient myths Medea leaves the community around her shattered and broken by the devastation, Big Henry's house in *Salvage* is magically spared and even encircled by fallen trees, becoming the communal hub that helps the people of Bois Sauvage come together after the hurricane. And while many a time the desperation of a marginalized and racially oppressed Medea-figure has led to the death of her children, Esch decides to keep her unborn child and to raise it even within the uncertain community of Bois Sauvage in "Katrina time." The model of "savage salvaging," initially indicative of the destitute economic climate in which the narrator finds herself, becomes the format of reception Esch adopts as her memory-driven retelling moves the narrative away from a restrictive ancient intertext. As Stevens argued, the novel advises not only the consideration but also the practice of a "necessary and yet potentially transformative" kind of reception.[76] And as the novel meta-textually considers its own mode of adapting antiquity, the tell-tale signs of the novel's place in the young adult genre Esch's developing relationship to her teenage pregnancy and her development into the storyteller within her community serve as complex metaphors for *Salvage*'s mnemonically refigurative relationship to the Medea myth and its sociopolitical reception history.

Notes

1 Ward, *Salvage the Bones*, 15–16.
2 Fritz et al., "Hurricane Katrina," 1.
3 Tierney, Bevc, and Kuligowski, "Metaphors Matter," 69, 74.

4. Hill and Darragh, "From Bootstraps to Hands-up," 63.
5. Smyth and Hansen, "Teaching Social Justice," 343. Specifically, *Salvage* may be categorized as a mythopoeic young adult novel due to its frequent invocations of classical myth as well as the magical realism its world is imbued with.
6. Ward, *Men We Reaped*, 8; qtd. in Railsback, "Grapes of Wrath," 193.
7. Qtd. in DeChavez, "Hidden in Plain Sight," 33–4. Cf. Anna Hartnell, who summarizes the prevalent assumptions that the victims of Katrina had chosen to stay and die in their homes (Hartnell, *After Katrina*, 5).
8. Cutter et al., "The Long Road Home," 11.
9. In his article on Medea in *Salvage*, Benjamin Stevens writes that "Esch's identification with Medea is a way of understanding her own experience as a young woman coming of age, entering motherhood and confronting the responsibilities it entails" (Stevens, "Medea in Jesmyn Ward," 158).
10. Moynihan, "From Disposability to Recycling," 551.
11. Railsback, "Grapes of Wrath," n.p.
12. Hartnell, "When Cars Become Churches," 217.
13. Stevens, "Medea in Jesmyn Ward," 160.
14. Ward, *Salvage the Bones*, 17.
15. Ibid., 16, 28.
16. Ibid., 125.
17. Ibid., 218.
18. Johnson, "*Salvage the Bones*," 493.
19. Ibid., 493–4.
20. Ibid., 494.
21. Ward, "Jesmyn Ward on Salvage the Bones," n.p.; qtd. in Johnson, "*Salvage the Bones*," 494.
22. Ward, *Salvage the Bones*, 219.
23. Ibid., 75.
24. Gutierrez, *Mixed Magic*, xviii, 5.
25. Erll, "Homer," 275.
26. For a detailed discussion of the "democratic turn," cf. Hardwick and Harrison's edited collection *Classics in the Modern World*.
27. Johnson, "*Salvage the Bones*," 494.
28. Ward, *Salvage the Bones*, 24.
29. These comparisons foreshadow one of the most explicit passages of social commentary toward the end of the novel. When Katrina is about to hit, Esch reminisces that

   > When Mama first explained to me what a hurricane was, I thought that all the animals ran away … But now I think that other animals, like the squirrels and the rabbits, don't do that at all. Maybe the small don't run. Maybe the small pause on their branches, the pine-lined earth, nose up, catch that coming storm air that would smell like salt to them, like salt and clean burning fire, and they prepare like us. (Ward, *Salvage the Bones*, 215)

   The continuous comparisons of the Batiste family to small animals serve to illustrate their poverty and powerlessness, further reinforcing the novel's aim at humanizing and creating empathy for those who were unable to evacuate during the hurricane. For a comparable reading, cf. Lloyd, *Corporeal Legacies in the US South*, 165.

30 Ward, *Salvage the Bones*, 84.
31 Ibid., 60, 93.
32 Ibid., 78.
33 Ibid., 242.
34 Cf. Ward, *Salvage the Bones*, 120, 203.
35 Hamilton, *Mythology*, 172.
36 Ward, *Salvage the Bones*, 17. For a reading of the wind imagery in this scene with reference to Apollonius' version of the Medea myth, cf. Stevens, "Medea in Jesmyn Ward," 166ff.
37 Ward, *Salvage the Bones*, 203. For a more extensive discussion of the equality and interdependence between Skeetah and China, cf. Lloyd, *Corporeal Legacies*, 151ff.
38 Ibid., 204.
39 Stevens, "Medea in Jesmyn Ward," 159.
40 Ibid., 162.
41 Ibid.
42 Ward, *Paris Review*, n.p., qtd. in Lloyd, *Corporeal Legacies*, 162.
43 Lloyd, *Corporeal Legacies*, 163.
44 Stevens, "Medea in Jesmyn Ward," 175.
45 Moynihan, "From Disposability to Recycling," 551.
46 Hamilton, *Mythology*, 169.
47 Ibid., 177.
48 Ibid., 180.
49 Ward, *Salvage the Bones*, 124.
50 Ibid., 102.
51 Particularly illustrative for the sexism in *Salvage*'s sociopolitical environment is the scene on the second day wherein the Batiste children and Big Henry come across a couple that had been in a car accident (cf. Ward, *Salvage the Bones*, 32, 34).
52 Ward, *Paris Review*, n.p.
53 Cf., for instance, Ward, *Salvage the Bones*, 70ff.
54 Ward, *Salvage the Bones*, 97.
55 Ibid., 140–1.
56 Cf. Ward, *Salvage the Bones*, 132.
57 Ward, *Salvage the Bones*, 74.
58 Ibid., 49.
59 Ibid., 228.
60 Hawkins and Maurer, "Bonding, Bridging and Linking," 1778.
61 Giroux, "Reading Hurricane Katrina," 174–5.
62 Ward, *Salvage the Bones*, 4.
63 Ibid., 46.
64 Giroux, "Reading Hurricane Katrina," 175.
65 Ward, *Salvage the Bones*, 90.
66 Chamlee-Wright and Storr, "There's No Place like New Orleans," 615.
67 Cf. Lauriola, "Medea," 397ff.
68 Ward, *Salvage the Bones*, 225.
69 Hartnell, *After Katrina*, 2.
70 Fritz et al., "Hurricane Katrina," 8.
71 Ward, *Salvage the Bones*, 255.
72 Ibid., 154.

73 Cf. Ward, *Salvage the Bones*, 52.
74 Ward, *Salvage the Bones*, 221–2.
75 For a discussion of maternal memory in *Salvage the Bones*, cf. DeChavez, "Hidden in Plain Sight," 44ff.
76 Stevens, "Medea in Jesmyn Ward," 175.

Bibliography

Chamlee-Wright, Emily and Virgil Henry Storr. " 'There's No Place Like New Orleans': Sense of Place and Community Recovery in the Ninth Ward after Hurricane Katrina." *Journal of Urban Affairs* 31, no. 5 (2009): 615–34.

Cutter, Susan L., Christopher T. Emrich, Jerry T. Mitchell, Bryan J. Boruff, Melanie Gall, Mathew C. Schmidtlein, Christopher G. Burton, and Ginni Melton. "The Long Road Home: Race, Class, and Recovery from Hurricane Katrina." *Environment: Science and Policy for Sustainable Development* 48, no. 2 (2006): 8–20.

DeChavez, Yvette Marie. " 'Hidden in Plain Sight': Loopholes of Retreat in Post-Katrina Literature and Performance." PhD Diss., University of Texas, 2017.

Erll, Astrid. "Homer: A Relational Mnemohistory." *Memory Studies* 11, no. 3 (2018): 274–86.

Fritz, Hermann M., Chris Blount, Robert Sokoloski, Justin Singleton, Andrew Fuggle, Brian G. McAdoo, Andrew Moore, and Chad Grass, Banks Tate. "Hurricane Katrina Storm Surge Distribution and Field Observations on the Mississippi Barrier Islands." *Estuarine, Coastal and Shelf Science* xx (2007): 1–9.

Giroux, Henry A. "Reading Hurricane Katrina: Race, Class, and the Biopolitics of Disposability." *College Literature* 33, no. 3 (2006): 171–96.

Gutierrez, Anna Katrina. *Mixed Magic: Global-Local Dialogues in Fairy Tales for Young Readers*. Amsterdam: John Benjamins, 2017.

Hamilton, Edith. *Mythology: Timeless Tales of Gods and Heroes*. New York: Grand Central, [1942] 2011.

Hardwick, Lorna, and Stephen Harrison (eds.). *Classics in the Modern World: A "Democratic Turn"?* Oxford: Oxford University Press, 2013.

Hartnell, Anna. "When Cars Become Churches: Jesmyn Ward's Disenchanted America: An Interview." *Journal of American Studies* 50, no. 1 (2016): 205–18.

Hartnell, Anna. *After Katrina: Race, Neoliberalism, and the End of the American Century*. Albany: State University of New York Press, 2017.

Hawkins, Robert L., and Katherine Maurer. "Bonding, Bridging and Linking: How Social Capital Operated in New Orleans following Hurricane Katrina." *British Journal of Social Work* 40 (2010): 1777–93.

Hill, Crag, and Janine J. Darragh. "From Bootstraps to Hands-up: A Multicultural Content Analysis of the Depiction of Poverty in Young Adult Literature." *Study and Scrutiny: Research on Young Adult Literature* 1, no. 2 (2016): 31–63.

Johnson, Andy. "*Salvage the Bones* by Jesmyn Ward (review)." *Callaloo* 39, no. 2 (2016): 493–5.

Lauriola, Rosanna. "Medea." In *Brill's Companion to the Reception of Euripides*, edited by Rosanna Lauriola and Kyriakos N. Demetriou, 377–443. Leiden: Brill, 2015.

Lloyd, Christopher. *Corporeal Legacies in the US South: Memory and Embodiment in Contemporary Culture*. Cham: Palgrave Macmillan, 2018.

Moynihan, Sinéad. "From Disposability to Recycling: William Faulkner and the New Politics of Rewriting in Jesmyn Ward's *Salvage the Bones*." *Studies in the Novel* 47, no. 4 (2015): 550–67.

Railsback, Brian. "A Twenty-First-Century Grapes of Wrath: Jesmyn Ward's *Salvage the Bones*." *Steinbeck Review* 13, no. 2 (2016): 179–95.

Smyth, Theony Soublis, and Angela Hansen. "Teaching Social Justice in Social Studies through Young Adult Literature." In *Social Justice Instruction: Empowerment on the Chalkboard*, edited by Rosemary Papa, Danielle M. Eadens, and Daniel W. Eadens, 339–46. Cham: Springer, 2016.

Stevens, Benjamin Eldon. "Medea in Jesmyn Ward's *Salvage the Bones*." *International Journal of the Classical Tradition* 25, no. 2 (2018): 158–77.

Tierney, Kathleen, Christine Bevc, and Erica Kuligowski. "Metaphors Matter: Disaster Myths, Media Frames, and Their Consequences in Hurricane Katrina." *The Annals of the American Academy of Political and Social Science* 604 (2006): 57–81.

Ward, Jesmyn. *Men We Reaped*. New York: Bloomsbury, 2013.

Ward, Jesmyn. *Salvage the Bones*. London: Bloomsburg, 2011.

Ward, Jesmyn. "Jesmyn Ward on Salvage the Bones." Interview by Elizabeth Hoover. *The Paris Review*, August 30, 2011. https://www.theparisreview.org/blog/2011/08/30/jesmyn-ward-on-salvage-the-bones/.

Contributors

Michelle Anya Anjirbag is a PhD candidate at the University of Cambridge, UK. Her research interests include the analysis of adaptations of fairy tales and folklore, focusing on cross-period approaches to narrative transmission across cultures and societies. Her current research is on depictions of diversity in Disney's fairy-tale adaptations from 1989 through the present. Her work appears in *Social Sciences*, *Jeunesse*, and *Adaptation*.

Saffyre Falkenberg is a doctoral student in the English Department at Texas Christian University in Fort Worth, Texas, USA. Her research interests include children's and young adult literature, fantasy, feminist theory, queer theory, asexuality studies, pop culture, video games, and female heroes. She has published most recently on recovering asexual history through Julia Ward Howe's *The Hermaphrodite* (2019).

Dalila Forni is a PhD candidate in Education and Psychology at the University of Florence, Italy. She obtained her MA in European and Extra-European Languages and Literatures at the University of Milan with a thesis entitled "A World of Pure Imagination: Cinema and Theatre Adaptations of Roald Dahl's *Charlie and the Chocolate Factory*." Her research interests include children's literature and culture, gender studies, and queer studies. She has recently published essays on family dynamics in children's fictions. She is currently researching how gender identities are represented in children's narratives, from picture books to video games.

Fiona Hartley-Kroeger is a doctoral candidate in English Literature at the University of Illinois at Urbana-Champaign, USA. Her research interests focus on children's and young adult literature, women's and gender studies, folklore and fairy tales, and transhistorical adaptation. She has published on gender and narration in young adult fiction, and she is a reviewer for the *Bulletin of the Center for Children's Books*.

Madeleine Hunter is a PhD candidate in Education at the University of Cambridge, UK. Her research interests include twenty-first-century children's media, intermediality in literature, and new media aesthetics and materialities. Her work has been published in international peer review journals and in edited book volumes.

Dana E. Lawrence is an assistant professor of English at University of South Carolina Lancaster, USA. Her teaching and research interests include adaptation, children's literature, Shakespeare, gender studies, and literary tourism. Her essay, "Isabella Whitney's 'Slips': Collaboration, Appropriation, and Coterie," appears in *A History of Early Modern Women's Writing*, edited by Patricia Phillippy (2018). She has also presented papers at numerous conferences, including Renaissance Society of America,

Children's Literature Association, and "Placing the Author: Literary Tourism in the Long Nineteenth Century" (Manchester, UK 2015).

Melanie A. Marotta is a lecturer in the Department of English and Language Arts at Morgan State University, USA. Marotta is an editor for the *Journal of Science Fiction*. Marotta's research focuses on Science Fiction, Young Adult Literature, the American West, contemporary American Literature (in particular African American), and ecocriticism. She is currently working on a monograph about young adult literature featuring African-American female characters. Her collection, *Women's Space: Essays on Female Characters in the 21st Century Science Fiction Western*, has been published in 2019 as part of the *Critical Explorations in Science Fiction and Fantasy Series*.

Amy L. Montz is an associate professor of English at the University of Southern Indiana, USA. She coedited the collection *Female Rebellion in Young Adult Dystopian Fiction* (2014) and has published in *Children's Literature Association Quarterly* and *Neo-Victorian Studies*, as well as collections on The Hunger Games and Elizabeth Gaskell. Her research includes material culture, British literature, and young adult literature.

Tara Moore is a visiting assistant professor of English at Elizabethtown College, USA. She has published on Christmas culture in *Victorian Christmas in Print* (2009) and *Christmas: The Sacred to Santa* (2014). Her research interests include representations of adoption in young adult literature.

Indu Ohri is an assistant professor, General Faculty in the University of Virginia's English Department, USA. She is working on a book project that examines how the ghosts in women's supernatural fiction reflect various unspeakable social concerns of late-Victorian and early-twentieth-century Britain. Her research and teaching interests include Victorian and Edwardian women's ghost stories, global literatures of the long nineteenth century, and neo-Victorianism. Her articles on these topics have appeared or are forthcoming in publications such as the *Victorians Institute Journal Digital Annex* (2014), *The Companion to Victorian Popular Fiction* (2018), *Preternature* (2019), and *The Wilkie Collins Journal* (2020).

Eileen Totter is an adjunct English instructor at the University of North Georgia, USA, and Athens Technical College, USA. Her research interests include eighteenth- and nineteenth-century British literature, and how gender and sexuality is presented in popular culture. She is especially interested in the critical reaction to Jane Austen.

Madeleine Tulip is a teaching associate at Warwick University, UK, in the Department of English and Comparative Literary Studies. Her research interests focus on classical reception and adaptation theory in modern and contemporary literature. She is in the process of publishing a coedited collection on the descent narrative in classical and modern literature. She also has a forthcoming monograph, entitled *Classical Memories: The Underworld in the Twentieth Century* (2020).

Lisa M. Valenzuela is a lecturer for the English Department at the University of the Incarnate Word in San Antonio, Texas, USA. Her research interests include contemporary adaptations of fairy tales and folklore, as well as Native-American literature. She has presented papers at several conferences on these topics, including the Modern Language Association and the Popular Culture Association Conferences.

Brett Carol Young is a lecturer of English at Valdosta State University, Georgia, USA. Her interests include neo-Victorian literature, Victorian studies, and children's and women's studies.

Maya Zakrzewska-Pim is a PhD candidate at the University of Cambridge, UK, and member of the Centre for Research in Children's Literature at Cambridge. Her research focuses on modern popular culture in adaptations of Charles Dickens's novels for children and young adults. Her research interests include Victorianism, adaptation theory, children's and young adult literature and culture. She has presented at international conferences; the International Research Society for Children's Literature Congress, the Child and the Book Conference, and the Annual Charles Dickens Symposium.

Index

Achilles 86, 215
"acts of god" 220
Adaptation and Appropriation (Sanders) 7, 12 n.24, 13 n.30, 91 n.6, 91 n.13
adaptations
  acknowledged vs unacknowledged 7
  and appropriation 7, 12 n.24
  as adaptations 140
  canonical 171
  children's adaptations 200–1
  Corrigan's idea about 8
  defined 1, 6–8
  embedded 173–4, 176–7
  as evolution v
  fairy tales 10
  feminist 18
  liberties of modern reader 170
  as literary progeny 2
  as palimpsest 7
  parallel 172
  and reader response 7
  in teen films, girl-centric approach 201–3
  and young adult novels 8–12, 19
  for young adults 1–2
Adapting Canonical Texts in Children's Literature 9
adolescence 12, 34, 50, 64, 70, 139, 148
adult–child relationship 84
Adventures of Dr. Franken, The 114, 123 n.18
After Juliet (Macdonald) 21–2; *see also Romeo and Juliet* (Shakespeare)
"afterlife" of texts 1
age gap between the lovers 99–100
agency 8, 22–4, 26
Age of Innocence, The (Wharton) 33, 45 n.4
Agnes 186
Aladdin (Disney) 141, 144
Alexander, Lloyd 108 n.44

Alice in Wonderland (Fritz and Day) 9
Alison/Alisoun (The Wife of Bath) 3
  childlike panties 5
  experience of statutory rape 3, 5, 6
  "face-off" with the Washington Monument 5–6
  "gap-toothed"/"gat-tothed" smile 3
  icon of freedom 5
  against Jankyn's misogynist attacks 4
  lost virginity 3–5
  prettiness 3
  sexuality 3–4
allusions to classics 217
Al-Mansour, Haifaa 117, 122
Alter, Robert 194 n.8
American culture 81–2
Americentrism 86–7
analogue 98
Anderson, Laurie Halse 104
animal abuse 34
Anjirbag, Michelle Anya 11, 139, 150 n.34
Apollonius 213, 214, 217, 219
Appearance of Annie Van Sinderen, The (Howe) 8, 11, 22–4, 26, 162–5
appropriation 7, 12 n.24; *see also* adaptations
Argonautica (poem) 213
Ash (Lo) 66–71
  female desires 70
  girls' sexuality 66
  heterosexual consummation 70
  homosexuality 68
  identity 68
  Kaisa, the King's huntress 68, 70–1
  "lesbian," "bisexual," or "pansexual" 68
  nonheteronormative relationships 69
  queer relationship 69
  same-sex couples 70
  same-sex relationships 68
  Sidhean 68
  stepmother and stepsisters 67–8

Index

Ashton, Brodi 98, 99, 108 n.14, 108 n.23, 108 n.27
As I Lay Dying (Faulkner) 215
As Old as Time 141, 144, 150 n.35
assimilation 84, 87–9
Astrophil and Stella (Sidney) 20
Austen, Jane 11, 102, 136 n.13, 136 n.18, 136 n.24, 136 n.27, 136 n.30, 136 n.32, 136 n.35, 136 n.39–41, 136 n.43, 137 n.60, 137 n.64, 161
authorial acknowledgment 7

Bacchilega, Christina 63, 74 n.1
Baetens, Jan 140, 149 n.4, 150 n.14
Balizet, Ariane 201, 209 n.26–7
Bardugo, Leigh 139
Barrow, Mare 106
Bates, Catherine 20, 29 n.22
Beauty and the Beast 141
Beckendorf, Charles 87
Beckwith, Charles E. 195 n.18
Beloved (Morrison) 221
Benincasa, Sara 10, 49–50, 60 n.7
Bennet, Elizabeth 11, 125
Bennet, Kitty 132
Bennet, Mary 128
Benson, Stephen 71
Benvolio 10, 17, 19, 23–8
Bevc, Christine 223 n.3
bi/lesbian characters 67
Biography of a Tenement House: An Architectural History of 97 Orchard Street (Dolkart) 159
Black, Holly 106
black Athena 216
Blackburn, Mollie V. 74 n.15, 75 n.17
Black Medea 215, 218–23
Bland, Guy 170, 179 n.3
Blankier, Margot 107 n.1
Blau, Sheridan 169, 179 n.1
Bly, Nellie 162
Book of Genesis, The 171
Book of Wicked Women 4
Borden, Lizzie 36
Bortolotti, Garry R. 97, 98, 107 n.3
Bottoms, Janet 209 n.25
Bradford, Clare 85, 91 n.23

Braswell, Liz 141, 150 n.35, 150 n.37, 150 n.41–7, 150 n.49–56
Bray, Libba 155–7, 166 n.1
Brennan, Sarah Rees 11, 194 n.12, 195 n.15, 195 n.20, 195 n.22, 195 n.28, 195 n.31, 195 n.43, 195 n.54, 195 n.59, 196 n.61, 196 n.63
Brightly Burning (Donne) 98, 101, 105–6; see also Jane Eyre
  Hugo Fairfax 98
  Jane's story 98, 104
  Rochester 98
Bright Smoke, Cold Fire 22
Bright Young Things (Godbersen) 156
Britt, Fanny 104
Brontë, Charlotte 10, 97, 104, 106, 108 n.11, 108 n.29, 108 n.37, 171, 181 n.13
  cultural selection 98
Brontë, Emily 170
Brontë-esque theme 104
"Brooch-Cameo" 168 n.47
Bryant, John 7, 13 n.31
Buchbinder, David 7–8, 13 n.32, 82, 91 n.11, 91 n.27, 97, 102, 107 n.2, 108 n.24, 125, 126, 127, 135 n.3, 135 n.9, 136 n.37, 137 n.82
Bullen, Elizabeth 209 n.28, 209 n.29
Busl, Gretchen 91 n.1
Butler, Guy 221
Butler, Judith 188, 195 n.27
Byronic hero 102
By the Bog of Cats (Carr) 220

Caine, Rachel 17, 25–7, 29 n.57–8
Calonita, Jen 141
Cambridge Companion to the Literature of New York, The (Patell) 158
cameo ring 164–5
Campbell, Joseph 80, 91 n.4
canonical literature 169
Canterbury Tales, The (Chaucer) 2
  Alison/Alisoun 3
  gender representation, inadequacy of 2
Carlsbad Caverns 87
Carr, Marina 220
Carraway, Nick 49, 60
Cart, Michael 75 n.40

Carter, Steve 221
Carwyn 186, 193–4
Case of Peter Pan, or the Impossibility of Children's Fiction, The (Rose) 84
"Challenging the Pluralism of Our Past: Presentism and the Selective Tradition in Historical Fiction Written for Young People" 158; *see also* Power, Chandra L.
Chamlee-Wright, Emily 221, 225 n.66
Charlie (Baz) 180 n.8
Chaucer, Geoffrey 2, 9, 12 n.7
children's literature 8–9, 18, 28 n.11, 84, 156–7, 200–1
Children's Literature and New York City (O'Sullivan and Whyte) 156
"Children's Literature and the Child Flâneur" 157; *see also* Tribunella, Eric L.
Children's Shakespeare, The (Nesbit) 18
Chiron 86
Chodorow, Nancy 184, 194 n.5
chromosomal sex 65
Chronis, Athinodoros 200–1, 209 n.18
Cinderella 10, 12, 66, 141; *see also* Ash (Lo); Tale of the Shoe, The (Donoghue)
 abuse, suffers 72
 heteronormative social standards 72–3
 queer interpretation 69–71
 rescuer 73
 self-discovery 74
 violence by stepmother and stepsisters 71–2
Clark, Caroline T. 74 n.15
Clarke, Mary Cowden 21–2, 29 n.33, 29 n.38
claustrophobic ladies 33
Coats, Karen 150 n.24
Cold Legacy, A (Shepherd) 115–16, 119, 120, 122
Coldwell, Andrea 1, 9, 12 n.2
Coleridge, Samuel Taylor 40
"collective consciousness" of assimilation 87
Collins, Suzanne 184
colonialism 84
Conceal, Don't Feel (Calonita) 141

Connolly, Tina 98, 106, 108 n.46, 109 n.48
'continuative' novelizations 140
Coppola, Maria Micaela 65, 75 n.22, 75 n.56
Corbett, Sue 150 n.22–3
Corrigan, Timothy 8, 13 n.33
cosmopolitanism 158
Cournault, Anne de 33
Couzelis, Mary J. 133, 137 n.69, 137 n.75
crass commercialism 140
Cristabel (Coleridge) 40
cultural markers 63
Cursed Child, The 9
Cutter, Susan L. 224 n.8

Daddy Long Legs (Webster) 120
Daisy 51
Dante, Alighieri 20, 171
Darcy, Fitzwilliam 130–1
Darragh, Janine J. 224 n.4
Darwinism 7
David Copperfield (Dickens) 187
Dawson, Delilah S. 139
Day, Sara K. 9, 13 n.38, 127–8, 136 n.26, 136 n.36, 195 n.58
Deadpool 102
Deitchman, Elizabeth A. 209 n.28
de la Peña, Matt 139
Delilah 51, 55–8
Demea (Butler) 221
desire 65; *see also* Ash (Lo); fairy tales; female sexual desire; *Tale of Two Cities, A* (Dickens)
DeStefano, Adriana 53
Dickens, Charles 11, 100, 172, 183–6, 190, 193–4, 194 n.10, 195 n.19, 195 n.38, 195 n.53, 195 n.60
Disney–ABC Television Group channel ABC Family 141
diversity 2, 10
Divine Comedy (Dante) 171
Diviners, The (Bray) 155
"Docile Bodies, Dangerous Bodies: Sexual Awakening and Social Resistance in Young Adult Dystopian Novels" 127–8; *see also* Day, Sara K.

Dodger (Pratchett) 172
Dolkart, Andrew S. 159, 167 n.20
Dombey and Son (Dickens) 186
domestic violence 34
Dominguez, Diana 105, 108 n.36
Donne, Alexa 98, 108 n.33
Donnelly, Jennifer 11, 159–62, 167 n.22, 167 n.32
Donoghue, Emma 66, 71, 73, 75 n.48, 75 n.55
Dr. Franken 114–15
Dreadfully Ever After (Hockensmith) 10, 126, 131
   Austen's treatment of race 133
   Bennet sisters 129
   dying England 135
   Elizabeth Bennet 126, 128–9
   Gurdaya's rescue 133
   Mary, breastfeeding 132
   Mary as zombie hunter 129
   Mary in 129, 130
   Mary's priggish nature 130
   revenge fantasy 131
   Sanditon 134
   zombie hunter 126
dream Romeo 207
Dreher, Diane Elizabeth 202, 209 n33
Duchess at Prayer, The (Wharton) 33
Dumplin (Murphy) 104
dystopia 11

Eclipse (Meyer) 170
Edelman, Lee 66, 75 n.26
Eleanor & Park (Rowell) 17, 104
Eliot, George 100
Elliott, Jane 98, 104, 140, 149, 150 n.19, 150 n.57
Elliott, Kamilla 8, 13 n.34, 149, 149 n.9, 149 n.13
Ellis, John 143, 150 n.29
embedded adaptations in young adult literature 171–3
empathy 64
Erll, Astrid 224 n.25
essays 1
Euripides 214
Everdeen, Katniss 106
Eyre, Jane 97

Faerie Queen character 106
Fairy Tale Reform School series (Calonita) 141
fairy tales 10, 63; *see also specific fairy tales*
   adaptations 10, 64
   awareness 65
   as educative tool 63
   gender diversity 64
   gender identity and sexual orientation 63–4
   queer adaptations or retellings 64–6
   queer desires 66–7
   self-discovery 65
Falkenberg, Saffyre 10, 79
false sexual freedom for young women 41
fan fiction 179 n.6
Faulkner, William 215
female love relationships 67
female purity 183
female sexual desire 67
female teen protagonists 157
femininity, representation 183–5
   love *versus* hatred 186–8
   performing femininity 191–3
   significance of titles 185–6
   woman in the twenty-first century 188–91
feminist movements 183
feminist psychoanalytic work 184
Fiedler, Lisa 22
Film Adaptation and Its Discontents: From Gone with the Wind to The Passion of the Christ (Leitch) 98
Fink, Bruce 60 n.2
Fitzgerald, F. Scott 49
Flood, Alison 91 n.16
Florence 186
fluid-text approach 7
folklore, Breton 34
Force Awakens, The (Disney) 139
Ford, Genevieve Larson 91 n.32
Forni, Dalila 10, 63
Frankenstein: The Monster Returns 114, 121
Frankenstein, Victor 111–12, 121, 122
Frankenstein-A Cold Legacy (Shepherd) 10, 111–12, 121
   Adaptation, Video Games, and the *Frankenstein* Franchise 114–17

cinematic adaptations 112–14
Elizabeth 111
female character as daughter and scientist 117–22
Frankenstein 122
Hemsley's body repair 111
Juliet, transformation of 111
Lucy Radcliff 111
mortal being 111
"sentimental family" 118
Frankenstein formula 112
freedom of movement 157
French Revolution 184
Fritz, Sonya Sawyer 9, 13 n.38, 156, 167 n.7, 223 n.2, 225 n.70
From the Mixed-Up Files of Mrs. Basil E. Frankweiler (Konigsburg) 156, 157, 166
"From 'Wizard' to 'Wicked': Adaptation Theory and Young Adult Fiction" 126; *see also* Buchbinder, David

Garber, Marjorie 208 n.1
Gaskell, Elizabeth 161
Gateway Arch 87
Gatsby, Jay 51, 52
gay assimilation 69
"gaze back" 84
Geerts, Sylvie 91 n.2
gender roles 63, 65
gender socialization 63
Genette, Gerard 107 n.1
Ghostbusters 103
Ghosts of Kerfol, The (Noyes) 10, 33
 abuse of cheating women 34, 42
 adaption to *Kerfol* 35
 Anne's carelessness 37
 Anne's death 36
 Anne's status as cheating woman 35
 captive woman, transmutation 34
 cheating woman 34
 ghost dogs 40–1, 44
 Grand-mère's version 39
 Hauntings of Kerfol 35
 Hervé de Lanrivain 35, 36
 Kerfol's haunting 35
 misogynistic beliefs 44
 necklace/collar and a pet dog 35
 Perrette 4, 33–40, 43–4
 perspectives from diverse young adult characters 36
 sexuality 40
 sexual maturity, emergence into 34
 Suze Cole, aesthetic and sexual objectification 39–42
 transforms Wharton's woman 43
 unfaithful women, punishments 35
 were/wolf 39
 woman excessively punished 33, 42
 Yves (Anne's husband) murder 35–6
 Yves's brutality 36, 38
 Yves's death 39
 Yves's presentation of the necklace 37
Gilbert, Sandra M. 22, 29 n.43, 105, 108 n.35, 194 n.1
Ginney 179 n.7
Girlhood of Shakespeare's Heroines (Clarke) 21
Giroux, Henry A. 220–1, 225 n.61, 225 n.64
Godbersen, Anna 156, 166 n.4
Godwin, William 117
Gordon, Charlotte 114, 123 n.13
Gothic: Ten Original Dark Tales (Noyes) 34
Grahame-Smith, Seth 10, 102, 125, 126–8, 136 n.13, 136 n.17, 136 n.19, 136 n.24, 136 n.27, 136 n.30, 136 n.32, 136 n.35
Grand Canyon 87
Grant, Catherine 143, 150 n.30
Grapes of Wrath (Steinbeck) 215
Great (Benincasa) 10, 49–59, 60 n.7; *see also* Naomi
 female narrator 50–1
 Gatsby and Daisy, affair between 49
 Naomi, and her struggle with identity 49
 power, theme of 50
 power in young adult novels 59
 self-discovery 50
 social constructs, boundaries of 49
Great Gatsby, The (Fitzgerald) 10, 12, 49
 dichotomy 51
 male narrator 50–1
 Trimalchio or *Trimalchio in West Egg* 52
Greek mythology 79
 adaption for young adults 81–2
 cultural inheritance 82

cultural tradition 79
diversity problem for young adult literature's 83–4
intertextuality 81
reinterpretations 81
Greek myths 217
Green-Barteet, Miranda A. 126, 135 n.8
Greenhill, Pauline 65, 74 n.4
Grier, Kasey 166 n.2
Guber, Susan 22, 29 n.43, 194 n.1
Gutierrez, Anna Katrina 216, 224 n.24

Haag, Claudia 86
Hamilton, Edith 214, 215, 225 n.35
Hamlet (Shakespeare) 201
Hand, Cynthia 98, 99, 108 n.14, 108 n.18, 108 n.23, 108 n.27
Harper, Suzanne 198, 209 n.4, 209 n.6
Harriet the Spy 156, 157
Harry Potter 3, 103
Hartley-Kroeger, Fiona 10, 17
Hartnell, Anna 215, 224 n.12, 225 n.69, 225 n.71–4
Hateley, Erica 21, 29 n.37, 201
Hawkins, Robert L. 225 n.60
Hazel 87, 88
Heath, Kay 100, 108 n.10
hegemonic femininity 188
Heinze, Rüdiger 202, 209 n.39
Hemsley 111
Hephaestus 87
Her Dark Curiosity (Dr. Jekyll and Mr. Hyde) (Shepherd) 111, 120–1
Herman, David 216
Heroes of Olympus, The (Riordan) 79–80, 85, 86, 87
  Frank Zhang 80
  Gaea 79
  Hazel Levesque 80
  House of Hades 80
  Leo Valdez 80
  sexuality and disability 80
heteronormativity 64
Hidden Adult, The (Nodelman) 84
Hill, Crag 224 n.4
Hilton, Mary 150 n.26
History of the Assizes of the Duchy of Brittany, A. Quimper, 1702 35

"History Writing That's 'Good to Think With': *The Great Fire, Blizzard! And An American Plague*" 158; *see also* Zarnowski, Myra
Hobbit, The 103
Hockensmith, Steve 10, 126, 128–35, 136 n.15–16, 136 n.42, 136 n.44, 136 n.47, 136 n.53, 136 n.55, 137 n.61, 137 n.65, 137 n.70, 137 n.73, 137 n.76
Hodge, Rosamund 22
Holderness, Graham 22, 29 n.44, 200, 209 n.16, 210 n.61
Hoover Dam 87
Howe, Katherine 11, 162–3, 167 n.36, 168 n.43
How the Other Half Lives: Studies among the Tenements of New York (Riis) 160
Hulbert, Jennifer 197, 209 n.3
human–animal divide 38
Hunger Games, The (Collins) 106, 184
Hunter, Madeleine 11, 139
Hurricane Katrina 12, 213–14, 220–1
  non-natural disaster 220
  retell the destructiveness 215
  "terrible mother" 215
Hutcheon, Linda 1, 6, 7, 8, 12 n.1, 12 n.22, 81, 91 n.8, 97, 98, 106, 107 n.3, 108 n.42, 114, 123 n.11, 123 n.15, 123 n.19, 123 n.23, 123 n.25, 140, 149 n.10, 150 n.31, 194 n.11
hypertexts 97, 107 n.1
hypotexts 107 n.1

identity 2, 7, 10, 12, 20, 23, 25, 63
imperialism 84
Independent, The 99
inexperienced reader 11
Ingram, Blanche 103
intertextuality 2, 7, 34
Ironside 106
Ironskin (Connolly) 98, 100; *see also* Jane Eyre
  analogue adaptation 98
  Dorie/Adele 98
  Jane Elliot 98
  Jane's facial wound 104
  Jane's new power 105
  Rochart/Rochester 98

Island of Dr. Moreau, The (Wells) 11, 173–4
  Prendick's narrative 174

Jacinta 51–3
Jagose, Annamarie 65, 74 n.13, 75 n.16
Jahnn, Hans Henny 221
James and the Giant Peach 157
Jane, the Fox and Me (Britt) 104
Jane Eyre (Brontë) 10, 97, 102, 106, 108 n.8, 108 n.21, 171
  adaption 101
  age gap between the lovers 99–100
  body image and 103–4
  feminist adaptation 107 n.7
  hypertexts 97
  Mrs. Rochester's "crimes" 101
  narrative 99
  Rochester's literary punishment 100–1
  Victorian proto-feminism 105
Jason 86
Jay, Stacey 17, 22–3
Jemisin, N. K. 139
Jenkins, Christine A. 67, 75 n.27, 150 n.15, 150 n.17
Jensen, Emma 117
Johnson, Joanna Webb 209 n.30, 209 n.38, 224 n.18, 224 n.27
Jones, Caroline E. 66, 75 n.21, 75 n.23
Juliet; The White Dove of Verona 21
Juliet Club, The 198–9
Juliet Immortal (Jay) 17, 22, 23

Katniss Everdeen 184
Keats, John 40
Kerchy, Anne 64, 74 n.6
Kerfol (Wharton) 10, 33; *see also Ghosts of Kerfol, The* (Noyes)
  Hunger Moon 36, 38
  reinterpretation of 36
  "romantic" nature and supernatural influence 40
  Victor 40
Keywords for Children's Literature (Lee) 8
King, Frederick D. 108 n.28
King Lear (Shakespeare) 7, 171, 179 n.7
Kissing the Witch (1993) 71
Kitty 129, 132–5, 137 n.83

Kugelmass, Jack 161, 167 n.31
Kuligowski, Erica 223 n.3

La Belle Dame 40
Lady's Maid's Bell, The (Wharton) 33
Lamb, Charles 18, 28 n.9
Lamb, Mary 18, 28 n.9
Lanier, Douglas 197, 208 n.2
Lanzendörfer, Tim 125, 130, 135 n.2, 135 n.5, 136 n.21, 136 n.29, 136 n.31, 136 n.34, 136 n.44, 136 n.51, 136 n.54
Last Man, The 112
Las Vegas Strip 87
Lavenza, Elizabeth 111
Lawrence, Dana E. 1, 11, 197
Lee, Alison 90, 108 n.28
Lee, Mackenzi 139
Lefebvre, Benjamin 9, 13 n.40
Leighton, Alexander 80, 81, 91 n.5, 91 n.9
Leitch, Thomas 98, 107 n.5
Leo 87
lesbian characters in fiction 66
Lester, Neal A. 63, 74 n.3, 74 n.9
Let It Go (Calonita) 141
Levesque, Marie 88
Lewis, Arabella Ludlow 165
Lewis, Francis 165
LGBTQIA (Lesbian, Gay, Bisexual, Transsexual, Queer, Intersex, and Asexual) 64, 66, 69
  readers 10
  licensed publishing 139
Lightning Thief, The 80
  Medusa 80
Lim, Elizabeth 141, 150 n.48
literary tourism 11, 157, 161, 198–203, 206
Little Dorrit 100
Little Mermaid, The 141, 145
Little Women 118
Lizzie Bennet Diaries, The 9
Llewellyn, Mark 107, 109 n.50
Lloyd, Christopher 225 n.43
Lo, Malinda 66, 75 n.32, 75 n.39
Lolita 5
London, Dickensian 172
Lost Hero, The 88
love triangle 170
Lu, Marie 139

Lucas, Charlotte 125
Ludlow, Gabriel 165

Maas, Sarah J. 139
Macdonald, Sharman 21–2
MacLeod, Anne Scott 118
Madman's Daughter, The (Shepherd) 11, 111, 118, 120, 171, 173, 177–9
Madsen, Lea Heiberg 108 n.17
Madwoman in the Attic, The (Gilbert and Gubar) 104
Madwoman Trilogy (Shepherd) 11, 120
Mahlknecht, Johannes 149 n.6, 150 n.32
male abuse 34
male "fantasy" 40
Manette, Lucie 184
mantle of poet-lover 21
Marchitello, Howard 200, 209 n.15
Marcus, Leonard S. 157, 167 n.12
Marotta, Melanie 10, 111
Marr, Melissa 106
Mary Shelley 114, 117, 123 n.43
Mary Shelley's Frankenstein 114
Maurer, Katherine 225 n.60
McCallum, Robyn 18, 28 n.8, 188–9, 195 n.24, 195 n.29, 196 n.62
McDonough, Megan 129, 130, 136 n.46, 136 n.52
Meadows, Jodi 98, 99, 108 n.14, 108 n.23, 108 n.27
Medea 12, 215–18
Medea. Stimmen (Wolf) 220
Medea (Euripides) 213–14
Medea (Jahnn) 221
medea myth 221
Men We Reaped (Ward) 214
Mercenaries 23
Merchant House Museum 155, 156, 157–8, 162, 164, 168 n.49
  "A CALL TO ARMS!" 165–6
  ghost tour 163
meta-retellings 11, 197, 198
#MeToo Movement 112, 194
Metropolitan Museum of Art 87, 155, 166
Milton, John 171
Miola, Robert S. 2, 12 n.3
Mirror, Mirror 141
Miskec, Jennifer 169, 179 n.2

modern Janes 105
Moison, Thomas 209 n32
Monin, Christan 102, 108 n.22
Montz, Amy L. 1, 11, 155, 167 n.29
Moore, Tara 10, 97, 108 n.45
Moreau, Juliet 111
Morey, Anne 82, 91 n.10, 91 n.26, 99, 107 n.6
Morrison, Toni 215, 221
Morrow, Christopher L. 7, 13 n.26
Mount Olympus 87
Moynihan, Sinéad 224 n.10, 225 n.45
Mulan, adaption of 141
Müller, Anja 8, 9, 13 n.35, 13 n.41
multitext 141
Murphy, Julie 104
Murray, Simone 149 n.2–3
Myers, Walter Dean 83, 91 n.15
My Plain Jane (Hand, Ashton, Meadows) 98, 99, 100, 101, 102, 105; see also *Jane Eyre*
  Alexander Blackwood 99
  Bertha 101
  Charlotte escapes starvation 99
  ghost characters 104
  Helen Burns (ghost) 99
  hypotext 99
  Kirkus Review 102
  neo-Victorian writing 101
  Thornfield Hall 99
"mythologizing" function 140
mythology 4, 10
Mythology (Hamilton) 215, 218

Nakamura, Ethan 87
Naomi 51–2
  coming-of-age moment 59
  Delilah, friendship with 52
  and Delilah Fairweather 51
  Hamptons, role in 56
  and her father 56
  privilege and lifestyle 59
  romance with Jeff Byron 55–7
  self-perception 51
  sexuality 55
  transformation 54
narrative
  novelties 139–42

for novices 142–3
schemata 216
National Anti-Vivisection Society 180 n.9
National Endowment for the Humanities Institute on Material Culture in Nineteenth-Century New York City 155
National Museum of Natural History 87
Nature Theater of Oklahoma 19
Nelson, Claudia 82, 91 n.10, 91 n.26, 99, 107 n.6
Nemesis 87
Nemeth, Emily 74 n.15
neo-Victorianism 9
neo-Victorian writing 101
Nesbit, E. 18, 28 n.10, 28 n.13
New York
  cosmopolitanism 158
  Gilded-Age New York City 160
  mythology 156
  Nineteenth-century New York 156
New York City 11, 155–66; *see also* Bray, Libba
  adolescent audience 157
  canonical text 155–6
  concept in literature 157
  female teen protagonists 157
  freedom of movement 157
  girls, restricted in movement 157
  historical moments to teen audiences 158–9
  individual and cultural growth 158
  literary tourism 157, 161
  nineteenth-century-set adaptations 157, 162
  paranormal mystery 155
  teenaged girls in the nineteenth century 155
New York Historical Society 156
'New York is a Great Place': Urban Mobility in Twentieth-Century Children's Literature (Fritz) 156
New York Tribune 162
Nezu 132–5, 137 n.83
Nikolajeva, Maria 50, 150 n.26
Nine Lives of Chloe King, The 141
nineteenth-century feminist 169–71
  connection 178–9
  embedded adaptations in young adult literature 171–3
  modern voice among the past 173–8
  in young adult literature 169–79
Nintendo 114
Ninth Ward (Rhodes) 214
Nodelman, Perry 84, 91 n.20, 91 n.22
nonheteronormative love stories 10
nonheteronormative novels 67
normative sexual dynamics 65
novelizations 139–40
Novy, Marianne 18, 28 n.4
Noyes, Deborah 10, 33, 45 n.5

Ohri, Indu 10, 33, 45 n.6
Oliver Twist (Dickens) 172
Once Upon a Dream 141, 144, 145
Opie Library 18
orientalism 84
Orme, Jennifer 75 n.18, 75 n.42, 75 n.44
O'Sullivan, Keith 156, 167 n.5
Othello (Shakespeare) 201
"Owl and the Pussy-cat, The" 41

Paradise Lost (Milton) 171
parallel adaptations 172; *see also* adaptations
parallel novels 197
Parley, Armelle 107, 109 n.47, 109 n.49
Parody, Clare 141, 150 n.18
Part of Your World 141, 145
Patell, Cyrus R. K. 158, 167 n.17
Pecong (Carter) 221
Percy Jackson and the Olympians (Riordan) 79–80, 85, 86, 87–9
  demigods 79–80
  dyslexia 80
  Kronos 79
  Nico di Angelo 80
performing femininity 191–3
Peter Pan 141
Petrarchan mistress 10, 18
Petronius 52
Phasma 139
Phegley, Jennifer 108 n.9, 108 n.13
points of contact 170
Polidori (Al-Mansour) 122
pop-Gothic aesthetics 144

"post-Carter generation" of fairy tales 71
post-Katrina environment 222
Power, Chandra L. 158, 167 n.19
Pratchett, Terry 172, 180 n.8
Pride and Prejudice and Zombies
    (Grahame-Smith) 125, 131; *see also*
    Dreadfully Ever After
  alien attacks 125
  Austen's novel of manners 127
  deadly heroine 128
  dystopian heroine 126
  Elizabeth as dystopian heroine 127
  Elizabeth Bennet 125
  fears of upper-class corruption 126
  lethal plagues 125
  natural cataclysms 125
  Santaularia 126, 127, 135 n.4, 136 n.22, 136 n.28, 136 n.38
  women forsaking independence 126
  young adult genre 126–7
  zombie hunter 128
  zombification of marriage 127–8
Pride and Prejudice (Austen) 10, 102, 103, 131; *see also Pride and Prejudice and Zombies* (Grahame-Smith)
Prince of Shadows (Caine) 17, 25–7
Princess Bride 103
Prindle, Alison H. 200, 209 n.14
prose retellings 200
Pulliam, June 184, 194 n.6, 195 n.26
puma-woman 174
Pygmalion (Ovid) 121

queerness 64–5, 69
queer retellings 65; *see also* LGBTQIA (Lesbian, Gay, Bisexual, Transsexual, Queer, Intersex, and Asexual)

Railsback, Brian 224 n.11
Rash, Ron 7
Red Queen 106
Red Violin, The (film) 35
Rees, Sara 183
Reflection 141, 144
Reimer, Mavis 90, 92 n.37
Reinventing Childhood Nostalgia: Books, Toys, and Contemporary Media Culture (Wesseling) 8

renaissance fair 206
revenge fantasy 131
re-vision 17, 18
revisions of plays 197
Reynolds, Jason 139, 150 n.28
Rhodes, Jewel Parker 214
Rhys, Jean 171, 180 n.7
Rich, Adrienne 17, 28 n.2, 28 n.6, 108 n.16
Riis, Jacob 160
Riordan, Rick 79, 81, 85, 86–7, 87–9, 90, 91 n.3, 91 n.25, 91 n.28–9, 91 n.33–4
Riordan *(Heroes of Olympus, The)*
  Nico di Angelo 80
  Piper McLean 80
  sexuality and disability 80
Rochere, Martine Hennard Dutheil de la 71, 75 n.41, 75 n.43, 75 n.45, 75 n.50, 75 n.54
Rokison, Abigail 18, 28 n.7
Roman mythology 79
Romeo and Juliet, Saving Juliet 11
Romeo and Juliet (Shakespeare) 10, 11, 17–21, 28 n.18, 28 n.26, 29 n.42, 172, 197–8, 201; *see also After Juliet* (Macdonald); dream Romeo; *Frankenstein-A Cold Legacy* (Shepherd); Rosaline, Petrarchan Mistress in Sonnet; *Saving Juliet* (Selfors); *William Shakespeare's Romeo + Juliet*
  cultural primacy 18
  meta-retellings 198
  resurrection 17
  re-vision 17–18
  Rosaline 19–27
  for teens 18–19
  Verona's tourism narrative 198
  young adult adaptations 19, 197
  young audience 18–19
Romeo-as-poet 20
Romeo Redeemed (Jay) 17, 22
Romeo's Ex: Rosaline's Story (Fiedler) 22
Rosaline, Petrarchan Mistress in Sonnet 17, 19–21
  embodied 21–3
  in Margins 25–7
  Prince of Shadows 25–7
  sexuality 27
  speaks 23–5

Rose, Jaqueline 84, 91 n.17
Rosencrantz and Guildenstern Are Dead 102
Rowell, Rainbow 17, 104
Rowling, J. K. 9, 28 n.1

Said, Edward 84
Salih, Sara 133, 137 n.71
Salvage the Bones (Ward) 12, 213–23
   Absyrtus 213
   Artemis 213
   Black Medea 215, 218–23
   Demeter 213
   Esch 213–14, 223, 224 n.29
   intertexts, collection of 215–18
   Io 213
   Jason 213
   Medea 213
   Randall 214
   Skeetah 214
Sanders, Julie 7, 12 n.24, 13 n.30, 18, 28 n.5, 81, 91 n.6, 91 n.13
Santaularia, Isabel 125, 135 n.4, 135 n.6, 136 n.22, 136 n.28, 136 n.38
Satyricon (Petronius) 52
Saving Juliet (Selfors) 198–9, 201, 202, 203
   literary tourism 198
   meta-retelling 203–8
   temporal tourism and rewriting Shakespeare 203–8
   Verona 207
Schickel, Richard 150 n.33
Schuyler, Anne 45 n.2
Scott-Douglass, Amy 200, 209 n.12
Seifert, Lewis C. 74 n.12
self, girls' definition 184
Selfors, Suzanne 11, 198, 209 n.9, 209 n.24, 209 n.341, 210 n.59, 210 n.62, 210 n.83
sensationalism 36
"sentimental family" 118
Serena (Rash) 7
Serle, Rebecca 22
Seven Types of Intertextuality (Miola) 2
Severn, John R. 7, 13 n.27
sexual and financial autonomy 41
sexual autonomy 33
sexual objectification 34

sexual orientations 63
sexual transgressions 34
Shakespeare, Williams 7, 9–11, 17–28, 28 n.18, 170, 199; *see also specific novels and adaptations*
   adapting as an enterprise 17
   for girls 201–3
   "teenpics" 202
   uber-canonical body of work 18
Shakespeare and Modern Culture 208 n.1
Shakespearean quill 207
Shakespeare as Children's Literature 28 n.11
Shakespeare's cultural authority 197
Shaw, George Bernard 121
Shelley, Mary 10, 123 n.8
Shepherd, Megan 10, 11, 111–12, 122 n.1, 123 n.39, 171, 173, 181 n.14
Sidhean 69
Sidney, Philip 20
Sierra Burgess Is a Loser (movie) 104
Simpson, Anne 85
Sixth Sense 103
Sleeping Beauty 141
Smiley, Jane 171, 179 n.7
Smith, Madeleine 36
Smyth, Theony Soublis 224 n.5
Snell, Heather 90, 92 n.37
Soares, Rebecca 125, 126, 135 n.1, 135 n.12, 136 n.23, 136 n.25
social inequalities 11
social influencer 53
socialite partygoer 54
social media 6, 10
social order 80
Sometimes We Tell the Truth (Zarins) 2, 12 n.4, 12 n.14
So This Is Love 141
source text 11
Stableford, Brian 111, 123 n.4
Stam, Robert 7, 13 n.29
star-crossed lovers 201
Star Trek 140
Star Wars 140
steampunk genre 9
Stein, Von 120
Steinbeck, John 170, 215
Stephens, John 18, 28 n.8
stereotyping 87–9

Stevens, Benjamin Eldon 224 n.13, 225 n.39, 225 n.44, 225 n.76
Stevenson, Robert Louis 117, 150 n.21
Steward, Susan 210 n.56, 210 n.63
Still Star-Crossed (Taub) 17, 23–5
Storied City: A Children's Book Walking-Tour Guide to New York City 157
Storr, Virgil Henry 221, 225 n.66
Stout, Daniel 194 n.9, 195 n.21
Straight on Till Morning 141
Suhr-Sytsma, Mandy 91 n.21
supernatural fiction 35
swine-woman 174

Tale of the Shoe, The (Donoghue) 66, 71–4
    erotic fulfillment 73
    girls' sexuality 66
    identity 71
    self-discovery 71
    sexuality 71
Tale of Two Cities, A (Dickens) 11, 183–96
    adapted for teenage audience 184
    desire for revenge 187
    Lucie as daughter 186
    Lucie as narrator 184
    Lucie's literal interpretation 186–7
    Marie 188
    maternal instincts 187
    modern Lucie 189–90
    "monstrous" femininity 187
    sans-merci's verdict 189–90
    self-discovery 184
Tales from Shakespeare (Lamb and Lamb) 18
Talley, Lee 8, 13 n.36
Taming of the Shrew (Shakespeare) 201
Taub, Melinda 17, 23–5
Taylor, Samuel 40
teenage fashion 53
teen readers 1, 12
Tell the Wind and Fire 183–96
temporal tourism 203–8
Ten Days in a Madhouse 162
Tenement Museum 155, 156, 159, 160, 161
10 Things I Hate About You 201
textual engagement 198
Textual Transformations in Children's Literature: Adaptations, Translations, Reconsiderations (Lefebvre) 9

Theory of Adaptation, A (Hutcheon) 1, 6, 12 n.1, 114
These Shallow Graves (Donnelly) 11, 159–62
    Eddie 159–62
    Fay 159–60
    Jo (heroine) 159–62
Theseus 86
Things I Hate About You 201
Thompson, Kristin 149 n.8
Thousand Acres, A (Smiley) 171, 180 n.7
tie-in merchandise 140
tie-in novels 139
Tierney, Kathleen 223 n.3
Tithe (Black) 106
tokenism 83, 87–9
Tosi, Laura 200, 209 n.13, 209 n31
Totter, Eileen 10, 125
tourism 6, 11, 161–2, 198–201
    imaginaries 200
transformative experiences 169
Transgressive Tales: Queering the Grimms (Turner and Greenhill) 65
transhistorical punishments, discrepancies 34
Tribunella, Eric L. 157, 167 n.10
Trimalchio, Jacinta 52
Trimalchio or *Trimalchio in West Egg* 52
Trites, Roberta Seelinger 50, 60 n.1, 118, 120, 123 n.26, 142, 150 n.27, 194 n.7, 209 n.34
Troy 203
true female characters 174
Trupe, Alice 74 n.7
Tulip, Madeleine 11–12, 213
"Turfing the Slum: New York City's Tenement Museum and the Politics of Heritage" 161; *see also* Kugelmass, Jack
Turner, Kay 65, 75 n.19
Twelfth Night (Shakespeare) 201
Twilight 3
Twilight Saga 169–70
Twisted Tales (Disney) 11, 139–43, 148–9
    endings and futures 148–9
    from Ur-stories to Your-stories 143–8

unannounced adaptations 7
"unequal" 100

upper-class wives 33
Ursula 141

Valenzuela, Lisa M. 10, 49
Van Parys, Thomas 150 n.16
Varnado, Christine 29 n.69
Venus 3
Verona 21, 198–201, 203–9
Vickers, Nancy 20, 29 n.25
Victorian feminism 176, 183
Victorianism 9–11
Victorian marriage market 100
Victorian proto-feminism 105
video games 6
Vindication of the Rights of Women, A (Wollstonecraft) 128–35

Waggoner, Zach 115, 123 n.22
Wagner, Katherine A. 129, 130, 136 n.46, 136 n.52
Walker, Alice 215
Walker, Steven 91 n.14
Waller, Alison 150 n.25
Wallingford, Mimi 198–9
Walt Disney 11, 139–49, 142
Wanted, The 52
Ward, Jesmyn 12, 213–23, 219, 223 n.1, 224 n.6, 224 n.14, 224 n.21–2, 224 n.28, 225 n.30, 225 n.36–7, 225 n.42, 225 n.49, 225 n.52, 225 n.57, 225 n.62, 225 n.65, 225 n.68
Wargo, Jon 69, 75 n.32, 75 n.36
Waters, Catherine 195 n.14
Watson, Nicola 199, 209 n.5, 209 n.11
Wells, H. G. 11, 117, 173–4, 209 n.17
Wesseling, Elisabeth 9, 13 n.37
Western civilization 86
West III, James W. L. 52
Wetmore, Kevin J., Jr. 197
Whalen, Catherine 166 n.2
Wharton, Edith 10, 33
When You Were Mine 22
White, Barbara 45 n.1
Whole New World, A (Braswell) 141, 144, 145

Whyte, Pádraic 156, 167 n.5
Wicked Lovely (Marr) 106
Wide Sargasso Sea (Rhys) 106, 171, 180 n.7
William Shakespeare's Romeo + Juliet 201
Wintergirls (Anderson) 104
Wolf, Christa 220
wolf-woman 174
Wollstonecraft, Mary 128
women, representation 183–5
love *versus* hatred 186–8
performing femininity 191–3
significance of titles 185–6
woman in the twenty-first century 188–91
Worthen, W. B. 19, 28 n.14
Wosk, Julie 121, 123 n.40
Writing of Fiction, The (Wharton) 33, 35, 45 n.3, 45 n.7
Wuthering Heights (Brontë) 170

Yearwood, Stephanie 111, 122 n.3
Yoon, Bogum 85, 91 n.24
York, Robert L. 197
Young, Brett Carol 11, 74 n.8, 75 n.28, 169
young adults
audiences 81, 177
emotional insecurities 64
female love relationships in fiction 66
identity and sexuality 64
imperialism and assimilation 84–6
literature 84, 142
novel adaptations 197
novels 1, 8–12, 10, 19
publishing market 142
readers 2, 10, 11, 34, 171
Younger, Beth 64, 75 n.38

Zakrzewska-Pim, Maya 11, 183
Zarins, Kim 2–6, 12 n.4, 12 n.14
Zarnowski, Myra 158, 167 n.16
Zhu, Yujie 200, 209 n.20
Zipes, Jack 63, 74 n.2
zombie hunter 128
Zombies 3, 10, 11, 102
zombification of marriage 127–8

Lightning Source UK Ltd.
Milton Keynes UK
UKHW022315010920
369185UK00003B/239